A
Century *of*
Arts & Letters

The History of the National Institute of Arts & Letters and the American Academy of Arts & Letters as Told, Decade by Decade, by Eleven Members

LOUIS AUCHINCLOSS

JACK BEESON

HORTENSE CALISHER

ADA LOUISE HUXTABLE

WOLF KAHN

R.W. B. LEWIS

RICHARD LIPPOLD

NORMAN MAILER

CYNTHIA OZICK

ARTHUR SCHLESINGER, JR.

JOHN UPDIKE, EDITOR

A CENTURY *of* ARTS & LETTERS

COLUMBIA UNIVERSITY PRESS   NEW YORK

COLUMBIA UNIVERSITY PRESS

Publishers Since 1893

New York   Chichester, West Sussex

Library of Congress Cataloging-in-Publication Data
A century of arts and letters : the history of the National Institute
of Arts and Letters and the American Academy of Arts and Letters as
told, decade by decade, by eleven members / R. W. B. Lewis . . . [et al.] :
John Updike, editor.
p.   cm.
ISBN 0–231–10248–8 (alk. paper)
1. National Institute of Arts and Letters (U.S.)—History.
2. American Academy and Institute of Arts and Letters—History.
I. Lewis, R. W. B. (Richard Warrington Baldwin)   II. Updike, John.
NX22.C46   1998   97-40940
700'.6'073—dc21

Casebound editions of Columbia University Press books are printed on
permanent and durable acid-free paper.

Printed in the United States of America

Designed by Linda Secondari

FRONT SHEET:
"The Ten," December 17, 1897. Artists who resigned from the Society of American Artists
to establish their own association. All of "The Ten" were eventually elected into the
Academy. Standing (l–r): William Merritt Chase, Frank W. Benson, Edmund C. Tarbell,
Thomas W. Dewing, Joseph R. DeCamp. Seated (l–r): Edward Simmons, Willard Metcalf,
Childe Hassam, J. Alden Weir, Robert Reid. (*Photo by A. E. Seler, Philadelphia.*)

ENDSHEET:
The last meeting of the old Academy, May 20, 1992, with
nineteen of the 50 Academy members present.
First Row (l–r): Jacob Lawrence, Elizabeth Hardwick, Louis Auchincloss, Lukas Foss,
Ada Louise Huxtable. Second Row (l–r): Jack Levine, Milton Babbitt, James Merrill,
Hugo Weisgall, Arthur Schlesinger, Jr., Saul Steinberg, William Gaddis. Third Row (l–r):
Alfred Kazin, Ralph Elison, C. Vann Woodward, James Dickey, Richard Wilbur,
Kurt Vonnegut, Harrison E. Salisbury. (*Niki Berg*)

c 10 9 8 7 6 5 4 3 2 1

CONTENTS

FOREWORD
John Updike
vii

ACKNOWLEDGMENTS
xiii

1898–1907
THE FOUNDERS' STORY
R. W. B. Lewis
1

1908–1917
IDEALISM *and* PATRIOTISM
Louis Auchincloss
28

1918–1927
AGAINST MODERNITY—
ANNALS *of the* TEMPLE
Cynthia Ozick
47

1928–1937
THE INFILTRATION *of* MODERNITY
Arthur Schlesinger, Jr.
86

1938–1947
DECADE *of the* ROW
John Updike
105

1948–1957
THE TESTIMONY *of* TWO ARTISTS
Richard Lippold and Wolf Kahn
136

1958–1967
ROUNDING CAMELOT
Norman Mailer
156

1968–1977
HOUSEKEEPING *in a* MESSY WORLD
Jack Beeson
198

1978–1987
HOLDING *the* HIGH GROUND
Ada Louise Huxtable
238

1988–1997
DECADE *of* REUNION
Hortense Calisher
264

APPENDIX: ACADEMY MEMBERS, PAST *and* PRESENT
293

INDEX
327

FOREWORD

John Updike

THE AMERICAN GRAIN somewhat resists formal organizations devoted to the arts. Just as religion should be kept separate from the state for the sake of impartial government and individual freedom, so the arts, perhaps, should be unclubbable and ungovernable. As is set forth in R.W.B. Lewis's initial chapter here, the idea of an "American Academy" was present in the mind of John Adams as early as 1780, when the new nation was still fighting for its existence. A number of nineteenth-century attempts at creating a formal group that would enhance "the public welfare" by "disseminating correct views" attracted some eminences but failed to be established. And, indeed, in a society inventing itself on a ground freed from European control, where personal liberty was valued more than traditional hierarchies and standards, what would "correct" artistic views be? Only a peculiarly American art could mirror and serve the New World, and by the 1850s Hawthorne, Melville, Thoreau, and Whitman were publishing brilliant departures from European models. Not that the colonies had ever been mere extensions of British sensibility: the Puritan divines in their stockaded pockets of the wilderness did not preach the same sermons heard beside the Thames and Isis—or, in a generation or two, preach with the same accents. The more extreme climate, the vast untamed land, the haunting, ambivalently regarded populations of "Indian" aborigines and Negro slaves all worked their differences in communal sensibility. As the colonies grew toward rebellion, the painter John Singleton Copley and the journalist, inventor, and practical philosopher Benjamin Franklin emerged as exemplars of a distinctively sharp American realism. Both Boston natives, as it happened, crossed the Atlantic eastward—Copley to become a London painter and member of the Royal Academy, Franklin to charm the French court during the Revolution—as if to show the Old World what polished specimens the New could now produce.

The native soil, though rich enough for the farmer, the merchant, and the fledgling industrialist, was for the artist thin both in economic opportunity and institutionalized approval. Reviewing an 1842 volume entitled *The Poets and Poetry of America: With a Historical Introduction*, by Rufus W. Griswold, Edgar Allan Poe complained, "That we are not a poetical people has been asserted so often and so roundly, both at home and abroad, that the slander, through mere dint of repetition, has come to be received as truth." It was untrue, Poe affirmed, even though "the idiosyncrasy of our political position has stimulated into early action whatever practical talent we possessed. . . . Because it suited us to construct an engine in the first instance, it has been denied that we could compose an epic in the second."[1] As he wrote, Boston and Concord were giving rise to a community of thought, artistry, and spiritual striving called (by an unsympathetic outsider) the Transcendental Club. Emerson in his secular sermons, bound together as books of essays, phrased the optimistic national mood into a philosophy, and his disciple Thoreau gave individualism its most poetic prose, bristling with opinions and particulars. In New York, by midcentury the most populous of the eastern ports, a thickening of print activity bred literary circles like that of the Duyckinck brothers, whose Saturday-night suppers—called the Tetractys Club—came to include Herman Melville. It was Evert Duyckinck who arranged the meeting of Melville and Hawthorne, in the famous picnic on Monument Mountain in August of 1850, which led to Melville's enthusiastic reading of his fellow American's work and his excited perception that an American Shakespeare was possible. In his rapturous review of Hawthorne's *Mosses from an Old Manse* he envisioned a community wherein "genius, all over the world, stands hand in hand, and one shock of recognition runs the whole circle around."[2] The hope of such electric moments—the encouraging creative spark leaping from soul to soul—underlies the assembling of artists together, even though for every Melville-Hawthorne contact there is a Hawthorne-Emerson fizzle and a Twain-James antipathy (the latter two did both enjoy a warm connection with William Dean Howells).

Writers, perhaps, stand in special need of collegial associations. Their work, drawing on private depths of knowledge and feeling, is necessarily conducted in isolation and silence, lacking the social, performative dimension of the musicians' art and the friendly craft aspect of painting and sculpture. The writer's education can take place at Bowdoin or on a whaling ship, whereas the education specific to the other arts tended to congregate apprentices and teachers; the expatriate artistic communities of Rome and Paris generated friendships that could be brought back to New York and Philadelphia. In any case, writers have dominated in number—though not always in administrative skill or public flair—the honorary institution whose century of existence is herein recounted.

The American Academy of Arts and Letters, as it is now called, was born of a breath, a hint, on a porch in Saratoga, New York, in 1898, to the effect that the American Social Science Association, which dated back to 1865, might well contain, along with its other departments of human endeavor, one devoted to literature and the arts. The suggestion came from Dr. H. Holbrook Curtis, a throat specialist, and found the receptive ear of the president of the association, Judge Simeon Baldwin. By February 1899 the first annual meeting of the "National Institute of Arts, Science and Letters" took place, on West 43rd Street in New York City. Within a year the word "Science" was dropped from its name, perhaps in deference to the older American Academy of Arts and Sciences, based in Boston and Cambridge; within that same year, before the century was quite spent, close to one hundred fifty members had been selected and had accepted membership in the fledgling organization.

What's in a name? The "Institute" of the original title evoked the Institut de France, a cultural institution founded in 1795 by the radical French Directory, replacing five learned societies that had been repressed by the Convention two years earlier. The name "Académie" was considered reactionary for a time in France, but as the revolutionary fury settled it crept back into the Institut's subdivisions, of which the best known is the Académie française, founded in the seventeenth century by Cardinal Richelieu. The word *academy*, then, was available in 1904, when a committee of three Institute members, seeking to infuse more energy and funds into the struggling young group, thought a smaller, even more select body chosen from within the Institute might prove attractive to prospective donors. The American Academy of Arts and Letters was thus conceived: thirty superexalted members out of one hundred fifty. Its formation was unanimously approved at a meeting of only twenty Institute members, and for ninety years the organization was thus twofold. When, in late 1907, the Academy voted to increase its members from thirty to fifty, the Institute swiftly decreed a proportional enlargement to two hundred fifty, the number that still obtains. Since all Academicians were chosen from, and remained within, the Institute, the arrangement might be likened to a ninety-years' pregnancy, with predictable internal discomfort. For creating a first-class status perforce creates a second class, for those Institute members not blissfully unaware of the invidious distinction. The name, also, of the overall society became confusingly compound and unmemorably lengthy.

The stratagem succeeded in its main object, however. Robert Underwood Johnson, assigned the title of Preliminary Secretary of the Academy, inaugurated his remarkably energetic campaign on behalf of an institution that, without him, might have lapsed into insignificance. A national charter was sought for both bodies, to enable them to receive gifts; the Institute's was granted in 1913, and the Academy's limpingly followed, after many sensible Congressional objections, in 1916. Even before the charter bill passed, however, Johnson had found, in Institute member Archer Huntington, a financial angel who would give the Academy-Institute the land and handsome buildings on West 155th Street it has occupied since 1923 and who would with patient generosity supply the funds that form the basis of the endowment whereby it still operates.

The bulk of Huntington's donations were to the Academy, and in 1939, displeased by some of the members newly elected to the Institute, he proposed, with the concurrence of Academy president Nicholas Murray Butler and most of the directors, that the Academy not be bound to elect its members from those of the Institute. He even offered, it is said, to buy the Institute its own building; the bifurcation of 1904 threatened to become a total split. The Institute, under the leadership of its president, Walter Damrosch, rallied, with the result that Huntington resigned and the duplex institution became less elitist, focused less on its own internal ceremonies and more on the granting of awards and fellowships to nonmember artists. In 1976 the Institute and the Academy, after more than seventy years of separate though adjacent functioning, merged into one institution with a single board of directors and budget, named the American Academy and Institute of Arts and Letters. The Academy, however, retained its own officers, its own lapel boutonniere, and its fifty carved Italian-walnut and leather chairs bearing the name of each successive occupant and arranged in arched tiers in an exquisite small auditorium with a view of Trinity Cemetery. After a number of aborted moves toward total unification, the Academy members voted in 1992 to give up all that; the Academy invited the entire Institute to join it and thus dissolved itself in all but name. From the first day of 1993, the body became that of the Institute, and the name the American Academy of Arts and Letters.

This saga of nomenclatorial transposition is but one of the strands in the pages that follow. *A Century of Arts and Letters* traces a hundred years of competing movements, of changing reputations, of altering concepts of art's function and artistic author-

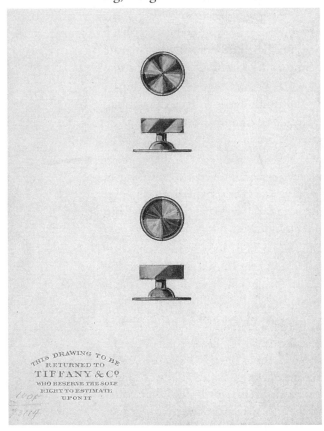

Tiffany designs for Academy and Institute lapel rosettes, circa 1909. Top, Institute; bottom, Academy.

ity's scope. Statesmen and military men are no longer elected members; a separate American Honorary category has been created for film directors, choreographers, jazz artists, photographers, and other significant adepts whose work falls outside the three departments decreed in 1898. The genteel tradition versus naturalism, representational art versus abstraction, diatonic versus twelve-tone music, ars gratia artis versus art as social propaganda: the progress of these battles can be seen in the record of elections and awards. Most, it seems safe to say, of the major American writers, artists, architects, and composers of the twentieth century have become members, though sometimes with a shameful belatedness. A distinguished list can be made of those who declined election: John Jay Chapman, Frederic Edwin Church, Richard Harding Davis, John Dewey, Thomas Eakins, Ernest Hemingway, Sol Le Witt, Cormac McCarthy, H. L. Mencken, Vladimir Nabokov, J. D. Salinger, Frank Stella, James Thurber, Edmund Wilson. A number who declined at first later accepted membership: Rockwell Kent, Sinclair Lewis, John Crowe Ransome, Karl Shapiro. There have been resignations, sometimes fiery: Thomas Hart Benton, Joseph Brodsky, James Branch Cabell, Finley Peter Dunne, Robert Herrick, Lewis Mumford, John O'Hara, Ezra Pound, Upton Sinclair, Yvor Winters. Many who accept and keep membership do no more than that; no dues are asked, no attendance is compulsory, no committee work is required. Yet the committee work grows, as the number of prize endowments increases. Election is first and foremost an honor, a tribute paid to outstanding work; secondarily it is an invitation to attend the year's four convivial events and to participate in the work of the institution, which primarily consists of the fostering of the arts through monetary awards and prizes and also by means of exhibitions and recordings.

A pleasant piece of work has been the planning for the Academy's centennial anniversary in 1998. Few individuals live to a hundred, and fewer institutions; those that do are obliged to celebrate. Part of that celebration, it was decided, should be the publication of a history of this organization. A single author could have been found and hired, perhaps, but a more festive and intimate approach suggested itself: divide the century into ten chapters, and have each written by a different member. The chairman of the centennial committee, looking for a range of voices, marshalled the obliging writers, who were presented with sheaves of newly organized and unearthed archival material. Eight of the contributors are from the literature department—historians, novelists, critics—but one composer, Jack Beeson, allowed himself to be enlisted, and not one but two artists, Richard Lippold and Wolf Kahn, agreed to present their version of the decade, the fifties, that saw American art set the international pace. Among these chapters, styles, lengths, angles of approach, and degrees of generalization vary, as is inevitable and fitting. A story gets told, and not just the story of an institution but of the cultural context it reflects, distills, absorbs, or repels, in a flicker of harmony and contrast. Other stories could, of course, be told: as many as twelve hundred, which is the total number of members since 1898.

From some few of these, the Institute and the Academy won hours and decades of devoted attention; for the great majority, the institutional activities were a pleasant grace note, a somewhat quaint marginal ornament as removed from their lives' main business as Audubon Terrace is from midtown Manhattan. Officers and committee members generally are asked for no more than three years of service. The institution's continuity, aside from the driving involvement of Robert Underwood Johnson, has been provided by the four salaried women—Grace Vanamee, Felicia Geffen, Margaret Mills, Virginia Dajani—who, over the years, under titles of which the latest is executive director, have kept the ballots and notices flowing. It is they, furthermore, who have kept in order the Academy's magnificent set of buildings, designed by McKim, Mead, & White and by Cass Gilbert, along with all the relics, the paintings and photographs and statues and furniture, accumulated in increments and preserved by inertia. For the first time in its history, the institution recently enjoyed an architect, Kevin Roche, as its president; with lavish expenditure of his own time, he has directed needful and beautiful improvements.

The buildings in their solidity and grandeur assure the Academy's members, awardees, and guests that the arts warrant a monument: that the resources of the democracy, rallied by improvised private means, can construct a place where artistic achievement, as judged by artists, is honored. Fashions in achievement change. Many honored in their lifetimes are forgotten, and some not honored are cherished by posterity: unpredictability goes with artistic endeavor. There is a quixotic comedy in the attempt to serve a grand ideal, and comic moments are not lacking in our chronicle. But the seriousness with which the members of this Academy have taken their responsibilities, nearly indefinable as they are, impressively marks this centennial history.

NOTES

1. *Boston Miscellany*, November 1842, reprinted in *Poe: Essays and Reviews* (New York: Literary Classics, Library of America, 1984), p. 549.

2. "Hawthorne and His Mosses," *Literary World*, August 17 and 24, 1859, reprinted in *Herman Melville* (New York: Literary Classics, Library of America, 1984), p. 1165.

ACKNOWLEDGMENTS

A Century of Arts and Letters was sponsored by the Centennial Committee of the American Academy of Arts and Letters: the committee's members were Will Barnet, Jack Beeson, John Guare, Elizabeth Hardwick, Ada Louise Huxtable, Jacob Lawrence, Jack Levine, Richard Lippold, Cynthia Ozick, Ned Rorem, Harrison Salisbury, Robert Venturi, Hugo Weisgall, and John Updike, chairman. The Academy members who composed this text could not have done so without the admirably thorough compilation, organization, and summation of the extensive Academy-Institute archives conducted by the institution's professional staff. Nancy Johnson was the scrupulous archivist and librarian during the bulk of this research; her able successors were Laura Stoland and Rossana Martinez. Katia Hadidian, Kathryn Talalay, Milena Chilla-Markhoff, and Jenni Kim all assisted. Lydia Kaim read back files and lent her invaluable personal knowledge of forty-seven years of the institution's existence. Betsey Feeley, besides undertaking editorial duties, sifted through the archives for photographs and supervised their selection. Virginia Dajani, the Academy's executive director, devoted many hours and much characteristic tact to steering the project through its many human channels. John Moore, Jennifer Crewe, Sarah St. Onge, and Ron Harris of the Columbia University Press provided abundant editorial care and wisdom. The greatest debt is owed to the members of the National Institute of Arts and Letters and American Academy of Arts and Letters, living and dead, whose words and decisions form the substance of this volume and the essence of its interest.

A CENTURY of ARTS & LETTERS

CHAPTER ONE

1898–1907

THE FOUNDERS' STORY

R. W. B. Lewis

THE INITIAL SUGGESTION for what would become the first enduring literary and artistic elite in America was made on a September day in 1898, on the veranda of a hotel in Saratoga, New York. The American Social Science Association—a large loose organization founded in 1865 and containing departments of jurisprudence, education, and others—was holding its annual meeting in Saratoga, and one of its members, H. Holbrook Curtis, approached the president of the ASSA, Simeon Baldwin, with the idea of sponsoring a subcompany of men in literature and the arts. The new entity, so it was argued, might model itself to some degree on the Institut de France. (The latter, with its four Académies, dated from the early nineteenth century, but it was dominated by its literary component, the Académie française, which had been set up by Cardinal Richelieu in the 1630s and consisted of forty *littérateurs*.) Neither Curtis nor Baldwin was a literary or artistic person: Curtis was a throat specialist from New York City, and Baldwin was a federal judge in Connecticut and would later serve as governor of that state. But the thought seemed a good one: "There were many men," Curtis would recall having said, "who spend their lives in research and in literary pursuit, who would value beyond pecuniary reward the entrance into . . . an academic institution of unquestioned origin and standard."[1]

Judge Baldwin submitted the proposition to the council of the ASSA, which approved it at a December meeting. Dr. Curtis and Charles Dudley Warner, an essayist and fiction writer who had collaborated with Mark Twain, were then asked to oversee the selection of charter members in what for the moment was called the National Institute of Art, Science and Letters.

The notion of such an institute was far from new. One way of tracing the course of the national self-image is to notice the successive initiatives of this kind. In

September 1780, when the country itself was in the process of being founded, John Adams wrote to the president of Congress to propose (in a nice run of verbals) an "American Academy for Refining, Improving, and Ascertaining the English language." Nothing came of this, but forty years later, in the first flush of the nationalist temper, when the issue of an American as against a wholly English speech was being debated, a language teacher in New York City named William E. Cardell promoted the creation of an "American Academy of Language and Belles Lettres," which was to have representation from the entire country. Both the title and the overriding concern with language reflect the ancestry of the Académie française. This institution actually got under way, with John Quincy Adams as president, Supreme Court justice Brockholst Livingston, and Washington Irving among its counselors and corresponding members from twenty-one states, but the whole thing ran out of money. In 1868, amid the intense if muddled post–Civil War search for sources of national unity, a move began to organize a "National Institute of Letters, Arts and Sciences," the aim of which (and here the phrasing anticipates rather than echoes) was to enhance "the public welfare" by "disseminating correct views" on the matters named in the title. William Cullen Bryant and the historian John Lothrop Motley got involved; the transcendentalist writer and editor George Ripley worked on its behalf, in the belief that such an institute might give "a healthy tone to literature in this country"; the landscape architect Frederick Law Olmsted and George Templeton Strong, much later known to be the greatest of the Civil War diarists, were on the board. This enterprise, too, collapsed for lack of funds.[2]

But a fascination with the native cultural achievement, and how to identify and assess it, was more than ever in the American air as the last quarter of the century went forward. In 1884 a New York literary journal invited its readers to send in "a list of forty American authors of the sterner sex whom they deem most worthy of a place in a possible American Academy."[3] The response was unexpectedly heavy. The "Forty Immortals" chosen by the readership began with O. W. Holmes, Sr., James Russell Lowell, John Greenleaf Whittier, George Bancroft, and William Dean Howells. Henry James came in twenty-second, Mark Twain twenty-third, Walt Whitman twenty-ninth. William Wetmore Story and Francis Parkman arrived last, but there were also votes for many others, among them F. Marion Crawford, Richard Watson Gilder, and Edward Eggleston. And though only sterner-sex writers were to be admitted, votes were cast as well for Harriet Beecher Stowe, Helen Hunt Jackson, Julia Ward Howe, and Constance Fenimore Woolson.

Another potent sign of cultural self-awareness was the opening to the public, on November 1, 1897, of the new Library of Congress building in Washington, directly across the east plaza from the Capitol. It was John Adams who had authorized a Library of Congress in 1800, with the first books arriving from England a year later. A separate building for the enormously expanded library was approved in 1886, and the vast Italian Renaissance edifice was ready for use after a decade's wrangling. A guidebook of the day declared that "America is justly proud of this gorgeous and palatial monument to its National sympathy and appreciation of Literature, Science and Art . . . a fitting temple for the great thoughts of generations past, present and to be."[4] The facade and interior were decorated by more than fifty American painters and sculptors, almost half of whom before long would enter the Institute. And what was stressed at every turn was the national, indeed the nationwide, character of the new building.

It was less than a year later that Curtis and Baldwin, in their talk at Saratoga, helped launch a New York–based organization that was to be similarly expressive of a "National sympathy" for literature and the arts. Scores of invitations were sent out across the country, and almost all of them were accepted. On February 11, 1899, there took place what was billed as "the first annual meeting of the National Institute of Arts, Science and Letters" at the Academy of Medicine on West 43rd Street in New York.[5] Charles Dudley Warner was made temporary president, and there was talk about whether to remain a department of the Social Science Association (enhancing its status—so Judge Baldwin pointed out—and enlarging its membership) or to become an independent body (which Curtis favored).

The crucial decision was made in September 1899, at a joint meeting of the new Institute and the old Association. The Institute proclaimed its independent status, and it was announced via Henry van Dyke—Princeton professor and tireless author of stories, poems, and essays—that the Institute was dropping the word "Science" from its name.

At the same meeting, a report was given on the acceptances to membership. Ninety of these were in the department of literature, which was declared complete. A number of hoped-for members in the department of art were residing abroad (in France, mostly) and were hard to reach, but forty-five artists would shortly be inscribed. The minutes contain no reference to the department of music; it would nevertheless list fourteen names. The size of the Institute had changed a couple of times over the year; a limit of 150 members was now postulated, and so it would remain until 1908, when the number was increased to 250.

The charter members, to repeat, were selected by Curtis, Warner, and the Council of the ASSA, with various knowledgeable persons being solicited for nominations. At an early stage, for example, Curtis wrote Baldwin about a recent conference with Augustus Saint-Gaudens, the architect Charles McKim, and the painter Edward Simmons. All three voiced enthusiasm for the venture and urged Curtis to ask John Singer Sargent in Boston and James McNeill Whistler in London to act as a subcommittee for candidates in art. (Sargent was taken into the Institute, a bit late, in 1905, but this, strangely, seems to be the only recorded reference in the extant annals to Whistler.)

The Institute, as composed, exhibited a decidedly mixed response to the American scene on which it took its place, and this very question—the viable relation between the Institute and the world outside it—was of intermittent concern to the first participants. At the first public meeting ("public" meant that ladies, escorted by gentlemen members, were invited), which was held at the start of the new century on January 30, 1900, President Warner led off with a statement of purpose that dimly hinted at some sense of the historical environment. The aim of the Institute, he said, was "the advancement of art and literature"; the criterion for membership was "notable achievement" in those fields; and the body, while keeping alive "the traditions of good literature," should also be "hospitable to all discoverers of new worlds."[6] But discoverers of new worlds—in literature and art and music—were in the small minority at the outset of the Institute's history.

As to the *actual* world in its turn-of-the-century form, it was characterized by rapidly and enormously expanding business and industry; by the increasingly urban as against the rural (New York City in 1900 had a population of three million, five times the number in 1860; Chicago had more than tripled over four decades to one million); and by very big money. The secular gospel of the age was in two parts: wealth and success (more simply, the successful pursuit of wealth). Even the religious gospel got drawn in. "Godliness is in league with riches," the bishop of Massachusetts announced to almost audible applause. He went on to say, in words that stir teasing reminders of political talk not long since, that "Material prosperity is helping to make the national character sweeter, more joyous, more unselfish, more Christlike." Indeed, the bishop said, "in the long run it is only to the man of morality that wealth comes"; and by a natural corollary—this was widely assented to—lack of money was an infallible sign of lack of morality.[7]

Hamlin Garland, writing to the Institute secretary in 1903, had some of this in mind, when he talked about the Institute and the hard-driving, monied world outside it. With the fervor he displayed in his best and earliest work, *Main-Travelled Roads* (1891), Garland argued that the ideals of the members were "higher than those of commerce or politics and more liberal and fruitful than those of the churchmen." The work of the Institute, he continued, should be to dignify art and to insist on the importance of poetry, to say—especially to young people—that "there are other things better worth while than acquiring millions or being elected Senator of a state."[8]

Among American writers in the epoch, Walt Whitman—who died half a dozen years before the Institute was born—had spoken most eloquently against the dominance of business and money in American life and had expressed most strongly the hope that literature would save the day. "The depravity of the business classes in our country," he wrote in *Democratic Vistas* (1871), "is not less than has been supposed but infinitely greater." But he clung to the belief that there would arise in America "a class of native authors . . . fit to cope with our occasions, lands, permeating the whole mass of American mentality." By the late 1880s he had given up any such thought and could see nothing on the literary horizon but "accomplish'd, good-natured persons," performing decorously in polite society, skilled in such matters as whether the sherry should precede or follow the stewed eels on a dinner menu, "but for real crises, great needs and pulls, moral or physical, they might as well never have been born."

There was no shortage of such socially knowing, good-natured, and adaptable folk among the charter members of the Institute, especially in its department of literature, where a sizable number were not really literary practitioners but instead high-quality magazine editors, professors, and other well-settled arbiters of taste. But there were some who recoiled in disgust from the American cultural panorama, with its showiness, anti-intellectualism, and sanctimoniousness, especially among men of "barbaric wealth."[9] The quoted phrase is from Charles Eliot Norton, Harvard art professor and stern moralist, and Norton, like Henry Adams and one or two others, found respite from the ill-bred turmoil of their time in the orderly attractions of the Middle Ages. For persons so disposed, the Institute could serve as a refuge, a place where opinions could be shared about the bad state of things.

The Institute, in its literary membership, also represented a third response—beyond amiable acquiescence or flight—to the cultural surroundings. This was the activity of what Lionel Trilling called "the opposing self" and that he defined as an "intense and adverse imagination of the culture in which [the self] has its being."[10]

Mark Twain, in his cunning and contradictory way, had an elaborately adverse imagination of his native culture, whether the imagination focused on the old southern slave society or the postwar reverence for business and money. Henry James, in his own imaginative workings, made evident (as did Edith Wharton) the violence, even the murderousness, that could lurk behind the well-mannered conduct of the socially adept. William Dean Howells is an example of the imagination that *became* adverse under the pressure of historical event: specifically the Haymarket Square riot in Chicago in 1886—one of a series of riots and strikes that terrified the country and energized the labor unions—and its aftermath, when three anarchists were hanged for bomb throwing with not the slightest evidence of their guilt. Howells, whose social conscience had been aroused at just this time by Tolstoy's declaration of Christian socialist faith, tried to galvanize the literary community, to no avail; indeed, the former abolitionist Whittier, speaking as it were for his entire literary and social class, turned Howells down indignantly, and in the end Howells was the only major man of letters in the country to speak out against the savage injustice. In his writings thereafter (*Annie Kilburn, A Traveller from Altruria*), Howells evinced a concern with social wrongs that had been only implicit in his fine earlier novels (*A Modern Instance, The Rise of Silas Lapham*).

But William Dean Howells was an agreeable kind of activist, essentially cheerful in temper (despite private griefs); a person given to taking part in protest marches but also to showing up at fashionable tea parties. For all of this, he was everybody's favorite in the Institute from the time it began. He presided over it, after the death of Charles Dudley Warner, from 1901 to 1904; he was the first individual elected to the Academy in 1904 and served as its president until 1920. "Don't let him resign to take a back seat," Garland begged the secretary in 1903, when Howells was inclined to step down from the Institute. "He belongs just where he is in the Chair. . . . Character and achievement both combine to fit him for the place."[11] Garland was also, for a period, the object of Howell's benevolent and right-minded literary influence: Howells had encouraged him in his early quasi-realistic work and had implored him to stick to that line. (Garland didn't: he vanished into the mystical American West of the *Middle Border* books.) Another Howell's protégé and charter member was Henry Blake Fuller, who followed a path similar to Garland's: after two estimable tales of Chicago life in the 1890s (*The Cliff Dwellers* and *With the Procession*), somewhat in the Howells vein, Fuller gave up and reverted to romances set in Italy.

Outside the Institute, several writers were manifesting a more vigorously adverse imagination than anyone in it. Among them was Stephen Crane, whose brilliant tales of lyrical realism (*Maggie, George's Mother*, and so on) appeared in the 1890s but who died in 1900, at the age of twenty-eight, before the Institute could take sufficient note of him. Frank Norris also died prematurely, in 1902, at the age of thirty-two, but it is doubtful if his novels of business and industrial greed and brutality (*McTeague, The Octopus, The Pit*) would have made him welcome at the National Institute. The whole breed of the new realists and naturalists in fiction, in fact, was rejected by one main element in the Institute, as jauntily represented by Thomas Bailey Aldrich, poet, editor of the *Atlantic Monthly* and the author, early on, of *The Story of a Bad Boy*. Aldrich versified about these writers:

> The mighty Zolaistic movement now
> Engrosses us—a miasmatic breath
> Blown from the slums. We paint life as it is,
> The hideous side of it, with careful pains,
> Making a god of the dull commonplace.[12]

Frank Norris carried the additional burden of being from the Far West: Chicago-born but settled at an early age in San Francisco. The Institute had not wholly neglected the regions to the south and west of the eastern seaboard, but the members who hailed from those parts were relatively few and almost exclusively in Literature.[13] There were half a dozen from the southern states, among them the Kentuckian John Fox, Jr., who gave the world *The Little Shepherd of Kingdom Come*, and the Virginian Thomas Nelson Page, a local colorist of no little fame. From Indiana came Edward Eggleston (*The Hoosier Schoolmaster*) and a couple of others. The tendency even of these noneasterners, however, was to end up in New York. The Californians presented a somewhat different picture.

In the earlier generation, Mark Twain came from Missouri to spend a period of time in San Francisco, and Bret Harte came there from Albany; neither made it a permanent home. The most conspicuous if not the most talented of the early San Franciscans was Joaquin Miller, the flamboyant and self-declared "frontier poet," whose accounts of his exploits as a horse thief and Indian fighter rivaled the later autobiographical fantasies of William Faulkner. Miller was wildly popular in England and lent a certain zest to the eastern establishment of the Institute. There was also the venturesome naturalist and explorer John Muir (*The Mountains of California*), who grew up in Scotland and studied in Wisconsin before moving west to California. But at the century's end cultural activity from and about the Far West seemed to be slack.

The area had no more concerned observer than Frank Norris. In a newspaper article of January 1902, he described the West as being in a "transitional period" somewhere between the "wild life" of the past, so often depicted in dime novels and exaggerated travel writings, and the "quiet life" of the future. And he believed, as he wrote Howells excitedly after the appearance of *McTeague* in 1899, that "there is a chance for somebody to do some great work with the West and California as background," a novel with a regional setting but with national implications. He did not live to write it, and the eastern literati meanwhile were unable to set their sights properly on so distant a scene.

Jack London may be another who suffered from his San Francisco background, though his seeming endorsement of socialism, especially in the powerful *The Iron Heel* (1908) and his flirtation with the anarchist Emma Goldman would have put him out of court. Another avowed socialist in the era was Upton Sinclair; no contemporary imagination was more adverse than his to the social and economic order (see *The Jungle*, 1906). The Institute held him at bay until 1944, when in his sixty-seventh year and in the midst of his entertaining and politically amenable series of Lanny Budd novels, he was elected. Above all, of course, there was the Midwest-born Theodore Dreiser, scarcely known and scarcely knowable in the 1900s but coming into view later as one of the country's literary titans, with his rugged novelistic visions of human individuals buffeted by naturalistic force. Dreiser was finally considered for membership in 1935, but he declined the honor.

In the department of art, the great majority of members, predictably, were painters. There were a handful of sculptors, among them the influential

Augustus Saint-Gaudens; Daniel Chester French, he of the Lincoln Memorial in Washington and the seated John Harvard in the Harvard University yard; and Frederick MacMonies, resident and teacher in Paris for a quarter of a century, nonclassical and even impressionistic in his figures. Charles McKim seems to have been the only architect in the founding group, but his partner Stanford White was elected in 1905 (the year before White was shot to death), as was Daniel Burnham, the urban planner and architect of high aesthetic ideals. But caution is necessary in describing the membership of this department: several artists, like the world-traveling and world-portraying Frederic Church, declined or tried to decline election, and almost a third of the original department have so completely disappeared from celebrity that their identities and achievements are virtually unrecoverable.

About half the painters in 1898 might be categorized as American impressionists, using the phrase flexibly. Leading the list were the definitive impressionists: Childe Hassam, William Merritt Chase, John H. Twachtman, and J. Alden Weir. Maurice Prendergast, for all his ceremonially colorful scenes of Venice and New York, was unaccountably left out. The two greatest American painters in the period, Winslow Homer and Thomas Eakins, were chosen only after a delay: Homer in 1905 (he was instantly elevated to the new Academy), and Eakins in 1908. (Eakins rejected the offer, possibly out of justifiable irritation at having been excluded for a decade.)

The dominance of the impressionists was to be expected. By the century's end, American impressionistic painting, with its beguilingly and sometimes arrestingly decorative treatment of surface (e.g., Twachtman's *The White Bridge* and Weir's still more artful, dreamlike *The Red Bridge*) had become familiar to native art lovers everywhere, though the Institute was ahead of public taste in recognizing Twachtman. The movement was devoid of the enjoyable scandal that had adhered to the French impressionists; by 1905 the American form could almost be called a "safe" and academic mode of expression. A kind of gentility was shown in the three-piece suits most of these artists wore in the studio (Hassam was an exception). They looked rather like businessmen or at least like people at ease in the business world.[14] But they were real painters, with a genuine appreciation of visual experience, especially of natural settings. Gentlemanly and to an extent Europeanized, they nonetheless worked hard and devotedly, and there is a kind of durable artistic assurance in their best work.

Just as the literature department looked askance at such hard-edged realists as Norris, Sinclair, and London, or looked right past them, so the Art Department was slow and tentative with those younger painters who pushed to new extremes the "realistic" treatments exemplified by Eakins. "The younger artists," writes Jules Prown, ". . . wanted to capture in their art the actual sensory feel of experience. . . . They wanted to go where the action was, and the action was in the city." Prown himself points to affinities between the young urban realists and "such contemporary naturalist writers as Theodore Dreiser and Frank Norris."[15]

The artists in question in 1900s America included Robert Henri (he was of French descent but pronounced his name "Hen-rye"), John Sloan, George Luks, Everett Shinn, and George Bellows. In 1907 a group of them tried to put on an exhibition of their work at the National Academy of Design in New York, but the effort was turned down. They then mounted a show at the Macbeth Gallery. It earned them considerable notoriety and derision, along with scattered applause; it also earned them the enduring label of "The Ashcan School." Some of these same Ashcan artists, in 1913, helped to put on the large independent exhibition of contemporary art in New York that has become known as the Armory Show and is generally reckoned the single most important public event in American art history.

The Institute was not entirely hostile to the Ashcan artists. Robert Henri was elected in 1908, but Henri, somewhat like Howells, was at once a radical of sorts and an establishment personality. He rejected impressionism as superficial and academic, and he liked to present himself as a philosophical anarchist. In reality, however, he worked and taught in the great tradition of Emerson, Thoreau, and Whitman, and he had a gift for communication with his cultural elders. Another decade would go by before another Ashcanner, George Bellows, was invited in; his monumental picture *Both Members of the Club*, of two prizefighters in violent combat—two men trying to kill each other, Bellows said of it—is probably the most famous single work of the group.

American architecture, or the then-commanding phase of it, came into its own a few years before the Institute's founding, in the resplendent White City, built for the World's Columbian Exposition in Chicago in 1893: another sign, along with the Library of Congress building and the Institute itself, of the national culture seeking to come into focus. Daniel Burnham was the chief designer of the City, and in his own dictum, "the influence of the Exposition will be to inspire a reversion to the pure ideal of the ancients."[16] The ancients were represented rather by their Renaissance emulators, by colossal Beaux-Arts buildings based on sixteenth-century Roman, Florentine, and Venetian models, most imposingly in the Brunelleschian Duomo atop Richard Morris Hunt's administration building. The panorama created an overwhelming impression on the hordes of visitors to the exposition (not the least on Henry Adams, who let himself believe that America's own cultural day had finally arrived), and sketches and photographs of the various sites can still arouse an artistic excitement. But pretty much neglected amid the Renaissance display was the architectural equivalent of Frank Norris and the Ashcan painters: the Transportation Building of Louis Sullivan, half hidden in the rear of the City. Larzer Ziff, in his study *The American 1890s*, puts it forcibly: the "polychrome stridency" of Sullivan's Transportation Building was that architect's answer to the "static idealization of the human condition" espoused by Burnham and his like. The White City was a glorious event in its way; but Ziff observes rightly that twentieth-century architecture developed rather "out of the ideas of Sullivan." Burnham, however, was elected to the Institute in 1906 (Hunt died just too soon for membership), and Louis Sullivan was never elected at all, though he lived until 1924.

The department of music in its first phase showed a mix of the comfortably established and the cautiously innovative similar to that of Literature and Art. It was the smallest of the departments by far—fourteen members in 1898, with one addition in 1905—and it suffered from less vigorous attention. There was, as well, a feeling among the musical participants that music in America was still in an uncertain stage. Writing to Hamlin Garland in March 1907, George Chadwick—composer (overtures, symphonies, choral works), director of the New England Conservatory of Music in Boston, and one of the most interesting of the charter members—remarked that "the musicians in this country who have accomplished enough serious work to be worthy of membership in the Institute are not very plenty."[17] And Horatio Parker, in a talk at the first public meeting of the Institute in January 1900, sounded what had become a familiar note: that music in America was still neglected; that Americans abroad might boast about their railroads and their grain elevators but never about their music; that America must in time "have a vigorous school of American music" (with an audible stress on "American"); and that "we must work out our musical destiny for ourselves."[18]

Parker played a leading role in the American musical world at the turn of the century, and in many ways he was typical of it. A New Englander by origin, he followed in the footsteps of the chief musical New Englander of the earlier generation, John K. Paine (also a charter member), who had spent four years studying in Berlin and adhered, as he said, to "the historical forms developed by Bach, Handel, Mozart and Beethoven," steering clear of the "complicated technics of . . . Wagner, Liszt" and their associates. In 1875 Paine became the first professor of music at Harvard; Horatio Parker in turn became the first professor of music at Yale in 1894. Among his early students was a young man from Danbury, Charles Ives, who would say of his former teacher that "his choral works have dignity and depth" but that in general Parker was too restricted by his German models and training.[19] Parker's most enduring work, as Ives implied, were his choral pieces, especially *Hora Novissima*, an hour-long composition in eleven movements, based on a twelfth-century Latin poem.

There were several other New England presences in the first music group. The most widely known member of all was the New Englander Edward MacDowell, composer of landscapes and seascapes (*New England Idylls*) and of the tremendously popular "To a Wild Rose," along with symphonic poems drawn from the Arthurian legends and from Shakespeare; MacDowell studied for twelve years in Germany and, by the end of the century and as the first professor of music at Columbia, was championing the new German music of Liszt and Wagner and offering rich chromatic harmonies of his own.

MacDowell, in addition, was the author of a work called *Indian Suite*, in which he undertook to depict Indian village life in America by drawing on Iowa, Kiowa, and Chippewa melodies. In fact, as a recent study has pointed out, MacDowell got his Indian material not from a visit to a tribal settlement but from a German dissertation (published in Leipzig) on American Indian music, and "after the opening horn call, there is little except the titles of the various movements to evoke tribal life or American culture."[20] Even so, it was a gesture in the right direction: the direction, at least, that certain voices outside the country were urging.

The most effective of these voices, needless to say, was Antonin Dvořák, particularly in an article in *Harper's New Monthly* for February 1895. On the basis of his experience in the United States, the composer of the *New World Symphony* was hopeful that the intense patriotism and enthusiasm he had encountered everywhere in America could now be addressed to the cause of music. Dvořák was dedicated to "music that is most characteristic of the nation whence it springs"; for America, he advanced the proposition that "inspiration for truly national music might be derived from the negro melodies and Indian chants."[21] He spoke of "the so-called plantation songs" that were "the most stirring and appealing melodies that have yet been found on this side of the water." "Plantation and slave songs," he went on, were "distinguished by unusual and subtle harmonies, the like of which I have found in no other songs but those of old Scotland and Ireland." The fact that some of these songs were written by a white composer, Stephen Foster, should not bother anyone, Dvořák added firmly. He said next to nothing about "Indian chants" beyond the reference to them; and he perhaps spent more time than necessary lecturing his American readers on the history and glories of music in Europe.

Dvořák's musical summons and MacDowell's halting example were followed up here and there: notably, by Arthur Farwell, who offered a *Navaho War Dance* in 1906, and by Henry F. B. Gilbert, author of *Comedy Overture on Negro Themes*, also in 1906. But neither Farwell nor Gilbert was mentioned at the Institute, and they had trouble publishing their work in America. The national spirit in music called for by Dvořák would really await the arrival of Aaron Copland (elected to the Institute in 1942). And this was, as it is always disconcerting to remember, because the profoundly, quintessentially national music of Charles Ives, though in existence from about 1900 onward, would not be performed until the 1940s and not be truly known for several decades after that. Ives went

to Yale, as has been said, and studied with Horatio Parker (as an undergraduate, he wrote tunes like *A Song of Mory's* and *The Bells of Yale*). Persuaded that music was a nonpaying vocation, Ives, like Wallace Stevens, worked for an insurance company and composed on weekends and vacations, composed particularly in the period 1905–1917, the time from which his great sonata "Concord, Mass. 1849–1860" derives, with its impressions of Emerson, Thoreau, Hawthorne, and the Alcotts. But even before that epoch of masterpieces, Ives completed works like "Harvest Home Church," probably in 1900, and "Procession" in 1901.

There were no women members during the first eight years of the Institute's existence. The issue was raised near the very outset, in August 1899, by Thomas Wentworth Higginson, the stalwart if now aging Cambridge-based social activist, whose admirable career had included the command of the first black regiment in the Civil War and the editorial support of Emily Dickinson's poetry and who had continued to speak out for equal rights for black Americans and voting rights for American women. When invited to join the Institute—his Brahmin background, as it were, making up for his radical per-formances—Higginson wrote Hamilton Mabie, the acting secretary, that much as he would like to be a member, there was "one fatal objection, that it comprises one sex only." He pointed out that other comparable organizations (he cited the Massachusetts Historical Society) admitted women, even if in small numbers, and that in some of these, women served "in high positions." Given these facts, he concluded, he must respectfully decline membership.[22]

The Institute officials pretended not to notice Higginson's refusal to join, and he was carried on the books as a founding member. In 1905 they went through the motions of reelecting him; he again declined, but a compromise of sorts was reached through a rewording of the Institute's constitution whereby women were not formally excluded. Higginson accepted what he called "replacement," and in the next year, in 1906, he nominated Julia Ward Howe for election. Mark Twain seconded the nomination, and Richard Watson Gilder, poet and editor of the *Century*, added his name. Mrs. Howe was duly elected on January 25, 1907, by a vote of thirty-five to four ballots. In 1908 she was elevated to the Academy.

Julia Ward Howe was eighty-seven years old at the time of her election, and though she had done conspicuously valuable work (of special appeal to Higginson) in abolition and women's suffrage, it is probable that most of the ballots were endorsing both an old friend and the author of "The Battle Hymn of the Republic." They were electing a song whose phrases had gone into the national language. Among those who held out against Mrs. Howe was Barrett Wendell, Harvard professor and early advocate of American literature, who told the Institute secretary that "I am so strongly opposed to the prece-dent of admitting women that even my affection for Mrs. Howe cannot change my opinion."[23] When notified of her election, Julia Ward Howe wrote the secretary asking him to convey to the proper persons "the assurance of my appreciation of the honor conferred upon me."[24]

In January 1905 Richard Watson Gilder approached the then-president of the Institute, the genteel poet and Wall Street broker Edmund Clarence Stedman, and urged him to hold a "formal discussion" on the question of women in both the Institute and the newly created Academy—a formal discussion, he said, rather than the "desultory talk among members" that was all there had been so far—and he observed, as Higginson had done, that "scientific, historical and art associations" were by now admitting women and that "in matters of art," indeed, "it is growingly the custom to make no distinction." He suggested the immediate nomination of "Mrs. Julia Ward Howe and Mrs. Wharton among writers" and "Cecilia Beaux among artists."[25] Higginson in turn, in late 1908, asked Gilder to join him in nominating Edith Wharton (Gilder had edited various of Wharton's nonfictional writings for the *Century*); Mark Twain and Edward Everett Hale were being asked to support the nomination.[26] Edith Wharton, nonetheless, was not elected for almost two more decades; in 1926 she entered the Institute, together with Mary Wilkins Freeman and the cultivated and witty essayist Agnes Repplier. (It might be added that the Académie française held back from admitting women until at last, in the 1980s, it elected the expatriate Marguerite Yourcenar, then herself in her eighties.)

In a much later retrospect, it is easy to identify a goodly number of women eligible on every count for membership in one or another of the three

Edmund Clarence Stedman, journalist, poet, literary critic, and Wall Street broker, was president of the Institute from 1905 to 1906 and one of the founders of the Academy. (Frederick Stuart Stedman, 1903)

departments. In literature, in addition to those just named (Mary Wilkins Freeman's superb *A New England Nun and Other Stories* had appeared in 1891), there were the highly accomplished Sarah Orne Jewett (*Deephaven*, 1877; *The Country of the Pointed Firs*, 1896), and Kate Chopin (*Bayou Folks*, 1894; and the alarming masterpiece *The Awakening*, 1899). In the field of American art, Cecilia Beaux (1863–1942), bold and original portraitist of Theodore Roosevelt, Clemenceau, and others was a likely nomination; but the greatest woman artist of the age was a person never once alluded to in Institute discussion: Mary Cassatt (1845–1926), who began to exhibit with the French impressionists in late 1870s Paris. She was almost unrivaled as a designer of surface space, and in the 1890s she created a set of colored prints, deriving from the Japanese, that in Jules Prown's opinion are "among the most beautiful works of graphic art ever produced by an American artist."[27] Again, a number of other names could be listed: at the Columbian Exposition, for example, some three score women artists were on show. In the world of music, one name at least should be emphasized: Amy Marcy Cheney Beach (she went by the name of her husband, the Boston physician H. H. A. Beach, a man well regarded among the intelligentsia—the ailing Henry James, Sr., had been one of his patients). Mrs. Beach, a follower, like many others, of John Kendall Paine, was a thoroughly professional composer in the romantic mode: piano works, chamber works, a symphony (the "Gaelic" of 1894), and about one hundred and twenty songs that were performed by international recitalists. She is generally regarded as the foremost American woman in music of her time.

If the possibility of admitting women was sometimes talked about in a desultory manner at Institute gatherings, no one, so far as can be discovered, ever proposed the nomination of a black person. In saying that, however, one must also acknowledge that the whole idea of minority representation—in a cultural context or in any other—was nowhere entertained in turn-of-the-century America, nor would it be for another seventy years or more. Yet several black writers of achievement were visible in the early 1900s, even granting that they are a good deal more visible to us today. Frederick Douglass had died in 1892, but on the horizon was Booker T. Washington, whose *Up From Slavery* came out in 1901 and whose presence in the organization could have matched that of such politically grounded white writers as John Hay and Theodore Roosevelt. Also on the scene were Paul Laurence Dunbar (1872–1906), whose volumes of poems in the late 1890s (*Oaks and Ivy* and others) made him prominent, in the language of the day, as "*the* 'Negro writer' "; Charles Chesnutt (1858–1932), whose two books of fiction (*Conjure Woman* and *The Wife of His Youth*) marked the arrival of the first unmistakably gifted black writer of fiction; and W. E. B. Du Bois, a man who created entire chapters of history in the American twentieth century but whose classic work *The Souls of Black Folks* appeared as early as 1902 and captured the interest, among other members of the Institute, of Du Bois's former teacher William James.[28] Du Bois was at last elected to the Institute in 1944, at the age of seventy-six.

Fewer names come to mind in the area of art, but one that does is Henry Tanner (1850–1937), Pennsylvania-born student of Thomas Eakins; a student and then a permanent resident in Paris; the creator of genre scenes such as "The Banjo Lesson" (1893, now in the Hampton Institute) and more typically of religious subjects such as "The Raising of Lazarus" (purchased by the French government). Tanner was elected to the National Academy of Design in 1909, the first black artist to be so recognized, but despite his beginnings with Eakins and his association with that unending stream of Americans at the Académie Julien in Paris (no few of them eventual Institute members), Tanner was never considered at the Institute. In music, the work and performances of the black musical artist Scott Joplin had been witnessed by 1910, but it would be many a year before the black rhythms and melodies enjoyed by Dvořák would be recognized in anything like the degree they warranted.

The absence of Jewish names on the Institute roster in its first decade is largely to be explained by the absence of Jewish writers and artists in the country at large. There had been Jewish members of the New World population since the 1660s, many of them in Newport (their beautiful cemetery there was visited and reflected upon by Longfellow in one of his best poems). But the great waves of Jewish immigration began only in the 1880s, following the savage pogroms in eastern Europe. These events led to the first notable work of poetry in America by a Jewish writer: *Songs of a Semite*, by Emma Lazarus, author as well of the address to the Statue of Liberty and a friend of Emerson (an admired acquaintance, too, of William James). Emma Lazarus died prematurely in 1887, before the Institute was conceived. The early work of Mary Antin, refugee from Russian Poland, could have been known in 1900, but her defining achievement, *The Promised Land*, an autobiographical account of European Jewish life, did not come out until 1912. In the same way, the fledgling novel of Abraham Cahan, *Yekl: a Tale of the Ghetto*, was published in 1896, but though it was, typically, noticed and praised by William Dean Howells, who reviewed it together with *The Red Badge of Courage*, it made little impression. Cahan's major work, *The Rise of David Levinsky*, a semiautobiographical narrative about a Jewish immigrant from Russia, did not make its appearance until 1917.[29]

The American Academy of Arts and Letters originated in a tiny Institute committee meeting—called to discuss some budgetary matters—in early January 1904. The Institute had been moving along somewhat haphazardly, with intermittent queries by members as to the purpose and value of the outfit and the occasional resignation of a dissatisfied member. Meetings continued, as many as four a year, though not often well attended (fourteen turned out for the January 1901 gathering). Talks were given with a certain regularity. There were several on drama: by the popular playwright Augustus Thomas, by Brander Matthews, professor of dramatic literature at Columbia, and—in a rambling and enjoyable discourse based on his own stage experience—by the much-loved Joseph Jefferson, the Rip van Winkle impersonator. There were discussions of painting and sculpture and a talk entitled "The Relation of the Fine Arts to the People." Horatio Parker surveyed the state of music in America, and Thomas Lounsbury considered correct pronunciation in English. One concern that was periodically raised had to do with finances, and this led to the committee meeting in question.

There was no cause for budgetary anxiety. Members were charged $5 a year in dues, and the treasurer, Congressman Perkins, invariably reported a favorable balance. In January 1903 the balance was so large ($800) that Perkins decided not to ask for dues that year. Expenses averaged less than $150 a year; the Institute dinner in April 1904, as an example, cost $45, the one in December of that year $41—something like $2.50 a head. There were printing bills from time to time, and the secretary's clerical assistance ran to $75 a year.

But a few restless souls in the Institute yearned for more costly activities. Robert Underwood Johnson, magazine editor and sporadic poet and probably the most dedicated figure in the entire history of the Institute and the Academy, had for some time been urging that the Institute should seek to raise an endowment. Such a thing, he said in a September 1902 letter, would make possible prizes for accomplishment in art, literature, and music and the publication of papers read at the dinners; it could pay for the entertainment of foreign visitors, and, closest to Johnson's heart, it could underwrite the building of a permanent *home* for the Institute, "a small beautiful classical building" that would serve as a clubhouse, even as the Players' club did for actors.[30] It was to look into Johnson's proposals that a committee showed up for the January 1904 meeting: MacDowell, Stedman, and Johnson. While they were considering how Institute members could best appeal for funds, MacDowell suggested that the Institute might be divided into two classes, one of which would be of greater weight and influence with donors. Stedman then reworked this idea by proposing that a smaller body actually be organized within the Institute, and that it be called an academy. This notion was received with enthusiasm by the other two men, and a few weeks later the creation of an academy was formally recommended. (The matter of an endowment was temporarily shelved.)

At the Aldine Association on Fifth Avenue, on a Saturday evening in April, with twenty of the one hundred and thirty members of the Institute present— Childe Hassam and Josiah Royce, for a rarity, among them—the formation of the Academy was approved unanimously. The new body would consist of thirty members chosen entirely from the Institute, and Johnson then orchestrated an intricate method of selection: seven members would be elected by ballot of the Institute; those seven would among them choose eight more; those fifteen would then choose five more; and finally those twenty would then choose the final ten. The process needs following in a certain detail. By December 2, 1904, the original seven members had been named, sixty-one people (about half the living membership) having sent in their ballots. Howells led, with fifty-three votes; then came Saint-Gaudens, with forty-six; Stedman, with thirty-eight; John La Farge, thirty-four; Clemens, with twenty-three;

John Hay, with nineteen; MacDowell, with seventeen. Charles Eliot Norton, with sixteen votes, fell just short, as did Henry James, with fourteen.

What was called "the first Conference of the Members of the Academy of Arts and Letters" was held at the Century Association on January 7, 1905. Two of the original seven could not make it: Howells was in Europe, and Clemens was ill. Robert Underwood Johnson was there as acting secretary. The five voting members moved swiftly to elect Henry James, Charles McKim, and Henry Adams. After a certain amount of give-and-take, four more names were added: Charles Eliot Norton, John Quincy Adams Ward, Thomas Lounsbury, and Theodore Roosevelt. There was general agreement on Thomas Bailey Aldrich, but a formal vote was delayed until Howells and Clemens could be consulted. Aldrich was later inducted.

Present at the January meeting and making careful notes was Robert Underwood Johnson, whom the group had named preliminary secretary of the Academy. This appointment, according to Grace Vanamee, close friend and great admirer of Johnson and herself connected with the Academy for twenty-six years, from 1915 on, was unquestionably the most important event in the history of the Academy. Johnson was excessively formal, to the verge of pomposity, and he was rigorously traditional in his own tastes, but he was tireless and meticulous, and Mrs. Vanamee was probably right to say that he did more to shape the Academy than any other member. He himself was elected in 1908.

With fifteen members, the makeup of the new Academy, in midwinter 1905, began to be apparent. Literature predominated: ten of the fifteen belonged to that department. But there were four in art: a painter of portraits and landscapes (John La Farge); an architect (Charles McKim); and two portrait sculptors of vigorous "naturalist" tendency (Saint-Gaudens and J. Q. A. Ward). Only one musician, Edward MacDowell, who told Johnson in his letter of acceptance that he regarded his election as an honor "Not only for myself but also for the recognition of the art of Music in this land."[31]

The literary members were a suggestive assembly. Of the ten, only four could incontestably be called writers: Howells, Mark Twain, Henry James, and Henry Adams. Two were academics: Charles Eliot Norton, of Harvard, and Thomas Lounsbury, a professor of English at Yale and author of a panoramic *History of the English Language*. The remaining two, John Hay and Theodore Roosevelt, were public figures, and their selection made apparent what had been implicit in the Institute's literary list: the sensible desire to have individuals of high public visibility and authority. John Hay, Lincoln's assistant secretary and currently secretary of state, was the author, with John Nicolay, of the ten-volume *Abraham Lincoln* (1890); a journalist, the author of dialect poems about Illinois frontier life, and a novelist, he might well have been chosen even if he had never served in government. In his letter of acceptance, from the Department of State in Washington, Hay declared with lively sin-

Henry James (ca. 1881), crayon drawing in the Academy's collection by Abbott Handerson Thayer, his boyhood friend and fellow Academician.

cerity that he was "equally surprised and gratified" by his election, which he took as "the greatest distinction I have ever received."[32] Theodore Roosevelt, the president of the United States, composed his four-volume *The Winning of the West* in the late 1890s while working as head of the New York City police; it is a well-informed study of the settlement of the Northwest territory, rhetorically and perhaps a bit anachronistically in the Parkman mode. Roosevelt also wrote *The Rough Riders* and *The Strenuous Life*, among others; he was as energetic with the pen as in public affairs. But he was an avid and to some degree discriminating reader of history, fiction, and poetry, and with Thomas Jefferson, the Adamses, and Abraham Lincoln, one of the relatively few occupants of the White House over two centuries to whom the word *literary* might be applied.

The creation of the Academy went ahead fairly swiftly with a meeting of eight of the fifteen—the others being variously on their travels—in late April at the Aldine Association. In a nice gesture, the dying Joseph Jefferson was

President Theodore Roosevelt, an avid reader, in his car in 1910. He was elected to the Institute in 1898 and to the Academy in 1905. (Courtesy of the Theodore Roosevelt Association.)

elected (he died the following evening). The group then balloted to elect John Singer Sargent, Richard Watson Gilder, and Horace Howard Furness, a Shakespearian scholar of the first rank and founder of the *New Variorum* edition. After some wrangling, during which, according to the record, William James was elected and then unelected, the vote was given to John Bigelow, newspaper editor, the effective American consul general in Paris during the Civil War, and editor of the writings of Benjamin Franklin.

About three weeks later, the election of the final ten members of the Academy took place, again at the Aldine Association, at eleven in the morning. Eight Academicians were present; seven more sent their ballots, with accompanying letters. The second ballot resulted in four names: Winslow Homer, Carl Schurz, Alfred Thayer Mahan, and Joel Chandler Harris. Schurz and to a lesser degree Mahan enlarged the presence of the publicly prominent. The German-born Schurz had been Lincoln's minister to Spain and Hayes's secretary of the interior (where he worked hard to improve the treatment of American Indians and to conserve natural resources); he had been a senator from Missouri and was coeditor of the *New York Post* and author of many collections of reminiscences and speeches. Mahan, a rear admiral, had produced the much-consulted *Influence of Sea Power Upon History, 1660–1783*.

William James was then "declared elected 'viva voce' ";[33] and in a complicated third ballot, five more names were added to complete the Academy membership of thirty. These final members were Daniel Chester French; John Burroughs, an ally of Walt Whitman and often said to be the greatest American writer about nature after Thoreau; James Ford Rhodes, prize-winning American historian; Edwin Austin Abbey, book and magazine illustrator and muralist (*The Quest for the Holy Grail*); and Horatio Parker.

On June 15, William James, writing from his Cambridge, Massachusetts home, informed Johnson that he could not accept membership in the Academy. He had, he said, just returned from three months in Europe—where (though he did not say so) he had been grandly celebrated at a philosophical conference in Rome, had met there with a group of devoted epigones headed by Giovanni Papini, and in Paris had enjoyed a session with Henri Bergson—and found awaiting him "the very flattering news" of his election. The thought of being associated with "so many illustrious names" tempted him to accept, but against that was his "lifelong practice of not letting my name figure when there is not some definite work doing in which I was willing to bear a share." He had preached all his life, he said, against the vanities of the world, especially of the academic world.

He could not discover that the Academy would engage in any significant kind of work and had, rather, the impression of an organization for the mere purpose of "distinguishing certain individuals (with their own connivance) and enabling them to say to the world at large 'we are in and you are out.' "

Then came the sentence that would ripple through many a later account of the affair: "And I am the more encouraged to this course by the fact that my younger and shallower and vainer brother is already in the Academy, and that if I were there too, the other families might think the Jameses' influence too rank and strong."[34] To drive the message home, William James took the step of resigning from the Institute as well. Johnson replied at once, with a picture (in James's words) of "the Academy's duties and functions," but it only confirmed James in his viewpoint and his decision. "I am going to stand fast by both my resignations," he concluded.[35]

William James was not the only person to decline membership in the Institute, or the Academy, or both. Charles W. Eliot, the president of Harvard, refused election to the Institute at the moment of its founding, declaring it to be too small and too exclusive to attract him; in 1908, asked to join the Academy, he described himself as "too old to take part in a new organization" (he was seventy-four), but he wished it well. The physician-novelist S. Weir Mitchell managed to avoid being taken into the Institute, and when he was nominated for the higher body in 1905, he wrote Johnson a chilly note to say "I do not want to belong to the Academy or to any more institutions than I do at present." The artist Abbot Thayer tried to "drop out of the Institute," as he put it (he needed "all my five dollarses for too many very vital things"), but his resignation was not accepted, and he was elevated to the Academy in 1909.[36]

There was, though, something special about the case of William James. His stated objection to academic honors did not hold much water: he had accepted a number of these from what might be called nonworking as well as working academic centers, and in the curriculum vitae he himself sent to the Institute in 1902 he listed membership in five such bodies. In his June 15 letter, there was an unmistakable note of badly wounded pride. He probably thought he was being humorous in his allusion to his vainer and shallower younger brother, but, fresh from his international triumphs, he was aware that the younger Henry had been elected to the Academy two meetings and three months ahead of him. What he presumably did not know, and what would have made matters sourer for him, was that Henry had not voted for William on either ballot that May morning.[37] The fraternal relationship, as it happened, was in one of its recurring periods of tension and even rancor that year, with William vocally resenting Henry's articles about the American scene (Henry was exploring it from coast to coast), which not only invaded what had long been William's cultural territory but also found severe fault with a lot of it. Henry's vanity, William implied, was made clear by his accepting the vanity of Academy membership, and his shallowness by his travel pieces.

Stedman must have intuited something of this. On the back of William James's second letter, he scribbled in pencil the following:

Old Ditty (in Chas. Reade)
So fare you well, my Lady Jane—
If you are proud, I'll be the same!
I make no doubt but I shall find
As pretty a girl unto my mind—

    Sing, fol-de-rol—de-rol—etc.[38]

The individual named by Stedman and his fellows to replace William James—whether equally attractive to their minds or not—was William Milligan Sloane, professor of history at Columbia, not much remembered today but the author of a once popular lavishly illustrated and nicely written life of Napoleon in four volumes.

William James's contention about the Academy's nonactivity was all too soundly based. Henry James himself, as late as 1914, was complaining in the same way. Commenting on a jubilant letter announcing the gift of a vast sum of money to create a permanent home for the Academy, James declared that, to his sense, the Academy should have made good on its "promises" before accepting large money gifts and that the "striking absence of anything to 'show' "—in the way of support for artistic and literary endeavors—gave him "very gravely to think."[39]

Promises of a sort had been put forward in a document drafted by Johnson and revised by Stedman and Howells and circulated between May and November 1905. It was called "The Work and Functions of an Academy in America" and was seemingly the report William James referred to in his second letter. The Academy, it propounded in the first of its sixteen numbered points, should be "representative of the best American achievement in literature and the arts" and should make itself "a center and rallying point of the best literary and artistic opinions." It should stand for "dignity, moderation and purity of expression" and oppose "vulgarity, sensationalism, meretriciousness, lubricity and other forms of degeneracy." It should resist "the tyranny of novelty" and might draw up "well considered lists of words or meanings *taboo*." It might, though only very occasionally, give public expression of opinion in "affairs of literature and the arts."

To most of these earnest platitudes, William James could reply, as he did, that he saw nothing in them that suggested work he could take part in. But there are other points in the paper that he might have gone along with. One was the repeated necessity of a permanent home, a local habitation, for the Academy: something "beautiful, simple, comfortable . . . with alcoves for quiet hours" and a library. James may have wondered at Johnson's hope that this be "the most beautiful small classic building in America," but he could approve the general idea of a place that would invite more frequent meetings and so help establish greater solidarity.

Perhaps the key positive paragraph was point five, which spoke of receiving and administering gifts of money "in the interest of the promotion of literature and the arts; to set on foot or assist enterprises of special promise; to protect and aid men of distinguished ability who for lack of means cannot pursue important enterprises ... to provide and bestow medals and to administer travelling or stationary scholarships and branch seats of the Academy abroad ... as for example for the study of music in Munich, of sculpture in Florence or of letters in England and in France; to establish prizes." It was not until about 1941 that anything like that handsome program was genuinely under way in the Academy and the Institute; then, many and varied awards began to be given regularly, works of art purchased, exhibitions mounted, musical productions underwritten, and fellowships in America and abroad conferred—and with recipients by this time of either gender.

Still, William James's dismissal of the Academy as a cluster of self-serving individuals anxious merely to assert their own exclusivity was not entirely accurate. Self-indulgences and bias, of a recurringly human variety, were patently at work: in the selection of members and in the tone and style of the proceedings. But the selection and proceedings also bore witness to a continuing concerted effort, at the turn of the century, to declare to the world the nature of American culture, its achievements, and its tendencies.

These actions of the Academy amounted to a historical statement, a statement not only about the condition of things cultural at an epochal moment in history but also about the persistent responsiveness *to* history displayed by the leading figures. The culture so imaged to a telling degree refuted the prophecies of Alexis de Tocqueville, who, in his classic study *Democracy in America* (1835 in France, 1838 in America), opined that the culture of a democratic people would never show much concern for the historical. In America, he said, "no one cares for what occurred before his time"; Americans had no interest in keeping records or retelling old legends, and so, in America as in other democratic nations, "each generation is a new people." Democratic art and literature, accordingly, would not examine human beings in historical social settings, Tocqueville said, but would deal rather with "Man himself, taken aloof from his country and his age and standing in the presence of Nature and God."[40]

Several of Tocqueville's pronouncements strike a resonant chord today; one has heard, one has even made, similar observations about the national habit of forgetfulness, and the indifference to history. But the study of history in America was beginning even as Tocqueville wrote, and sixty years later a sophisticated knowledge of history was almost the mark of the cultivated person. The reasons for such a development are far to seek, but central among them is the colossal event of the Civil War. There is much to be said for Robert

Penn Warren's argument that, for Americans, history—the consciousness of it as something alive and powerful—was the legacy of the Civil War.[41]

In any case, by the century's end, the American mind at its best was becoming imbued with history. Of the original Academicians, no few could be classified as historians, indeed, as historians of the American experience: Henry Adams, John Hay, Theodore Roosevelt, and James Ford Rhodes (who followed a history of the United States with a history of the Civil War); and to these may be added the naval historian Mahan and the historian of language Lounsbury. The fiction writers, meanwhile, provided vivid impressions of social reality in moments of critical transition: William Dean Howells was particularly good at this; Henry James realized belatedly that his novels of the 1900s foretold the social cataclysm of 1914; Mark Twain exposed strains in the country's racial past. Even among the artists, the historical alertness was notable: St. Gaudens, for example, was a historian of sorts in sculpture, with his portrait of Robert Shaw and the 54th Black Regiment and his portrayals of Lincoln, Sherman, Howells, Stevenson. John La Farge gave his countrymen their first views of contemporary Japanese life and scenery; John Singer Sargent and Winslow Homer managed to catch representative Americans of the age, highborn or seafaring, in characteristic postures.

"Man himself . . . standing in the presence of Nature and God" had indeed been the great subject for the literary imagination in the romantic period, and something of that ideal being still appealed to the native artist. But as the twentieth century made its start, the native artistic attention was drawn far more often to men and women in the very midst of the historical life. This it was that the founding members of the Academy exemplified, by and large, and this it was that they honored and recognized in their selections and gatherings, with whatever narrowness of vision and stuffiness of manner. What it added up to was a collective image of America watching itself come of age.

In 1905 the Institute's Literature members brought in another half-dozen members, the most notable of whom was Brooks Adams, whose best-known work today, *The Degradation of the Democratic Dogma*, was still in the future. Since Henry Adams's other brother, Charles Francis, Jr., historian of railroads and former president of the Union Pacific, was already a member, the Adams family influence was thereby stronger if not ranker than anything the Jameses might have feared or aspired to.

During the same January 1907 meeting in which Julia Ward Howe was official voted into the Institute, a resolution was passed supporting a petition to Congress from the American Copyright League on behalf of a pending copyright bill. The motion was the slow consequence of discussions at the Institute over a number of years, the matter being the one public issue to which the members sought some way of responding. The bill itself would greatly extend the legal protection of authors, both native and foreign. The Institute's declaration asked that "provision be made for the full security of the composer in all commercial reproduction of music"; and it asked for the "abolition of duty on works of art."[42]

Earlier in the evening, the members (seventeen were on hand) passed a resolution that a medal be given annually to an American judged to "have rendered most distinguished services to any of the arts in the creation of original works"; Institute members would be eligible. Reporting on both the evening's measures, Secretary Johnson (with William James's words, it seems, in his head) remarked that "they make the beginning of a policy of practical usefulness on the part of the Institute to the various professions represented in its membership."[43] It cannot be said that this "beginning" had any swift or substantial follow-up: the first Institute medal was not awarded until 1909, and the first Academy medal not until 1915.

What did follow, as the Institute's first decade came to an end, was a decision to expand its numbers. In December 1907 the Academy, voted to increase its members from thirty to fifty, and taking note of this, the Institute on December 16 voted to enlarge its membership limit to two hundred and fifty, with an eye, so President Sloane proclaimed, to taking in people from new sections of the country and so to make the Institute, as its name would have it, a national entity.

NOTES

Unless otherwise specified, all materials cited are located in the Academy files, which are also the source of any unannotated archival sources in the text.

1. Typed statement, including document of February 15, 1899, describing formation of the National Institute of Arts and Letters.

2. Allen Walker Read, "The Membership in Proposed American Academies," reprinted from *American Literature* 7, no. 2 (May 1935): 145, 146, 153, 154, 155.

3. Ibid., p. 155.

4. John H. Cole, *Jefferson's Legacy: A Brief History of the Library of Congress* (Washington: D. C.: Library of Congress, 1993), p. 81.

5. Academy minutes, first annual meeting of the National Institute of Arts Sciences and Letters, February 11, 1889.

6. Address before the meeting of the National Institute of Arts and Letters in New York City, January 30, 1900.

7. Bishop Lawrence of Massachusetts, quoted in *American Literature: The Makers and the Making*, edited by Cleanth Brooks, R. W. B. Lewis, and Robert Penn Warren (New York: St. Martin's Press, 1974), pp. 1202–03.

8. To Hamilton Mabie, January 25, 1903.

9. *American Literature* (see note 7), p. 1208.

10. Lionel Trilling, *The Opposing Self* (New York: Viking, 1955), p. x.

11. To Mabie, January 25, 1903.

12. From "At the Funeral of a Minor Poet" by Thomas Bailey Aldrich, *The Poems of Thomas Bailey Aldrich*, vol 2. (Cambridge: Riverside Press, 1897).

13. Thomas Bailey Aldrich, incidentally, accused the Institute of being parochial on the grounds that it did not sufficiently recognize the cultural achievements of Boston people (to Robert Underwood Johnson, November 15, 1904).

14. In one extant photograph, Cass Gilbert looks less like a businessman than like a middle-aged Hollywood actor playing the part of a businessman (whose daughter, perhaps, against father's wishes, wants to marry Cary Grant). In the same picture, the sculptor Herbert Adams seems to be a diplomat, perhaps attached to the French embassy.

15. Jules Prown, *American Painting* (Geneva: Skira, 1969), p. 126.

16. Larzer Ziff, *The American 1890's: Life and Times of a Lost Generation* (New York: Viking, 1966).

17. To Hamlin Garland, March 20, 1907.

18. January 30, 1900, given at Mendelssohn Hall.

19. H. Wiley Hitchcock, *Music in the United States*, 3d ed. (Englewood Cliffs, N.J.: Prentice-Hall, 1988), p. 149.

20. Barbara Tischer, *An American Music: the Search for an American Musical Identity* (New York: Oxford University Press, 1986), p. 30.

21. Anton Dvořák, "Music in America," *Harper's New Monthly Magazine* 90 , no. 807 (February 1895): 432.

22. August 16, 1899.

23. To Robert Underwood Johnson, October 8, 1906.

24. February 22, 1907. Franklin B. Sanborn, the Concord abolitionist and author of studies of Emerson, Thoreau, and Hawthorne, wrote James Breck Perkins in 1899 that he would not even consider membership in the Institute "until women are actually functioning as members" (James Breck Perkins to Mabie, November 25, 1899). The conservative New York congressman and charter member James Breck Perkins, coming upon this letter, remarked about it to Hamilton Mabie that "the expression seems to me as odd as the sentiment" (ibid.). Perkins was unyielding in his opposition to women; as to Sanborn, he never did accept membership.

25. January 21, 1905.

26. October 26, 1906.

27. Prown, *American Painting*, p. 120.

28. In 1903 Du Bois published an article in the anthology *The Negro Problem* called "The Talented Tenth," in which he named some of the leading black figures on the cultural scene. His contention was that "the Negro race, like all other races, is going to be saved by its exceptional men"—in fact, by the talented ten percent in the then contemporary black population. Among those Du Bois mentioned were Dunbar and Chesnutt in literature and the artist Henry Tanner.

29. Bret Harte was in fact of Jewish ancestry, intermingled with Dutch and English. His grandfather Bernard Harte was a well-known Jewish merchant in New York City in the early nineteenth century. His father, Henry Harte, a scholarly individual, brought other strains into the family with his marriage in 1830 to Elizabeth Rebecca Ostrander. The Jewish background had no obvious effect on Bret Harte's writings—"The Luck of Roaring Camp," "The Outcasts of Poker Flat," and others—nor did Harte have any visible relation to the slowly developing Jewish literary community. In any case, Harte died in 1902, after spending the last part of his life in Scotland and London.

30. To Mabie, September 11, 1902.

31. December 11, 1904.

32. To Edmund Clarence Stedman, December 15, 1904.

33. Notes on Academy elections, May 13, 1905.

34. To Johnson, June 17, 1905.

35. To Johnson, June 26, 1905.

36. To Gilder, November 13, 1908; March 8, 1905; to Mabie, June 8, 1905.

37. His handwritten ballots are in the Academy archives.

38. This "old ditty" has not thus far been located among the writings of Charles Reade.

39. To Johnson, June 13, 1914.

40. Alexis de Tocqueville, *Democracy in America* (New York: Knopf, 1945), 2:27, 76.

41. Robert Penn Warren, *The Legacy of the Civil War* (New York: Random House, 1961).

42. Academy minutes, eighth annual meeting of the Institute, January 25, 1907.

43. Circular letter to the members of the Institute, March 1, 1907.

CHAPTER TWO

1908–1917

IDEALISM AND PATRIOTISM

Louis Auchincloss

IN 1908, the same year that the membership of both the Institute and the Academy was raised to the numbers that would endure until the 1993 merger—fifty for the Academy and two hundred fifty for the Institute—the Academy drafted its constitution. This provided that it would act as a counseling body on the arts to the federal government, advise the public on matters of taste regarding literature and the fine arts, "assist in securing just dignity and importance for refinement, culture, and the creative imagination,"[1] and stimulate activity in the arts by giving prizes, which the Institute began doing with its Gold Medal the following year.

It now became evident that both bodies were going to need a national charter to enable them to receive gifts. The Institute received its in 1913,[2] but the Academy had much more trouble, though the bill was sponsored in the Senate by Henry Cabot Lodge and in the House by James Breck Perkins, both Institute members, and heartily lobbied for by Professor William Milligan Sloane, author of a famous life of Napoleon. Opponents first objected that the charter for the Institute should be enough for both bodies. Then it was argued that the Academy's name was too similar to that of the already chartered American Academy of Arts and Sciences, of Boston, and the latter organization indeed entered a protest, which aroused the ire of poet Robert Underwood Johnson, the indefatigable and ever-conscientious permanent secretary of the petitioning Academy. He wrote to the historian James Ford Rhodes of Boston: "Were there ever smaller potatoes and fewer in a hill than those revealed by the protest against our Academy charter by the American Academy of Arts and Sciences? For grown people to go on record as opposing as good a thing as our Academy seems to me almost unbelievable. Will you be good enough to procure for me a list of the members of the Boston Institution."[3]

The third but by far the most important objection raised in Congress to the Academy's charter, particularly by western senators and representatives, was that the membership was too heavily drawn from the Atlantic seaboard. The Institute had a hundred members from New York State alone, and of the Academy's fifty, twenty were from New York, fifteen from Boston or elsewhere in the New England states, and only one from the area between the Alleghenies and the Rockies. A West Virginia senator suggested privately to Lodge that "two good men" from his state be elected.[4] (Some opponents also pointed out that only a single woman, Julia Ward Howe, had been elected, but in those benighted days little was made of this.) The Academy riposted by showing that of the seventy-six members of the Academy elected since its foundation, twenty-four had been born in New England, twenty-six in the central states, ten in the Middle West or West, and eleven in the South. Five were naturalized citizens.

The bill had to pass the Senate four times and be four times favorably reported by the Library Committee of the House before the latter body finally approved it in 1916. And before that occurred Henry James's name had to be removed from the list of members attached to the proposed charter after the news arrived that he had become a British subject to demonstrate his disappointment that his country had not yet declared war on Germany.

The Academy and Institute had learned that it would be wise in the future to give the organization more visibility outside New York, and in the years following, before they had their own home on Audubon Terrace in upper Manhattan, they embarked on a policy of holding their annual meetings outside New York City and inviting local dignitaries to attend receptions and hear lectures by members. Thus in 1909 they met in Washington, in 1912 in Philadelphia, in 1913 in Chicago, and in 1915 in Boston.

The charter bill had still not passed when, in 1914, Institute member Archer Huntington, heir to a railroad and shipping fortune, offered the Academy eight city lots on West 155th Street and $100,000 in endowment funds, contingent on the Academy's raising sufficient funds by 1919 to construct a building on the site. A New York State charter had to be obtained before the gift could be accepted. This happened soon enough, but the Academy had also to establish itself as an educational foundation to be exempt from real estate taxes. An annual series of lectures was set up in 1915, and tax exemption was granted.

At the same time a collection of literary and art memorabilia was solicited in order to establish a public museum of American art. A plea to Academician Henry Adams elicited this sad reply: "I have no manuscripts for one of my weaknesses has always been not to take myself seriously or to believe that my work would ever be regarded as serious beyond my own day. I have left to my brothers all care for fame, and you can still make my brother Brooks, who is the most capable of us all, take charge of such duties as seem good."[5] George de Forest Brush declined to contribute one of his own paintings, but for a very different reason. "To ask an artist to give away his best work or to give something which he does not value, discloses in my mind, a poor estimate of the work."[6]

Other plans for educational ventures were discussed but never materialized, including having a conference with related bodies "with a view to forging a basis of sympathy and action," taking the lead in calling a meeting of American poets in an effort to encourage an interest in American poetry, establishing relations with literary departments of colleges and universities, and founding art museums in states where none exist.[7]

As the primary original purpose of the Académie française had been to preserve the French language from the corruption of contemporary misuse, there were always those who advocated that a similar care for the much more endangered English language should be a goal of the Academy and Institute. William Milligan Sloane, a particular enthusiast in this cause, recommended semiannual meetings in which the Academy would "discuss and decide questions prepared in advance by a small committee from the section of letters relating to verbal criticism, literary usage and literary structure."[8] But he engendered very little enthusiasm among his brethren, and William Crary Brownell seems to have put the matter to rest with an apt quotation from Matthew Arnold: "I feel no disposition to pass all my own life in the wilderness of pedantry, in order that a posterity which I shall never see may one day enter an orthographical Canaan."[9] The battle, Brownell believed, had already been lost when the universities had begun to emphasize literature over usage, any too strict treatment of the latter being popularly considered not only unadventurous but undemocratic.

There was considerable disagreement among members as to the extent to which the Academy-Institute should take public stands on public events not directly or even indirectly connected with it. In 1917 the Sulgrave Institution, successor to the Centenary Peace Commission, proposed to send as gifts to London and Paris, to be located presumably in appropriate squares, replicas of George Gray Barnard's statue of Abraham Lincoln, recently erected in Cincinnati. Several members of the Academy-Institute were outraged that this "slouchily dressed" figure, which had appalled the martyred president's surviving son, Robert, should represent American commemorative art abroad, and a protest was duly published, despite the warning of Frederick MacMonnies that the members should remember that they were not omniscient.[10] And indeed had they been possessed of crystal balls they would have seen Barnard receiving the Institute's Gold Medal for sculpture in 1936 and read his grateful response: "Your encouragement brings light to many dark and doubtful years."[11]

The Gold Medal established by the Institute in 1908 was to be awarded for excellence in a variety of categories, rotating yearly among sculpture, history, biography, music, poetry, architecture, drama, painting, fiction, and belles lettres, in that order. No awardee was to have been dead for more than a year at the time of the award. The first award went posthumously to Augustus Saint-Gaudens.

In 1915 the Academy established its own Gold Medal, to be given in three broad categories: literature, art, and music. Considerable vexation was felt by Daniel Chester French, chairman of the committee in charge of the design and execution of the new medal, when after its composition the decision was made to add the word "Achievement" to "Inspiration and Opportunity." "I suppose no one but an artist," he wrote the permanent secretary, "appreciates how a little change like the one suggested in the inscription involves no end of trouble."[12] But Robert Underwood Johnson, "as timidly as I can," insisted.[13]

Not all plans to provide (or pursue) honors were deemed acceptable. The idea of offering a prize for a new national hymn was happily quashed by Walter Damrosch who wrote to Johnson: "I am inclined to think that our great 'National Hymn' will be borne in full armour, like Minerva from the head of Jupiter, under the stress of some great national movement or danger."[14] And in 1911 Johnson took the position that the Academy should not endorse any of its members for the Nobel Prize or for any other foreign honor.[15]

In 1917, however, the Academy agreed to play an important role in the judging of the Pulitzer prizes. Under the will of Joseph Pulitzer, the trustees of Columbia University were to award four prizes annually in the field of arts and letters: for history, biography, the novel, and the drama. It was arranged that the Academy should choose a jury of three for each of the specified categories from its own and the Institute's members to make the nominations to the trustees, with whom, of course, the final decision rested.

The desire to promote standards occasionally reached beyond the strict confines of art, literature, and music. Johnson sought unsuccessfully to inter-

Gold Medal of the Academy (2 11/16 inches diameter), designed by James Earle Fraser in 1916.

est Mrs. August Belmont (the former actress Eleanor Robson) to fund a medal for fine diction on the stage, "to promote drama of the best type in the face of the ruinous commercial competition of the moving picture."[16] He was more successful with Evangeline Wilbour Blashfield, wife of the mural painter Edwin H. Blashfield, who gave a total of $3,000 to assist the Academy in "the preservation of the English language in its beauty and integrity, and its cautious enrichment by such terms as grow out of modern conditions."[17] This was perhaps broader than Professor Sloane's conceived agenda, and the money has been used for lectures on language.

Confusion as to the different identities of the Academy and Institute existed not only among the public but among the members themselves. George de Forest Brush, responding to Johnson's notification of his election to the Academy, wrote: "I don't know whether to accept with thanks or whether to give it away that I have been a member almost ever since it started. Which had I best do?" To which Johnson retorted: "The joke is on you. You never were a member of the American Academy of Arts and Letters until June 1, 1910. You were only a humble, retiring and unwilling member of the National Institute of Arts and Letters from the membership of which, 250, the Academy of 50 is recruited."[18]

Resignations from either body were rare, but not unknown. Charles W. Eliot resigned because he was "too old" and was "not at all clear in my mind" as to the purposes of the two institutions,[19] Andrew West because he couldn't attend meetings,[20] and William Gedney Bunce "as he has received no benefit that he is aware of."[21] But Henry James, who could not attend meetings as he rarely crossed the Atlantic, was nonetheless most conscientious about the problem of voting. It disturbed him that he knew so little about the candidates, the Academy-Institute having then no staff to prepare biographical sketches. In 1913 he wrote to Johnson that he had searched the envelopes in vain for the least light:

> But I confess I am glad to remain thus indulgedly in the dark rather than be faced by either of the alternatives that have too often come up for me: the voting for a candidate of whom I know nothing, sometimes to the extent of really never having heard of him, and as to whom at this distance I can obtain no information; and the presumptuously, or with a different ignorance, committing myself on the subject of some composer, architect or plastic Artist of whatever sort, as to whom I hold my right of determinant appreciation absolutely nil. As to a gentle Writer I am willing to pass for more or less qualified—but as to those other candidates I am not in the least so willing to pass, seeing what depends on my action. I have so painful a consciousness of our absence of common ground as a markedly heterogeneous association—I mean technically

common ground, not socially or sociably, of course, which has nothing to do with it—that I am only too thankful to profit by any loophole for not taking action.[22]

The sole woman elected to the Academy in this period was Julia Ward Howe, and her elevation came only in 1908, two years before her death at the age of ninety-one. She was chosen, one gathers from the tribute of Bliss Perry, largely on the basis of a single poem:

> She wrote essays, verses, sermons and a play, but her fame as a writer rests almost wholly upon her *Battle Hymn of the Republic*. The poem was scribbled hastily in the gray dawn after a sound night's sleep. It was composed, like many of the songs of Burns, to a well-known tune. It interpreted, as no other lyric of the war quite succeeded in interpreting, the mystical glory of sacrifice for freedom. Soldiers sang it in camp; women read it with tears; children repeated it in school, vaguely but truly perceiving in it, as thirty years before their fathers had perceived in Webster's *Reply to Hayne*, the idea of union made "simple, sensuous, passionate."[23]

One wonders how Brooks Adams reacted to her election. He seems to have felt that women were particularly guilty in what he described in an address as "the Revolt on Modern Democracy Against Standards of Duty." He stated:

Julia Ward Howe, suffragette and author of "The Battle Hymn of the Republic," was elected to the Institute in 1907 at the age of eighty-eight and to the Academy one year later. No other woman was admitted until 1926.

Since civilization first dawned on earth the family has been the social unit on which all authority, all order, and all obedience has reposed. . . . To preserve the family, and thus to make society stable, the woman has always sacrificed herself for it, as the man has sacrificed himself for her upon the field of battle. The obligations and the sacrifices have been correlative. But I beheld our modern women shrilly repudiating such a standard of duty and such a theory of self-sacrifice. On the contrary, they denied that as individual units they owed society any duty as mothers or as wives, and maintained that their first duty was to themselves. If they found the bonds of the family irksome, they might renounce them and wander whither they would through the world in order to obtain a fuller life for themselves.[24]

On reflection, however, he may have deemed that Mrs. Howe's fine domestic record and her glorification of the sacrifice of men in battle compensated even for her noted work for equal suffrage organizations.

It was becoming more and more apparent that with so many members and no permanent home or endowment the Academy-Institute was going to have to embark on extensive fund raising. Operating without a headquarters presented many problems of administration for the Institute's treasurer. After one of the evening gatherings he had to cope with letters like the following:

> I enclose you herewith the itemized bill of the Institute of Arts and Letters dinner at the University Club. I have made careful inquiry, and the numbers of cocktails drunk and cigars smoked seem, while excessive, actually to have been properly consumed by members of the Institute.
>
> I enclose the wine cards of those members who are not members of the University Club. Each card shows the name of the man, and the price, in the upper right-hand corner, of what he consumed. Your clerk can easily, I suppose, drop a card to each, mentioning the amount, and they will refund to you. . . . The flowers, cocktails, cigars and cigarettes will, I suppose, have to come out of the general funds of the Institute.[25]

But these "general funds," alas, were exiguous. Annual dues of five dollars were imposed and resented by many. Carroll Beckwith asked that the treasurer "merge" his check "into the expense account of the Institute" as he did not like the idea of paying "annual Dues" in a society that he looked on as being "distinctly an honor."[26] But even so famous a member as the humorist Finley Peter Dunne received this terse communication from the treasurer: "Dear Sir: I am instructed by the Council of the National Institute of Arts & Letters to notify you that unless your indebtedness to the Institute, according to the enclosed bill, is paid within thirty days that your name will be dropped from the list of members."[27]

Eventually, Robert Underwood Johnson began a vigorous campaign to win an endowment, writing letters to members, wealthy bankers, widows, captains of industry such as Henry Ford, even to Thomas Edison. His efforts were thwarted at every turn, especially by the outbreak of World War I. In 1917 he reluctantly noted that

> in accordance with the general feeling, it has been thought inadvisable to make any systematic effort to obtain an endowment during the present war. The vast sums being obtained by popular subscription for national loans, the work of the Red Cross and YMCA, in addition to the many worthy funds, have made the times singularly unpropitious for the

urging of our claims, though we might well maintain that the foundation of a great institution to establish and promote the best standards in ideal work is of the essence of patriotic effort. It is thus indeed that every nation has nourished its own principles and policies.[28]

During the war the Academy-Institute protested the destruction of works of art in Europe and proclaimed its readiness to interest itself "instantly and effectively" whenever called upon to advise or assist. "For example, on request it could secure the aid of historians to ascertain underlying facts in obscure international relations, or of painters to improve the methods of protective coloration for the navy and the merchant marine, or of writers and speakers to make plain to the people the principles of national policy."[29] It does not appear that he was much taken up on this inventive offer.

Still, the arts were not forgotten in the war. In 1916 Johnson invited the Kneisel Quartet to play for the Academy-Institute, with this suggestion: "Now, my dear Kneisel, do put on your thinking cap and give us the most distinguished programme you can, including something unpublished, and something new to New York by an American composer."[30] But Kneisel replied: "Just now there is no manuscript work by an American composer at hand which would likely proof [*sic*] significant enough to present it on this occasion—in fact we have nothing in view by American writers for a performance at any of our public concerts during the coming season."[31] Walter Damrosch, a vocal member of the concert committee, would not accept this dismissal of American composers and insisted that the Kneisel quartet look further for works by Institute members. Compositions by members George W. Chadwick, Arthur Foote, and Henry K. Hadley were finally agreed on and played by the Kneisel quartet at the annual meeting on November 16, 1916. A day later, in a concert of music inspired by Greek mythology and drama that Damrosch organized at the Colony Club, an American note was struck with the inclusion of five excerpts from Damrosch's own *Iphiginea in Aulis*.

The First World War is now seen by many as an unmitigated catastrophe that would have been better stalemated than won. Instead of having an enduring and democratic peace Europe was plagued with communism and dictatorships, and atrocities were and still are committed on a scale that makes the Kaiser's rape of Belgium seem a relatively humane affair. And in the conflict itself the pointless butchery in the trenches, where hundreds of thousands of men were sacrificed for a few yards of gain or the straightening out of a sector, led to mutiny and despair. Some British tommies complained that when home on leave they simply could not discuss their experiences realistically without being accused of lack of patriotism. For never in history had the home front been more at variance with its fighting men. The world has never seen anything quite like the hysteria of that war's noncombatants, both in the United States and among its allies. In our Civil War there were not only draft riots; it was actually respectable in many places to be a copperhead. In World War II German opera was tolerated at the Metropolitan, and any public support of our stand in Vietnam was frowned on by the majority of our youth. For these reasons the belligerent utterances of members of the Academy and Institute during the years 1914–1918 make interesting reading today.[32]

John Burroughs made a plea for the ostracism of all things German:

> We do not want their ideas or their methods. Their ideas are subversive of our democratic ideals, and their methods enslave the mind and lead to efficiency chiefly in the field of organized robbery. . . . They invent nothing, but they add a Satanic touch to the inventions of others and turn them to infernal uses. They are a heavy, materialistic, grasping race, forceful but not creative, military but not humanistic, aggressive but not heroic, religious but not spiritual; brave it may be, but not chivalrous, utterly selfish, thoroughly scientific and efficient on a low plane, as organized force is always efficient. Kant was a great philosopher, but he had a Scottish mother.[33]

Nicholas Murray Butler struck a nobler note. To him, as to Woodrow Wilson, the war had to be a crusade. It was unimaginable that no good could come out of such horror: "The war which now involves the whole world is on the part of the Allies avowedly a war not for conquest, for revenge, or for economic advantage, but a war to restore the rule of law and to establish durable peace. No other war has ever been fought for a like motive."[34]

Robert Grant blows Siegfried's horn:

> Our flag will wear new glory
> Before our boys return,
> Its crimson stripes be gory,
> Its stars like planets burn,

Naturalist John Burroughs, elected to the Institute in 1898 and to the Academy in 1905, at Woodchuck Lodge in Roxbury, New York.

And many will be sleeping
upon a foreign shore;
Yet still within thy keeping,
Jehovah! God of War.[35]

Arthur T. Hadley echoes Butler and Wilson:

It is sometimes said that wars are waged for commercial reasons. This
may be true of little wars, but it is not true of great ones. Every great war
establishes some principle. The wars of the French Revolution established the principles of civil liberty. The wars in the middle of the last
century established the principle of nationality. I believe that this war
will establish the principle that character and performance must go hand
in hand; that morals and brains must be conjoined; and that a civilization
which attempts to base itself on either to the exclusion of the other is
fundamentally incomplete.[36]

William Dean Howells was bemused by the perversity of the German
people: "What is the fell magic which holds them liege to their oppression
in a dream of ruthless dominion, and makes them as eager to shed their own
blood as the blood of their fellowmen? What has so possessed their souls
with the love of their own slavery that they should wish to die in the
endeavor to make it universal, and so holds them to it that they cannot wish
to break from it?"[37]

Henry Cabot Lodge opined that the war might have the beneficent effect
of ending the division of our people into race groups that strive to direct the
course of the United States in the interest of some other country. "Whatever
suffering and misery war may bring, it will at least sweep these foul things
away. Instead of division into race groups, it will unify us into one nation, and
national degeneracy and national cowardice will slink back into the darkness
from which they should never have emerged."[38]

And Horatio Parker found the prejudice of the American public and its
officials against modern German music (he exempts Bach) "perhaps justifiable." This generation of Teutons, he asserted, had lowered their objects of
devotion. "Instead of the ethereal heights of Bach we find concrete, detailed
specifications of human affairs, often weaknesses or uglinesses. Austerity of
thought has given way to luxuriance." And in his condemnation of Richard
Strauss's "childish" love of trivial details he anticipated the harsh views of
the Nazis.[39]

An examination of the various papers on aesthetic subjects written by members of the Academy-Institute and published in its *Proceedings* during this decade
does not reveal much evidence that many members would have welcomed the
coming movements of abstract art, free verse, or naturalistic novel writing.

There is a distinct greatest common denominator of lofty idealism, fervent patriotism, and belief in conservative deportment in sexual and social matters.

The painter Carroll Beckwith found little to be gained from the acceleration of change in styles of painting in France. Revolution in art to him was regressive:

> We then come to another period, the latest revolution—that of Cézanne and Matisse, who have occupied the headlines. From my point of view, not only have values and form been disregarded, but awkwardness seems to be sought for, and the rules of skilled craftsmanship have been defied. It is now a sin to be a skillful draftsman. It is considered obnoxious in the schools of Paris to draw too well. It is not natural. Nature draws clumsily. We have a distinguished illustration of this tendency in the work of the very great sculptor Rodin. Until twenty years ago, Rodin was undoubtedly proud of his technique and skill. To-day he makes his figures heavy, ponderous, and oftentimes shapeless.[40]

Thomas Wentworth Higginson, writing of his fellow Academician Charles Eliot Norton in an address subtitled "A Link Between the Old and New Worlds," quoted Norton as having told him, a half century before, in 1856, that "no nation on the American continent, which stretched from the Atlantic to the Pacific, could ever be intellectually great, but only physically comfortable." "For science and art," Norton had maintained, "we must look to countries penetrated by gulfs, bays and rivers, and interrupted by mountains, so that all could communicate easily with one another, as in Europe." But Higginson went on to point out that Norton had seen fit to change his view, for in his eightieth year he had written to a friend that "if his life were to be lived again, he thought that he should like to live it in Chicago."[41]

Bliss Perry, in his memorial to Higginson in 1912, did not show Norton's ability to keep pace with the times. He commended Higginson as a war hero, a stylist, a scholar, a natural bookman, and, above all, an essayist, but he ended his tribute on this questionable note of enduring fame.

> No contemporary of any writer can solve what Higginson once called "the equation of fame." That equation contains too many unknown quantities. Lamb's "Essay on Roast Pig," which has simply a good deal of Charles Lamb in it, is now as sure of immortality, as far as we can see, as Gibbon's *Decline and Fall of the Roman Empire*. At least we can say, here are a dozen volumes into which Thomas Wentworth Higginson has put a great deal of himself, clear-grained, seasoned, sun-bathed stuff. They will outlast our day and many days.[42]

But they haven't. What has solely made Higginson immortal is his article on meeting Emily Dickinson, which appeared in the October 1891 issue of the

Atlantic Monthly, and his editing, with Mabel Loomis Todd, of the first posthumous volume of her poetry.

Of course, we have hindsight today, and it is easy to poke fun at those of our predecessors who peered into what *The New Yorker* called "The Cloudy Crystal Ball." But Emily Dickinson's poetry had been known for nineteen years when Perry chose to ignore the role that she had played in Higginson's life. I think that what we begin to discern in many of the literary and artistic judgments shown in these papers is a feeling that great art is intimately tied up with high-mindedness, nobility of character, idealism, clarity of thought, and a gentlemanly masculinity.

I quote, for example, from Robert Underwood Johnson's poem in tribute to the late Augustus Saint-Gaudens:

> The hand that shapes us Lincoln must be strong
> As his that righted our bequeathed wrong;
> The heart that shows us Lincoln must be brave,
> An equal comrade unto king or slave;
> The mind that gives us Lincoln must be clear
> As that of seer
> To fathom deeps of faith abiding under tides of fear.[43]

In keeping with this view of art and the artist, John Bigelow would not have considered the mind of Alexandre Dumas, with whom he breakfasted in 1864 while he was minister to France, as one qualified to opine on a great subject. Speaking of Dumas (who had a black grandmother) at the Academy half a century later, he recalled the slipshod character of the French novelist's work habits: "There was where the African came in. He had no reflective faculties. The moment he began to correct he became confused, and the train of his thought was irrecoverably broken. He had to run down, like a clock, as he was wound up, and without stopping. It is the peculiarity of the African that, for want of the reflective and logical faculties, he is incapable, except in rare instances, of measuring distance, size, or time, or of thoroughly mastering the common rules of arithmetic."[44]

Nicholas Murray Butler, in an address entitled "The Revolt of the Unfit," made it very clear that he would tolerate no denigration of the natural nobility of man by any theory of evolution, no equating of homo sapiens with "earthworms . . . climbing plants and . . . brightly colored birds." Man revolts, he insisted, against the implication of the doctrine of evolution and objects both to being considered unfit to survive and succeed and to being forced to accept the only fate that nature offers to those who are unfit for survival and success. Indeed, he concluded, man "manifests with amazing pertinacity what Schopenhauer used to call 'the will to live.' "[45]

George Washington Cable, in "A Novelist's Philosophy," came out strongly in favor of the importance of character in art.

A novelist should have as clear a conviction of how to live as how to write, and on occasion may state it with the freedom of an actor answering a curtain call.

In either case originality is not the supreme necessity, and so I would say that the chief element in a life worth living is what the preachers call character, and that in character the three paramount constituents must be courage, fidelity, and affection.[46]

Lorado Taft, speaking on "Recent Tendencies in Sculpture," emphasized the importance of the note of the eternal that he found in Saint-Gaudens's hooded figure over the grave of Mrs. Henry Adams. "When shall we sculptors learn that the greatest asset of our art is its hint of eternity? That look of serene permanence which is so dependent upon mass and simple contour is what impresses one in the great works. It is not the feverish, gesticulating figure that is convincing. Is it not, rather, the quiet nature of an Adams memorial, so still that it seems to move?" This he contrasted with decadent tendencies abroad: "In place of a self-respecting art worthy of its ancient lineage, we find in Paris to-day the puerile effronteries of Matisse and of Maillot, delighting through their very ineptitude a public avid of new sensations. Realism and unbridled cleverness have run their course, and the jaded critics find refreshment in willful bungling and pretense of naivete."[47]

Indeed, did we have to look beyond our native shores for the finest inspiration? Edwin Howland Blashfield, conferring on John Singer Sargent the Gold Medal of the Institute, declared that, as a painter, he was greater than any man alive.[48] Hamlin Garland, speaking of "Local Color as the Vital Element of American Fiction," welcomed the decline of provincialism, which he defined as "the dependence upon a mother-country which marks a colony." Yet he conceded that not all of our writers were of this mind:

> Some of them still despise or fear the local, the democratic; but they seem to me to stand outside the normal development of our art. Is it not in a sense unnatural and sterile when an American steps aside to write novels of the Old World, of distant lands? Can there be lasting vitality, national significance in such work? What sort of figure would we present to the historian, if all our writers were still composing poems, dramas, and novels upon French or English or Russian themes?
>
> I assert that it is the most natural thing in the world for the young writer to love his birthplace, to write of it, to sing of it.[49]

One wonders where Henry James came out in all of this, but we find that Birge Harrison took care of him in "The American Temperament." First, he quoted James's dismay at witnessing the discharge, at Ellis Island, by five huge ocean liners of their human freight. "It seemed to me that there was something hostile, threatening, almost appalling about this slow-moving, murmuring, never-ending throng; and finally it burst upon me that this was an invasion—silent and furtive, but nonetheless sinister, formidable, and irresistible. It is a disaster, gentleman; a flood, a human inundation, which, if unchecked, is destined to submerge the old Anglo-Saxon stock, to engulf and utterly destroy the fine old Anglo-Saxon civilization." But Mr. Harrison did not agree: "Out of the admixture of so many and such diverse race units, grafted upon the old Anglo-Saxon stock, there should develop during the next century or two a new people—a people more powerful perhaps than any the world has heretofore known. And in due season these new Americans, following the universal law, would develop an art of their own which would be brilliant and forceful and beautiful in proportion to the force, the brilliancy, and the love of beauty in the race itself."[50]

Who would not prefer that prophecy to Henry James's?

Brand Whitlock was equally patriotic in his defense of the all-American point of view: "The Russian realists viewed humanity in despairing pity. The French realists, and especially Flaubert, viewed it in contempt and disgust. The American realist, I should say, would view it much as the American humorists have viewed it: they have known most of its defects, but they have viewed it tolerantly, sympathetically, and with respect for the dignity and the right there is somewhere in every man simply because he is a man."[51]

William Lyon Phelps, in "Realism and Reality in Fiction," was equally suspicious of specific and lubricious details in the work of certain foreign novelists: "A work of art may be conscientiously realistic,— —few men have had a more importunate conscience than Zola—and yet be untrue to life, or, at all events, untrue to life as a whole. Realism may degenerate into emphasis on sensational but relatively unimportant detail: reality deals with that mystery of mysteries, the human heart."[52]

It remained for Theodore Roosevelt, to whom it meant "very little" to have an Egyptian obelisk in Central Park, to put the final stamp on the doctrine of "Nationalism in Literature and Art":

> Of course an over-self-conscious straining after a nationalistic form of expression may defeat itself. But this is merely because self-consciousness is almost always a drawback. The self-conscious striving after originality also tends to defeat itself. Yet the fact remains that the greatest work must bear the stamp of originality. In exactly the same way the greatest work must bear the stamp of nationalism. American work must smack of our own soil, mental and moral, no less than physical, or it will have little of permanent value.[53]

This statement by the hero of San Juan Hill might be taken as the ultimate expression of a decade of patriotism whose fervor was beginning to grate and whose concern was turning insular. Ahead for the Academy-Institute lay the challenges of free verse, abstract art, naturalist novels, and atonal music. A whole new set of critical standards would be required.

NOTES

Unless otherwise specified, all materials cited are located in the Academy files.

1. "Report of the Executive Committee," John Bigelow, chairman, a circular letter to the members of the Academy, February 5, 1908.

2. It was at this time that Albert Jaegers, the sculptor, was elected to the Institute under bizarre circumstances. Jaegers, writing on December 17, 1912, to Henry D. Sedgwick, accepted election to the Institute and explained,

> I take this opportunity however, to make a statement, which in justice to myself I should make. On the occasion of modelling a portrait bust of Ex speaker Cannon, I became pleasantly acquainted with him and also with Representative Mann of Illinois. In a most kindly spirit these gentlemen inserted my name in a list of members of the Nat. Inst. of Arts and Letters, when a bill for a charter for that body was before Congress. This was done without my request or knowledge and if my election was partly caused by this, it was through a circumstance beyond my control.

Jaegers was thereafter duly elected, but not without one member's commenting on his ballot that his blood was made to "boil" by Cannon's "impudence" and that the candidate should resign, if elected under such circumstances, out of self-respect (Herbert Adams to Robert Underwood Johnson, July 8, 1912).

There are times, in thumbing through the Academy-Institute files, when one feels that both bodies, in those years before they had a building of their own, were sustained almost singlehandedly by the busy and often frustrated poet-secretary. Johnson could be as sharp to slackers within as to attackers without. Here he is writing to John Burroughs on April 23, 1909, which he notes is Shakespeare's birthday: "I regret to notice that you did not vote at the last Academy election. The failure of two or three to do so resulted in no choice, and a lot of heavy work on me. It seems a very little thing to do for you to look over a list and select your preferences. Living as you do a bucolic life, you do not realize what such an organization can do for the profession. . . . You can bring Pegasus to the Pierian Spring but you can't make him drink" (April 23, 1909).

3. February 28, 1913.

4. Lodge to Johnson, quoted in "The Charter Campaign: January 12, 1909–April 17, 1916," an unsigned, unpublished article by Grace D. Vanamee.

5. Adams to Johnson, April 18, 1915.

6. To Johnson, May 20, 1915.

7. Minutes of an Academy board of directors meeting, April 22, 1915.

8. William Milligan Sloane, "The American Academy and the English Language," in *Academy Papers: Addresses on Language Problems by Members of the American Academy of Arts and Letters* (New York: Scribner's, 1925), p. 37.

9. William Crary Brownell, "The Academy and the Language," in *Academy Papers*, p. 42.

10. Frederick MacMonnies wrote to Robert Underwood Johnson on September 6, 1917, stating, "1st I think Barnard's Lincoln is a sincere and original work and I see in it a remarkable effort to be beautiful. 2nd I should feel that the Academy had become a serious menace if it attempted to put the arts into leading strings, by an assumption of omniscience. It seems to me its criticism should be constructive and follow the French Academy in crowning fine effort and discouraging none."

The attack on the statue was led by sculptor F. Wellington Ruckstull, an Institute member, who in 1917 published a series of articles condemning the portrait in his ultraconservative magazine, *The Art World*. In an August piece entitled "Lincoln: Was He a Slouch?" he refers to "this slouchily dressed and presumably democratic despiser of elegant social forms [who] will certainly give to every European reactionary and enemy of democracy a justification for saying: 'Do you see the disgusting fruit of the vulgar social life of a Democracy?' " In the same issue Ruckstull suggested that the Sulgrave Institution call on the Academy to advise it on this matter. Robert Underwood Johnson, who was in sympathy with Ruckstull, wrote to members of the art department, asking their opinion; the response was divided. Though the Academy never took a stand on the issue as an organization, many members signed a protest that appeared in the November number of *The Art World* under the title "A Calamity in Bronze! Mr. Barnard's 'Lincoln' Once More."

11. Telegram to the National Institute of Arts and Letters, January 16, 1936.

12. To Johnson, July 21, 1916.

13. To Daniel Chester French, November 29, 1916.

14. November 11, 1908.

15. To Sloane, March 13, 1911. Johnson wrote that he "will do anything I properly may for [Henry] James" but noted "privately" to Sloane that he did not think an American would get the prize after Theodore Roosevelt aroused the ire of the Swedish Academy by failing to accept his 1906 Peace Prize in person. Nonetheless, Johnson continued, "When it comes to the Academy uniting in an action of this kind, recommending one of its members for a prize, it seems to me that is a pretty dubious undertaking and would lay us open to the charge of log-rolling. Whatever may be done by us individually may well be done, and other people may say that we are members of the Academy, but there should be on the face of it, it seems to me, no use of the organization's name, don't you think so?"

16. Report of the permanent secretary, attached to the minutes of the annual meeting of the Academy, November 18, 1915.

17. The offer of gift from Mrs. Edwin Howland Blashfield was quoted in the minutes of an Academy board of directors meeting, November 15, 1916, and in the preface to *Academy Papers*.

18. June 4, 1910; June 6, 1910.

19. To Richard Watson Gilder, November 12, 1908. Eliot went on to say, however, "I dare say the young men, like yourself, are quite right in organizing these two bodies devoted to letters and the arts, and in endeavoring to find real functions for them." Eliot was seventy-four; Gilder, sixty-four.

20. To Samuel Isham, February 12, 1914. West noted that he was resigning not "from any dissatisfaction, but solely because I find no convenient opportunity to attend any of the meetings."

21. Archibald A. Welch, for Bunce, to Arnold W. Brunner, November 12, 1914.

22. May 5, 1913.

23. Bliss Perry, "Thomas Wentworth Higginson, Julia Ward Howe, Francis Marion Crawford, William Vaughn Moody," in *Commemorative Tributes of the American Academy of Arts and Letters, 1905–1941* (New York: American Academy of Arts and Letters, 1942), p. 34.

24. Brooks Adams, "The Revolt of Modern Democracy Against Standards of Duty," delivered at public meetings of the Academy and Institute at Jordan Hall, Boston, on November 18, 1915, and published in *Proceedings of the American Academy of Arts and Letters and the National Institute of Arts and Letters (1914–1921)* 2, no. 9 (1916): 10.

25. Robert Bridges to Arnold W. Brunner, November 24, 1914.

26. April 23, 1916. Beckwith continues, "It would seem to me like paying dues to belong to the Institute de France—but I am always willing to contribute to the expenses of postage &c to the extent of my purse."

27. March 25, 1915.

28. Report of the permanent secretary, attached to the minutes of the annual meeting of the Academy, November 21, 1917. Also in 1917 the Institute hailed the accomplishment of the Russian revolutionaries with an enthusiasm that subsequent events may have proved premature: "With one master stroke the leaders of the Russian people have made the greatest reinforcement of half a century in the cause of popular government." On April 23, the Institute held "A Meeting of the Authors, Artists and Musical Composers of the United States under the auspices of The National Institute of Arts and Letters To offer Greetings and Congratulations to the Men of Letters and Artists of Russia who have contributed so largely to the Emancipation of their Country." The meeting included speeches by Augustus Thomas, George Kennan, and Nicholas Murray Butler (published in "The Institute's Greetings to Russia," *Art World*, June 1917), as well as "The Adoption of a Memorial Address to the Men of Letters and Artists of Russia," from which the quotation is taken.

29. "The Adoption of a Memorial Address to the Men of Letters and Artists of Russia."

30. Ca. August 31, 1916.

31. Louis Svecenski, violist for the Kneisel Quartet, for Kneisel, to Johnson, September 5, 1916.

32. In 1919 the Academy published a slim volume entitled *The World War: Utterances Concerning Its Issues and Conduct by Members of the American Academy of Arts and Letters*. A note on the title page indicates that it was "printed for its [the Academy's] Archives and for Free Circulation." Publication of the volume was authorized at a meeting of the Academy board on January 11, 1918, and on February 12, Robert Underwood Johnson wrote a "Special, Confidential and Immediate" letter to the members of the Academy asking for "extracts from the published utterances of members of the Academy relating to the present world conflict," which would be published by the Academy to "make record of individual expressions of a patriotic character, which, collectively, may be of further influence upon public opinion, and also to enable the Academy to take part as a body in the struggle for civilization. . . . It is believed that such presentation will not only be a stimulus to the patriotic spirit

of the country, but also a support of the claim of the Academy to a reason for existence as a public influence."

33. John Burroughs, "Can Peace Make Us Forget? A Plea for the Ostracism of All Things German," in *The World War*, p. 10.

34. Nicholas Murray Butler, "The Road to Durable Peace: An Address Delivered Before the Chamber of Commerce, St. Louis, Missouri, February 1, 1918," in *The World War*, p. 12.

35. Robert Grant, "A Hymn," in *The World War*, p. 17.

36. Arthur T. Hadley, "A Conflict of Ideals: From an Address on the Price of National Liberty, Providence, March 15, 1917," in *The World War*, p. 18.

37. William Dean Howells, "The Incredible Cruelty of the Teutons," in *The World War*, p. 21. This piece originally appeared in the "Easy Chair" section of the August 1918 issue of *Harper's Magazine*.

38. Henry Cabot Lodge, "Speech in the United States Senate, April 4, 1917, on the Declaration of War," in *The World War*, p. 27.

39. Horatio Parker, "A Note on German Music and German Ideas," in *The World War*, p. 40.

40. Carroll Beckwith, "Taste and Technique," an address delivered at public meetings of the Academy and Institute held at the New York Historical Society, December 13, 1912, and published in *Proceedings of the American Academy of Arts and Letters and the National Institute of Arts and Letters (1909–1913)* 1, no. 6 (1913): 28.

41. Thomas Wentworth Higginson, "Ruskin and Norton: A Link Between the Old and New Worlds," delivered at the first public meetings of the Academy held in Washington, D.C., December 14 and 16, 1909, and published in *Proceedings* 1, no. 1 (1910): 23, 24.

42. Bliss Perry, "Higginson, Mrs. Howe, Crawford, Moody," a commemorative paper read before the Academy at a special meeting in New York, December 13, 1912, and published in *Proceedings* 1, no. 6 (1913): 64.

43. Robert Underwood Johnson, "Ode: 'Saint-Gaudens,' " read at a meeting at the Fine Arts Society "to Confer Upon the Work of Augustus Saint-Gaudens the Gold Medal of the Institute," November 20, 1909, and published in *Proceedings* 1, no. 2 (1911): 14.

44. John Bigelow, "A Breakfast with Alexandre Dumas," delivered at public meetings of the Academy and Institute held at the New Theatre, New York, December 8, 1910, and published in *Proceedings* 1, no. 4 (1911): 7.

45. Nicholas Murray Butler, "The Revolt of the Unfit: Reflections on the Doctrine of Evolution," read at public meetings of the Academy and Institute held at the New Theatre, New York, December 8, 1910, and published in *Proceedings* 1, no. 4 (1911): 21.

46. George Washington Cable, "A Novelist's Philosophy," read at public meetings of the Academy and Institute held at Aeolian Hall, New York, November 20, 1914, and published in *Proceedings* 2, no. 8 (1915): 41.

47. Lorado Taft, "Recent Tendencies in Sculpture," delivered at public meetings of the Academy and Institute held at the New Theatre, New York, December 8, 1910, and published in *Proceedings* 1, no. 4 (1911): 50, 46.

48. "Conferring on John Singer Sargent of the Gold Medal of the Institute," speech by Edwin Howland Blashfield delivered at public meetings of the Academy and Institute held at Aeolian Hall, New York, November 20, 1914, and published in *Proceedings* 2, no. 8 (1915): 45.

49. Hamlin Garland, "Local Color as the Vital Element of American Fiction," delivered at public meetings of the Academy and Institute held at the New Theatre, New York, December 8, 1910, and published in *Proceedings* 1, no. 4 (1911): 41, 43.

50. Birge Harrison, "The American Temperament," delivered at a public meeting of the Academy and Institute at the Bellevue-Stratford, Philadelphia, January 26, 1912, and published in *Proceedings* 1, no. 5 (1912): 52, 59.

51. Brand Whitlock, "The American Quality in American Literature," delivered at public meetings of the Academy and Institute held at Jordan Hall, Boston, November 19, 1915, and published in *Proceedings* 2, no. 3 (1916): 47.

52. William Lyon Phelps, "Realism and Reality in Fiction," delivered at public meetings of the Academy and Institute held at the New York Historical Society, December 13, 1912, and published in *Proceedings* 1, no. 6 (1913): 31.

53. Theodore Roosevelt, "Nationalism in Literature and Art," delivered at public meetings of the Academy and Institute held at the Ritz-Carlton Hotel, New York, November 16, 1916, and published in *Proceedings* 2, no. 10 (1917): 17.

CHAPTER THREE

1918–1927

AGAINST MODERNITY——ANNALS OF THE TEMPLE

Cynthia Ozick

A CENTURY, like any entrenched institution, runs on inertia and is inherently laggard. Even when commanded by the calendar, it will not easily give up the ghost. The turn of the century, as the wistful phrase has it, hardly signifies the brisk swing of a gate on its hinge: a century turns, rather, like a rivulet—a silky, lazy, unwitting flow around a silent bend. Whatever the twenty-first century (seemingly only minutes away) may bring, we, entering it, will go on being what we are: creatures born into, and molded and muddied by, the twentieth.

And the twentieth, too, did not properly begin with the demise of the nineteenth. When the fabled Armory Show introduced modern art to New York in 1913, the American cultural establishment (to use a term typically ours, not theirs) was in the governing hands of men born before the Civil War, men who were marked by what Santayana, as early as 1911, had already condemned as "the genteel tradition." Apart from the unjust condescensions of hindsight, and viewed in the not-so-easily-scorned light of its own standards, what *was* the genteel tradition? Its adherents, after all, did not know themselves to be premodernist; they did not know that a volcanic alteration of taste and expression was about to consume the century; they did not know that irony and pastiche and parody and a conscious fever of innovation-through-rupture would overcome notions of nobility, spirituality, continuity, harmony, uncomplicated patriotism, romanticized classicism. It did not occur to them that the old patterns were threadbare or could be repudiated on grounds of exhaustion.

To be able to say what the men of the genteel tradition (its constituents were nearly all men) did know, and what they saw themselves as, and what they in fact were, would lead us directly to the sublimely conceived fellowship they established to embody their ideals: a kind of latter-day temple to the Muses. And the word *temple* is apt: it calls up an alabaster palace on a hill; an elite priesthood; ceremonial devotions pursued in a serious though lyrical frame of mind—a resolute thoughtfulness saturated in notions of beauty and virtue, and turned from the trivial, the frivolous, the ephemeral. The name these aspirants gave to their visionary society—a working organization, finally, with a flesh-and-blood membership and headquarters in New York—was the American Academy of Arts and Letters.

The cornerstone of what was to become the Academy's permanent home, a resplendent Venetian Renaissance edifice just off Riverside Drive on West 155th Street, was laid on November 19, 1921, by Marshal Ferdinand Foch of France. The commander-in-chief of the Allied forces in the First World War, Foch was summoned to wield a ritual trowel not only as the hero of the recent victory over the Kaiser but—more gloriously still—as an emissary of French cultural prestige. The nimbus of power that followed him from Paris to this plot of freshly broken ground along the remote northern margins of Manhattan was kindled as much by his membership in the French Academy as by his battlefield triumphs.

The venerable French Academy, founded by Cardinal Richelieu to maintain the purity of the French language and limited to forty "Immortals," had preceded its New World counterpart (or would-be counterpart) by some two-

November 19, 1921. French war hero Marshal Foch (in uniform) and Academy president William Milligan Sloane (to Foch's right) walk down West 155th Street from Broadway for the laying of the building's cornerstone. (Paul Thompson Photos, NY)

Archer M. Huntington, Hispanic scholar and railroad heir, endowed the Academy and paid for its buildings.

—*Anna Hyatt Huntington, circa 1925*

Photomontage of Audubon Terrace from Broadway.

—*Byron Company, circa 1925. Courtesy of The Hispanic Society of America.*

Exhibition of works by the living artist members of the National Institute of Arts and Letters in connection with the opening of the art gallery of the new building of the American Academy of Arts and Letters, November 13, 1930, through May 13, 1931.

—*Probably Frank J. (Colonel) Crasto, Jr., Academy librarian*

William Hunt Diederich, who in 1947 became the only member ever expelled. He sent out anti-Semitic mailings stamped "With compliments from Members of the National Institute of Arts and Letters."

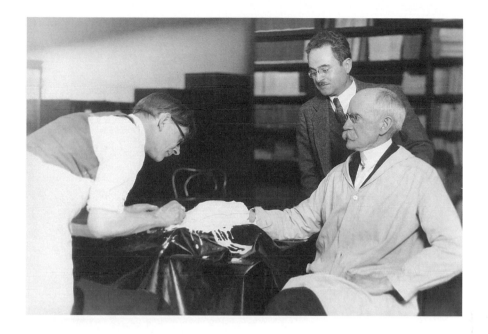

ABOVE: Painter Edwin H. Blashfield submits to having a plaster cast of his hand taken.

BELOW: Foreign Honorary Member Charles Chaplin, elected 1976, poses for Jo Davidson in 1924. —*Hagelstein Brothers, New York*

Samuel Langhorne Clemens (Mark Twain) in
Dublin, New Hampshire, 1906. Clemens was
a charter member of the Institute in 1898, and
of the Academy in 1904. He seconded the
nomination of Julia Ward Howe.

—*Albert Bigelow Paine*

Portrait of Edith Wharton in the Academy's collection, painted in Paris by Edward Harrison May in
1881, when she was eighteen. Her election to the
Institute was stymied in 1918 by a tabling of a motion
to admit women, but occurred, with that of three
other women, in 1926. In 1930 she became the first
female member of the Academy since Julia Ward
Howe.

Childe and Maude Hassam at the opening of Hassam's 1927 exhibition at the Academy. Hassam's legacy of 400 of his works endowed the Academy's Purchase Program.
—*Probably Frank J. (Colonel) Crasto, Jr.*

Sculptor F. W. Ruckstull (elected 1898), with his bust of Institute president Nicholas
Murray Butler, circa 1933.   —*Probably Frank J. Crasto, Jr.*

Grace Vanamee (circa 1925), executive
director of the Academy from 1915 to 1940,
felt obliged to resign after the Row.
        —*Probably Frank J. Crasto, Jr.*

Ezra Pound in the garden of his Paris studio, 1923. Pound was elected in 1938 and, never satisfied with the purposes of "the Insteroot," resigned in 1958.

—*International News Photos Inc.*

Paul Manship (elected 1920) in his studio with two works he completed in the 1930s: *Celestial Sphere* and a bronze polar bear for the Bronx Zoo Gateway.   —*Walter J. Russell*

1959 Ceremonial. Arthur Miller and his wife, the actress Marilyn Monroe, when he received the Gold Medal for Drama. —*Ray Shorr*

Ceremonial 1969. (l to r) Hugh Kenner, John Ashbery, L.E. Sissman, and Allen
Ginsberg, who all received Academy–Institute Awards in Literature.

1967 Ceremonial. Norman Mailer at the reception following his induction. *—Congrat Butlar*

1949 Ceremonial. Dame Edith Sitwell and Yasuo Kuniyoshi (middle) following their induction as Foreign Honorary Members. Two years later Sir Osbert Sitwell (left) was inducted. Institute member Glenway Wescott on right.   —*World Wide Photos*

Eero Saarinen (on left, elected 1954) congratulates Louis I. Kahn (elected 1964) on
winning the 1960 Brunner Prize in Architecture.   —*United Press International*

1952 Ceremonial. Pearl S. Buck presents the Gold Medal for Fiction to Thornton Wilder.   —*Acme Photograph*

Award recipients backstage of the auditorium following the 1944 Ceremonial.
(l to r) Samuel S. McClure (Award for Distinguished Service to the Arts), Willa Cather
(Gold Medal for Fiction), Theodore Dreiser (Award of Merit Medal for the Novel),
Paul Robeson (Medal for Spoken Language).

Drawing of Charles Ives (1874-1954, elected 1946) by David Levine, created for the Academy's Centennial Portfolio, published in 1998.

and-a-half centuries. Though this august company of scholars and men of letters was to serve as inspiration and aristocratic model, American democratic principles demanded a wider roster based on a bicameral system; hence membership in the American Academy was open to as many as fifty, and these fifty were selected by ballot from the two hundred and fifty distinguished authors, painters, sculptors, architects, and composers of the National Institute of Arts and Letters, the lower (and older) body. And while the "chairs" of the French Academy were phantom chairs—metaphoric, platonic—American pragmatism (and one Mrs. Cochran Bowen, who donated the requisite five thousand dollars) supplied *real* chairs, with arms and backs of dark polished wood, each with a plaque for its occupant's name.

The homegrown Richelieu of this grand structure of mind and marble was Robert Underwood Johnson, a powerful magazine editor and tireless poet who, though not precisely the organization's founder, was present at the Academy's earliest meetings, and as permanent secretary was its dominating spirit for the first three decades. In 1920 he disappeared, temporarily, having been appointed U.S. ambassador to Italy. A 1922 newspaper photograph of Johnson— occasioned by a dispute with the Internal Revenue Department over unpaid taxes on ambassadorial meals and lodgings—shows a determined elderly gentleman with a steady yet relentless eye and a rather fierce pince-nez, the ribbon of which flows down over a full white beard and high collar. Unfortunately, no mouth is visible; it would be instructive to see the lips that so often speechified at Academy events or adorned the hour with original verse. In still another portrait—a wood engraving by Timothy Cole, artist and Academy member—the Johnsonian mouth is again concealed under a cloud of furry whiskers, but the stiff cravat, scimitar nose, straight spine, and erect head are eloquent enough. They declare a fine facsimile of a Roman bust, attentive to what is noble and

Robert Underwood Johnson, secretary of the Academy for over thirty years, was the institution's primary engine, single-handedly raising its endowment and enforcing, in many a peppery letter and memo, a conservative artistic agenda.

what is not, the face and figure of a man of established importance, a man who knows his worth: editor of *The Century*, ambassador to Italy, director of the Hall of Fame, secretary of the American Academy of Arts and Letters.

Above all it is the face and figure of the nineteenth century, when the ideal of the publicly Noble could still stir the Western world. Together with the Harmonious, the Noble spoke in lofty statuary, in the balanced configurations of painting and music, in the white pilasters of heirloom architecture—but nowhere more melodiously than in the poetry that descended (though somewhat frayed by overhandling) from Keats.

The cornerstone affixed by Marshal Foch—in high-laced boots and full uniform—on that rainy November afternoon in 1921 was a hollow repository. In it Brander Matthews, chancellor of the Academy and a professor of literature at Columbia University, placed numerous historic articles and documents: congratulatory messages from the president of the United States, from the governor of New York, from the academies of Belgium, Rome, Spain, and Brazil; papers recording the Special Symposium on Diction; *Utterances by Members of the Academy Concerning the War of 1914–1918*, bound in purple; replicas and photographs of medals, including one presented to Marshal Foch by the American Numismatic Society (located next door); minutes of meetings; commemorative addresses; and a holographic copy of a dedicatory poem by Robert Underwood Johnson:

The Temple

If this be but a house, whose stone we place,
   Better the prayer unbreathed, the music mute
   Ere it be stifled in the rifted lute;
Better had been withheld those hands of grace,
Undreamed the dream that was this moment's base
   Through nights that did the empty days refute.
   Accurs'd the fig-tree if it bear no fruit;
Only the flower sanctifies the vase.

No, 'tis a temple—where the mind may kneel
   And worship Beauty changeless and divine;
     Where the sage Past may consecrate the stole
Of Truth's new priest, the Future; where the peal
   Of organ voices down the human line
     Shall sound the diapason of the soul.[1]

And there it was: the echoing legacy of Keats. But Keats's season of mists and mellow fruitfulness had long since passed into fog and desiccation; the Romantic exhalations of the last century—a century more than twenty years gone—could not be kept going by pumping up a useless bellows that had run out of breath. The cornerstone may have received the pious mimicry of "The Temple" as its chief treasure, but modernism (one of its names was Ezra Pound) was pounding at the Temple's gates, shattering the sage Past and slighting the old forms of Beauty.

The Temple was not unaware of these shocking new vibrations: it derided and dismissed them. In 1925, in an address before the Academy-Institute (as the two closely allied bodies came to be called), three years after the publication of *The Waste Land*, Robert Underwood Johnson pointed to T. S. Eliot as one of the "prominent apostles" of "this so-called modern American poetry" and scolded him for prosiness and lack of taste and humor, while praising "the dignity and beauty of Landor's invocation to an English brook." (Walter Savage Landor, it might be noted, was born in 1775 and died in 1864, when Johnson was eleven years old.) Quoting lines from Marianne Moore, Johnson asked, "What is the remedy for this disease?" "The Academy's chief influence," he concluded, "will come from what and whom it recognizes, what and whom it praises, and what and whom it puts forth."[2]

In the extraordinary literary decade that followed the Great War, the Academy neither recognized nor praised nor put forth nor took in T. S. Eliot, Ezra Pound, Marianne Moore, William Carlos Williams, Hart Crane, Wallace Stevens, Conrad Aiken, H.D., Louise Bogan, John Crowe Ransom, or E. E. Cummings: revolutionaries, in their varying degrees, of voice, theme, and line. Not since Whitman had there been such a conflagration of fresh sound in American verse; it engulfed the poets of the Harlem Renaissance—Langston Hughes and Jean Toomer among them—and burned brilliantly, though in another language, among the American Yiddish imagists of the In Zikh movement farther downtown. Beauty, it seemed, was turning out to be neither changeless nor divine: it could take the form of the Brooklyn Bridge and manifest itself in idioms and accents that an unreceptive Temple, immaculately devoted to the difference between *can* and *may* (the Academy's task, Johnson said, was to preserve this distinction),[3] might be oblivious to at best, or at worst recoil from.

The Academy was incorporated by an act of Congress on April 17, 1916; its first president, who served from 1908 to 1920, was William Dean Howells, one of the few early Academicians whose names are recognizable to later generations. *The Rise of Silas Lapham* may not be much read today—not, say, as *The Great Gatsby* is read, zealously and regularly—but Howells (who was long ago dropped from routine high school curricula) is nevertheless permanently lodged in American literary history. He was succeeded as president (in a term lasting until 1928) by William Milligan Sloane, a professor of history at Columbia University, the author of a mammoth four-volume *Life of Napoleon Bonaparte* and of seven other equally ambitious works. A public presence—an eminence—in his time, Sloane must now be researched in the *Dictionary of American Biography*.

And so it is with numerous others. The cycle of generations dims if not eclipses even the most illustrious, and if an examination of the Academy-Institute's membership reveals nothing else, it surely affirms the melancholy wisdom of Ecclesiastes. Yet one need not go to the Preacher to learn how there is "no remembrance of former things"; sometimes biblical perspective comes without waiting so much as a day.[4] In 1923—the very year the Academy moved into its just-completed Renaissance palace—Burton Rascoe, a journalist with the *New York Tribune*, targeted the Temple's newest anointed: "When Mr. Johnson handed me a list of the fledglings upon whom the organization had just conferred harps and wings and other eternal impediments, I was even more startled to observe that scarcely one of the twenty outstanding literary personages of America was included, but a whole roster of nobodies whose careers were so limited and obscure that I had to spend an hour or so in the morgue after I got back to the office to find out what they had done or written."[5] Rascoe's literary nobodies of 1923 included John Spencer Bassett, James Bucklin Bishop, Owen David, Burton J. Hendrick, Rollo Ogden: names that, if they meant nothing to Rascoe, are merest dust to us. But Eugene O'Neill was on that same list, and Don Marquis (the celebrated progenitor of Archie the Cockroach); and if Rascoe—himself reduced now to one of the nobodies—had looked back a few years, from 1918 on (i.e., from the end of the war), he would have encountered literary somebodies we still remember and sometimes even read: James Gibbon Huneker, Edgar Lee Masters, Irving Babbitt, John Erskine, Joseph Hergesheimer, and Bernard Berenson.

William Dean Howells, journalist, novelist, playwright, and poet, served as the first president of the Academy from 1908 to 1920. The Academy honors his legacy with the Howells medal, given every five years to the most distinguished work of fiction published during that period.

Still, the forgotten Burton Rascoe is not mistaken about the forgettable among his own contemporaries or about the deadly absence of "outstanding literary personages." During the Academy's third decade of life—the vital cultural period between 1918 and 1927—the single major American writer to attain membership was Edith Wharton. (A belated elevation that took place in 1926, after an effort toward securing the admission of women finally prevailed over an acrimonious opposition.) Whereas in the world beyond the Temple—to confine our inquiry at this moment to literature only—there was an innovative ferment so astounding (and exhilarating) that no other segment of the twentieth century can match it.

Consider: 1918 saw the publication of Willa Cather's *My Ántonia*, Lytton Strachey's *Eminent Victorians*, the first installments of James Joyce's *Ulysses*, volumes by Rebecca West and H. L. Mencken; *The Education of Henry Adams* won the Pulitzer Prize; the Theater Guild was founded in New York; in Germany, the Dada movement began; in Russia, Aleksandr Blok was writing poetry in praise of the Bolshevik Revolution (without suspecting that its dissolution eight decades later would draw equal praise). The following year brought *Winesburg, Ohio*, by Sherwood Anderson; *Jurgen*, by James Branch Cabell; *The Arrow of Gold*, by Joseph Conrad; *La Symphonie pastorale*, by André Gide; *Demian*, by Hermann Hesse; *The Moon and Sixpence*, by Somerset Maugham—and Carl Sandburg won the Pulitzer. Finally, the next eight years—1920 to 1927—introduced a torrent of works by F. Scott Fitzgerald, John Galsworthy, Katherine Mansfield, Max Beerbohm, H. G. Wells, Sigrid Undset, John Dos Passos, Aldous Huxley, D. H. Lawrence, George Bernard Shaw, Luigi Pirandello, Bertolt Brecht, T. S. Eliot, Sinclair Lewis, François Mauriac, Virginia Woolf, Stefan Zweig, Rainer Maria Rilke, Italo Svevo, Robert Frost, Colette, S. Ansky, E. M. Forster, Edna Ferber, Thomas Mann, Maxwell Anderson, Michael Arlen, Theodore Dreiser, Maxim Gorky, Franz Kafka, Gertrude Stein, Edwin Arlington Robinson, Ernest Hemingway, W. E. B. Du Bois, T. E. Lawrence, Sean O'Casey, William Faulkner, Jean Cocteau, William Butler Yeats, Thornton Wilder, Henri Bergson. Mixed though these writers are in theme, genre, nationality, and degree of achievement, they represent, on the literary side, what we mean when we speak of the twenties: an era staggering in its deliverance from outworn voices and overly familiar modes and moods. Not all were "experimental"—indeed, most were not—but all claimed an idiosyncratic distinction between their own expectations of language and art and the expectations of the author of "The Temple."

Some of the Americans among them did finally gain admission to the Academy-Institute, but not without opposition. To combat the new streams of expression, Harrison Smith Morris—a writer elected to the Institute in 1908— proposed a resolution:

The National Institute of Arts and Letters in its long established office of upholder of Taste and Beauty in Arts and Letters in America, welcomes the approach of a return to the standards made sacred by tradition and by the genius of the great periods of the past.

The National Institute feels that the time has arrived to distinguish the good from the bad in the Arts, and to urge those who have loved the literature and painting that are accepted by the winnowing hand of time to turn away from the Falsehoods of this period and again to embrace only the genuine expressions of man's genius.

And the National Institute calls upon all those who write or speak on this essential subject of our culture as a nation, to ask their hearers to join in abhorrence of the offences, and to insist on the integrity of our arts.[6]

Though the archives of the Academy do not yield information on how the members voted (or at least I have been unable to uncover the results), the resolution itself was in profound consonance with the views held by the permanent secretary: Robert Underwood Johnson himself. And Johnson in effect ran things, despite the status of the men at the top (Howells, then Sloane, later Nicholas Murray Butler); Johnson was the Academy's primary engine. A first-rate organizer and administrator, he single-handedly acquired an endowment for the Academy—or, rather, he acquired the friendship and loyalty of Archer Milton Huntington, an extraordinarily wealthy donor with a generous temperament and a serious interest in Spanish culture. In addition to donating the land and ultimately the funds for the Academy's permanent headquarters, Huntington showered the Academy with periodic gifts[7] ($475,000 in 1923, $100,000 in 1927, $600,000 in 1929),[8] so that within a very short span a membership that was only recently being dunned for dues found itself cushioned and cosseted by prosperity.

At the annual meeting of 1925, Johnson spoke of Huntington as "a permanent friend of the Academy who desires to remain permanently anonymous." This was certainly true; yet Huntington—who quickly became a member of the Academy and whose second wife, a sculptor, was herself eventually elected—was not without intimations of immortality. In an autographed poem dedicated to the Academy, entitled "Genius," and in a style reminiscent of Johnson's own, he wrote in praise of "this oriflamme of glory":

High mystery prophetic that men cry!
The splendid diadem of hearts supreme,
Who shape reality from hope's vast dream
And gild with flame new pantheons in the sky!
Thus are we led to nobly raise on high
An edifice of deeds that may redeem

The lowliness of being, 'neath the gleam
Of mists all colorless where life must lie.[9]

(There was a follow-up stanza as well.)

Huntington was Johnson's organizational masterstroke: a funding triumph with recognizably lofty verbal credentials, capable of gilding new pantheons with cash. But Johnson's executive instincts pulled off a second administrative coup in the shape of Mrs. Grace Vanamee, who was enlisted as the permanent secretary's permanent deputy in the fall of 1915. A widow in her forties, Mrs. Vanamee was a kind of robust Johnsonian reverberation: if he was exuberantly efficient, so was she; if he was determined that no concern, however minuscule, should go unresolved, so was she. Mrs. Vanamee was, in brief, an unflagging enthusiast. She is reputed to have been a woman of large dimensions (though there is no one alive who can claim to have set eyes on her) and even larger energies. Like Johnson, she could successfully concentrate on several activities at once. On the side, so to speak, Johnson oversaw New York University's Hall of Fame; Mrs. Vanamee directed the Organization of Soldiers' Families of America. A public lecturer herself, she was also chair of the Republican Women's State Speakers' Bureau[10] and founder of the Women's National Republican Club; during the war she served as secretary of the Italian War Relief Committee, for which she earned a medal from the Italian Red Cross.

Her career as celebrated Academy factotum (a combination of executive director and chief housekeeper) began in a "sordid little office"[11] at 70 Fifth Avenue, equipped with an ancient second-hand typewriter bought for twenty dollars. Huntington soon provided a more suitable venue, a building he owned on West 81st Street, which was rapidly refurbished with offices, an auditorium, and living quarters for Mrs. Vanamee. There was, in addition, a President's Room decorated with a mahogany desk and green leather chairs and fine carpeting, at a cost of fifteen hundred dollars. Only two years later, when the West 155th Street edifice was ready to be occupied, all this would be dismantled.

But in the meantime, Mrs. Vanamee was in charge of caring for the now lavishly outfitted interim building—though not alone. A certain Frank P. Crasto emerges here as her indispensable assistant and sidekick; it is possible that he may represent our history's love interest. (The archives, it goes without saying, are silent on this point; but in Castro's obituary, intimacy is given a delicate license: he is described as Mrs. Vanamee's "foster-brother.") Mrs. Vanamee's early widowhood was enlivened by an open and famously zippy character, and her correspondence with this or that member of the Academy occasionally bordered on the flirtatious. In the middle of so much dense Victorian formality, she was even capable of an indiscreet anecdote: if not for Mrs. Vanamee, posterity would still be in the dark about the Pinching of the Trowel. In her account of

Marshal Foch and the West 155th Street building's cornerstone ceremony—"President Sloane almost white with excitement, Mr. Johnson radiant because his dreams had come true"—she describes how "the little Maréchal was tired and had to hurry away, and as he did so to our great amusement and consternation we saw that he had absent-mindedly thrust the lovely little silver trowel into his hip pocket, but we never saw it again."[12]

This cheery neglect of reverence for the great French military leader did not extend to Frank P. Crasto, himself a military man. Mrs. Vanamee identified him as "a Captain in the Reserves [who] knows what it is to inspect buildings and equipment and to maintain discipline as well as order and cleanliness" and added, with the esteem due such things, that "he understands all about printing, and is an expert proofreader."[13] He was also found to be useful in handling the heavy work. Captain Crasto became Major Crasto, and Major Crasto was promoted to Colonel Crasto: ascending titles that Mrs. Vanamee noted with veneration. His maintenance responsibilities were perhaps less lofty than his officer status would suggest; at the Academy Board meeting of May 11, 1921,[14] for instance, he reported that 138 of the 310 light bulbs at West 81st Street were out. Eventually he was raised to the post of librarian, but his rise in Mrs. Vanamee's affections had evidently occurred long before. In times of sickness they spelled each other. In 1923, when she was seriously ill in a Brooklyn hospital (she in fact lived until 1946), all inquiries concerning her condition were directed to the colonel, and it was she who in 1925 packed him off on a recuperative steamer trip to New Orleans after a heart episode: "there is nothing pressing at the Academy,"[15] she urged. One gets the inescapable impression of a pair of turtle doves under the Temple's eaves.

Mrs. Vanamee, the colonel, and, of course, the permanent secretary all moved on together to West 155th Street. Huntington sold the West 81st Street building (he intended to use the profits as endowment funds) despite pressure from Witter Bynner of the Poetry Society of America, who hoped to rent it as a meeting place for "all the Poetry Societies of America." The idea was discussed by the Academy board early in 1922 and quickly rejected. Brander Matthews dismissed such a convention of poets as "a large body of very small people," and Robert Underwood Johnson declined to place "the Academy's stamp of approval on the lack of standards of the Poetry Society."[16] (Its membership at the time included Stephen Vincent Benét, Carl Sandburg, and Edwin Arlington Robinson, all of whom Johnson scorned.)

It was in this same year that Sinclair Lewis, elected to Institute membership, angrily rejected it, unwilling to place *his* stamp of approval on the Academy or any part of it. Seven years later, accepting the Nobel Prize for literature before the Swedish Academy in Stockholm, he excoriated its American counterpart: "It does not represent literary America of today. It represents only Henry Wadsworth Longfellow."[17] (And in 1979 Witter Bynner had *his* revenge, albeit posthumously, with the establishment of the Academy's Witter Bynner Prize for Poetry.) The Academy was offended by Lewis but unruffled. The board went on to review a roster of quotations that might be appropriate to stand as a frieze across the brow of the new building. Aperçus by Cicero, Lucian, Pericles, Plato, Aristotle, and Emerson were proposed, none of which satisfied—whereupon Johnson remarked that a member might be moved (he may have been thinking of himself) to write something original. The wording for the frieze was not determined until 1924, a year after the opening of the building.[18] Brander Matthews made the selection: HOLD HIGH THE FLAMING TORCH FROM AGE TO AGE. When the architects asked for a second quotation, Matthews supplied them with ALL ARTS ARE ONE ALL BRANCHES ON ONE TREE. (The sources for both lines are unknown.)

The estimated cost of the finished Temple as presented to the Academy by the architects—McKim, Mead, and White, all three of whom were members—was $380,223.04, though the final bill probably exceeded half a million. The doors were heavy bronze. An early sketch of the facade before completion shows a pair of neoclassical sculptures in embrasures, and while these draped female figures, goddesses or Muses, at length vanished from the plans and were never executed, their spirit stuck fast. Stanford White was the designer of New York University's neoclassical campus on University Heights, and Charles F. McKim presided over Columbia's beaux arts buildings on Morningside Heights; both were visionaries of an ideal acropolis conceived as an echo (or rebirth) of older cities grown legendary through literature and art.

It was the same echo that had sounded in Robert Underwood Johnson's ear since his days at Earlham College,[19] a small Quaker institution in Indiana that emphasized Latin and "the human element of Virgil, Horace, Tacitus, Cicero." Even the college-boy jokes were in Latin: a classroom was dubbed *Nugipolyloquidium,* "a place of talkers of nonsense." Out of all this came the lingering faith that the classical is the eternal, and that the past, because it *is* the past, holds a sacred and per-

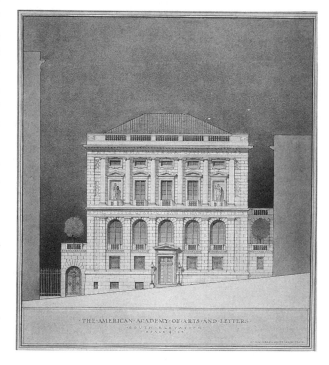

A 1920 rendering of the Academy building on West 155th Street by William Mitchell Kendall, office of McKim, Mead & White.

manent power: a view that differs from the historical sense, with its awareness (in contradistinction to Truth and Beauty) of evolution, displacement, violence and oppression, migration of populations, competing intellectual movements, the decline and fall of even contemporary societies and cultures. The achievement of such a serene outlook will depend on one's distance from strikes, riots, destitution, foreign eruptions, the effects of prejudice, immigrants pressing in at Ellis Island, and all the rest.

Inland Earlham in 1867, when Johnson was a freshman there, is deservedly called "tranquil"—"Tranquil Days at Earlham" is a chapter in Johnson's autobiographical *Remembered Yesterdays*, self-published in 1923 (just when Marshal Foch was pocketing the silver trowel)—and tranquility was the goal and soul of Johnson's artistic understanding. "We were charmed by the mountain scenery of the Gulf of Corinth, every peak and vale of which is haunted by mythological associations," he writes in a chapter entitled "Delight and Humor of Foreign Travel." "The Bay of Salamis gave us a thrill and at Eleusis we seemed to come in close touch with classic days, for here was the scene of the still unexplained Eleusinian mysteries." Living Greeks—at their rustic best, since "the urban Greek is undersized and unimpressive"—are admired solely as an ornamental allusion: "Some of them resembled fine Italian types, one or two reminding me of the elder Salvini," an Italian tragedian. More gratifying than these Greeks in the flesh are the crucial landmarks: "I stayed up until one o'clock at night to catch sight of the beacon on the 'Leucadian steep' which marks the spot from which Sappho is reputed to have thrown herself." "One may well imagine that three fourths of the time we spent in Athens was passed on the Acropolis."[20]

This was the sensibility that dreamed and labored over and built the American Academy of Arts and Letters. Johnson came to this task—this passion—after forty years at *The Century*, the magazine that succeeded *Scribner's Monthly*. Its editor-in-chief was Richard Watson Gilder, a poet hugely overpraised by his contemporaries ("An echo of Dantean mysticism . . . he wanders in the highest realms of spiritual poetry")[21] and wholly dismissed by their descendants. As editor-cum-poet, he was uniquely qualified to be mentor and model for Johnson, whom Gilder appointed associate editor in 1881. Gilder's own mentor and model was Edmund Clarence Stedman, himself a mediocre poet of the idealist school; both Stedman and Gilder were Academy members. Although Alfred Kazin (a present-day Academician) describes Gilder as "a very amiable man whom some malicious fortune set up as a perfect symbol of all that the new writers [of the twenties] were to detest," he was, for Johnson and his generation, the perfect symbol of all that belles-lettres and an elevated civilization required.[22]

Nor were Johnson and his generation misled. *The Century* was the most powerful literary periodical of its time, a genuine influence in the formation of American letters. In 1885, for example, the February issue alone carried—remarkably—excerpts from Mark Twain's *Huckleberry Finn*, Howells's *The Rise of Silas Lapham*, and James's *The Bostonians*. Gilder was a believer in purity of theme, which drew him away from certain subjects; Johnson was Gilder's even more cautious copy. In 1904, when, despite the editorial risk, Gilder wanted to publish Edith Wharton—he was shrewd enough to see that she was "on the eve of a great popular success"[23]—Johnson demurred: Wharton had written stories about divorce. At Gilder's death in 1909 Johnson took over as editor-in-chief. The decline of *The Century* is usually attributed, at least in part, to his inability to respond to changing public taste and expectation. The trustees, at any rate, found him inflexible; he resigned in 1913.

He was then sixty years old, in full and effective vigor, with a strong activist bent and an affinity for citizenly service. He was an advocate, a man of causes. At *The Century* he had promoted the conservation of forests and was instrumental in getting congressional sanction for the creation of Yosemite National Park.[24] It was he who persuaded a coolly reticent General Ulysses S. Grant to set down an emotional memoir of the battle of Shiloh. As secretary of a committee of authors and publishers, Johnson lobbied for international copyright and fought against the pirating of foreign books. His ardor spilled over into nine volumes of verse, all self-published, on subjects both sublime and civic, often interwoven:[25] "The Vision of Gettysburg," "The Price of Honor: The Colombian Indemnity," "The New Slavery (On the Expatriation by Germany of Civil Populations of Belgium)," "Armenia," "Henrik Ibsen, The Tribute of an Idealist," "To the Spirit of Luther: On Learning of the Reported Appeal of Germany to Matrons and Maidens to Give Themselves 'Officially' to the Propagation of the Race, Under Immunity from the Law." There are poems on the Dreyfus Affair: "The Keeper of the Sword (Apropos of the Dreyfus Trial at Rennes)" and "To Dreyfus Vindicated." The talent may have been middling, but the goodwill (and the prophetic vigilance) was mammoth.

If, as Emerson insists, the shipbuilder is the ship, then Robert Underwood Johnson was, long before its founding, the American Academy of Arts and Letters. There can be no useful history of the Academy that fails to contemplate Johnson's mind. Whatever ignited his enthusiasm, whatever struck him as repugnant: these formed the mind of the Academy. It was not that Johnson was dictatorial; on the contrary, he was elaborately courtly, and punctilious as to protocol. (As permanent secretary, he sent himself a deferential letter announcing his election to the Academy and, with equal deference, wrote back to accept the honor.) He did no violence to the opinion of others; rather, his opinion was generally the opinion of the membership, and vice versa. It may have been the Muses themselves who nurtured such unanimity; or else it was the similarity of background of these cultivated gentlemen, similarly educated, similarly situated in society, each with his triplet of rhythmically interchangeable names, all of them patriots, yet all looking toward an older Europe for continuity of purpose—with one urgent European exception.

The exception was Germany in the Great War. The Academy, most notably in the person of Robert Underwood Johnson, threw itself indefatigably into the war effort against Germany, contributing $100,000 to Italy and over one hundred ambulances presented in the name of the poets of America. Though the hostilities had come to an end with the November armistice of 1918, the Academy's hostility remained white-hot into the following year, with the publication of its World War *Utterances*. Here patriotism overreached itself into unrestrained fury. In an essay called "The Incredible Cruelty of the Teutons," William Dean Howells—the most benignly moderate of novelists—asked: "Can anyone say what the worst wickedness of the Germans has been? If you choose one there are always other crimes which contest your choice. We used at first to fix the guilt of them upon the Kaiser, but event by event we have come to realize that no man or order of men can pervert a whole people without their complicity."[26]

Luminary after luminary joined the cry, under titles such as "Can Peace Make Us Forget? A Plea for the Ostracism of All Things German"; "The Shipwreck of Kultur"; "The Crime of the *Lusitania*"; "Germany's Shame." "The nation which had invited our admiration for its *Gemütlichkeit* instantly aroused our abhorrence for its *Schrecklichkeit*," wrote Brander Matthews. And Nicholas Murray Butler, condemning Germany's "principle of world domination," compared German conquest and subjection of peoples to Alexander the Great, the legions of Rome, Charlemagne, Bonaparte, and, finally, "the Hebrews of old." (As the author of Columbia University's notorious and long-lasting Jewish quota, Butler—quite apart from his Academy activities, where such views were only rarely expressed—apparently also feared conquest by later Hebrews.) Woodrow Wilson, who had campaigned for the presidency with the slogan "He kept us out of war"—to the disgust of his more belligerent colleagues at the Academy—now spoke of Germany as "throwing to the winds all scruples of humanity" while engaged in "a warfare against mankind." In his "Note on German Music and German Ideas," Horatio Parker, one of the period's nearly forgotten composers, could not resist making a plea for German music, especially Bach, Richard Strauss, and Mendelssohn ("It is as useless to deny the beauty and greatness of classical masterpieces by Germans as it is to deny the same qualities in their mountains"); nevertheless he concluded that "prejudice of the public and of officials in this country against modern German music is perhaps justifiable."[27]

In these exhortations to hatred and ostracism, the Academy's impulse was no different from the anti-German clamor that was everywhere in the American street. From our distance, the bitter words may seem overreactive and hyperchauvinist. Still, reading these papers now three-quarters of a century old, one feels a curious displacement of rage: a vertiginous sense of the premature, as of an hourglass set mistakenly on its head. The sinking of the *Lusitania*, merciless act of war though it was, was not yet Auschwitz. If Howells, say, had written as he did not in 1918 but in 1945, after the exposure of the crematoria, how would we judge his judgment? It is sometimes an oddity of history that the right thing is said at the wrong time.

And it may be that, in the third decade of its life, many right things were spoken at the Academy at the wrong time. When the war was over, Johnson turned his energies once again to the celebration of a type of high culture. And again there looked to be a displacement of timing. In 1919 race riots broke out in Chicago and a dockworkers' strike hit New York; the eight-hour workday was instituted nationally; President Woodrow Wilson won the Nobel Peace Prize and presided over the first meeting of the League of Nations in Paris; the Red Army took Omsk, Kharkov, and the Crimea; Mussolini founded the Italian fascist movement; Paderewski became premier of Poland. Henri Bergson, Karl Barth, Ernst Cassirer, Havelock Ellis, Karl Jaspers, John Maynard Keynes, Rudolf Steiner—indelible figures—were all active in their various spheres. Short-wave radio made its earliest appearance, there was progress in sound for movies, and Einstein's theory of relativity was borne out by astrophysical experiments. Walter Gropius developed the Bauhaus in Germany and revolutionized painting, architecture, sculpture, and the industrial arts. Kandinsky, Klee, and Modigliani were at work, and Picasso designed the set of Diaghilev's *The Three Cornered Hat*. Jazz headed for Europe; the Los Angeles Symphony gave its initial concert; the Juilliard School of Music opened in New York, and the New Symphony Orchestra, conducted by Edgard Varèse, inaugurated a hearing for modern music. A nonstop flight across the Atlantic was finally accomplished. Babe Ruth hit a 587-foot home run. The Nobel Prize for literature went to Knut Hamsun.

In short, 1919 was the beginning of a deluge of new forms, new sounds, new ventures, new arrangements in the world. And in such an hour the Academy undertook to mark the centennial of James Russell Lowell, who had died twenty-eight years before. In itself, the choice was pleasant and not inappropriate. A leading American eminence of the nineteenth century, a man of affairs as well as a man of letters, a steady opponent of slavery, Lowell was poet, critic, literary historian. He was vigorous in promoting the study of modern languages, which he taught at Harvard. He was, besides, the *Atlantic Monthly*'s first editor and (with Charles Eliot Norton) a founder of the *North American Review*. He served as American ambassador to the court of Spain and afterward as emissary to Britain. His complete works—both verse and prose—occupy ten volumes. According to Lowell's biographer, Horace E. Scudder—member of the Institute and author of a laudatory *Encyclopaedia Britannica* article on Lowell that is virtually contemporaneous with the Academy's celebratory event—Lowell "impressed himself deeply on his generation in America, especially upon the thoughtful and scholarly class who looked upon him as their representative."[28] Johnson unquestionably looked on Lowell as his representative; Lowell's career—poet, editor, ambassador—was an ideal template for Johnson's own.

The centennial program, subtitled "In Celebration of the Unity and Power of the Literature of the English-speaking People," was intended to emphasize the ongoing link with the Mother Country. To further this connection, invitations went out to, among others, Prime Minister Herbert Asquith, Robert Bridges (the poet laureate), Rudyard Kipling, James Barrie, Arthur Conan Doyle, Gilbert Chesterton, Gilbert Murray, Arthur Quiller-Couch, Edmund Gosse, Alfred Noyes, and John Galsworthy. Ambitious though this roster was (it ran after nearly every living luminary of that scepter'd isle), only the last two accepted and actually arrived—Galsworthy with the proviso that he would attend the gala luncheon "*so long as this does not entail a speech.*"[29] Stephen Leacock came with a troop of notables from Canada, and Australia was represented by one lone guest.

Still, a demonstration of the unity and power of literary Anglo-Saxonism was not, as it turned out, the whole purpose of the centennial. Nor was it precisely as an act of historic commemoration that Johnson sought to honor Lowell. On February 13, 1919, a New York newspaper, the *Evening Post*, explained: "James Russell Lowell, who was born a hundred years ago next week . . . would not have liked vers libre or modern verse in general, says Robert Underwood Johnson. . . . Mr. Johnson knew Lowell personally." The *Post* went on to quote the permanent secretary's reminiscences—"I remember hearing Lowell once say, when asked if he had read the latest novel, 'No, I have not yet finished Shakespeare' "—and followed with a considerable excerpt from the rest of Johnson's remarks:

> Mr. Lowell represented in himself, as it is sometimes necessary to remind the current generation, the highest plane of learning, scholarship, and literary art, the principle of which he expounded in season and out of season in his critical writings. . . . His critical works furnish a body of doctrine in literary matters which is certainly preëminent in American criticism at least. In these days, when the lawlessness of the literary Bolsheviki has invaded every form of composition, it is of tonic advantage to review Lowell's exposition of the principles of art underlying poetry and criticism. . . . No man studied to better purpose the range of expression afforded by the English classics or would have been more outraged by the random and fantastic productions which are classified with the poetry of the present time under the name of vers libre. While no doubt he recognized the force of Whitman, he refused to recognize

him as a poet, and once retorted, when it was suggested that much of Whitman's poetry was between prose and poetry, that there was nothing between prose and poetry.

Johnson concluded with a pledge that the Academy would take on the "agreeable duty to endeavor to accentuate the treasures of American literature which have fallen into neglect" and hoped that the occasion would "incite our college faculties and their students to a study of the heritage which we have in the beautiful poetry and the acute and high-minded criticism of James Russell Lowell."[30]

To suppose that the times were ripe for a return to the prosody of Lowell was a little like a call to reinstate Ptolemy in the age of Einstein. The Lowell centennial was not so much a memorial retrospective—i.e., an unimpeachable review of a significant literary history—as it was that other thing: an instance of antiquarianism. Or—to do justice to Johnson's credo—it was a battle cry against the onrushing alien modernist hordes, the literary Bolsheviki.

The difficulty was that the Bolsheviki were rampant in all the arts. Young American composers—Virgil Thomson, Marc Blitzstein, Elliott Carter, Marion Bauer, Roger Sessions, Herbert Elwell, Aaron Copland, George Gershwin—were streaming toward Nadia Boulanger's studio outside Paris for instruction in harmony (much as young American writers were streaming toward Gertrude Stein's Paris sitting room for lessons in logic) and coming back home with extraordinary new sounds. Boulanger introduced Copland to the conductor Walter Damrosch (later president of the Academy at a time when its laces were far less strait), who joked about Copland's *Symphony for Organ and Orchestra*, "If a gifted young man can write a symphony like that at twenty-three, within five years he will be ready to commit murder." What Copland called the "jazz spirit," with its irregular rhythms and sometimes exotic instruments, was received by the more conventional critics as a kind of symphonic deicide: the old gods of rational cadence struck down by xylophones, tom-toms, Chinese woodblocks. Copland was charged with releasing a "modernist fury" of "barnyard and stable noises." "New York withholds its admiration," Virgil Thomson wrote of the critical atmosphere, "till assured that you are modeling yourself on central Europe."[31]

But experiment was unstoppable: George Gershwin was blending concert music and jazz in works commissioned by Damrosch, and Serge Koussevitsky, conducting the Boston Symphony, was presiding over Copland's barnyard noises. Edgard Varèse, who came to the United States from Paris in 1915—reversing the flow—declared his belief in "organized sound," or "sound-masses," and employed cymbals, bells, chimes, castanets, slapsticks, rattles, chains, anvils, and almost every other possible percussion device, "with their contribution," as he put it, "of a blossoming of unsuspected timbres."[32] His scores were often marked with "*hurlant*," indicating howling, roaring, wild and strident clamor: any sound, all sounds, were music.

In the prosperity and optimism of the twenties, proponents of the new music were turning their backs (and not without contempt) on traditionalists like Frederick Shepherd Converse, Edward Burlingame Hill, George Whitefield Chadwick, Reginald De Koven, Arthur Foote, Victor Herbert, and John Powell, all members of the Academy and all continuing to compose in nineteenth-century styles. The maverick among them was John Alden Carpenter, nearly the only Academician to venture into blues, ragtime, and jazz. But in the world beyond the Academy, the matchless Louis Armstrong and other eminent black musicians were revolutionizing the American—and European—ear, and by 1927 Duke Ellington's band in Harlem's Cotton Club was devising original voices for trumpet and trombone.[33] The twenties saw an interpenetration of foreign originality as well: Sergei Rachmaninoff arrived after the Russian Revolution, and in the winter of 1925 Igor Stravinsky appeared with both the New York Philharmonic and the Boston Symphony. Three years earlier, Darius Milhaud was lecturing at Harvard, Princeton, and Columbia. Ernest Bloch, noted for chamber music and an enchantment with Hebrew melodies, became an American citizen in 1924. Arnold Schoenberg, inventor of twelve-tone technique and a refugee from Nazi Germany, emigrated to the United States in 1933, but his influence had long preceded him.

Meanwhile, Henry Cowell, a native Californian, was not only trying out novel sounds on the piano—sometimes treating it like a violin—but was inventing a new instrument, the rhythmicon, "capable of producing very complex combinations of beat patterns."[34] The quarterly Cowell founded, suitably named *New Music*, was hospitable to the work of the most arcane innovators, including Charles Ives, whose composition teacher at Yale in 1894 had been the mild but uncomprehending Horatio Parker. It is one of the ironies of the Academy's later history, and also one of its numerous triumphs over its older self, that grants and fellowships are now awarded to young composers in Charles Ives's name and out of the royalties of his estate—though Ives's polytonality, quarter tones, and disjointed melody lines would surely have appalled the Academicians of the twenties.[35] In February 1923, Richard Aldrich, a member of the Institute since 1908 and music critic for the *New York Times*, wrote in a bitter column called "Some Judgments on New Music":

> It is nothing less than a crime for a composer to write in any of the idioms that have been handed down, or to hold any of the older ideas of beauty. . . . Any who do not throw overboard all the baggage inherited from the past, all transmitted ideas of melody and harmony, are reactionaries, pulling back and hindering the march of music. . . . Whatever is presented to [the receptive new audiences] as acrid ugliness or ram-

bling incoherence is eagerly accepted as emanations of greatness and originality. It never occurs to them that it might be simple, common-place ugliness.[36]

These are lines that might have emerged from Robert Underwood Johnson's own inkpot. But it fell to John Powell, a Virginian elected to the Institute in 1924, to catch the Johnsonian idiom entire. The modernists, Powell said, were "nothing more or less than cheap replicas of the recent European Bolshevists." Powell was a composer of moods, beguiled by the picturesque and the nostal-gic, especially as associated with Southern antebellum plantation life. The intro-ductory wail of his *Rapsodie Nègre* is intended to capture a watermelon peddler's cry, a telltale image that, apart from its melodic use, may possibly bear some rela-tion to his distaste for racial mixing and new immigrants.[37] His musical prefer-ence was for what he termed "the Anglo-Saxon Folk Music School," and he shunned *Cavalleria Rusticana* and *Tristan and Isolde* not because he disliked opera but because he disapproved of marital infidelity.

The new music, with its "acrid ugliness and rambling incoherence," may have been the extreme manifestation of what the Academy idealists were up against. Among the other arts, though, the idealists did have one strong ally, which steadfastly resisted—longer than music and longer than painting—the notions of freedom of form and idiosyncratic or experimental vision that modernism was opening up to the individual artist. Sculpture alone contin-ued to profess public nobility and collective virtue in service to a national pur-pose.[38] "Sculpture" meant statuary dedicated to historical uplift and moral seriousness. Even architecture, through its functional aspect, was more inclined to engage in individual expression—but virtually every statue was intended as a monument. The Armory Show of 1913, the catalyst that revolutionized American painting, barely touched the National Sculpture Society, which had settled on Augustus Saint-Gaudens and his successors, in their advance from marble to bronze, as "The Golden Age of American Sculpture." (Saint-Gaudens died in 1907.) Colossal multifigured structures, exhibition palaces (often fashioned from temporary materials and afterward dismantled), foun-tains, celebratory arches, symbolic themes indistinguishable from spiritual cre-dos: all these were in full consonance with Robert Underwood Johnson's dream of an American Temple. Nearly fifty years before the Armory Show, the sculptor Erastus Dow Palmer had declared: "No work in sculpture, however wrought out physically, results in excellence, unless it rests upon, and is sus-tained by, the dignity of a moral or intellectual intention."[39]

This dogma remained intact until the rise of the modernists, who repudi-ated not only its principles but its techniques. The Paris beaux arts tradition depended on studio assistants; a sculptor was a "thinker," a philosopher who conceived the work and modeled it in clay, after which lower-level technicians were delegated to carry out its translation into finished form. Modernism, by contrast, brought on a rush of hand carving, the kinetic and aesthetic interaction of sculptor with tools and material. But it was not until the twenties were almost out that individual style began to emerge as a recognizable, though clearly not yet dominant, movement. It was a movement that purposefully turned away from Old World models and looked to the "primitive," to African and pre-Columbian as well as Sumerian and Egyptian sources. While the Academy itself clung to the civically earnest, advanced taste was (once again) headed for unfamiliar territory. Thomas Hastings, a beaux arts adherent elected to the Academy in 1908, had designed a victory arch—adorned with abundant inspirational statuary—for the soldiers returning after the First World War to march through. In 1919 it was executed in temporary materials, and the soldiers did march through it. But public sentiment failed to support a permanent rendering in stone, and the arch was taken down. Monuments to a civic consensus were slipping from popularity; work steeped in lofty aims met indifferent, or perhaps jaded, eyes.

Yet the new sculptors were not recognized by the Academy, and the strikingly fresh shapes and experiments of the twenties streamed past the Temple only to attract its vilifying scorn. Saul Baizerman, whose innovative studies of contemporary life, *The City and the People*, were hammered out between 1920 and 1925, was never invited into the Institute, while even more notable sculptors of the period had to wait for a later generation's approbation. Bruce Moore was not admitted until 1949; William Zorach became a member only in 1953, and Robert Laurent only in 1970, the year of his death. Within the Academy of the third decade, it was Daniel Chester French (admitted in 1908) who was preeminent: the prized sculptor of the Lincoln Memorial in Washington, D.C., the creator of a female *Republic* (with staff, globe, and dove) and of Columbia University's *Alma Mater*, himself a grand symbol of the grand symbolic statuary that preceded the modernist flood and was finally—if belatedly in the Academy—overwhelmed by it.

In a tribute delivered on French's death in 1931, Royal Cortissoz, an Academician who was art critic for the *New York Herald Tribune* from 1891 on, observed with just precision that French "was thoroughly in harmony with [the Academy's] spirit" in a life "dedicated from beginning to end to the production of noble work....A beautiful seriousness of purpose animated him."[40] As an example he offered French's figure of *Memory*, "a seated nude reminiscent of antique ideas." Cortissoz was reflecting exactly what William Milligan Sloane had prescribed in his address at the opening of the Temple in 1923:

> We are a company seeking the ideal....We do not forget that our business is conservation first and foremost, conservation of the best and but incidentally, if at all, promotion of the untried. We are to guard tradition,

not to seek out and reward innovation. . . . We are sternly bound as an organization to examine carefully any intellectual movement striving to break with tradition. . . . Our effort in word and work must be to discover and cherish the true American spirit and keep it pure, in order to prevent inferior literature and art from getting the upper hand.[41]

What, then, was Cortissoz about when he labeled modern art "a gospel of stupid license and self-assertion," if not preventing the inferior from getting the upper hand?[42] Still another Academician, the painter and critic Kenyon Cox, wrote: "There is only one word for this denial of all law, this insurrection of individual license without discipline and without restraint; and that word is anarchy."[43] The Armory Show, Cox announced, was a "pathological museum" where "individualism has reached the pitch of sheer insanity or triumphant charlatanism." Gauguin was "a decorator tainted with insanity." Rodin displayed "symptoms of mental decay." If Cortissoz thought Matisse produced "gauche puerilities," Cox went further and condemned "grotesque and indecent postures" drawn "in the manner of a savage or depraved child."

Eleven years after the Armory shock, the Academy, still unforgiving in 1924, published three papers attacking "Modernist Art," one each by Cortissoz and Cox and the third by Edwin Howland Blashfield.[44] All three blasts had appeared in periodicals in 1913 and 1914, in direct response to the Armory Show, but the Academy—while asserting that modernism's influence was "on the wane"—saw fit to reprint them in the interests of dislodging "eccentricities" from "the tolerance of critics." Here again was Kenyon Cox: "The real meaning of the Cubist movement is nothing else than the total destruction of the art of painting"; Cézanne "seems to me absolutely without talent"; "this kind of art [may] corrupt public taste and stimulate an appetite for excitement that is as dangerous as the appetite for any other poisonous drug"; "do not allow yourselves to be blinded by the sophistries of the foolish dupes or the self-interested exploiters of all this charlatanry." And Cortissoz on the postimpressionists: "Work not only incompetent, but grotesque. It has led them from complacency to what I can only describe as insolence"; their "oracular assertion that the statues and pictures are beautiful and great is merely so much impudence."[45] Blashfield, finally, after deploring "a license to omit painstaking care, coherent thinking, an incitement to violence as compelling attention," simply ended with a cry of self-defense: *there is no dead art.*[46]

Thus the Temple on the coming of the New. And thus the Academy's collective impulse toward vituperation—delivered repeatedly, resentfully, remorselessly, relentlessly; and aimed at the New in music, painting, sculpture, literature. And not only here. Whatever was new in the evolving aspirations of women toward inclusion and equality was repudiated. New immigrants (no longer of familial Anglo-Saxon stock, many of whom were to enrich American literature, art, and music) were repudiated. Any alteration of nineteenth-century standards of piety or learning was repudiated. In a 1922 address, Owen Wister, author of *The Virginian*, ostensibly lauding "the permanent hoard of human knowledge," offered a list of "certain menaces to our chance for great literature": "We are developing ragtime religion. Homer and Virgil were founded on a serious faith. . . . The classics are in eclipse. To that star all intellect has hitched its wagon. Literature has become a feminine subject in our seats of learning. What female Shakespeare has ever lived? Recent arrivals pollute the original spring. . . . It would be well for us if many recent arrivals would become departures."[47]

Across the water Virginia Woolf, too, was speculating on the absence of a female Shakespeare, though from another viewpoint. And in the very bowels of the Academy, in a letter to President Sloane on October 22, 1921, loyal Mrs. Vanamee herself—in the name of the logic of precedent—was protesting the exclusion of women:

> You will be astonished to learn that I found a volume of Institute Minutes which was once loaned to Mr. Johnson and in looking through it this morning we found a record of [Julia Ward] Howe's election to the Institute. It seems she was regularly [i.e., routinely] nominated and regularly elected for at that time [1907] there was no ruling against women's being elected to the Institute. Mrs. Howe's name has always been included among the names of "Deceased Members of the Institute." Of course this makes the ruling of yesterday entirely out of order.[48]

Mrs. Vanamee recommended that "any record of what occurred" (meaning the entire set of minutes of the meeting ruling against admission of women) be expunged in a little act of hanky-panky. Accordingly, the culpable minutes were somehow spirited away, never again to emerge; but the issue continued to fester, and it would be another five years before enough ballots could be counted in favor of admission. Julia Ward Howe's membership—for the three feeble years before her death at age ninety-one—was argued against as "an error of procedure."[49] Besides, as the author of "The Battle Hymn of the Republic" she was less a woman than a national monument, one of those ideal female symbol figures specialized in by Daniel Chester French.

In the ballots of 1923—asking directly, "Do you favor the admission of women to the National Institute of Arts and Letters?"—sometimes a simple *no* was not enough to satisfy the spleen of elderly gentlemen born before or during the Civil War. "NO I DO NOT," roared the painter Whitney Warren. "A categorical NO," announced the composer Arthur Bird, and followed up with a tirade:

> To express my decided antipathy against this proposed innovation you will notice that I have added *categorical*. I have lately in the Chicago Musical

Leader ventilated my opinion on this subject in a short exposé. The occasion of a woman attempting to conduct the Philharmonic orchestra here at a symphony concert gave me a long awaited opportunity to mount a short but vigorous sally . . . against the attempts of a certain clan of womanhood to try to do things the feminine gender is by nature utterly incapable of doing and hooting at those things for which it is by nature predestined. What on earth *have or ever will have women* to do with science, art and letters (in the highest sense of the words) or are they satisfied to play a very mediocre second fiddle? It is needless to hide the naked fact, conceal the plain truth, that the moment the fair sex drops its skirts, throws aside guiltiness, modesty, refinement, all that gentility that we know and love so much, *don the leather breeches, beat the drum*, then lackaday to all the poetry of this life, away with the sentiments so expressive in Heine's poem so prettily and cleverly translated by our Longfellow, "The sea hath its pearls," etc. Then we shall say "For women must work and fight, men weep and spin." Id est—the world turned upside down.[50]

Tirades on the one hand, gloatings on the other. "I rejoice exceedingly," the writer James Ford Rhodes wrote in 1918 to Robert Underwood Johnson (who, surprisingly, favored women's admission), "that you were beaten on the women question. What would you do with the 'wimmin' at the dinners at the University Club? . . . A hysteria is going over the country, showing itself in women's suffrage and Prohibition."[51] (The Temple may have been able to do without women at dinner, but it rarely permitted itself to do without booze, and regularly circumvented the Eighteenth Amendment, *viz.*, "My dear Cass, Please send the bottle of Gin for the Institute dinner, carefully wrapped up so as to conceal its identity"; "My dear Thorndike, Will you please send the bottle of Gin, carefully wrapped up so that it will not look suspicious.")[52]

In the midst of all these fulminations and refusals and repudiations (always excepting the gin), there was, nevertheless, one moment early in the Academy's third decade that hinted at a glimmer of doubt, perhaps even of self-criticism. It was, in fact, a kind of bloodless insurrection or palace coup and took place behind Robert Underwood Johnson's formidable back. The rebel in the case was Hamlin Garland, author of *A Son of the Middle Border*, a school classic of the last generation. Wisconsin-born, Garland grew up in the drudging privations of farm life, at home in the unpolished—and impoverished—regions of Iowa, California, and the Dakotas. Unlike Johnson (out of whom the last traces of Indiana had long since been squeezed), Garland could never have been mistaken for a formal easterner. His perspectives were wider and more sympathetic than many of his colleagues'; he was a liberal who wrote seriously on social reform. His name was irrefutably linked with narrative realism, but he was a realist in the more everyday sense as well: he looked around and saw an

Academy of fatigued and retrograde gentlemen stuck fast in a narrow mold. "We must avoid the appearance of a club of old fogies," he warned, and kept an eye out for a chance to invigorate the membership.[53]

The chance came in 1920, when President Wilson (an Academy member since 1908) appointed Johnson to be ambassador to Italy and Garland stepped in as the Academy's acting secretary. In Johnson's absence, Garland's first target was Johnson himself: "We cannot become a 'one man organization,' no matter how fine that man may be." To Brander Matthews he wrote, "Now is the time to make the Academy known. If we let this chance pass we shall be a Johnson Institution for the rest of our lives. . . . We can't be run by a volunteer member seventy years of age. . . . We are called . . . that Johnson thing."[54] He noted "the age and growing infirmity of many of our members who are losing interest in the organization" and "the fact that our membership is scattered as well as aged and preoccupied." "We should draw closer," he advised, "and take the future of the Academy much more seriously than we have heretofore done. . . . We must not lose touch with youth. We should not be known as 'a senile institution.' We must assume to lead in the progress of the Nation."[55]

Yet Garland's ideas for Academy programs turned out to be less than revolutionary: "The Academy by a Lecture Foundation should offer to the Nation a series of addresses on American Arts and Letters in which the most vigorous propaganda for the good as against the bad should be carried forward. We should stand against all literary pandering, all corrupting influences," an exhortation that might easily have been uttered by any of the old fogies had it not concluded with a call to "make it plain that we are for progress, that it is our plan to hasten and direct the advance. That we intend to recognize the man of genius whether in the Academy or not."[56] He proposed the election of honorary foreign members, so that the Academy's "penumbra can extend throughout the world." As for the native membership, he warned against "the choice of a scholar who is known only to a few other scholars." "There is always the danger of electing too many men who are merely college professors. The Academy," he insisted, "cannot afford to elect a classicist in preference to the man of original genius." And there was only one kind of genius he really wanted: "The Academy membership must be kept predominantly literary or the Academy will lose power. The moment the Academy is overbalanced on the art side it loses standing, a result which may be unjust but it is true." He pushed for fame: "A man may be chosen who is recognized by the great public as a figure. Edwin Markham for example does not have to be explained. He is in Who's Who. Some of the Academy elections have to be explained even to members." He pushed for zeal: "Men who will come to the meetings. . . . Every time the Academy takes in a man who has a sort of contempt for what it is trying to do it weakens the organization." He pushed above all for the Academy as "an inspiration to young men" and called for the establishment of annual awards to "young workers in the five arts."[57]

And as a final push, though Johnson was still safely in Italy, Garland considered how to suppress him on his return: "Johnson is ex-officio on all committees," he conceded, but "should not be Chairman." In the course of time Garland proposed an even more radical solution: the Academy should get rid of Johnson altogether. "The returning secretary is an old man, preoccupied (as the rest of us are) with personal work of his own. He cannot give his entire mind to the Academy and as he is a member, it is not desirable that he should. It is not a good thing to have any one member known as the manager of the organization. The managing Secretary should be an outside man on a salary."[58]

At the end of the day Garland was happy to have Johnson back. The truth was that Johnson *could* give his entire mind to the Academy and had always been eager to do exactly that. The administrative minutiae that Johnson reveled in ultimately made Garland grumble; he was clearly sick of contending with old-fogy letters like the two that arrived a month apart in the fall of 1921 from Abbott Lawrence Lowell, the president of Harvard: "I do not know whether I shall be able to be present at the meeting on November 2nd; but I want to suggest that it would be well for the Academy, which stands for Letters, to use the best English in its communications to members, and say 'I shall,' or 'shall not, be present,'—not 'I will, or will not' ";"I do not know what the duties of the Education Committee of the American Academy of Arts and Letters are. I am very glad to serve on the Committee; but it seems to me that it would be a great mistake for the Academy to attempt to do anything or express an opinion about education."[59]

Like Lowell, the membership, reluctant to be more activist than they had been under Johnson, resisted Garland's pressure for broader concern and greater participation. "The lack of interest and cohesion is pitiful," he wrote to President Sloane. And to Matthews he complained, "I am just downright discouraged. . . . The truth is we are a lot of 'elderly old parties' who don't care very much whether school keeps or not—we'd rather not if it involves any janitor work on our part. . . . I cannot be a party to a passive policy."[60] The Academy, it seemed, liked it well enough that Johnson ran a one-man establishment, and Garland himself was feeling more and more the imposition on his own literary productivity. "I am carrying so much of the detail work of the Academy at this time," he moaned one year into his service as acting secretary, "that I have no leisure for my own writing."[61] Two years later he was in a state of full surrender and could hardly wait for the finish of Johnson's ambassadorial stint. "As I see it now there will be no one but Johnson to carry on the work and I withdraw all opposition to him."[62] And: "I've been a nuisance to little effect and shall turn the Office of Secretary over to Johnson the moment he reaches the building. It is a thankless task for any man."[63]

Thankless for any but Robert Underwood Johnson. Though his beard may have grown whiter, he resumed his position at the helm as energetically as before: it was as if Italy had never intervened. Despite Garland's efforts to introduce notions of "progress," everything Johnson had left behind was still in place, every prejudice intact, the familiar projects ongoing: the preoccupation with standards of English diction; public addresses entitled "The Literature of Early American Statesmanship," "Kinship and Detachment from Europe in American Literature," "The Emotional Discovery of America," "The Relations of American Literature and American Scholarship in Retrospect and Prospect" (all these in 1924, to mark the Academy's twentieth anniversary); the annual Evangeline Wilbour Blashfield Lecture, in honor of the wife of Edwin Howland Blashfield, sculptor of *The Evolution of Civilization*. At her death she was eulogized not merely for her "nobility of character" but more particularly for her faith "in the furtherance of sane and useful movements in literature and the Arts."[64]

Perhaps the most Johnsonian display of taste burst out in 1924, the year Robert Frost won the Pulitzer Prize for poetry and the Academy voted not to award its Gold Medal to anyone at all. According to the minutes of October 10, Johnson protested this decision, "favoring as the recipient Miss Edith M. Thomas, whose seventieth birthday has just occurred. Mr. Johnson spoke in high appreciation of the substance and style of Miss Thomas's work, which he regarded as the summit of contemporary American poetry."[65] Not that this was Johnson's first salvo on behalf of the summit. He had begun to urge Miss Thomas's cause six years earlier; apparently he regarded her as his most incendiary weapon in the war on free verse. "Aside from her professional merits and the nobility of her character," he pressed, "the spiritual tone of her work . . . would be all the more timely because of the widespread misconceptions in the public mind concerning the art of poetry, due to the vogue of formless, whimsical and eccentric productions, which by reason of their typographical form are generally classified as poetry by publishers, librarians, critics and readers. That the Academy should honor a poetic artist of so fine a strain as Miss Thomas would be to throw the force of its influence against the lawlessness of the time that has invaded all the Arts."[66] And even by 1926—it was now four years since the landmark appearance of *The Waste Land*—Johnson was still not giving up on Edith Thomas: "I believe that in some respects she has seen more deeply and reported more melodiously the evanescent phases of the borderland of the soul than any other American poet except Ralph Waldo Emerson."[67]

In 1925 the vote for the newly established William Dean Howells Medal, given "in recognition of the most distinguished work of fiction published during the preceding five years," went to Mary E. Wilkins Freeman for her depiction of "Old New England, New England before the coming of the French Canadian and the Italian peasant. . . . The body of her work remains of the

Anglo-Saxon order."[68] (Other American fiction published in that annus mirabilis of 1925 included *The Professor's House*, by Willa Cather, elected to the Institute in 1929; *In Our Time*, short stories by Ernest Hemingway, never admitted to membership; *The Great Gatsby*, by F. Scott Fitzgerald, also never admitted; *An American Tragedy*, by Theodore Dreiser, another nonmember; *Manhattan Transfer*, by John Dos Passos, admitted in 1937; and *The Making of Americans*, by Gertrude Stein, who of all American writers was least likely to be nominated.) At the same time the vote in the Institute for the Gold Medal for Belles Lettres landed on William Crary Brownell, an Academy member who had the distinction of serving as Edith Wharton's editor at Scribner's. Wharton herself was still unadmitted. In 1926 the Gold Medal for Sculpture was presented to Herbert Adams, the Academician who had designed the bronze doors for the Academy's terrace entrances, with their inscription: GREAT MEN ARE THEY WHO SEE THAT THOUGHTS RULE THE WORLD. In 1927 William Milligan Sloane won the Gold Medal for Biography and History; Johnson had successfully nominated the Academy's president for the Academy's own award.

The Academy was also engaged in other forms of self-recognition. There was the question of a bookplate, insignia, regalia: all the grave emblems of institutional Importance. The bookplate—an airy Pegasus rearing among clouds, framed by a wreath resting on a book, below which appears the Academy's motto: OPPORTUNITY, INSPIRATION, ACHIEVEMENT—was devised by the architect Henry Bacon and engraved by Timothy Cole. The airiness was Cole's contribution—"a delicate light style," he said, "that I have been at great pains to secure"—but Bacon rejected it, preferring the "heavy strong manner" of Piranesi, the eighteenth-century Italian neoclassicist.[69] Bacon died in the middle of the dispute, so Pegasus continued

Genius of Inspiration at The Gates of the Academy Collecting Soap Bubbles to cleanse the Mouths of Detractors

Herbert Adams.

Detail of bronze doors by Herbert Adams, north gallery. Adams wrote the caption on image.

to fly lightly, as Cole rendered him. No lightness attached to the issue of regalia, however: odd-looking caps and shroudlike gowns were supplied to the Academicians (a photograph attests to their discomfort) and then discarded. From 1923 on there were various experiments with insignia; at one point the current small rosette was in disfavor for grand occasions, and a great floppy badge was introduced: a giant purple satin ribbon trimmed with gold scallops and tiny bows. (A box of these relics, accompanied by cards of unused ribbon, matching thread, and even needles and pins, is still being thriftily stored in the Academy's archives.) And there were Roman-style busts of the Academicians themselves: F.Wellington Ruckstull, an Academy sculptor, was commissioned to immortalize both Nicholas Murray Butler and Wilbur Cross, a governor of Connecticut whose name, familiar as a highway leading to New England, may prove that asphalt is more lasting than bronze.

But it would be misleading to infer that the Academy was fixed only on itself in these years. One ambitious plan for the general enlightenment was to establish an art museum in every state lacking one. "The commanding motive," Johnson explained in 1925, was to bring "knowledge of the best painting and sculpture to populations that are not able to visit the great centers." Doggedly optimistic, Johnson traveled from city to city searching for donors and making speeches; "I am well, but a bit tired of my own voice," he reported to Mrs. Vanamee. The idea fell through, possibly because, as Johnson noted, "there is an impasse between the artistic and the commercial temperament."[70] A second attempt to widen the Academy's purview—its affiliation with the American Academy in Rome—was more efficacious, and endured.

The course of public lectures the Academy launched in Boston, Cleveland, Chicago, Philadelphia, and other venues frequently aspired to a global embrace: "The Literature of Japan"; "The Spirit of Italy"; talks on Scandinavia, France, Russia; and, following the war, an entire series on "The Failure of German Kultur" (though these were rather more punitive than embracing). Relations were kept up with the Belgian and French academies. Letters of invitation—and homage—went often to

A 1930 Cass Gilbert drawing of induction medal and ribbon (never realized).

British men of letters. In 1919 Maurice Maeterlinck, the 1911 Nobel Laureate, visited the Academy as an honored literary guest from Belgium. The novelist Vicente Blasco Ibáñez came from Spain.

Spain, Italy, Belgium, France, Canada, and Britain all sent laudatory messages to the Academy's William Dean Howells memorial meeting in March 1921; Rudyard Kipling's contribution, representing England, brought a vigorous insight into the American literary past—with more conviction, possibly, than some of the narrowly Anglophile Academicians themselves (always conscious of what they saw as American marginality with regard to European models) could wholeheartedly summon. Despite the international tributes solicited from overseas, and despite the number of speakers and subjects ("Howells the Novelist," "Howells the Dramatist," "Howells the Humorist," etc.), some indeterminate trace of the intramural nevertheless clung to the Howells commemoration—a touch of the gentleman's club; Howells, after all, had been the Academy's first president.[71] The event rises out of the record less as a national literary celebration than as an Academy period piece. The speakers, Academy members all, were once again identifiable by their common idiom: the idiom of backward-looking gentility, hence of diminishment. Press attention was meager.

Three years later, H. L. Mencken, in an article headlined "No Head for Howells' Hat" in the Detroit *News* of March 23, 1924, took up a different approach to Howells. "Suppose," he wrote, "Henrik Ibsen and Anatole France were still alive and on their way to the United States on a lecture tour, or to study prohibition and sex hygiene, or to pay their respects to Dr. Coolidge . . . who would go down the bay in a revenue cutter to meet them . . . who to represent American literature?" Represent it, he explained, "in a tasteful and resounding manner." "So long as Howells kept his legs," Mencken went on, "he was chosen almost automatically for all such jobs, for he was dean of the national letters and acknowledged to be such by everyone. Moreover, he had experience at the work and a natural gift for it. He looked well in funeral garments. He had a noble and ancient head. He made a neat and caressing speech. He understood etiquette."

But the price of Mencken's esteem for Howells, however soaked in the Mencken satire, was disesteem for the Academy:

> Who is to represent [American literature] today? I search the country without finding a single candidate, to say nothing of a whole posse. Turn, for example, to the mystic nobles of the American Academy of Arts and Letters. I pick out five at random: William C. Brownell, Robert Underwood Johnson, Hamlin Garland, Bliss Perry, and Henry van Dyke. What is wrong with them? The plain but dreadful fact that no literary foreigner has ever heard of them—that their appearance on the

deck of his incoming barge would puzzle and alarm him and probably cause him to call for the police.

These men do not lack the homely virtues. They all spell correctly, write neatly and print nothing that is not constructive. In the whole five of them there is not enough sin to raise a congressman's temperature one-hundredth of a degree. But they are devoid of what is essential to the official life; they have, so to speak, no stage presence. There is nothing rotund and gaudy about them. No public and unanimous reverence bathes them. What they write or say never causes any talk. To be welcomed by them jointly or severally would appear to Thomas Hardy or Gabriele d'Annunzio as equal to being welcomed by representatives of the St. Joe, Mo., Rotary Club.

On the heels of the Howells commemoration came the Academy's 1922 memorial to John Burroughs, the naturalist, a member since 1905. This was

Academy meeting, December 6, 1923, in Members' Room with Academy chairs. Seated, left to right: *Robert Underwood Johnson, Owen Wister, Bliss Perry, Joseph Pennell, and Archer M. Huntington.* Standing, left to right: *Nicholas Murray Butler, Charles Dana Gibson, John Charles Van Dyke, Arthur Twining Hadley, Hamlin Garland, Augustus Thomas, and Daniel Chester French.*

marked by a lengthy address entitled "The Racial Soul of John Burroughs," by Henry Fairfield Osborn (who was *not* an Academy member), a talk of a certain brightness and charm until it discloses its dubious thesis: the existence of "racial aptitudes." "The *racial* creative spirit of man always reacts to its own historic racial environment, into the remote past."[72] "Have we not reason to believe that there is a racial soul as well as a racial mind, a racial system of morals, a racial anatomy?" In short, it was his northern heredity that drew Burroughs to become "the poet of our robins, of our apple trees, of the beauties of our forests and farms" and "the ardent and sometimes violent prophet of conservation."[73] There is no evidence that any of Osborn's listeners demurred from a theory linking conservation of forests to northern European genes. And a decade later similar ideas of race, less innocently applied than to an interest in robins, would inflame Europe and destroy whole populations.

In the spring of that same year the Academy turned once again to Europe, anticipating Mencken's nasty vision of distinguished "literary foreigners" being welcomed at the docks by a Temple nonentity. The nonentity in this instance was not an Academician but rather a Mr. Haskell, unknown to history and apparently a Columbia University factotum sent to the pier by Nicholas Murray Butler to meet the S.S. *Paris*. Aboard were Maurice Donnay and André Chevrillon, director and chancellor respectively of the Académie française. The pair had been imported to attend the three-hundredth anniversary of the birth of Molière—"In Celebration of the Power and Beauty of the Literature of France and Its Influence upon That of the English-speaking Peoples"[74]—and were feted at luncheons and dinners in New York, Princeton, Boston, Philadelphia, and Washington. The official Academy dinner included oxtail soup, appropriately dubbed "Parisienne"; the appetizer was a quatrain by Richard Watson Gilder:

Molière

He was the first great modern. In his art
   The very times their very manners show;
But for he truly drew the human heart
   In his true page all times themselves shall know.

The public meeting honoring Molière—or his latterday representatives—was held at the Ritz-Carlton Hotel on April 25, 1922. A day earlier the visitors had been taken uptown to see the site of the new Temple, and then were conducted back to the temporary Academy building at 15 West 81st Street for tea and a speech by Butler: "I well recall that in his subtle and quite unrivaled study of French traits, our associate, Mr. Brownell, pointed out that while among the French the love of knowledge is not more insatiable than with us, it is infinitely more judicious. . . . Precision, definiteness, proportion, are certain marks of what is truly French." "The aim of the American Academy," he continued, "must for long years to come be to rescue a people's art and a people's letters from what is vulgar, from what is provincial, from what is pretense, and to raise a standard to which the lovers of the beauty of loveliness and the lovers of the beauty of dignity may, with confidence and satisfaction, repair."[75]

Precision, definiteness, proportion were truly French; vulgarity, provinciality, pretense were truly American. The literary foreigners may have been flattered by what seemed to be homage born of New World insecurity, but since Butler's list of American flaws covered not only homegrown philistinism but also international modernism ("pretense"), the French were surely implicated in the latter. It was France, after all, that had produced Matisse and Milhaud and Jules Laforgue (who had influenced Eliot), not to mention the French infatuation with jazz and Paris's harboring of suspect American types like Gertrude Stein. And if the laughing ghost of Molière had come to the feast, would it have chosen to side with the deadly predictable purveyors of "the beauty of loveliness" or with the syncopated ironists of modernism?

In 1925 Robert Underwood Johnson was still incorrigibly at war with the new poets. The recoil from modernism he enshrined as a cause; and what was Johnson's cause was bound to become the Academy's cause, very nearly its raison d'être. (The first cracks in antimodernism would not occur until late in the decade and then—torrentially—in the 1930s and 1940s.) On November 23, 1925, in a letter to *Who's Who in America*, presenting himself as an incarnation of the Temple's eternality, Johnson requested that he be identified as "an antagonist of free verse and author of a criticism of it in an address before the Academy entitled 'The Glory of Words.' " "The modernists," he complained in that talk, "wish to exalt into poetic association words that heretofore have not been considered poetic. . . . Naturally such an attempt is conspicuously deficient in the glory of words." The "metrical product of the revolutionists," he went on, was "unimaginative," "monotonously conventional," and "objectionably sophisticated—individualism run to seed." And: "They are determined to make silk purses out of sows' ears." "Because the Muses no longer rule there must be no allusion to Parnassus; the Muses are not 'factual' and must go by the board." "The chief promise of poetry is to express the pervasive and permanent spiritual forces of all time."[76]

Although Johnson's zeal on behalf of Miss Thomas had failed to win her an Academy honor, his fight against Robert Frost did not abate. To Booth Tarkington he wrote:

> I am very strongly opposed to Frost's nomination on principle (I have never met him and have no personal feeling). . . . I think both he and Edwin Arlington Robinson who has been nominated are in the main mediocre in their work . . . they are not worthy of consideration for the

Academy. . . . We have other men in the Institute who ought to be put forward for the quality of their poetry—Percy MacKaye, Clinton Scollard, Richard Burton, Brian Hooker, Don Marquis, Charles deKay and John Finley. Each one of these men has done beautiful work.[77]

To our ears these are largely unrecognizable minor deities. Johnson's own Parnassus has not gathered them to its bosom. And if Polyhymnia, having anointed (sparingly) Edward MacDowell and Victor Herbert, remains cool to Frederick Shepherd Converse and George Whitfield Chadwick, while smiling palely on Horatio Parker chiefly for his connection with Charles Ives, what of the painters' Muse? Edith Thomas as poet and John Powell as composer may be confined to the category of antiquarian curios, but (for instance) Joseph Pennell and Childe Hassam are not. (Anyone examining the superbly evocative Pennell drawings that accompany Henry James's *Collected Travel Writings*, reissued in 1993 by the Library of America, will be stirred by what we call permanence in art: that which cannot "date.")

Repeatedly infuriated by the encroachments of new modes of literary expression and helpless before its tide—Robinson and Frost were both admitted to the Academy, in 1927 and 1930, respectively—Johnson was determined that the Temple should make an indelible statement at least in the graphic arts. One effort toward that end, the attempt to put a museum in every state, fizzled. A second idea both survived and prospered: this was to establish a collection by Academicians and other American painters. Johnson worked closely with the earliest Committee on Art, then known as the Committee on Art Censorship, a name that may suggest the prescriptive tastes of its three members: the painter and critic Kenyon Cox, the sculptor Herbert Adams, and the architect Cass Gilbert. Paintings were solicited from private collectors and through bequests. Since one of Johnson's motives was to promote and augment the influence of the Academy,[78] it is no wonder that portraits dominated or that the collection was based, by and large, on the products of its own members. Johnson was relentless in going after contributions, especially from the freshly widowed wives of deceased Academicians. The collection expanded to cover etchings, lithographs, engravings, small sculptures, photographs, memorabilia, and manuscripts.

To display the Academy's riches, the year 1927 saw four public events: separate exhibits honoring Academicians Childe Hassam, Timothy Cole, and Joseph Pennell, and an "Exhibition of Manuscripts Representing the First Century of American Independence," which included the notebooks of John Burroughs and letters by Academy members Henry Adams, Charles Francis Adams, Thomas Bailey Aldrich, Julia Ward Howe, William Dean Howells, Thomas Wentworth Higginson (the very Higginson who had chided Emily Dickinson for "spasmodic" and "uncontrolled" verse), Henry James, Henry Charles Lea,

Edmund Clarence Stedman, and Richard Henry Stoddard. Manuscripts by Emerson, Hawthorne, and Whitman were also on exhibit. As a mendicant on behalf of the Academy, Johnson was astoundingly tireless.

A few days after the Timothy Cole event, Huntington presented the Academy with a gift of $100,000 as an endowment for future exhibits.[79] The permanent collection and the new plan for ongoing showings by painters were designed to set a standard for American cultural aspiration. So were the concerts and recitals sponsored by the Academy during the decade of the twenties: what was to be emphasized, George Whitfield Chadwick urged, was "the development of *American Music* (not by foreign musicians, no matter how accomplished)."[80] But the pressure for indigenous American achievement—a sign of the early Academy's sense of its own inferiority before the age and weight of Europe's cultural cargo—was nowhere more pronounced than in

Academy meeting, November 10, 1927. Left to right: John Huston Finley (writer, elected 1908), James Earle Fraser (artist, elected 1915), Sir Reynolds Rodd (not a member), Nicholas Murray Butler (writer, elected 1909), Edwin Howland Blashfield (artist, elected 1898), Booth Tarkington (writer, elected 1908), and John Charles Van Dyke (writer, elected 1908) in front of Edwin Blashfield's painting, Academia.

the preoccupation with American speech. President Sloane warned of "a stream of linguistic tendency, prone to dangerous flood and devastating inundation," alluding no doubt to the postwar immigration.[81] Yet native-born journalists were almost as perilous a threat as foreigners spilling into the country: "How are we to justify the diction of the press," William Roscoe Thayer inquired, "through which pours an incessant stream of slang, vulgarism, grammatical blunders, and rhetorical crudity?"[82] Responding, the press—in the shape of the *Boston Herald* of December 15, 1926—pretended to take up the case of an instance of ambiguity in the use of "is" and "are," which was being placed before the Temple for adjudication: "After having brought half the dilettantes and intellectuals of the nation in futile disagreement, one of the worst sentences ever written will soon arrive at the Academy of Arts and Letters in search of further trouble."

Further trouble? Such playfulness—or mockery—could hardly sit well with the permanent secretary. The function of the Academy, Johnson grandly noted, was to reject "invasions from the ribbon counter" and to "stand against the slovenly, and for the dignified and effective use of words."[83] This meant also the *sound* of words. In a radio talk invoking the Academy's various causes, Mrs. Vanamee testified to the excitements of clear enunciation: "There is a medal for good diction on the Stage which was awarded to Walter Hampden in 1924 and last spring to Miss Edith Wynne Matthison whose perfect diction was never more perfectly in evidence than in her superbly simple and touching acceptance of the medal from the hands of Robert Underwood Johnson, the Secretary of the Academy, and after he and its Chancellor, Dr. Nicholas Murray Butler had paid high tribute to Miss Matthison's work."[84]

Mrs. Vanamee was plainly not in line for a medal honoring Style.

The ribbon counter, along with the Academy's defunct ribbon badge, has vanished; it is a different Academy today. For one thing, though born of the Institute, the Academy has swallowed up its progenitor. What was once two bodies, joined like Siamese twins in any case, is now a single organization: diverse, welcoming, lavishly encouraging to beginners in the arts. Yet what Hamlin Garland remarked on long ago remains: a quantity of seasoned gray heads, few of whom, however, are polemically inclined to retrogressive views. Crusty elitism is out. The presence of women goes unquestioned. Ethnic parochialism is condemned. No one regards experiment as a revolutionary danger. And by now modernism, which seventy years ago seemed so disruptive to the history-minded, is itself an entrenched tradition with a lengthening history of its own—even fading off into the kind of old-fashionedness that derives from repetitiveness, imitation, overfamiliarity. Modernism has grown as tranquil as Robert Underwood Johnson's Parnassus; and what postmodernism is, or will become, we hardly know.

Do these white-bearded, high-collared gentlemen of the old Academy—who lived out the nineteenth century's aesthetic and intellectual passions right up to the lip of the Great Depression—strike us as "quaint"? Condescending and unholy word! Unholy, because it forgets that death and distance beckon us, too: our turn lies just ahead. Possibly we are already quaintly clothed, as unaware that we are retrograde as Kenyon Cox and Royal Cortissoz before Matisse or Robert Underwood Johnson in the face of T. S. Eliot and Marianne Moore. Despite our ingrained modernist heritage, we may, after all, discover ourselves to be more closely linked to the print-loyal denizens of the twenties Temple than we are to the cybernetic future. If a brittle and browning 1924 Mencken clipping testifies to the cultural irrelevance of the official humanists of two generations ago, the loss of a fixed and bound text, if it occurs—bringing a similar disorientation to fixed expectations—may be as cataclysmic for us as cubism was to the votaries of beaux arts.

And if time has reduced Robert Underwood Johnson and his solemnly spiritualized colleagues to toys for our irony, what does that signify? Probably that (given our modernist habits) we value irony more than dignity, and what does *that* signify? The "mystic nobles," as Mencken called them, of the Academy's third decade lacked irony, but they also lacked cynicism. When they sermonized on "nobility of character," they believed in its likelihood, and even in its actual presence. When Johnson honored "Beauty changeless and divine," he took it for granted that the continuity of a civilization is a sacred covenant. A review of *American Poetry: The Nineteenth Century*, a pair of Library of America volumes published in 1993 and edited by John Hollander, a contemporary Academician, adds this perspective: "Just as the spare acerbity of early modernism must have looked bracingly astringent to writers and readers grown weary of nineteenth-century rotundities, so today . . . these relics of another age are deeply refreshing."[85]

We who are postmodern inheritors of the violent whole of the twentieth century no longer dare to parade—even if we privately hold them—convictions of virtue, harmony, nobility, wisdom, beauty; or of their sources. But (setting aside irony, satire, condescension, and the always arrogant power of the present to diminish the past), the ideals of the Temple, exactly as Johnson conceived them, *are* refreshing to an era tormented by unimaginable atrocity and justifiable cynicism. Nor are those ideals precisely "relics." Suppose Johnson had chosen Frank Lloyd Wright as architect for the new building; what might the Academy have looked like then? If it is good to have the Guggenheim Museum's inventiveness, it is also good to have the Academy's Venetian palace, just as Stanford White and Charles McKim dreamed it.

Or what if the Academy's art committee had allied itself with, say, Alfred Stieglitz's "291" gallery, the heart and muscle of the modernist cause? What if Robert Frost and Charles Ives had been admitted to membership in 1918? Or H. L. Mencken?

Such speculations instantly annihilate the history of the Temple's credo between the Great War and the Great Depression. Worse, they wipe out the name and (noble) character of the redoubtable Robert Underwood Johnson, and who would want that?

NOTES

Unless otherwise specified, all materials cited are located in the Academy files, which are also the source of any unannotated information in the text.

1. *Proceedings at the Laying of the Cornerstone of the American Academy of Arts and Letters, New York City, November 19, 1921* (New York: American Academy of Arts and Letters, 1922).

2. *Academy Papers: Addresses on Language Problems by Members of the American Academy of Arts and Letters* (New York: Scribner's, 1925), pp. 277–78.

3. Robert Underwood Johnson, "The Glory of Words," in ibid., pp. 255–282.

4. Eccles. 1:11.

5. "A Bookman's Day Book," *New York Tribune*, November 11, 1923, p. 26.

6. Undated.

7. Archer Huntington.

8. Charles Fenton, "Literary Rags and Riches in the 1920s," *South Atlantic Quarterly* 58, no. 4 (autumn 1959): 572–86.

9. Huntington.

10. Geoffrey T. Hellman, "Some Splendid and Admirable People," *The New Yorker*, February 23, 1976, pp. 43–81.

11. Mrs. Vanamee.

12. Ibid.

13. Hellman, "Some Splendid and Admirable People."

14. Buildings.

15. Mrs. Vanamee.

16. Academy minutes, January 2, 1922.

17. Fenton, "Literary Rags and Riches," p. 585.

18. Events, 1924.

19. Robert Underwood Johnson, *Remembered Yesterdays* (New York: self-published, 1923), p. 63.

20. Ibid., pp. 463–65.

21. Herbert F. Smith, *Richard Watson Gilder* (New York: Twayne, 1970), p. 40.

22. Ibid., p. 153.

23. Ibid., p. 154.

24. *Dictionary of American Biography* (New York: Scribner's, 1958), s.v. "Robert Underwood Johnson."

25. Robert Underwood Johnson, *Poems of Fifty Years: 1890–1930* (self-published).

26. *The World War: Utterances Concerning Its Issues and Conduct by Members of the American Academy of Arts and Letters* (New York: American Academy of Arts and Letters, 1919), 20.

27. Ibid., pp. 35, 12, 74–75, 40.

28. *Encyclopaedia Britannica*, 13th ed.

29. February 12, 1919.

30. *New York Evening Post*, February 13, 1919.

31. Barbara L. Tischler, *An American Music: The Search for an American Musical Identity* (New York/Oxford: Oxford University Press, 1986), pp. 102, 99. See also p. 101.

32. H. Wiley Hitchcock, *Music in the U.S.A.: A Historical Introduction* (Englewood Cliffs, N.J.: Prentice-Hall, 1988), pp. 194–96.

33. Charles Hamm, *Music in the New World* (New York: Norton, 1983), p. 548 ff.

34. Hitchcock, *Music in the U.S.A.*, p. 198.

35. Tischler, *An American Music in Search*, p. 39.

36. Ibid., p. 106.

37. Nicholas E. Tawa, *Mainstream Music of Early Twentieth Century America: The Composers, Their Times, and Their Works* (New York: Greenwood, 1992), pp. 127–29.

38. "Statues to Sculpture," *Two Hundred Years of American Sculpture* (Boston: Godine, 1976), p. 112 ff.

39. Ibid., p. 118.

40. *Tributes of the Academy, 1905–1941* (New York: American Academy of Arts and Letters, 1942), p. 27.

41. Proceedings at the formal opening of the permanent home, pamphlet, February 22–23, pp. 2–4.

42. Milton Brown, *American Art from the Armory Show to the Depression* (Princeton, N.J.: Princeton University Press, 1955), p. 57.

43. Ibid., p. 54.

44. *Three Papers on "Modernist Art"* (New York: American Academy of Arts and Letters, 1924).

45. Ibid., p. 32.

46. Ibid., p. 57.

47. Proceedings, Molière, pp. 69–70.

48. Sloane.

49. Vanamee to Henry de Forest Baldwin, attorney, December 3, 1925.

50. Letter, December 10, 1923.

51. February 10, 1918.

52. Letters, January 17, 1920.

53. Garland, purpose, policy.

54. Garland, 1921.

55. Nancy Johnson, summary of third decade.

56. To William Sloane, 1921.

57. "Suggestions Concerning the Academy's Opportunities," annual meeting, November 18, 1921.

58. Garland, purpose, policy.

59. Garland.

60. October 1921.

61. To Elihu Root, September 1921.

62. To Brander Matthews, October 1921.

63. To Sloane, October 23, 1921.

64. Projects, awards.

65. Ibid.

66. To members of the Academy, December 10, 1918.

67. Academy annual meeting, 1926.

68. Garland, presentation of Howells Medal for Fiction.

69. Cole to Gilbert, February 25, 1924.

70. To Vanamee, March 9, 1925.

71. Proceedings, Howells memorial meeting, March 1, 1921.

72. Pamphlet, *Public Meeting of the American Academy and the National Institute of Arts and Letters in Honor of John Burroughs* (New York: American Academy of Arts and Letters, 1922), p. 17.

73. Ibid., pp. 14, 13.

74. Events.

75. Academy minutes (prepared by Robert Underwood Johnson), April 24, 1922.

76. Johnson, "The Glory of Words," pp. 262–67 passim.

77. September 1925.

78. Lillian B. Miller and Nancy A. Johnson, *Portraits from the American Academy and Institute of Arts and Letters* (Washington, D.C.: Smithsonian Institution, 1981), p. 21.

79. Report of the art committee, April 21, 1927.

80. Letter, November 19, 1921.

81. Quoted in paper by Allen Walker Read, in "Proceedings at the Special Meeting Held at the University Club," February 22, 1917, pp. 13–14.

82. Ibid., p. 27.

83. Johnson. "The Glory of Words," p. 277.

84. "Radio Talk on the American Academy of Arts and Letters by Mrs. William Vanamee," pp. 5–6, WGBS, September 12, 2 P.M., Vanamee.

85. Carol Iannone, *Commentary* (March 1994): 54.

CHAPTER FOUR

1928–1937

THE INFILTRATION OF MODERNITY

Arthur Schlesinger, Jr.

ON APRIL 23, 1929, the American Academy of Arts and Letters held a grand banquet at the Ritz-Carlton Hotel in New York City to celebrate its twenty-fifth anniversary. Established for half a dozen years in the monumental temple on West 155th Street, the Academy had achieved, through the generosity of its benefactor, Archer Milton Huntington, both architectural solidity and financial stability. Its officers now thought that it could properly aspire, like the Académie française, to national cultural leadership.

The Academy's new president, elected after William Milligan Sloane's death in 1928, was Nicholas Murray Butler, the president of Columbia University. "It is our ambition as an Academy," Butler said, "to set standards, to defend ideals, and to appeal to the multiplying public mind."[1] Butler was a vigorous sixty-seven in 1929, and Robert Underwood Johnson (this was the era of the triple-barreled name), the Academy's first and thus far only secretary, was as vigilant as ever at seventy-seven. Both saw the Academy, and themselves, as guardians of aesthetic tradition against subversive tendencies of experiment and insurgency in arts and letters.

Johnson had served briefly as Woodrow Wilson's last ambassador to Italy. He was director of the Hall of Fame, a once-celebrated memorial to notable Americans, and a prolific writer of fourth-rate verse, but his heart belonged to the Academy. Because he was always there, because he cared so much, and because he was so pontifical in his certitudes, the secretary dominated Academy policy. His assistant, Grace Davis Vanamee, was his loyal ally and cheerleader. A strong-minded woman, she had feminist inclinations and political aspirations. In 1929 she was designated as Republican candidate for the office of register on a ticket headed by Congressman Fiorello H. LaGuardia for mayor and Fredric R. Coudert, Jr., for district attorney. (Jimmy Walker won the election by nearly half a million votes.) In 1932, after the Lindbergh kidnapping, Mrs. Vanamee proposed in the *New York Times* the formation of women's vigilance committees to aid the police in running down clues that "a woman might handle better than a man."[2]

Johnson and Vanamee had begun planning for the twenty-fifth anniversary months before the great night. Huntington agreed to pick up the check. Foreign academies were alerted; foreign dignitaries appraised. Arnold Bennett, G. K. Chesterton, and Robert Bridges "would do very well indeed" as guests, Butler wrote Vanamee, "but I should gravely deplore asking Bertrand Russell. He has a most unbalanced mind and an unspeakable character."[3] When Butler then proposed Elinor Glyn, Johnson could not contain his astonishment. "I take it for granted," he told Butler, "that you do not realize that Elinor Glyn is the author of a nasty book called 'Three Weeks' . . . one of the first of the scandalous sex stories." Her presence, the letter continued, "would reflect discredit upon the Academy and upon us all and be the source of just and damaging criticism."[4] Elinor Glyn was not invited.

When the great night arrived, representatives appeared from nine foreign academies. King Alphonso XIII of Spain and Grand Duke Alexander of Russia cabled greetings; so too did, among others, Bennett, Chesterton, Rudyard Kipling, W. B. Yeats, John Galsworthy, E. M. Forster, Lytton Strachey, J. M. Barrie, and Dr. Fridtjof Nansen; nothing, however, from Bertrand Russell or Elinor Glyn.

Butler was sidelined by sickness, so in his place Cass Gilbert, an architect of the old school who was designing the Academy's new auditorium and art gallery, delivered the major address. "This is no cloistered society," Gilbert told the black-tie audience after their dinner of *suprêmes de bass de mer portugaise* and *côtes de pintade Eugénie*. "If it is to uphold its purpose and be worthy

The opening of the north gallery, on November 13, 1930. Left to right: Cass Gilbert, architect of the north gallery (entrance pictured) and the auditorium; Nicholas Murray Butler, president of the Academy; Herbert Adams, sculptor of the bronze entrance doors.

of its claim to existence, it must . . . set up and maintain standards of taste in Art and Letters." Times, Gilbert acknowledged, were changing. "The movement of today is not the slowly unfolding panorama of our father's generation, but the electric flash of the movie and the radio. . . . The rapid pace of modern times may lead to Parnassus or to the precipice, and if ever there was a nation, or a time, when leadership was necessary it is now." Would America become materialistic, self-indulgent, and vulgar under its "new and vast prosperity" and with its unassimilated immigrant population? Or would it be "the last fine hope of the great white race which for a thousand years has moved forward in the march of civilization. If we would see our best hopes fulfilled we must do our part."[5]

Gilbert's "new and vast prosperity" was not long for this earth. Six months after the banquet Wall Street laid its famous egg. Though the stock market crash went unmentioned in the minutes of the Academy and the Institute, the consequences gravely affected both institutions.

To understand the finances of the 1930s, a word must be said about dollar values. Consider the 1937 invoice from the society caterer Louis Sherry charging the Institute $163.20 for a dinner for thirty. A five-course meal preceded by two Martinis or Bacardis and followed by two cigars—all included—cost $5 per person.[6] One dollar in the 1930s, in short, was equivalent to about

Exterior, auditorium on 156th Street between Broadway and Riverside Drive, designed by Cass Gilbert, 1930.

Interior detail of the auditorium, designed by Cass Gilbert, 1930. (Cervin Robinson 1993)

eleven-and-a-half dollars in the debased currency of the 1990s. When Archer Huntington subsidized the twenty-fifth anniversary celebration, his $20,000 amounted to about $230,000 in 1998 dollars.

Huntington had already been a most bountiful angel. A wealthy man with serious credentials as a Hispanic scholar and collector, he was elected to the Institute in 1911 and the Academy in 1919. He paid for the West 155th Street temple and for Cass Gilbert's additions in 1930. Beginning in 1923 he made annual contributions of $20,000. His gifts in cash, bonds, and real estate in the 1920s amount to $23 million in 1997 dollars.

As the Great Depression began, Huntington increased his budget subsidy to $40,000 in 1931. He gave $25,000 in 1932 and 1933 and $20,000 each year from 1934 to 1937: a total in 1998 dollars of nearly $2 million. Unlike other philanthropists, Huntington had no interest in getting public credit for his good deeds. Butler proposed in 1931 that an Academy building be named for him. Huntington replied that he was flattered by the idea of the Academy's assuming "the friendly burden of my name," but "I am filled by no ambition to be celebrated, and it has been a life-long practice to attach my name to no

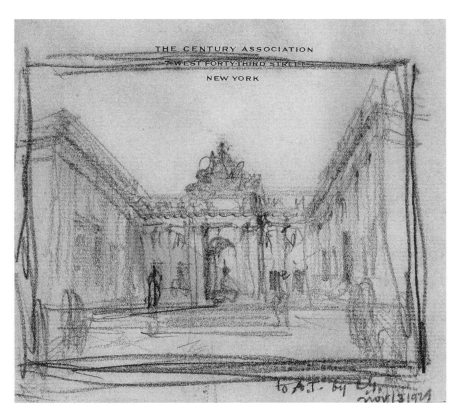

A 1929 proposal (never executed) by Cass Gilbert of an arched facade to connect the north and south galleries.

monument, and I am stirred to no sense of pleasure with the thought of self-contemplation in a mirroring pool filled by the silver drippings of a cheque book!"[7] No doubt his generosity gave him a proprietary interest in Academy policy, but he shared the ideals of Butler and Johnson, and, so long as they were in control, he would continue his angelic work.

The Academy budgets in the 1930s averaged around $50,000 a year, but income from both investments and gifts fell sharply as the Depression deepened. The collapse of the Harriman National Bank was a particular blow. "A few years ago, at the urgent request of my longtime friend Joseph W. Harriman," Butler explained to Huntington in February 1933, the Academy entrusted Harriman's bank with the Academy's funds.[8] The bank then used $75,000 of the money to buy its own stock, a terrible investment and one that involved the Academy in double liability. The bank went into receivership, and the Academy was dunned for 100 percent assessments. "The Harriman National Bank officers," Butler grimly concluded, "practically stole our money."[9]

Times were indeed hard, "The simple fact of our situation," Butler said in 1931, "is that we have not money enough to run the Academy properly." Four months later: "The most important thing is to exercise the most extreme economy."[10] The Institute, financially dependent on the Academy, was even worse off. On January 1, 1932, its bank balance was $340.95; on May 1, 1935, it was $343.11. "I should tell you," Grace Vanamee informed Harrison S. Morris, the Institute's treasurer, in August 1935, "that there is only $90.00 in the Institute bank account and very little more to come in this fiscal year."[11]

In 1935–36 Huntington sought to assure an adequate annual income by establishing a joint trust fund with the nominal value of $741,000 ($8.5 million in 1998 dollars). (One side effect was the abolition of dues—$5 per year—which members in any case did not always pay; Robert Frost and Finley Peter Dunne—the creator of "Mr. Dooley"—were notorious delinquents.) But the Huntington trusts did not perform as well as anticipated, producing barely $6,000 in 1937, thereby reducing the income for that year by $32,750 and foreshadowing a loss in 1938 of $75,450.[12] Without consulting Butler, Vanamee wrote Huntington pleading for a gift of $65,000 to see things through the next two years.[13] With characteristic generosity, Huntington resumed his $20,000 annual subsidy.

The Depression affected members as well. In 1932 the artist Augustus Thomas requested a loan of $2,000, offering two paintings as security. Though an appraiser said that the paintings would bring no more than $1,000 at auction, the Academy's directors made the loan.[14] Other hardship cases appeared, and by 1937 the Institute established a relief fund of $1,500 for members "in extreme cases such as threatened eviction and saving of home and in case of serious illness."[15] An early beneficiary was Don Marquis, poet, columnist, and chronicler of *archy and mehitabel*.

The Academy and Institute records show little interest in the larger impact of the Great Depression. One finds hardly any references, pro or con, to Franklin D. Roosevelt and the New Deal. Nor did foreign affairs intrude. In 1933 an anti-Hitler resolution was offered. "Was it a Jew who uttered it?" asked Harrison S. Morris.[16] (It was Van Wyck Brooks.) No further concern about Nazism is to be found in this period. The two bodies seemed almost hermetically sealed against all but artistic politics, and even here New Dealish writing or painting provoked the automatic disapproval of the officers. Instead they persisted in trying to realize the dream of cultural leadership in the genteel cause of Beauty and Taste.

Their first initiative had been a campaign to improve the use of language. In 1924 the Academy had started an award for good diction on the stage; the onset of radio stimulated Hamlin Garland, the old veritist and populist of the 1890s and one of the last survivors of the Institute's original membership, to propose in 1928 a similar award for radio announcers. In the same year the conductor Walter Damrosch, president of the Institute, suggested that a committee of authorities on English speech should pick out words variously pronounced, decree the correct pronunciation, inscribe it on phonograph records, and distribute the records in public schools "and other places where the growing masses can readily be reached."[17]

"The preservation of our English speech in its purity," Butler said in announcing the radio award, "is for the Academy a matter of high concern. To resist the inroads of carelessness, of slovenliness and of vulgarity is deemed by the Academy a task to which we must constantly and with every effort set our

The Medal for Good Diction on the Radio (2 inches in diameter), designed in 1929 by John Flanagan, was given from 1929 to 1935.

hand."[18] Johnson took his duties so seriously that he even rebuked George Pierce Baker, Yale's famed professor of drama, for using the word *wisecrack* in an address to the Academy: "The Academy ought to be very slow in admitting so recent and so slangy a term. I think we are not open to the charge of pedantry in considering it as a phrase to be placed in quotation marks."[19]

From his first volume of *Prejudices* (1919), H. L. Mencken, the champion of the American language, had chosen Academicians as favorite whipping boys, and he watched their crusade with enormous pleasure. "Not many of them show any capacity for sound writing, whether in English or in American," he observed, "but they nevertheless propose in all solemnity to convert themselves into a sort of American counterpart of the Académie Française, and to favor the country, from time to time, with authoritative judgments in the matter of speech."[20]

But NBC and CBS, happy for respectable attention, hailed the radio award. So did more than a hundred newspapers around the country. "At last account," Hamlin Garland said in the spring of 1929, "we had had nearly four thousand inches of publicity space."[21] Even the austere Irving Babbitt was drafted for the award committee, and professors of speech in over sixty universities served as talent scouts.

In time, however, the award to radio announcers seemed administratively cumbersome and perhaps substantively trivial. In 1936 the Academy dropped it. In the meantime, an effort to establish an award for good diction in the pulpit failed to get financial support. (In 1944 the campaign for good diction was revived with the more ingratiating "Medal for Spoken Language," first awarded to Paul Robeson and soon extended to radio and television performers, honoring among others Edward R. Murrow and Alistair Cooke. The medal was never offered, however, to the pulpit; nor was it even considered for movies.)

Increasingly Johnson directed his efforts less to educating the barbarians than to repelling them, especially when nominated for membership. In 1929 Robert Frost was proposed for a vacancy in the Academy. Johnson considered Frost's poetry to be "rhymed narrative of the most commonplace sort" and wanted the seat to go to Edwin Markham, author of "The Man With the Hoe."[22] He had his way, but Frost was nominated again the next year. This time Johnson tried to beat him with William Lyon Phelps—"Billy Phelps"—of Yale, the most amiable and uncritical of critics.[23] But Johnson's influence was beginning to wane: Frost was elected, and Phelps did not make the final club until 1931.

As for the waiting club, still called the National Institute of Arts and Letters, "How we do need to strengthen the Institute on the literary side!" Johnson wrote in October 1931. "Art and Music is [*sic*] pretty well represented. But let's keep away from the eccentrics and semi-eccentrics or the Old Academy will go up in smoke!"[24] He had no inhibitions about intervening to exclude the unworthy. When the poet Stephen Vincent Benét was proposed for the Academy in 1932, Johnson, who detested *John Brown's Body*—"not only not distinguished poetry, but not poetry at all"—sent out a circular letter asking Academicians to join in turning him down. Benét's election, Johnson wrote his colleagues, "would lower the standard of poetry in the Academy set by such men as (to mention only the dead) [Edmund Clarence] Stedman, [Thomas Bailey] Aldrich, [Richard Watson] Gilder."[25]

Such intervention nettled even men of Johnson's age and reared like him in the genteel tradition. Bliss Perry—born in 1860, professor of English at Harvard, and formerly editor of the *Atlantic Monthly*—was outraged. When Johnson asked why he had not replied to his anti-Benét circular, Perry responded with vigor,

> I was too angry to write. That the Secretary of the Academy should attempt to influence the opinion of a member on the merits of a candidate for election seems to me a gross impropriety. This is the second or third time you have sent me your personal opinion of a candidate before the voting took place, and the last time it happened I resolved to absent myself from future meetings of the Academy. That the Secretary, occupying an honorable and confidential position, should attempt to influence an election to the Academy seems to me intolerable.[26]

When the Academy assembled to elect new members, Judge Robert Grant of Boston, author of *Unleavened Bread* and *The Chippendales*, novels in the Howells school of realism, now in his eightieth year, spoke out in downright Yankee fashion: "It seems to me plain treachery to the members who nominated Benét to have the Secretary take advantage of his official office weeks before the ballots were mailed, to descend to influence the members against the candidates." Grant then submitted a resolution declaring it "inconsistent with the fiduciary nature of the Secretary's office for him to take an active part in support of or opposition to candidates nominated for membership." While the secretary should be free to express an opinion when asked, Grant's resolution continued, he "is debarred by his official control of the machinery from inspiring or conducting a campaign animated by his own preferences." Owen Wister of Philadelphia, author of *The Virginian* and *Philosophy Four* and Benét's sponsor, seconded Grant's motion.

Johnson stoutly defended himself, denying that he had pursued "a course of intrigue and treason to the Academy." Paul Elmer More, the high priest of humanism, called the wrangling undignified. Cass Gilbert moved to table Grant's resolution and refer any further controversy to the board of directors. Grant observed that, if tabling was to be interpreted as sanctioning Johnson, he would feel it his duty to circulate the resolution in order to inform the Academy and the Institute "as to how the members are elected to the Academy." Johnson responded, "Of course, gentlemen, you know that if the [Grant] resolution is passed I shall at once resign as Secretary of the Academy." Gilbert's tabling resolution then succeeded, with only the old judge voting "nay."[27]

Johnson was thus enabled to continue his fight against the barbarians. The next May he wrote the council of the Institute stigmatizing two candidates as "quite out of relation and sympathy with the objects and standards of the Institute." T. S. Eliot, he said, "has written some of the worst free verse that has yet been produced,—eccentric and in very bad taste." As for H. L. Mencken, he was one of those "clever writers who are opposed to the principles and standards that have governed the best products of English literature." There is such a thing, Johnson concluded, "as being so 'liberal-minded' that the whole value and purpose of the Institute would be lost."[28]

Things kept getting worse. "I have just discovered," Johnson wrote in October 1933, "that Carl Sandborg [*sic*] is proposed for the Institute. Ye Gods! What a quartet—Eliot, [Robinson] Jeffers, Sandborg and M_____! Surely the radicals will soon have control. I think the only thing for me to do is to resign. I have written more than 40 letters against H.L.M., but my fight for the old standards is a lone one."[29] Three days later: "It is now easier to get into the Institute than into the National Peanut Roasters Institute. I hear strong disapproval of [Carl] Becker, [Claude G.] Bowers and [Samuel Eliot] Morrison [*sic*], besides the four to whom I am greatly opposed, Mencken, Jeffers, Sandburg and Elliott [*sic*]."[30]

Johnson was losing his touch. Even Nicholas Murray Butler favored Eliot, "one of the most remarkable poets of our time,"[31] though Eliot, it turned out, had become a British subject and was therefore ineligible. Becker, Sandburg, and Morison were all elected over Johnson's protest; Bowers and Jeffers had to wait till 1937. Johnson need not have worried about Morison, who promptly declined membership (he acquiesced thirty years later, accepting election to both the Institute and the Academy in 1963).

Some thought Morison's declination symptomatic of deeper troubles in the Institute. "I have some sympathy with him," wrote the Institute's secretary, the drama professor Walter Prichard Eaton. Eaton, who had got nowhere with his proposal of Ring Lardner the previous January, was increasingly irritated by the old guard. "So long as our medals and awards go so often to people who are remote from the real currents of present day life, and so long as we celebrate with great todo the anniversaries of men who were, even in their own day, third rate as artists [Eaton clearly had in mind the Academy's centennial celebration for Edmund Clarence Stedman],[32] and so long as we admit to membership people of small artistic consequence while leaving out many who conspicuously ought to be in, we shall suffer rebuffs."[33]

An even more conspicuous nonmember, at least to present eyes, was F. Scott Fitzgerald. Nominated for the Institute in 1934, the author of *The*

Great Gatsby lost while the historical novelist Kenneth Roberts was elected. In 1936 Pearl Buck, Hervey Allen (*Anthony Adverse*), Christopher Morley, and Robert Nathan were elected; still no Fitzgerald. In 1938 the naturalist William Beebe made it, and even Walt Disney, though not elected, had more votes than Fitzgerald.

Samuel Eliot Morison was not alone in refusing the honor. Rockwell Kent declined in 1930, objecting to the clause in the Institute's constitution providing for the expulsion of members "guilty of unbecoming conduct." Kent wrote that "a man's personal conduct has absolutely nothing to do with the honors his professional achievements may win him." He added, "Knowing my life to be consistently of such a nature that if the American Institute of Arts and Letters were aware of it, they must instantly debar me from membership . . . I am privileged to take that drastic action into my own hands. Therefore, knowing myself to be frequently guilty of what must be considered 'Unbecoming Conduct' I regretfully decline the honor."[34] (Like Morison, Kent reconsidered and accepted membership in 1964.) In 1931 Finley Peter Dunne paid up $30 of back dues (six years' worth) and resigned from the Institute.[35]

As for Mencken, Johnson's forty letters argued fiercely against him on grounds of his "opposition to the purposes of the Institute to promote the best literary traditions."[36] This fusillade produced mixed results. The playwright Austin Strong agreed that Mencken was "a pernicious influence" and that "his scorn for good English" should keep him out of the Institute.[37] The novelist Margaret Deland, the author of *John Ward, Preacher*, a best-seller of the 1880s, appreciated, she said, the "extraordinary agility" and "poignant cleverness" of Mencken's mind, but these qualities would not promote the " 'best literary traditions.' . . . If he is elected, I should feel that the standards of the Institute were quite definitely altered."[38]

When a centennial celebration of Mark Twain's birth was planned for 1935, John Erskine, the founder of Columbia's famed "great books" course and the author of racy novels like *The Private Life of Helen of Troy*, objected to Butler's idea that G. K. Chesterton give the major address; he threatened not to come if Chesterton were chosen and proposed Mencken along with Sinclair Lewis and Eugene O'Neill as alternatives. "The absence of my erratic friend, John Erskine, would not affect the Celebration unfavorably," Butler said, adding that he himself wouldn't come if any of Erskine's nominees were chosen. In the end William Lyon Phelps gave the address.[39]

Many members, including coevals of Johnson and Butler, were in favor of Mencken. Wilbur L. Cross of Yale, editor of the *Yale Review* and biographer of Fielding and Sterne, who was elected president of the Institute in 1931 (and governor of Connecticut the same year), told Johnson tactfully that, while he agreed that Mencken's candidacy required careful consideration, "I cannot, however, agree with you in your estimate of his work."[40]

For Mark Antony DeWolfe Howe, the perennial Boston biographer gently parodied as Mr. Willing in J. P. Marquand's *The Late George Apley*, Johnson's anti-Mencken letter had precisely "the contrary effect." He had not meant to get into the Mencken controversy at all, he explained, but "if the Institute cannot tolerate a critical spirit within its own membership, there would seem to be something very much the matter with it. My only fear would be that this particular candidate might decline an election." Judge Grant, Howe added in a postscript, "asked me today to say on his behalf that he shares heartily in my feeling about this matter."[41] Walter Prichard Eaton observed that, if Mencken would accept, "I'd like to record my own complete accord with Howe's sentiments. I am very much for Mencken, and not a little annoyed at the nature & source of the opposition to him."[42]

Mencken was bad enough, but, for Johnson, Sinclair Lewis was the greatest menace of all. Lewis had committed three unpardonable sins: He had declined election to the Institute in 1921 when Hamlin Garland, Billy Phelps, and Judge Grant nominated him. He had condemned the Academy in 1926 when, rejecting the Pulitzer Prize, he had named the Academy as a prime source of the "compulsion . . . put upon [American] writers to become safe, polite, obedient and sterile."[43] Worst of all, he had denounced the Academy and its members before the Swedish Academy when he picked up the Nobel Prize for Literature in 1930.

The announcement of the Nobel award to Lewis had provoked Henry van Dyke, clergyman, diplomat, fisherman, founding member of the Institute, and Academician since 1908, to declare that the Swedish Academy, in honoring a scoffer at the American way of life, had thereby insulted America. "I am, actually, extremely grateful to the fishing Academician for having somewhat condemned me," Lewis told his audience in Stockholm. "For since he is a leading member of the American Academy of Arts and Letters, he has released me, has given me the right to speak as frankly of the Academy as he has spoken of me."

Lewis proceeded to exercise that right with relish. The Academy, he conceded, did have "such a really distinguished university-president as Nicholas Murray Butler" (Lewis was not being sarcastic), "so admirable and courageous a scholar as Wilbur Cross," and such "first-rate writers" as Edwin Arlington Robinson, Robert Frost, Edith Wharton, Hamlin Garland, and Booth Tarkington. Yet the Academy found room for "three extraordinarily bad poets, two very melodramatic and insignificant playwrights, two gentlemen who are known only because they are university presidents, a man who was thirty years ago known as a rather clever humorous draughtsman, and several gentlemen of whom—I sadly confess my ignorance—I have never heard." Where were Theodore Dreiser, Ernest Hemingway, Willa Cather, William Faulkner, John Dos Passos, Eugene O'Neill, Carl Sandburg, Edgar Lee Masters, Robinson Jeffers, Sherwood Anderson, Ring Lardner, Upton Sinclair, Edna Ferber?

An Academy recruited on existing principles, Lewis continued, "cuts itself off from so much of what is living and vigorous and original in American letters, can have no relationship whatever to our life and aspirations. It does not represent literary America of today—it represents only Henry Wadsworth Longfellow." He then added mysteriously: "Let me again emphasize the fact— for it is a fact—that I am not attacking the American Academy." Rather, he was attacking the entire conventional culture, the "tea-table gentility," of which the Academy, he felt, was only one conspicuous example. Universities were no better. "Our American professors," Lewis said, "like their literature clear and cold and pure and very dead." Most Americans "are still afraid of any literature which is not a glorification of everything American."[44]

For Johnson, Lewis's speech was a wanton assault on all he valued and idealized, rendered more unforgivable by the ad hominem attack on Academicians and further compounded by its delivery before a foreign academy. He found a measure of agreement. Lewis's performance offended at least one among those he praised. Edna Ferber, the author of *So Big* and *Show Boat* and an occasional collaborator with the satirist George S. Kaufman, had planned as a nonjoiner to decline her recent election to the Institute. She now oddly and rather ungratefully wrote, "The utterances of Mr. Sinclair Lewis, on the occasion of his receiving the Nobel Prize, have caused me to change my mind. I accept the election."[45]

Others, even some of the old guard, were less concerned. William Lyon Phelps, while deploring Lewis's "undergraduate" tone, called his address in its entirety "inspiring" and said he "fully deserved" the Nobel Prize.[46] Wilbur Cross told the press he had "a high opinion of [Lewis's] contribution to American literature."[47] Alarmed by what he feared was a growing possibility that the Institute might actually elect Lewis, Johnson warned Walter Damrosch in December 1934 of "the impending degradation of the Institute from a conservative supporter of high literary standards, style, dignity, taste, sincerity, personal character, to a hotbed of radicalism. . . . Sandburg, a wretched poet and MacLeish a flash poet are already members and the Committee now proposes Dreiser, who avows there is nothing in life but sex, and is a nasty _____ _____. Also Lewis . . . Mencken the mocking and flippant poseur, Hemingway, lacking in taste and distinction. . . . Truly we are headed for Gertrude Stein, thought worthy of consideration by the Yale Review."[48]

Damrosch replied courteously, "Even you must acknowledge that although in the past we did not have any members of vicious tendencies, yet some of them made mighty dull reading, music or painting."[49] Stephen Vincent Benét was less courteous, noting in his diary after an Institute meeting, "Stuffed imbecile R. U. Johnson & other incompetent old men try as usual to elect mediocrities and suppress ability."[50]

As the annual meeting of the Institute approached in January 1935, Johnson sought to rally the old guard. The reliable Hamlin Garland voted no on almost all the nominations: "I felt that the pornographers were altogether too numerous in the list. . . . The membership will soon be filled with writers of this stamp. They will then bring pressure to bear on the Academy. We have two Jews and we shall have more. It all looks pretty depressing."[51] But Mencken, Dreiser, Hemingway, and Lewis, to Johnson's horror, received enough votes to put their names on the ballot for election to the Institute.

Mencken promptly indicated that he was not interested. Hemingway could not be located but was assumed not to be interested either. Dreiser asked Mencken what he should do. Mencken replied sarcastically that it was "a great honor, and if you were a man properly appreciative you'd burst into tears." After all, Mencken said, membership would elevate Dreiser into the company of such immortals as Struthers Burt, Edna Ferber, Hermann Hagedorn, and Hamlin Garland. Dreiser said no.[52]

But Sinclair Lewis did not object; his name went on the ballot, and he was duly elected. He explained to the *Herald Tribune* that the Institute had become "very much more vital. In the last few years they have elected some splendid and admirable people."[53] Wilbur Cross applauded Lewis's decision and expressed the hope that Mencken, Hemingway, and Dreiser would soon be members too.

In 1935 a heart attack struck down Johnson, confining him to his apartment for the rest of his life (save for summers in the Berkshires at the home of his son, Owen, the author of *The Varmint* and *Stover at Yale*). Still, in spite of a weak heart and failing eyesight and hearing, Johnson signed letter after letter spurred by an indomitable determination to secure the Academy against the terrors of modernism.

He could no longer, however, count on the Academicians. Even William Lyon Phelps wrote in 1936, at the age of seventy-one. "If we elect another man over seventy years old to the Academy, it will be a disaster, a calamity. We *must* get in younger men, or we shall be a laughing-stock, and perhaps not even that."[54] The Academy now had a dozen vacant seats, and the modernists appeared set to take over.

Johnson's last stand was against the candidacy of Sinclair Lewis, nominated in 1937 by Eugene O'Neill, the playwright Sidney Howard, and a strong team of old-timers: Damrosch, Cross, Grant, Wister, and Phelps. The establishment itself was raising the white flag. "I am now aroused to the danger to Academy standards involved in twelve vacancies," Johnson wrote in September 1937. "This is a year of peril for the Academy, as Dr Butler recognizes. . . . The first thing, I think, is to defeat Lewis."[55] But it was apparent that a majority wanted Lewis. Rather desperately, Johnson suggested that, in view of the Stockholm insults "the kindest thing to Mr Lewis" and to the "dignity and self-respect of the Academy" would be to withdraw his nomination "in the hope that, at some future meeting when Mr Lewis shall have made the 'amende honorable,' his work could be considered on its merit."[56]

This was an evident nonstarter. Johnson next proposed an amendment to the bylaws that would prevent the election of a candidate who received ten or more blackballs, and he spent the summer of 1937 writing letters designed to round up the vital ten. A few Academicians supported him. "S. Lewis," wrote Booth Tarkington, "should never become a member of the Academy after what he said of it when he danced naked before the Swedes in rapture over himself, and I don't think he deserves it anyhow."[57]

But most disagreed. Judge Grant, still young in his eighty-sixth year, announced his opposition to the amendment. Damrosch wrote Grant that he too had been "amazed" by Johnson's proposal and planned to protest vigorously against it.[58] Though Johnson told Grace Vanamee that nearly all the Academy's directors favored the amendment, she saw, when she read their polite letters, that in fact none of them really did; they were only trying to let the old man down easily.

For most Academicians the exclusion of Lewis, the first American writer to win the Nobel Prize, only discredited their Academy. Sidney Howard, who had been elected to the Academy in 1935, was especially embarrassed, realizing "that I, who have earned so much of my living of recent years by adapting no fewer than three of his books for the stage and the screen [*Arrowsmith*, *Dodsworth*, and *It Can't Happen Here*], should be a member of the Academy when he is not."[59]

Johnson was too frail to attend the crucial meeting. In order to spare his feelings, the Academicians voted to table rather than defeat his amendment. Then they proceeded to elect his bête noire to the Academy. In a charitable desire to relieve Johnson's mind, his nurse told him that the amendment had passed. "His face brightened," she said later, "and he said, 'Good, that will keep him out.' "[60] When Johnson died a week later, he was presumably a happy man.

Had he known that his amendment had failed, Johnson already had his fallback position, in which he was supported by Butler, to whom he had confided as early as 1935 his idea that the Academy "should quickly take steps . . . to elect new members of the Academy not from the membership of the Institute alone, but from the entire field of workers in the whole field of letters and the arts."[61] This proposal, backed by Butler in order (it was said) to get General John J. "Black Jack" Pershing into the Academy, led to the great row of 1940–41 and the defections of Butler and Archer Huntington.

But even Butler was capable of heresy. When Huntington wondered in 1937 whether Herbert Hoover ought not to be elected, Butler responded crisply, "The gentleman suggested in your concluding paragraph as a member of the Institute and Academy is simply ridiculous. He is not even intelligent."[62]

The challenge of white modernist males was accompanied by a less powerful but still significant challenge of minorities. The number of women members in the two bodies increased in the 1930s. Julia Ward Howe, it is true, had been elected to the Institute in 1907 and to the Academy the next year. "Did it ever occur to you," Henry Adams wrote Johnson at the time, "that if we put Julia Ward Howe on our membership lists, we are subject to much criticism for neglecting other women? I do not see how we justify omitting Edith Wharton, for example, and I've no doubt that a dozen more would claim much higher literary credit than Mrs Howe can claim."[63] But Adams protested in vain. The author of "The Battle Hymn of the Republic" seemed too much a patriotic icon, and therefore a special case, to constitute a precedent. For years after Mrs Howe's death, in 1910, the old guard succeeded in keeping women out.

At last in 1926 the Institute took in Wharton, Mary E. Wilkins Freeman, Margaret Deland, and the essayist Agnes Repplier. The sculptor Anna Hyatt Huntington (Archer Huntington's wife) was elected in 1927. Willa Cather and Edna St. Vincent Millay did not make it until 1929. Others followed: in 1930 Edna Ferber and the artist Cecilia Beaux; in 1931 the novelists Dorothy Canfield Fisher and Anne Douglas Sedgwick and the artists Laura Fraser and Bessie Potter Vonnah. Ellen Glasgow came in in 1932; the playwright Rachel Crothers in 1933. It was still no more than a trickle,

As for the Academy, in 1930, a long twenty years after Henry Adams's protest, Wharton became the first woman since Julia Ward Howe to attain the inner sanctum. Anna Huntington followed in 1932, Cecilia Beaux in 1933, and then no women until Willa Cather and Ellen Glasgow were tapped in 1938. In the same period, over thirty men, most of them far less memorable than Wharton, Cather, and Glasgow, became Academicians. Yet during this time, the first four William Dean Howells Medals, awarded every five years to "the most distinguished work of American fiction" published in that period, all went to women: Freeman in 1925, Cather in 1930, Pearl Buck in 1935, Glasgow in 1940.

Once women were admitted, how to make them feel at home? In 1931, when Cecilia Beaux was the only woman accepting an invitation to the spring luncheon, Vanamee asked Nicholas Murray Butler whether it might not be a "kindness" to tell her that. Butler replied: "I should not trouble about Miss Beaux; she will not be in the least embarrassed by being the only woman present and I am glad that we may have even that many."[64] He was right: Beaux turned out to be an intrepid pioneer, and at the annual meeting in November 1931 William Lyon Phelps gallantly proposed formal greetings to her as the first woman member ever to attend this august occasion.

The next year, when only Beaux and Bessie Potter Vonnoh accepted the invitation to the annual meeting, Walter Prichard Eaton, as the Institute's secretary, wrote Edna Ferber, and no doubt others, that President Wilbur Cross and the members of the council were "especially eager" to increase attendance "on the distaff side. The Institute may have begun in a masculine world, or what it assumed was a masculine world; but its officers and membership no longer have any such delusion." The presence of women, Eaton continued, would "add so much to the social pleasure of the occasion, and contribute so much to its deliberations, that a special plea is hereby made to you that you try to attend."[65] But the record does not suggest that female members in the 1930s took an active part in the governance or in the contentions of the two bodies.

A few members, like Hamlin Garland, worried about the admission of Jews. The poetaster and steelmaster Harrison S. Morris, treasurer of the Institute from 1925 to 1936, was a special worrier, writing of the "folly to propose the Semites that crowd us out." In connection with an art exhibition, he exhorted Grace Vanamee, "Do keep out the Semitic rot." (She replied, "We hope to keep out what you call the 'Semitic rot.' ")[66] But Clayton Hamilton, the dramatic critic, expressed the more characteristic sentiment of the members when, nominating Elmer Rice and George S. Kaufman in 1936, he noted, "These two candidates are Jews. I insist that there should be no anti-semitic prejudice in this organization, which is not a 'social club.' "[67] Rice and Kaufman were elected in 1938.

The question of black Americans attracted less attention. When the architect John Mead Howells, son of the novelist, proposed a black for the staff, Vanamee replied, perhaps recalling an attack by a black burglar when she was a young woman, "We do not employ any colored help. . . . We have found it better not to raise the race question."[68] On membership it was again Clayton Hamilton who pressed the issue. "The time will come," he told a dinner meeting in December 1936, "when men of the highest creative ability of the Negro race will be and should be elected to the Institute. . . . The Institute is not primarily a social institution. . . . Today there are men with Negro blood who are doing better creative work than many members now in the Institute."[69] Despite this plea, no black was elected in the 1930s; the first, W. E. B. Du Bois, only made it in 1944.

Robert Underwood Johnson's long reign finally at an end, Henry Seidel Canby, the editor of the *Saturday Review of Literature*, became secretary of the Institute in 1935. Canby offered urbane transition into the new era. "It is not easy," he wrote in 1937, "for men of established reputation, as they grow older, to keep in sympathy with a newer generation doing work that in many respects is bound to be different from their own." But, he sternly added, it was "the duty of such men to temper austerity with toleration in order to be sure that rejections are not based upon a dislike of change."[70] So the Institute and Academy made their stormy way into the twentieth century. The department of literature blazed the trail. The election in 1937 of Sherwood Anderson, John Dos Passos, Robinson Jeffers, Joseph Wood Krutch, and Thomas Wolfe signaled the Institute's belated recognition of modernity. In December 1937 the Institute even elected Ezra Pound.

The departments of art and music remained more wedded to past gentilities. In 1931 the painter Childe Hassam nominated John Sloan for the Academy. Cass Gilbert refused to second the nomination because Sloan, he wrote, "has been rather closely affiliated with the more 'radical' group in the arts" and his views would not be "in harmony with the ideals and standards of the Academy."[71] "We had that same impression here," Grace Vanamee replied. "Nevertheless Mr Hassam is quite persistent and I think the nomination will be completed."[72] But the painters were a conservative lot, and Sloan did not make the Academy until 1942. In the meantime, the department of art passed over such possible candidates for the Institute as Edward Hopper, Thomas Hart Benton, John Steuart Curry, and Reginald Marsh.

As for the composers, they could in these years find only six new men fit for membership, ignoring Charles Ives, Aaron Copland, Douglas Moore, Virgil Thomson, and William Schuman. The 1930s were a glorious period in American musical comedy, but the department of music never, then or later, anointed George Gershwin, Irving Berlin, or Cole Porter.

Still, the winds of modernism had shaken—and shaken up—the Academy and Institute. A diverting chapter in American literary politics had resulted in fatal setbacks to the ancien régime. The genteel tradition had its back against the wall. But its guardians had one more fight left before the triumph of modernity could be complete.

NOTES

Unless otherwise specified, all materials cited are located in the Academy files.

1. Nicholas Murray Butler's address at the ceremony to mark the new building of the Academy, November 13, 1930.

2. Grace D. Vanamee, letter to the editor, *New York Times*, May 18, 1932. She also called for "the repeal of the Eighteenth Amendment to assist in ridding the country of the insidious rule of gunmen, bootleggers and lawbreakers."

3. February 28, 1929.

4. March 19, 1929.

5. Address by Cass Gilbert, April 23, 1929.

6. F. J. Thibold to Vanamee, March 2, 1937.

7. To Vanamee, April 1, 1931.

8. February 25, 1933.

9. To Vanamee, April 27, 1937.

10. To Vanamee, September 25, 1931; January 7, 1932.

11. August 16, 1935. The Institute's bank balances are from the Institute treasurer's report.

12. Vanamee to the Administration Committee, September 22, 1937.

13. September 23, 1937.

14. Butler to Vanamee, November 11, 1932.

15. Henry Seidel Canby to members of the Institute, March 5, 1937; report of Revolving Fund Committee, December 6, 1937.

16. To Vanamee, December 1, 1933.

17. Institute council meeting, March 14, 1928.

18. Radio address, December 17, 1928.

19. July 17, 1930.

20. Quoted by Geoffrey Hellman, "Mencken and Other Problems," unpublished MS.

21. Academy meeting, April 23, 1929.

22. To Henry van Dyke, November 14, 1928.

23. To Hamlin Garland, August 9, 1929.

24. To Charles Dana Gibson, October 31, 1931.

25. To Bliss Perry, September 1, 1932.

26. October 24, 1932.

27. Minutes of the Academy meeting, November 10, 1932.

28. May 8, 1933.

29. To Harrison Smith Morris, October 1, 1933.

30. To Vanamee, October 4, 1933.

31. To Vanamee, January 14, 1933.

32. The Stedman centenary was so pious an occasion that the address by the eminent Yale professor of literature Chauncey Brewster Tinker was subjected to censorship. "I cannot readily put out of memory," Tinker protested,

> the fact that I was denied free speech in the American Academy. Nothing that I had to say was really discourteous to Stedman's memory. He cannot go down to posterity protected by his friends and by members of the Academy. His work must in time be submitted to the cool judgment of posterity; it was an approach to such a judgment that I attempted in my essay. I was forced to make a last-minute revision under the eye of [William Lyon] Phelps. The only reason for making the address in its expurgated form was that Phelps made a personal appeal to me, as a friend of long standing. I did for him what I would not have done for anyone else, and I have sometimes regretted that.
>
> (TO VANAMEE, APRIL 27, 1934)

33. To Vanamee, November 23, 1933. See also letter of January 17, 1933.

34. To Burton J. Hendrick, December 10, 1930.

35. Finley Peter Dunne to Morris, January 22, 1931.

36. To Albert Bigelow Paine, 1933.

37. To the council of the American Academy, October 3, 1933.

38. To the council of the Institute, October 4, 1933.

39. To Vanamee, February 7, 1935. Wilbur L. Cross discussed Erskine's comments in a January 30, 1935, letter to Dorothy Canfield Fisher. The most perceptive contribution was a message from Rudyard Kipling, calling Mark Twain "beyond question, the largest man of his time, both in the direct outcome of his work and more important still if possible, in his indirect influence as a protesting force in an age of iron philistinism. He never seems, to me, to have said one tenth of what was in his mind in this

direction (even in the implications of Puddinhead Wilson) but it was there for later generations to take and use" (to Butler, February 18, 1935).

40. October 2, 1933.

41. To Walter Prichard Eaton, October 4, 1933.

42. To Vanamee, October 7, 1933.

43. "Sinclair Lewis Changes Mind, Enters Institute," *New York Herald Tribune*, January 18, 1935.

44. Sinclair Lewis, address before the Swedish Academy, December 12, 1930.

45. To Hendrick, December 30, 1930.

46. "Dr. Phelps Praises Lewis Prize Speech," *New York Times*, December 15, 1930.

47. "Governor-Elect Cross in Defense of Lewis," *New York Times*, December 19, 1930.

48. December 7, 1934.

49. December 19, 1934.

50. Charles A. Fenton, *Stephen Vincent Benét: The Life and Times of an American Man of Letters, 1898–1943* (New Haven: Yale University Press, 1958), p. 318.

51. To Vanamee, January 10, 1935.

52. Richard Lingeman, *Theodore Dreiser; An American Journey* (New York: Wiley, 1993), p. 491.

53. "Sinclair Lewis Changes Mind."

54. To Vanamee, September 5, 1936.

55. To Vanamee, September 15, 1937.

56. To Vanamee, n.d. [October 1937].

57. To Johnson, August 6, 1937.

58. Robert Grant to Walter Damrosch, September 22, 1937; Damrosch to Grant, September 23, 1937.

59. To Vanamee, June 11, 1937.

60. Grace Vanamee, "Robert Underwood Johnson," unpublished MS.

61. Butler to Vanamee, November 18, 1935.

62. To Vanamee, November 15, 1937.

63. October 4, 1909, reprinted in J. C. Levenson, Ernest Samuels, Charles Vendersee, and Viola Hopkins Winner, with Jayne N. Samuels and Eleanor Pearre Abbot, eds., *The Letters of Henry Adams* (Cambridge: Harvard University Press, 1988), 6:283.

64. April 18, 1931.

65. October 17, 1932.

66. October 22, 1936, May 31, 1937; Vanamee to Morris, June 2, 1937.

67. On nomination form, October 14, 1936.

68. February 25, 1931.

69. Minutes, December 9, 1936.

70. Untitled memorandum, January 27, 1937.

71. To Vanamee, September 15, 1931.

72. September 16, 1931.

CHAPTER FIVE

1938–1947

DECADE OF THE ROW

John Updike

THE YEARS 1938 TO 1947 were eventful and transformative for both the United States and the National Institute and American Academy of Arts and Letters. The nation emerged from World War II as the world's richest and strongest, prepared to shoulder global responsibilities; the Academy-Institute, which for decades had been maintained as a rather posh club for its elected members, emerged from a sharp internal struggle as a representative body whose principal service to the arts was the distribution of grants and prizes to nonmembers. In this decade the interdependence of the Institute and Academy was reconfirmed, with the parent Institute dominant, and the tradition of a joint ceremonial, where prizes were given to members and nonmembers both, was established.

The Departure of Archer Huntington

Archer Milton Huntington, born in 1870, was the adopted son of the railroad baron Collis Potter Huntington, a forty-niner from Connecticut who found his gold in developing the Central Pacific Railroad of California and, later, the Southern Pacific.[1] Archer had been born to a single mother, Belle D. Yarrington of Richmond, Virginia; she took the name Worsham, from the man who fathered her child without marrying her.[2] The illegitimacy of Archer's birth contributed, possibly, to his shyness of publicity. At the height of "the Row" that he was to precipitate within the Academy-Institute, the two principal antagonists, Walter Damrosch and Nicholas Murray Butler, "both agreed regarding Mr. Huntington's peculiarities and that in spite of his many fine and generous qualities, his enormous wealth and certain early experiences made him more or less a recluse and not normal in his relations with other men."[3]

Belle, who had changed her name to Arabella, was first the mistress, maintained in a Fifth Avenue mansion, and then the second wife of Collis Huntington; when they married in 1884, Collis legally adopted the fourteen-year-old Archer. The youth early showed a bookish and scholarly bent. He was tutored in languages and taken on tours of Europe's art treasures; he attended, but did not earn degrees from, Yale, Harvard, Columbia, and the University of Madrid.[4] His feeling for Spanish culture was strong; tall and vigorous, he traveled though its rugged hinterlands by carriage, mule, and on foot. He mastered not only the Spanish language but Catalan, Arabic, Portuguese, and Old Spanish. In his travels and archaeological expeditions he accumulated the large collection of Spanish artifacts, manuscripts, and works of art now housed in the Academy's neighbor on Audubon Terrace, the Hispanic Society of America. The young scholar gained access to the unique medieval manuscript of the *Poema del Cid* in Madrid and prepared a dictionary-concordance of the Old Spanish vocabulary as well as a scrupulous, though stiff, English translation, published in three volumes from 1897 on.[5] In *A Note-Book in Northern Spain* (1898), he wrote feelingly of the lonely, austere land that had captivated him: "The imagination has wings in this place. Soon one is breathing the unreal. Fanaticism is natural, chivalry a necessity. . . . The senses grow keener and quicker. The clear, calm air is filled with a vitality not of the body. And in the long silence, when sound is forgotten, we seem to *hear something*."[6] It was by virtue of his writings on Spain, and not of his high-flown poetry, that he was elected to membership in the Institute in 1911, followed by elevation to the Academy in 1919.

He had earned this elevation, in part, by giving the Academy, in 1915, a piece of a large lot he owned on West 155th Street, near Riverside Drive, while pledging a $100,000 endowment if funds could be found to erect a building. When no funds forthcame, he and his mother (who in 1913 had married her late husband's nephew, merging two Huntington fortunes into one) provided $200,000 more for erection of the present administration building. Between 1921 and 1930 Archer Huntington further donated around two million of that era's dollars in checks, securities, and real estate; he supposedly financed the building of the auditorium, completed in 1930, with the sale of Rembrandt's *Aristotle Contemplating the Bust of Homer* (inherited from his mother, a considerable collector) back to Sir Joseph Duveen for $700,000.[7] Between 1930 and 1936 Huntington bestowed a million more. Small wonder that, in 1939, he might have thought he had earned the right to have his way in a relatively minor matter.

He had come to think that the Academy, which he had housed and supported so baronially, should be free to select its members from outside the Institute as well as from within it. At an Academy directors' meeting of October 13, Huntington introduced a resolution that would strike from its constitution the sentence "Only members of the National Institute of Arts and Letters shall be eligible for election to the Academy."[8] The Academy president, Nicholas Murray Butler, and three of the four other directors present concurred. Only eighty-seven-year-old Judge Robert Grant, of Boston, author of *An Average Man* and other society novels, voted against the amendment. He reminded those present that the Academy was an offshoot of the Institute; such an amendment might destroy "the existing harmony between the two bodies," and "Mr. Huntington's noble endowment might be jeopardized by what might seem an affront to members of the Institute."[9] According to the eight-page statement that Arthur Train, the treasurer of the Institute, prepared after several meetings in December 1939, Dr. Butler gave the impression that Huntington "was very obstinate, and that he had it so much at heart that if the amendment were not passed, he would resign from the Academy and would alter the provisions of his will." Train also describes "an hour's talk" with his friend Huntington—"long, rambling and personal"—in which the millionaire implied that the proposal originated with Butler but allowed, "I think it ought to be done. I think the dignity of the Academy demands it, but you know I am out of all this. I start these things and then I expect others to run them. I do not know what the directors will do and I don't much care."

But in a letter to Walter Damrosch, the president of the Institute, Butler with a suave ominousness concluded, "My impression is that if the pending amendment be not adopted, both the Academy and the Institute may be gravely embarrassed in the not distant future." He described the amendment as harmlessly intended "to make possible the election from time to time to the Academy of some outstanding man of letters, artist or musician who might not at the time be a member of the Institute. The proposal . . . has been under informal consideration for a long time past."[10] According to Malcolm Cowley's account,[11] Huntington wanted to elect the hero of World War I, General John J. "Blackjack" Pershing, whose artistic and literary accomplishments would scarcely have qualified him for the Institute even when public men were frequently elected. Did not the Académie française include generals, statesmen, and prelates? Also, Butler, the president of Columbia since 1901 and of the Academy since 1928, had a number of pet professors whose Academization would not have displeased him. One member, Jonas Lie, was quoted as saying, "Butler is trying to fill the Academy with second rate Columbia professors."[12]

Discontent with the Institute had been intensifying among certain Academy stalwarts. As early as 1918, Robert Underwood Johnson had written to Harrison S. Morris of Philadelphia, a poet, industrialist, and art critic of congenially nonprogressive views, "If the Institute doesn't stand for standards and principles the Academy will be obliged to cut loose and choose its members from outside as well."[13] Butler had been indignant to hear, upon the report of

Grace Vanamee, who served as secretary to both the Academy and the Institute, that at the annual meeting of the Institute in January 1939 five new members—Charles Beard, William Beebe, William Faulkner, Marjorie Rawlings, and John Steinbeck—had been elected by declaration rather than through the procedures detailed in the bylaws. At the Academy's board of directors meeting, which firmly resolved that these new members "be elected in accordance with the by-laws of the Institute," Butler spoke of allowing the Academy to elect non-Institute members.[14] From far-off Hollywood, Academician Hamlin Garland wrote to Mrs. Vanamee, "I dont like the way the Institute is going. . . . All the most eminent of the pornographers will soon be in. Later they will be voted into the Academy. We may expect to have all the celebrants of incest, promiscuity, and the bestial side of women put in nomination. I hate the popular music, and most of the successful fiction and drama of today."[15]

A month later, Garland, a son of the Midwestern farmlands who, under the influence of Howells, had done yeoman service for realism in fiction, expanded on these sentiments in his 1938 Blashfield address, "Literary Fashions Old and New."[16] He thought back fondly to his youthful days as a writer and to those contemporaries whose works came to market with his: "They were all Anglo-Saxon in their derivation. They wrote with understanding sincere interpretations of a life which was still essentially pioneer in spirit. They treated of women in the English tradition. They held to their courtesies and inhibitions built up by centuries of English law and custom. They all had, indeed, a certain social verity and, at their best, an epic sweep of purpose." Nevertheless, "even before the Great War, it had become fashionable with certain biographers to sneer at our New England forefathers, to deprecate our national heroes while acclaiming books of pornographic content." As early as 1910, Garland said, he had noted in print "the centralization of our literary forces in New York City, many of whose reviewers and critics were of European ancestry and increasingly concerned with the pathologic side of life." In his backward glance, "novels dealing with female libertines" fed upon the rapacity of publishers and the sinister side of the feminist movement:

> Publishers . . . discovered that women more and more applauded "daring" books and "frank" plays, and the production of such books multiplied. Interest shifted from the virtuous woman, the modest young girl, to the women who defied the social conventions. Nudity, coarseness and cynicism came into social life and plays. It became the fashion to be shameless and tough.

He relates this literary coarsening to the rise of motion pictures: "They have not only pandered to the taste of the public, they have profoundly influenced the novelist who kept in mind as he wrote the possible sale of his motion picture rights." Since the aim of the movie producer "was to reach the largest possible throng of patrons, he naturally sought the lowest common denominator.

He bore in mind the mentality of the mob." His productions "were not demo-cratic in the sense prophesied by Whitman; they were democratic only in the sense that they reflected for the moment the taste of millions." Movies, plays, and books were "in fact, a calculated excitation of sexual passions." Garland, however "depressed by the nudity, crudity, and lewdness of present day litera-ture," concluded on a note of guarded hope: "Despite the moronic recreations of our people and the crudities of our literature, American life remains essen-tially sane. . . . Ultimately the river of our national life will clear itself of its scum and its slime, and our men of letters will record that change."

Disarmingly couched in accents of personal modesty, Garland's defense of "the English tradition" betrays an almost "pathologic" horror of female sexual-ity and a xenophobic, if not explicitly anti-Semitic, animus, especially in regard to the film industry. Garland was not alone in his unease; Harrison Morris, writ-ing to Butler at the height of "the Row," used language uncomfortably close to that of the Nazis in speaking of "the invasion of the unelect, who muscled into the Institute in spite of the efforts of R. U. J. and myself. . . . It was plain that the forces of degeneracy in all the arts were bent on capturing the whole outfit."[17]

One searches in some puzzlement for the recent elections to the Institute that might have excited a sense of alien invasion. In 1933 Carl Sandburg had been elected, against the fierce opposition of Robert Underwood Johnson, who impishly miscalled him "Sandborg." In 1935 Sinclair Lewis accepted—after an initial refusal—membership in the Institute. In 1936 Pearl Buck and Robert Nathan were elected; in 1937 Sherwood Anderson, James Branch Cabell, John Dos Passos, Thomas Wolfe, and Robinson Jeffers, followed in 1938 by George S. Kaufmann, Elmer Rice, Lewis's wife, Dorothy Thompson, and Ezra Pound. Faulkner and Steinbeck were to follow in 1939, in the contested election by declaration. By our present lights there is nothing like a pornographer in the lot: Erskine Caldwell, whose play *Tobacco Road* and bawdy novels of Georgia hillfolk were sensations of the early thirties, was not elected until 1942; the elec-tions of Henry Miller, Anaïs Nin, and William Burroughs were far in the future. But after the gangster brutalities and reckless hedonism of the Prohibition years and the mass suffering of the Depression, "courtesies and inhibitions" in art had lost some of their priority. Harvard professor Howard Mumford Jones might say, "I am bored by these novels. I have had my fill of cruelty, rape, seduction, lynching, and murder and general hellishness," but that didn't stop hellishness from happening and being described.[18] While the teapot tempest in Archer Huntington's noble temple was brewing,[19] the leading best-seller was John Steinbeck's *Grapes of Wrath*; indeed there was much in that book, and in Faulkner, Dos Passos, and Wolfe, not for the squeamish and the snobbish.

Johnson and Butler and Huntington had a vision of the American Academy as an equivalent to the French Academy: a static and luminous elect who, by their very existence, set standards and exemplified dignity. The word *dignity* insistently recurs in the debate, on both sides, but by 1939 dignity had faded as an ideal, along with the use of triple names; the liberations and scandals of modernism and the social ferment of a world slipping into cataclysm had variously tainted the membership of the Institute, and one-fifth of that membership composed the Academy. The battle was joined when the octogenarian Judge Grant—fighting, it was later said, "with the enthusiasm of a young man of thirty"[20]—sent out, on his Boston stationery, a letter to all the Academy members describing the October meeting when Huntington's amendment was proposed and inviting them to write him or the secretary of the Academy "if you feel that passage of the amendment would be unwise."[21] Grant counted twenty-nine responses agreeing with him that it would be unwise.[22] "A completely cockeyed idea," wrote Stephen Vincent Benét.[23] "In some manner, which I cannot explain," Ellen Glasgow wrote from Richmond, "it seems to me to detract from the importance, and I may add, the dignity of the Academy."[24] From Washington, Walter Lippmann issued the opinion "I am not aware that anyone whom the members of the Academy wished to elect would be refused election to the Institute. For that reason, I can see no point to this amendment."[25] In Cambridge, Bliss Perry wrote, "I suspected that there was some deal or other back of the proposal, but I was too ill to step into any fight."[26] "Something very unpleasant about the $ $ $ angle of it," Charles Dana Gibson scrawled in New York.

When Damrosch, on February 29, 1940, sent a letter to the members of the Institute outlining the controversy, more responses came in. Ezra Pound, from Fascist Italy, typed in his typical frenetic style:

> Nicholas Murray Butler belongs to a group of men unfit to live. . . . I trust that someday the legal forces of the country will find means of dealing with him, if he don't die first [appended in hand: "& the sooner the better."]. It took 'em some time to nab Capone. That the Academy as now constituted is a disgrace to the Institute might well be sustained, but that these fossilized old jossers shd/ be given any more power is against all decency.[27]

Nevertheless, Butler's board of directors at a meeting of April 12, 1940, passed the amendment, five to one, with only Charles Dana Gibson voting against it. Judge Grant was traveling in the Pacific, and William Lyons Phelps, who might have joined him in opposition, was also away. Grant wrote to Damrosch, "The action taken by the Directors on the 12th strikes me as cold blooded and dastardly."[28] "I am thoroughly disgusted," Eugene O'Neill wrote from California. "At first it seemed such an unreasonable proposal I never took it seriously."[29] James Truslow Adams inveighed against the Academy's "luxurious building in what is still a very inaccessible location" and the concert hall's "magnificent organ which . . . is never used." He rises to heights of indignant thrift and Stoic pride:

I thoroughly agree with you that the Academy should live in comparative poverty or at least in decent simplicity instead of bowing to the will
of one man who happened to inherit many millions as the adopted son
of a railroad magnate of a not very savory period of American finance. If
he, who has never done anything himself of note in the Arts, is to tell the
fifty members who are supposed at least to have done something, exactly
what they shall do or he will stop his contributions, I would personally
be inclined to sell the confounded building and thumb my nose at it.[30]

In a quavery hand from Indianapolis, Booth Tarkington pleaded for the good
intentions behind the amendment and begged his "Dear Colleagues" to moderate their passions: "We are of an age and disposition to come to agreements
without heat or heartburn, surely."[31] On the response form that the anti-
amendment forces had provided, he cautiously changed the words "I disapprove of" to "I am doubtful of the value of."

But twenty-six Academicians signed the form without qualification: a clear
majority. A minority felt otherwise. Sinclair Lewis, the former bête noire of the
Academy conservatives, wrote the Academy secretary, William Lyon Phelps,
that the proposed amendment "would, in general, give flexibility and natural-
ness to the election of the Academy members, and these are qualities more
important then even reasoned tradition."[32] He, the novelist John Erskine, the
artist Cecilia Beaux, and a number of sculptors beholden to Huntington's bene-
factions supported the director's actions. The defender of the English tradition,
Hamlin Garland, began a letter to Mrs. Vanamee with the sentence, "I am
inclined to think that Robert Grant's objection to the change in our by-laws is
sound," went on to voice once more his dislike of "pornography and gagg," and
ended, "I am nearly done with politics of any kind and shall *make* no *protest*
against any action of the Directors."[33] The man whose fortune and will were at
the heart of the controversy left little trace in the copious file of letters; a note,
chilly in its brevity, from Huntington to Arthur Train says implacably, "I need
not enter into the machinery of possible change. The point is that I believe it is
exceedingly harmful for both the Academy and the Institute to remain in their
present relationship. . . . It seems clear to me that the future of both institutions
will be greatly harmed if separation is not made plain."[34]

He and Butler had a bull by the horns, in the person of Institute president
Walter Damrosch. In the mass of correspondence and memoranda as the year
1940 carried "the Row" toward its climax, the clarity and increasing purpose-
fulness of Damrosch's letters is striking. He and Butler, born the same year, were
both approaching eighty, but "Papa" Damrosch was vigorous. Born in Breslau,
Prussia, he had come to this country at the age of nine, when his father,
Leopold, had accepted the directorship of a German-American male chorus
named the Arion Society. Early trained in many aspects of musicianship, Walter
was only twenty-two when his father's mortal illness thrust him into the role

of conductor of *Die Walküre* and *Tannhäuser* at the Metropolitan Opera. He
became a promoter of Wagner and a popularizer of classical music, especially
the German repertoire; he toured the United States with the Damrosch Opera
Company and then the New York Symphony, conducted concerts for the
American troops in Europe in the First World War, and pioneered children's
concerts, as well as composing operas and songs. His great fame arrived with
the advent of radio: beginning in the midtwenties, he conducted broadcast
concerts for NBC, including a weekly program, *NBC Music Appreciation Hour*,
beamed at classrooms on Friday mornings. His genial commentaries, delivered
in his "clear, resonant, slightly metallic voice"[35] with "its dash of Teutonic flavor,"[36] reached an audience numbered in the millions, including, by shortwave
radio, listeners in Latin America, Africa, and Asia. He received as many as thirty
thousand letters a week. He was a media celebrity, who in his distinguished
fashion was taming the vast, not quite Whitmanesque democratic audiences
whose tastes offended the artistic and monied elite. Shy, secretive Archer
Huntington, though eight years younger, came from an older order, of unquestioned privilege and genteel oligarchy.

Efforts at compromise were made on both sides. At the informal conference
among Butler, Damrosch, Train, and Adams at Butler's office at Columbia in late
November 1939, Damrosch (in Train's account) "asked what Dr. Butler's attitude would be to electing one member of the Academy every two years from
outside the Institute. Dr. Butler jumped at this suggestion and said he thought
he could have no difficulty in persuading Mr. Huntington to accept this compromise."[37] At one juncture, Malcolm Cowley states, Huntington "offered to
give the Institute a million dollars and a fine building of its own if it would separate itself from the Academy." At the annual Institute meeting of January 1940,
Charles Dana Gibson, in remarks omitted from the minutes, said: "We have all
accepted a great deal. It has been very useful to have these material things. We
don't know what happens to a man when he gets very rich. Humor the old
man. Pat him on the back, if there is some way to do that. We do not have to
worry about our dignity. . . . We have accepted his gifts. Say he is sick. I am sure
if you cajole him a little, he'll be happy as a child with a toy."[38] Then the uninhibited Gibson asked, "Can't a man be elected in the Institute in the morning
and in the afternoon, be elected in the Academy? Why wouldn't this help the
situation?" James Truslow Adams told him, "They wouldn't accept that now."

At an Academy directors' meeting of May 14, confronted with a rising tide
of protest from two-thirds of their membership, the board unanimously passed
Huntington's conciliatory motion that "the Directors, acting for the Academy,
for the time being, waive the right to elect members outside of the
Institute."[39] But the language, granting a "right" that was being contested as
illegal, did not placate the opposition; Damrosch called the motion a "stop gap
to allay opposition" and said it offered "no protection for the future."[40] Butler,
in a weary memorandum of June 8, 1940, confessed himself "perplexed by

the present wholly chaotic situation" and pointed out that the amendment did not provide for the election of members outside the Institute, but only for their nomination; without a majority of the Academy voting for such a candidate, no election was possible.[41]

There was no going back. The Huntington-Butler side insisted that the Academy—the possessor of the buildings and much the larger endowment—should be independent of the Institute. The other side, as Damrosch bluntly framed the issue in a letter to Walter Lippmann, asked "whether the Academy should lose its idealistic purpose and shall be turned over completely to become the toy of a very rich man."[42] He went on to describe his battle plan:"Although we have a strong majority who think as we do, we must get them to the meeting in order to finish this matter once and for all by electing a Board who will properly represent us and immediately rescind the obnoxious amendment."

Damrosch made good on this plan: at the annual meeting of the Academy in November 14, 1940—the best-attended in its history—the mixed slate of directors, which included Butler, Huntington, and their ally Wilbur L. Cross, the former governor of Connecticut, together with Damrosch and four insurgent allies, was unanimously elected, while Butler presided. Meeting fifteen days later, the new board voted, five to three, to restore the bylaws to their previous condition. Huntington resigned on the spot, claiming that the written resignation had been on his desk since his recent seventieth birthday. The board moved to reject the resignation, and Huntington said, "My decision is final. I shall never enter the Academy buildings again, and I shall not reply to any letters concerning the Academy."[43] Mrs. Vanamee, who had long been fluttering in dismay around the shaken nest that she and Colonel Crasto had woven in the eaves of Huntington's munificence, resigned as assistant to the president of the Academy; she had resigned as assistant secretary-treasurer of the Institute the previous December. She and the colonel cosigned with their initials a handsomely printed poem titled "Farewell Academia," which began,

> We who had thought our life-work fixed.
> Who hoped for years to come
> To serve Academia, now must go,
> And of our own volition.
> With eyes tear-dimmed, and hearts
> Too sad for any words to say,
> Remembering "Noblesse Oblige," we cannot stay.[44]

Governor Cross also resigned, while Butler merely asked to be soon relieved of the "onerous duty of the office of President."[45]

Though Butler had autocratically misread the temper of the institution that he had headed for thirteen years, he presided over his own defeat with good grace: Damrosch complimented him on "the great courtesy and fairness with which you conducted the meeting on November 29th."[46] In a letter to Gibson,

Damrosch confided, "Cross and Huntington lost their tempers badly, but Butler throughout acted with great fairness and courtesy."[47] At the next director's meeting in January, Butler, Huntington, and Cross had all vacated their positions, and Damrosch was elected president of the Academy. To the new president's vexation, Mrs. Vanamee did not attend; she had flown off in a flurry of raises that she and Butler in their last days awarded their loyal staff. She, with Crasto, retired to St. Petersburg, Florida, on a $40,000 severance gift from Archer Huntington, who, as good as his word, never set foot in the Academy again. His benefactions—but for a mysterious $50,000 in 1951[48]—ceased.

For Damrosch and his allies, it was a remarkably complete triumph, and the occasion for an energetic remaking of the Academy-Institute. A note of proud accomplishment reverberates through Damrosch's president's report of May 8, 1942. The board of directors had met thirteen times since the meeting in late 1940 when Huntington had resigned (Damrosch, for all his years, was simultaneously busy with the productions of a revised version of his opera *Cyrano* and of a new work, *The Opera Cloak*). The staff at the Academy buildings, he reports, was reduced from nineteen to eight, and $26,000 less was spent in 1941 on salaries and upkeep. (He had written in early 1941 to Charles McLean Andrews, "It seems that an enormous office force has occupied that building for many, many years, virtually almost only twirling their thumbs, and their salaries and upkeep of the building swallowing our entire income.")[49] Not only was the Huntington amendment revoked, but the powers of the Academy directors were curtailed, reserving any future amending of the bylaws to a general vote by the membership. The Institute, now headed by the lawyer and popular writer Arthur Train, had for the first time sponsored a public Ceremonial, held in Carnegie Hall on January 18, 1941. Train welcomed the public folksily: "Just as an example of our inborn modesty, let me tell you that during the 42 years of our existence, this is the first Ceremonial to which we have ever invited the public, and it is in your honor that we have put on our best bib and tucker, including the purple and gold scarf which we wear across our manly chests, and our women members wear on their—well, the Greeks had a word for it."[50] In May the following year, the Ceremonial was held in the Academy's auditorium and sponsored by the Academy and Institute both. Ten joint grants of $1,000 each were bestowed on "gifted non-members, to further encourage creative work in the arts."

There were numerous lesser signs of new life: the publication of the commemorative tributes in book form; the first comprehensive exhibition of works of members in the renovated museum; a contract with a firm of art dealers for the sale of the paintings donated by Childe Hassam; a complete catalogue of the library and museum holdings; and a joint donation of £1,000 for the purchase of thirty-five paintings by contemporary British artists "as a gesture of deep sympathy."[51] Felicia Geffen, who as Damrosch's personal secretary had been handling Institute business since 1939, assumed all of Mrs. Vanamee's duties and both of her titles: assistant to the president of the Academy and assistant secretary-treasurer of the Institute. She was to hold these positions for the next thirty-two years. The bicameral institution had taken on the form and style it would carry far into its second half-century.

Pound and Purposes

Ezra Pound, whose name first came up in nominating-committee discussions in 1934, was nominated by Archibald MacLeish and elected an Institute member in 1938. Pound was and is an indispensable figure in early twentieth-century English literature, not only for his frequently exquisite poems and translations and his scattershot but often penetrating critical utterances but for his generally shrewd taste, his advisory role in the formation of Eliot's *Waste Land* and William Butler Yeats's late poems, and the contagious fervor of his call to "make it new." But by 1938 Pound had gone from being a visionary to being a crackpot whose professed Jeffersonianism found fulfillment in Mussolini's Fascism. Having lived in London and Paris, he took up residence after 1924 in Rapallo, Italy, and from there directed toward West 155th Street a series of strident missives like no others in the archives. In his letter accepting his election, he wrote:

> The PURPOSE of the Institute is alluded to very casually and only in Article X.
>
> The composition of the Academy is such that DEAD hand [*sic*] must be very strong in any process of carrying out that purpose.
>
> I dont quite make out what the Institute DOES. Is it a purely otiose body having merely a name? Or does it in any way strive or even languidly conduce to the greater health of American letters and music?
>
> Is it a body to which its individual members can in any way look for action against patent evils and infamies and deadnesses in the present mercantilist treatment of letters?[52]

The last question hints at the eccentric economic theories that were to lead Pound from a pugnacious aestheticism into a vicious anti-Semitism, but the other questions were ones that members and nonmembers had often reasonably asked, if less pungently.

The economies effected by Damrosch and Train and the new Academy treasurer, the historian and former banker James Truslow Adams, provided some disposable income, and discussions began in 1941 as to how best to spend it. Exhibits, improvements to the library, and a midtown meeting place for members were among the suggestions. Van Wyck Brooks suggested the financing of "a comparative study of academies, relating all the various projects they have entertained since the word 'academy' was originally uttered."[53] One concrete proposal carried out was the printing of a pamphlet, for distribution only among members of the Institute, of "letters and excerpts from letters received from members in answer to a resolution passed at the meeting held on April 2, 1941 that they be requested to state what in their opinion the aims and purposes of the Institute were or should be."

Some of the replies were pages long, and others as brief as Edna Ferber's "the purpose and policy of the members of the Institute of Arts and Letters should be the preservation of the democratic form of government in the United States of America." Certain issues recurred. The Académie française, with its pomp of uniforms, its governmental stipend to members, and its power to regulate the language, was frequently mentioned, usually followed by a rueful admission that this isn't France. "Regarding Mr. Strong's proposal . . . that we should attempt to dictate the American language, I think it is quite impossible, even if it were desirable, which I doubt," wrote the composer Daniel Gregory Mason, who went on, "Our civilization is much more go-as-you-please than the French." The inconvenient location of the Academy-Institute buildings was often deplored: "the waste halls of 155th Street," "the building which so inadequately houses [the Institute's] activities—or rather, which houses so adequately its non-activities," "the present beautiful and admirable but inconvenient building—so inconvenient in its location that most members of the Institute never go near it from one year to another." The playwright Austin Strong was quite funny about it, in a little skit he imagined between a member and John Q. Public:

MEMBER: Congress gave us a charter.

J.Q.P.: What did you do with it?

MEMBER: We framed it.

J.Q.P.: But what do you do, that's what we want to know?

MEMBER: Well . . . we give gold medals to Radio announcers.

J.Q.P.: Oh yes, I remember that . . . I liked that . . . did a lot of good.

MEMBER: And we have a museum and a library and an art gallery and a marble theatre!

J.Q.P.: You don't say? Where is it!

MEMBER: On the way to Albany!

Sinclair Lewis thought the organization should be broken into specialized academies, whereupon the writers "could, like the French Academy, serve as a Supreme Court to accept or reject novelties in the American vocabulary and rhetoric." Donald Peattie came out against "all banquets, speeches, honorific installations, etc. It sounds like a cross between the Supreme Court and the local Masonic Lodge." A number of correspondents didn't want to be mistaken for "stuffed shirts." George McLean Harper admitted, "I cannot see how we are to take any concrete measures," and Carl Becker expressed the nub of the problem: "Only individuals can promote art and letters."[54]

Uncertainties of purpose went back to the beginning. Charles Dudley Warner, at the Institute's first public meeting in January of 1900, said, "It is believed that the advancement of art and literature in this country will be promoted by the organization of the producers of literature and art. This is in strict analogy with the action of other professions and of almost all the industries." But are the arts analogous to other industries? In even this turn-of-the-century heyday of industrial expositions, how could there be a useful congress of producers whose products are so individual, inward, and wayward? Warner himself, amiably, having asserted that "no one doubts that literature and art are or should be leading interests in our civilization," predicted that "the association of persons having this common aim cannot but stimulate effort, soften unworthy rivalry into generous competition, and promote enthusiasm and good-fellowship in their work." Robert Underwood Johnson, who made the institution his personal cause, spoke loftily of "maintenance of the dignity and the insistence on the value of literature and the arts. . . . To be in this way a fount of honor."[55] Harrison S. Morris, Johnson's faithful correspondent, translates the "fount of honor" formula into anti-Marxism:

> We are victims of the Marxian revolt against property both in wealth and nobility of life. The hatless and brainless mob would divide property, but it can not divide intellect and the instincts that create property, and the National Institute must discover ways to overcome the canaille. . . . We must therefore watch keenly the material we take into our ranks.

But in fact the Academy-Institute's most significant innovation *was* a bit Marxian: the annual distribution of some of Archer Huntington's money to nonmembers. Perhaps

Composer Walter Damrosch (1862–1950), served as president of the Institute, 1927–1929 and 1936–1941; he was president of the Academy from 1941–1948. Mr. Damrosch rallied the Institute in the Row with the autocratic leadership of the Academy. —Pirie MacDonald.

Douglas Moore, taking office as Institute president after the death of Arthur Train, summed up the organization's purposes most succinctly and realistically, at a meeting of the Committee on Progress of the Institute, in February 1946:

1. It gives the members a wonderful opportunity to get together, to have a good time, and to get acquainted with the practitioners in the other arts.

2. It does fine work in awarding Grants (together with the Academy), which this year have been increased from 15 to 23, to include members of the Armed Forces.[56]

A benign result of the grants program was a reduction of the gulf that existed between the Academy-Institute and large segments of the artistic, especially the literary, community. A writer receiving a grant in his twenties or thirties was not likely to refuse election in his forties or fifties. In the first seven years of the Academy-Institute awards, recipients in literature included Edgar Lee Masters, Muriel Rukeyser, Carson McCullers, Karl Shapiro, Eudora Welty, Tennessee Williams, Jean Stafford, Gwendolyn Brooks, Kenneth Burke, Malcolm Cowley, Peter De Vries, Langston Hughes, Marianne Moore, Arthur Schlesinger, Jr., Irwin Shaw, Nelson Algren, Eleanor Clark, and Robert Lowell; in art, Peggy Bacon, Isabel Bishop, Gertrude Lathrop, Peter Dalton, Raphael Soyer, Jack Levine, Dorothea Greenbaum, Joseph Hirsch, and Peter Blume; in music, William Schuman, David Diamond, William Bergsma, Marc Blitzstein, Norman Dello Joio, Otto Luening, Peter Mennin, Robert Ward, and Ulysses Kay: all were later elected to the Institute. By tangibly benefiting nonmembers— over objections that plenty of prizes and fellowships already existed and that "it is silly for the Institute to spend its money and its energy in merely doing in a small way what is already being done in a much larger way by other organizations"[57]—the Academy-Institute took a step in the infant art of public relations.

Ezra Pound's impression of "fossilized old jossers" and "a purely otiose body" was widely shared in this decade. A number of impressive figures declined membership. John Dewey in early 1940 wrote that "it is too late for one of my advanced years to become a member of the Institute."[58] Later that year Edmund Wilson told Henry Seidel Canby that "he could not see the Institute was doing anything much and thought he ought not to join"; years later, he told Conrad Aiken, "The only distinction I can ever be sure of is not to have belonged to the Institute."[59] The poet E. E. Cummings in 1941 wrote Canby perhaps the shortest, if not the rudest, turndown ever: "Dear Dr. Canby—no sale."[60] (His acceptance in 1949 was friendlier but scarcely less arrogant; to Archibald MacLeish he wrote, "No doubt you have lots of Xmas presents, but I would like to send you my change of mind.")[61] In 1945 James Thurber wrote Canby a long letter of declination, pleading his bad vision and a dim sense of the Institute's "basis of selection or the work it is engaged in." Further, he wrote, "the only members of the Institute I have talked to appear to be singularly disinterested in the organization" and "one or two writing colleagues of mine, who appear to be outside the Institute, deserve ahead of me the distinction I have been offered."[62] This hint led promptly to the election of its presumed subject, E. B. White, who wrote, "I do not decline invitations for the sheer fun of declining them, or because it seems a brisk and cocky thing to do. The fact is, I have no membership in any society or organization, and this non-joining comes naturally to me."[63] Years later, he remembered the incident in a letter to an inquirer: "I did not like being the bait the Institute would have to swallow in order to catch Thurber."[64] White, however, unlike Thurber, did become an Institute member, in 1962, after winning the Gold Medal for Essays and Criticism—though he never visited the premises.

And there were resignations, too. Margaret Deland, a novelist and short-story writer, wrote Arthur Train, "I never quite understood the purpose and significance of the organization."[65] The sculptor Cecil Howard resigned in 1942 because of his "mortification" when the Institute did not include in its Ceremonial exhibit a portrait bust whose subject he had invited to come view it there.[66] Katherine Anne Porter resigned from the Institute in 1943 in part because two candidates were identified in parentheses as "Negro" but also because "I do not feel at home there." She stated, "Chiefly my discomfort as member has been the absence from the membership of most of the poets, critics, and novelists whom I consider as the best we have."[67] She was persuaded to stay, however, and was elected to the Academy in 1966.

The "Negro" gaffe occurred on a list of possible candidates circulated to members in the department of literature. The names of W. E. B. Du Bois and J. Saunders Redding were so identified, and a number of members, including Porter, Elmer Rice, and Helen Keller, protested. Felicia Geffen hastened to explain this "horrible mistake" to the membership: "I had instructed the office to send out a list of the names of candidates received, and one of the girls inserted the word 'negro' because the sponsors of Mr. Du Bois and Mr. Redding had mentioned their race in the letters. My terrible error was not to have seen a proof of the list before the list was mailed to the members."[68] Du Bois was elected the next year, although one voter for him, Clayton Hamilton, wrote on his ballot: "Emphatically yes, but our general membership should be informed that he is a negro. If we have to have a fight upon this question, let us face it now."[69] Elsa Maxwell had admonished the Academy in a militant column, "Jim Crow Eat Crow," in the November 16, 1943, New York *Post*:

For generations the conventional and learned citizens of this republic have stood stolidly silent while the American Negro has been vilified, libeled, and denied almost all access to the privileged places of sweetness and light.

The solid south has stood as dumbly solid as a block of granite. The American Academy of Arts and Letters has not taken up the good fight nor has the sacrosanct Daughters of the American Revolution.

But a black native of St. Kitts, Edward Margetson, had won an Academy-Institute grant for music the previous year, and in November 1943 the Academy directors unanimously awarded the Medal for Good Diction on the Stage to Paul Robeson. He received it, and Du Bois—"Distinguished. Handsome. Almost overbearing," Felicia Geffen later recalled[70]—was inducted at the same Ceremonial in 1944. The Academy-Institute, not without some awkwardness, had integrated itself, a few years before the armed forces did so, but long after the Harlem Renaissance.

A smoldering anti-Semitism, as Jewish artists became unignorable, was a recurrent issue, though rarely overt. The correspondence of Harrison S. Morris, however, went beyond innuendo: upon the award of the 1939 Loines Award for Poetry to Joy Davidman, he wrote Mrs. Vanamee, "I did not see any notices of the last award to Miss Davidman. There is an odor of Semitism in both cognomens. Where have we fallen to." The assistant secretary replied in the same spirit, "Miss Davidman is certainly a Jewess. She has not yet deigned to send me an acknowledgment of my special delivery letter containing the check for $1,000." Morris responded, "That other recipient of a thousand dollars [Edward Doro], also a Jew, has acted true to racial habit. Perhaps such is Hitler's excuse."[71] An anonymous member wrote to the Institute in March 1942 complaining that the organization was "catering to the alien in our midst—the jew!" The letter went on,

> It is an historical fact—and a significant one, that every institution dominated by jews has eventually fallen into disrepute and an ignoble retreat from prominence—except of an unsavory sort!
>
> Continuation of this dangerous policy of pandering to the jew will result in the complete elimination of any inducement to persons of consequence to affiliate themselves with an organization which degrades itself thus!

President Train wrote "Pfui!" at the bottom and signed the comment with his initials.[72]

More than "Pfui!" was needed to settle the miserable affair of Hungarian-born sculptor Hunt Diederich, a member who in the spring of 1947 sent out anti-Semitic material in hand-addressed wrappers on which was typed "With compliments from / Members of the National Institute of Arts and Letters / 633

West 155th St. / New York, N.Y." The enclosures consisted of (1) privately printed speeches by Hon. Kenneth S. Wherry of Nebraska, arguing that under the plan of Henry Morganthau, the former Secretary of the Treasury and a Jew, sufficient food was being denied the people of occupied Germany; (2) the apocryphal "Benjamin Franklin's Jewish Prophecy," concluding that "Jews are Asiatics, and a menace to this country if permitted entrance, and should be excluded by this Constitution"; (3) a mimeographed statement claiming that the recently issued three-cent stamp depicting Joseph Pulitzer symbolized "Our new Jewish hero worship" and "appeasement to the terrorists in Palestine." A handwriting expert identified the hand on the wrapper as Diederich's. At a May meeting of the Institute held at the residence of Dr. Philip James, Deiderich did not deny he had mailed the material but defended himself by pointing out that his wrapper did not say "*The* Members of the National Institute." With Deiderich not voting, it was unanimously resolved "that by the vote of the membership of the Institute he has forfeited the rights and privileges of membership and is expelled from the organization, and the Secretary is instructed to erase his name from all lists."[73] When in 1969 George Biddle asked if the Institute's council would agree to restoring Diederich's name to the yearbook's list of deceased members, his request was denied.

Expulsion of a member was unprecedented, and a resolution for an amendment providing for expulsion had been proposed. Yet Diederich was expelled without the amendment having been voted in, and it never was. Edna St. Vincent Millay, in a four-page letter to "My dear fellow-members of the National Institute of Arts and Letters," eloquently argued against it: "I see this amendment as a blot for ever on the page of our history, like a drop of ink spilled in nervousness and haste. . . . Since it is not for their good manners that we admit men to membership in the Institute, we may not, by the same token, expel them from the Institute for their bad manners." She cited Baudelaire, who was denied admission to the Académie française though his genius warranted it; she cited Villon, Verlaine, Sappho, Catullus, Shelley, all as social renegades who might have failed election to "a group of timid persons of mediocre talent, but of impeccable social behavior."[74] She did not, but might have, mentioned Ezra Pound.

Pound's letters to the Institute were so outrageous that one looks for a glint of deliberate mischief in them. On March 3, 1938, he wrote to Colonel Crasto (as "Mr. Cresto"), saying that Crasto's earlier letter raises the possibility that "the Institute is a joke," describing the Academy president as "the still unjailed N. M. Butler" and adding in postcript:

It is not for men of letters to support a bloated usuriocracy If America can not support her own writers she is an uncivilized country/ fit only for the inhabitation of Hoovers (Herbert H/ I mean) Hardings, Wilsons and other vermin.

In great agitation, Mrs. Vanamee wrote to Damrosch, then president of the Institute, claiming that "the letter may seem to you facetious, funny, or merely eccentric," and expressing the opinion that "President Butler is too big to pay any attention to the intended insult to him," but delivering the ultimatum that she would "refuse to cooperate with any institution who will keep as a member a man who indulges in such vulgar abuse and who writes to an employee of the Academy in such a manner concerning its President."

She goes on to state, somewhat in excess of the occasion: "My loyalty is to the Academy and its President. Please therefore consider this as a letter of resignation of my position as Assistant Secretary-Treasurer of the Institute."[75] Both Damrosch and Butler tried to smooth over her sense of affront: Damrosch wrote her that Pound's letter was "so evidently the outpouring of a diseased mind that I am amazed that you should take any notice of it,"[76] and Butler called it "a characteristic outburst from one who has long been known to be a psychopathic case." He added, "The fact that anyone should have been willing to nominate him for the Institute is to me quite inexplicable."[77] Henry Seidel Canby, as Institute secretary, wrote Pound in response to his letter to Crasto, saying:

> The Institute was glad to recognize your services to literature by an election to its membership, but if you do not like its scope and activities, as to which you do not seem to be very well informed, it is always possible for you to resign. In any case, I would suggest that scurrilous attacks upon its members and officers are not the best means of elevating American culture.[78]

This satisfied Mrs. Vanamee for the time being, but the cracks of the coming split had shown themselves. Within the coming year, Academy discontent with the Institute would seek a formal separation, and Mrs. Vanamee would show her basic loyalty to Butler and Huntington by permanently resigning her Institute duties.

On the far side of the split, in April 1941, Pound was still mailing in his irrepressibly scurrilous letters, now to the new Institute president Arthur Train: "I am curious to know whether the world has at last been freed of the distressful presence of Nic Butler and hell (if it exist) manured by his remains, or whether the Academy has at last come to its senses and some sense of civic decency and kicked him OUT."[79] He had two nominations to offer: E. E. Cummings and William Carlos Williams. Their absence from the rolls was a "disgrace to the Institute." He also suggested George Santayana and T. S. Eliot, though aware they were not U.S. citizens, and in a postscript sought once more to enlist the Institute in his inscrutable Jeffersonian crusade:

> It ought to combat the utterly filthy ignorance of our own history, it ought to stimulate the publication of the thought and acts of our

founders and preservers. Marx, Lenin, Trotsky, Stalin are available at ten cents and $.25. But NO handy volumes of the thought of J. Adams, Jackson, Van Buren, Jefferson, Lincoln. . . . What in gord'z name DOES the Insteroot talk of at its meetings?

The new, cooler style at the Institute is reflected in Felicia Geffen's letter informing Pound, "I am immediately forwarding your interesting letter to Mr. Arthur Train who is now in Bar Harbor, Maine, for the summer."[80] American entry into the world war, with Italy one of the enemy Axis powers, drew the curtain on Pound's helpful effusions. But by 1943 word had come back on the poet's poisonous and treasonous wartime broadcasts. Institute member Hendrik Willem Van Loon telegraphed Train, "EZRA POUND HAS BRAVELY AND DEFINITELY GONE OVER TO THE SIDE OF THE ENEMY AND IS UNWORTHY TO BE ANY LONGER IN THE COMPANY OF DECENT AMERICANS."[81] That same day, Train wrote Francis Biddle, the attorney general of the United States,

> We are informed that he has been consistently guilty of broadcasting from Italy derogatory statements regarding the United States calculated to give aid and comfort to its enemies. If records of such broadcastings have been made, and it is consistent with your duties to allow me to do so, I should appreciate an opportunity to examine, and perhaps copy a few sentences, indicating that Pound is in sympathy with those forms of government which deny to their peoples the right of free artistic expression.[82]

The chief of the Special War Policies Unit, War Division, Lawrence Smith, wrote back to Train that "it is not the policy of this Department to reveal any information in its files to private persons or organizations."[83] To an inquiry from Felicia Geffen, Smith answered that "we have no information that Mr. Ezra Pound has renounced his American citizenship and is now an Italian citizen" (which would have been a convenient reason for dropping him from membership).[84] In July 1943 Pound and seven other American citizens were indicted by a District of Columbia grand jury for treason, and a New York *Times* story of March 8, 1944, was headlined INSTITUTE TO KEEP POUND AS MEMBER. Against pressure public and private, including statements of protest from such Institute members as S. N. Behrman, Joseph Wood Krutch, and Bliss Perry, Train, a lawyer best known for his stories in the *Saturday Evening Post* about the lovable legal codger Ephraim Tutt, held firm. In a *PM* article, he was quoted as stating: "Until and unless Mr. Pound is convicted by a jury of the charges against him, his relationship to and his privileges in our organization cannot be impugned."[85] In a letter to Mark Van Doren, who had been listed by *PM* among the protesters, Train added that if Pound were ejected without a legal proceeding "any of us might be ruined personally or socially by the arbitrary action of our associates in the Institute or any other body."[86]

By the time the war was over and Pound was captured and brought to trial, Train had died; the verdict reached by a federal district court jury in Washington was that Pound was of "unsound mind" and incapable of standing trial for treason.[87] An unsound mind, of course, was no reason to expel a member of the Academy-Institute, and during the twelve years in which Pound was confined to St. Elizabeth's Hospital in Washington, his name was carried, with that address, in the annual yearbook. He did not, however, receive the organizational mailings, though he was visited by such Institute members as Robert Frost and Archibald MacLeish. A group led by these two, with Conrad Aiken, Cummings, Robert Penn Warren, and Malcolm Cowley, helped secure his release in 1958, whereupon the mailings resumed and Pound did at last resign. Asked by two successive Institute presidents to reconsider, he replied from Rapallo in unrepentant accents that neither president had "adduced ANY reason, valid or even invalid, for my continuing to associate with a gang of writers opposed to every principle that I think valid, or, indeed, that wd/, in a civilized era, be considered as claim to membership in humanity."[88] At MacLeish's suggestion, the long-suffering Institute sent Pound $500 from the Revolving Fund.[89] The whole tortuous episode did, perhaps, serve a purpose: it demonstrated the majestic forbearance of an institution that honored artistic achievement in spite of an individual artist's tiresome foibles and repellent ideology.

The Arts in Wartime

It was as if the vast violence of the time infiltrated even the sleepy, ample quarters at 633 West 155th Street. The expulsion of a member, an open revolt against the elected leadership of the Academy, the precipitate resignation and southward flight of a librarian and paid executive: such things had not happened before. Death dramatically invaded the stage in the 1943 Ceremonial, when Albert Stoessel, a forty-eight-year-old violinist and conductor, collapsed in full view of the audience while conducting fifteen members of the New York Philharmonic Symphony Orchestra in a composition by Damrosch, his rendering of Robert Nathan's ballad, "Dunkirk." Stoessel, a good friend of Damrosch, died backstage, attended by his wife and a physician from the audience. "An hour earlier," the *New York Herald Tribune* reported, "he had told the musicians he felt a strange pain across his back."[90] William Lyon Phelps wrote Felicia Geffen, "The death of Mr. Stoessels [*sic*] was one of the most frightful events that I have ever been so unfortunate as to see."[91] Austin Strong, writing to Damrosch, took a more exalted view: "Though our afternoon was darkened by tragedy—there was something fine and heroic about it. An artist, struck down at the height of his career—among his brothers—what better way to pass into eternity? How splendid [*sic*] your Dunkirk was going. It had a splendor and real beauty. This is to express to you my deep sympathy in the passing of your friend, for I know how much he meant to you through the years."[92]

Being composed of, besides its female members, men generally well past draft age, the Academy-Institute pursued its routines throughout the war. The Ceremonials, after the opener in Carnegie Hall, were held each May under joint Academy-Institute auspices in the splendid, underutilized auditorium that Archer Huntington had built with the proceeds from his mother's Rembrandt. The organization contributed out of its funds to the war effort, financing triptychs for the chapels and recreation rooms of the Army and Navy Air Force, purchasing libraries of classical music for the far-flung outposts of the armed forces, investing in war bonds, and extending grants to refugee artists and members of the armed services. Members individually participated in war work: Thornton Wilder, for example, was in 1942 too busy to accept Damrosch's invitation to write an "amusing playlet" for an Academy evening: "I am employed in providing sound-track commentaries for some government propaganda movies, and I am afraid that most of our members will be found singularly [similarly] occupied. . . . A number of official and semi-official tasks resulting from my journeys to South America and to England prevent my being able to give sufficient time to the writing and finally to the staging of such an entertainment."[93] Damrosch proposed in 1942 a Forum on War and the Arts, but the plan was rejected as too ambitious and of dubious value to the war effort; nor did anything come of Edna Ferber's suggestion, at a dinner meeting in 1945, that "the Institute cancel all dinners and exhibitions for 1946 and use the money thus saved to help the artists of Europe who are dying of starvation and cold."[94] Over their cups and dessert plates, the members reluctantly agreed that such a step "would not make any appreciable dent in the alleviation of suffering in Europe" and "would curtail the important functions which the Institute performs for the furtherance of arts and letters, one of which should, of course, be a responsibility for the morale of the artists in Europe."

And indeed there is reassurance to be gained from examining the handsomely printed Ceremonial programs for those catastrophic years. The programs, with music before, after, and in the middle, ran long. At the 1943 Ceremonial, so shockingly terminated by the death of Alfred Stoessel, there was not only a Blashfield address by Van Wyck Brooks, entitled "Thomas Jefferson—Man of Letters," but another by Elmer Davis, the director of war information—"The Survival of European Culture" (read by Deems Taylor)"—plus music by Taylor, Paul Creston, William Schuman, and Damrosch. In the matter of awards, the Academy-Institute, as usual, had some catching up to do. The 1944 Award of Merit Medal to Theodore Dreiser at the age of nearly seventy-three was surely a tardy tribute to a writer who now seems the epitome—in his occasional clumsiness and wordiness as well as in his unblinking, Darwinian hon-esty—of American naturalism, which itself now seems less a particular school than the essential mode of our fiction in the century's first half. But Dreiser had been especially detested, for his sexual frankness, by Robert Underwood Johnson, and Dreiser's old ally Mencken was the Academy's most vociferous debunker. "I can only deplore the fact that you are having any truck with that gang," he wrote the novelist when he heard of the prize. "If they have actually offered you a hand-out, I hope you invite them to stick it up their rainspouts."[95]

Dreiser, like Hamlin Garland, had wound up living in southern California. Looking sheepish and unwell (he was to die the next year), he did show up in New York and listened to a citation, by Professor Chauncey Brewster Tinker, that some auditors thought defensive and condescending. Before handsomely acknowledging Dreiser's "tireless and unflinching devotion to the representa-tion of American life," Tinker took some pains to state that the Academy "sponsors no school, and has no programme. . . . Had it existed in the 17th cen-tury, it would have wished to bestow its recognition upon Pascal as well as upon Voltaire." Then, as if with tongs of even-handedness, he gave the prize to Dreiser as "an acknowledged leader of the Naturalist School in America."[96] Dreiser had brought a speech of acceptance in his pocket—on a pet topic, "the creation of a Secretary of the Arts, who should function as a member of the President's Cabinet"—but instead mumbled his thanks informally.[97] It was later said that he had been discouraged by members of the Academy from delivering unreviewed remarks or that his remarks were known to be contro-versial, but Felicia Geffen did not remember this and affirmed that acceptance statements were not reviewed. At any rate, the speech he meant to give found its way into the Academy files, with its plea that "if any nation, as we see today, can afford to spend endless billions in connection with wars—self-preservative or otherwise—it can surely afford at all times to look after at least a percent-age of those deserving and always struggling children of the arts."[98] Though not the most graceful of occasions, Dreiser's appearance on the Academy stage marked a significant rapprochement between the palefaces and redmen of American letters.

Next year's award of the Howells Medal to the ailing Booth Tarkington was a gesture to the past, to one of the "discoverers of America in literature—lov-ing his country, proud of it, mocking it, singing it, and always being it" (these words by Sinclair Lewis, who had become an amiable Academy regular).[99] The Award of Merit Medal for Poetry to W. H. Auden was a salute to a brilliant immigrant, one of the many European artists who came here in these years and one of the relatively few who stayed. In 1946 two "vans" were honored—Van Wyck Brooks, for essays and criticism, and John van Druten, for drama—and Senator William Fulbright in his Blashfield address on "Our Foreign Policy" expressed, for the first time in public, his distrust of Soviet intentions, warning,

"It is highly important that the world know that while we do not seek war, yet we are willing and able to fight whenever we believe any power threatens the right and opportunity of men to live as free individuals under a government of their own choice."[100] The cold war was settling in. Austin Strong afterward wrote Felicia Geffen that "I still think the Blashfield talk should be squeezed down to ten minutes as Fullbright [sic] did repeat himself. . . . Apparently the loud speaker went dead on us as I heard many complaints they couldn't hear."[101] The large-spirited Helen Keller, deaf and blind since the age of two, gave the 1947 Blashfield address; Glenway Wescott left a vivid account in his diaries:

> Grotesque and heartbreaking address by Helen Keller on "The Power of Speech." During the processional music she stretched her hand out before her and down toward the floor and made sweeping gestures not in time with the music, like some insane orchestra leader; which was to intercept the sound waves, I was told. When she made her speech, her companion stood just beside her and behind in a close embrace, and occasionally she prompted her or communicated with her by fingering up and down her back. Her voice is the most terrible sound on earth: a great soft gurgling and croaking with a note of anguish, only comprehensible here and there. Nerve-racking. Marianne Moore and Anne McCormick shed tears, but Mr. Damrosch, aged almost ninety, lost his temper, muttering aloud, "It's too long, too long," and stamping his foot.[102]

Damrosch would preside at no more Ceremonials, though he lived until 1950. In his dozen years as head of the Institute and then the Academy, he had seen their membership grow more fairly representative of the state of the arts in this country, though still heavily weighted with white males from the Northeast. Innovations take time to sink in, personal friendships inevitably influence votes, and an organization centered in New York will be overstocked with Easterners, but a survey of the honorees and new members after 1938 discovers few holes as gaping as those left, earlier, by the nonelection or declinations of Dreiser, Mencken, Edmund Wilson, Thurber, Hemingway, Fitzgerald, and Hart Crane. A genteel aristocracy of Academy directors no longer sought to set an exalted standard removed from the riffraff of the Institute. Of course, the hindsight of contemporary literary fashion discovers, even among the medal winners, forgotten and faded names. The poetry of Stephen Vincent Benét and the plays of Robert Sherwood are no longer highly esteemed, despite their gold medals in 1941 and 1943. And among major American poets, Frost was elected early and Wallace Stevens not until thirty years later, in 1946, though the greater vogue is now Stevens's.

The years 1938 to 1947 were, in this nation distracted by global upheaval, something of a breather in the arts. The vigorously populist but formally conservative mood of the 1930s carried into the war years and beyond. Scanning the titles of notable books published in those years, one notices few that still compel high praise. The first books by Saul Bellow and Vladimir Nabokov gain luster from their later careers, and the debut short-story collections by Eudora Welty and John Cheever received praise at the time. The brief career of Nathanael West, ended in a car accident when he was thirty-seven, produced its fourth and last novel in *The Day of the Locust* (1939), and Carson McCullers, another bleak, darkly poetic talent out of the mainstream, published her best novels in the early forties. The big literary books were Steinbeck's *The Grapes of Wrath* (1939) and Hemingway's *For Whom the Bell Tolls* (1940). Though still read and admired, both have the coarsely sentimental streak found in populist fiction. Hemingway's *The Fifth Column and the First Forty-nine Stories* in 1938 marked the high tide of his talent, which was great but fragile and easily parodied, even by himself. Posthumous works by Thomas Wolfe and F. Scott Fitzgerald testified to other truncated, intensely ambitious careers, while the later novels of Sinclair Lewis and Pearl Buck continued to satisfy their publics. Louis Bromfield and John Marquand smoothly penned best-sellers; Richard Wright exercised a lonely, scathing black voice; James Gould Cozzens in his early novels showed a brilliance that slowly dimmed; John Hersey, in *Into the Valley* (1943) and *A Bell for Adano* (1944), made the first contributions to a literature of the war and was elected to the Institute and then the Academy before he was forty. Faulkner was still in his prime, but even *The Unvanquished* (1938), *The Hamlet* (1940), and *Go Down, Moses* (1942) do not astonish as does his fiction prior to 1938. There is nothing in his decade to match Faulkner's explosive mix of Southern moonshine and hardcore modernism in the early thirties, or the honed best of Hemingway and Fitzgerald in the twenties, or the shimmering egocentric narratives of *The Adventures of Augie March*, *Invisible Man*, and *Lolita* from the fifties. O'Neill continued to dominate drama, though Thornton Wilder's *Our Town* (1938) and *By the Skin of Our Teeth* (1942) won Pulitzer Prizes and still entertain small-town and summer-theater audiences. In this decade, poetry yielded up the epic ambitions of the Benét brothers and early MacLeish and Robinson Jeffers and then began to settle, as the young poets returned from war and took advantage of the GI Bill, into its lyric intimacy with academia, where the "New Criticism" reigned. Reading fiction was still a middle-class recreation; writers reaped both profit and loss from the largeness of the respectful audience that purchased "family" magazines and two-dollar hardbounds. If the literature of the period must wear a single epithet, the word *workmanlike* comes to mind.

As for pictorial art, the style of the mural—large, crowded, stylized, message-bearing, and blunt if not chalky in color—set the tone even for easel painting in the thirties. Specifically American subjects, past and present, were favored. Grant Wood's immaculate, rounded farmscapes, Thomas Hart Benton's restless scenes of mass activity, and John Steuart Curry's majestic evocations of a remembered and reconstructed Kansas were the high points of a patriotic regionalism that saw countless local post offices and government buildings enriched with murals paid for, after 1935, by the Treasury Relief Art Project and the Federal Art Project of the Works Progress Administration (the WPA). Wood's *Spring in Town* (1941), Benton's *Threshing Wheat* (1939), and Curry's *The Tragic Prelude* (1938–1939) are exemplary late works of the "American Scene" school; indeed, Curry's outsize, open-mouthed, prophetically mesmerized figure of John Brown in this mural is, along with the pained, prim couple of Wood's *American Gothic* (1930), one of the decade's most memorable images. Amid all this rural emphasis, an opposed but kindred school arose in the cities; called social realists, they could not but observe the conditions of Depression misery, from sweat shop to bread line. Accused, not always wrongly, of Communist sympathies, its exponents could point in retort to the similarity between American Scene idealizing and Hitler's demand for a "pure" German art. Many of the social realists were Jewish—Ben Shahn, Max Weber, Jack Levine, Raphael and Isaac and Moses Sawyer—and some —Jacob Lawrence, Archibald

Motley—were African-American. Both schools shared, however, a rejection of Parisian modernism; their collectivist spirit helped prepare the nation for its united war mode. The mural artist Tom Lea, for instance, became one of *Life* magazine's outstanding "war artists," and the covers and posters of Norman Rockwell show a commercial genre style turned into superb pro-American propaganda.[103]

Mural art was uncomfortably close to "mere" illustration. The fin-de-siècle idea at the root of modernism, Art for Art's Sake, had by 1947 triumphantly returned to reestablish painting as self-delighting, self-justifying, and preferably abstract. Throughout the thirties, there had been countercurrents. The paintings of Edward Hopper, though primarily of urban scenes,

John Hersey, elected in 1950 to the Institute and in 1953 to the Academy, served as Academy secretary from 1961 to 1976. (Elliott Erwitt/Magnum Photos)

had been meditative, uncrowded, and apolitical. The work of Reginald Marsh rejoiced in steamy urban squalor as a manifestation of human vitality and female opulence. Stuart Davis reflected the ubiquitous clutter of metropolitan advertising to the point of creating abstract art, a direction in which Charles Sheeler and Charles DeMuth were also led. All the painters named above, except for Demuth, Motley, Isaac Soyer, and Grant Wood, eventually became members of the Institute. The contentious world of art heals its rifts, eventually; in this decade were belatedly elected a number of contributors to the wildly controversial Armory Show of 1913: Guy Pené duBois, at the age of fifty-eight; Jo Davison, at the age of sixty-one; Edward Hopper, at the age of sixty-three; Eugene Higgins, at the age of sixty-nine; John Marin, at the age of seventy-one.[104] Arshile Gorky, however, an immigrant from Armenia who committed suicide in 1948, died too soon to be honored for his critical double role as the last of the European surrealists and the first of the American abstract expressionists. Action Painting, by the end of the forties, had relegated representational art to the sidelines and had shrunk the teeming humanity on display in American Scene painting to the humanity of the painter alone; the painter—his brushstrokes, his wrestle with paint—became the only presence on the canvas. More personal, the art became less provincial, and for the first time Americans would be leaders, not followers, in world art. Paris and Rome now looked to New York. The wartime presence in the United States of so many artists, in every discipline, escaping Hitler's Europe had itself an incalculable deprovincializing effect.

Although "Papa" Damrosch, in a presentation at the 1943 Ceremonial, mentioned changes, "especially in musical composition, [that] are considered quite revolutionary in character," the department of music, the smallest and most collegial of the Institute's three, seemed to reflect well enough the major developments of the time. Like painting, music had turned with a vengeance to the American experience. The musicologist H. Wiley Hitchcock claims, of the "Eastman Group" of younger musicians, that "all seemed to share an aim to write the Great American Symphony by way of the Depression-era overture."[105] American folk songs, banjo tunes, hoedown melodies, New England singing-school music, and Protestant hymns were embodied in orchestral music. Aaron Copland's western-flavored ballet scores for *Billy the Kid* (1938) and *Rodeo* (1942) and his famous *Appalachian Spring*, dealing with rural life in early nineteenth-century Pennsylvania (1944); Ross Lee Finney's choral work *Pilgrim Psalms* (1945); Otto Luening's *Prelude to a Hymn Tune* (after William Billings); Douglas Moore's opera *The Devil and Daniel Webster* (1938); William Schuman's *American Festival Overture* (1939); Roy Harris's *Gettysburg Address Symphony, No. 6* (1944) and *American Ballads* (1942): these were typical celebrations of the American inheritance. The discovery of the work of Charles Ives, dating from John Kirkpatrick's premier performance of the "Concord" Sonata in 1939, enriched the inheritance, and Ives's eventual bequest of most of his copyrights to the Academy-Institute enriched the institution. The populism of the so-called American Wave in music included a willingness to work in popular forms: Copland produced film scores; Marc Blitzstein wrote for radio and the Broadway musical theaters; and Virgil Thomson composed scores for documentary films, as well as two operas with librettos by Gertrude Stein. The second of these, *The Mother of Us All* (1947), concerned women's-rights activist Susan B. Anthony. Thomson described the score as "a memory-book of Victorian play-games and passions . . . . with its gospel hymns and cocky marches, its sentimental ballads, waltzes, darned-fool ditties and intoned sermons . . . a souvenir of all those sounds and kinds of tunes that were once the music of rural America."[106] The avant-garde impulse was felt most strongly on the West Coast, where John Cage and Lou Harrison followed the experimental example of Henry Cowell. Throughout the country, composers increasingly found livelihood in association with colleges and universities, broadening musical education away from the conservatories of the eastern seaboard.

Meanwhile, the "hot jazz" of the twenties had become swing; the larger bands and fuller, more sophisticated arrangements brought jazz closer to the music of the concert hall. In 1938 Benny Goodman's orchestra gave an epochal concert in Carnegie Hall. Duke Ellington, the nonpareil of jazz composers, was at his peak in the late thirties and the forties and in 1970 took a place in the Institute, the first jazz artist to be so honored. Not so much the color line as the music department's rule against performance artists, and the difficulty of singling out individuals within group improvisations, has delayed recognition of this indigenous musical form, in which performance and composition are mingled. Swing succeeded with a wide public and danced the nation though World War II but had its deleterious effects on jazz: it was white-dominated, and its rigid performance conditions inhibited improvisation. During the war and after, a few subway stops from the Academy-Institute but in quite another world, young black musicians, playing after-hours for themselves, invented bebop. It is symptomatic of our organization's cautiously widening reach that one of bop's leading spirits, Dizzy Gillespie, was elected, toward the end of his life in 1993, to the Institute (by this time named simply the Academy) and that a great bop drummer, Max Roach, is one of ten American Honorary Members: "persons of great distinction in the creative arts whose works falls outside that of the three Departments of Art, Literature, or Music."[107]

The very invention of the "Honorary" category hints at growing pains. The Academy-Institute's first half-century coincided with the growth of jazz, from its roots in Negro spirituals, field songs, and blues, through ragtime and Dixieland, into an intricate and self-conscious music attracting intellectual analysis. The first serious critical attention came abroad, notably in France and Germany; to most Americans jazz was familiar but subcultural. Created and developed primarily by black males of little formal education, in sometimes sordid settings, this music testifies to the unruly demotic energy of art, which arises not where an elite would have it but where creative passion gathers. In these same fifty years, the cinema grew from its crude nickelodeon beginnings into an art form of profound expressiveness as well as great popularity. One can build a mansion for art to come and dwell in, only to have it flourish out by the alley. In a democracy above all, an institution dedicated to the advancement of the arts must wait upon the event and trust the future to confound the past.

NOTES

All archival materials are in the Academy files unless otherwise specified.

1. *Encylopaedia Britannica* (1969), s.v. "Huntington."

2. *Portraits from the American Academy and Institute of Arts and Letters* (Washington, D.C.: National Portrait Gallery, 1987), p. 18.

3. Memorandum, Walter Damrosch, "Conversation between Dr. Butler and myself at his house on Thursday, October 31, 1940."

4. *Portraits*, p. 18.

5. Facts from Academy tribute by Van Wyck Brooks at the meeting of December 14, 1956; "Archer Milton Huntington," by Beatrice Gilman Proske (New York: Hispanic Society of America, 1963); Geoffrey T. Hellman, "Some Splendid and Admirable People," *The New Yorker*, February 23, 1976.

6. Archer Milton Huntington, *A Note-Book in Northern Spain* (New York/London: Putnam's, 1898), p. 2.

7. Hellman, "Some Splendid and Admirable People," p. 44.

8. Ibid., p. 73.

9. Judge Grant's statement attached to his letter to the members of the Academy, dated November 8, 1939.

10. November 17, 1939.

11. " 'Sir: I Have the Honor': Notes on the History of the National Institute and the American Academy of Arts and Letters," by Malcolm Cowley, *Southern Review*, n.s., 8, no. 1 (winter 1972): 8.

12. Frank P. Crasto, Jr., to Grant, November 10, 1939.

13. November 20, 1918.

14. Cowley, "Sir: I Have the Honor," p. 9.

15. April 5, 1938.

16. Reprinted in American Academy of Arts and Letters, *Academy Papers: Address on the Evangeline Wilbour Blashfield Foundation of the American Academy of Arts and Letters* (New York: Spiral, 1951), 2:134–47.

17. March 11, 1940.

18. Hamlin Garland quoted Howard Mumford Jones (without citation of the original text) in his 1938 Blashfield address.

19. "It may turn out to have been a tempest in a teapot, but what a tempest!" (Vanamee to Grant, November 28, 1939); "I think the whole thing is a tempest in a

teapot, and I don't want to see the Academy wrecked by what really is a triviality"
(William Lyon Phelps to Damrosch, November 7, 1940).

20. Walter Damrosch, with blank salutation, May 23, 1940.

21. November 8, 1939.

22. Grant to Damrosch, April 26, 1940.

23. November 10, 1939.

24. November 10, 1939.

25. November 14, 1939.

26. November 21, 1939.

27. April 7, 1940.

28. April 23, 1940.

29. May 4, 1940.

30. May 8, 1940.

31. To "Dear Colleagues," May 12, 1940.

32. November 18, 1939.

33. November 14, 1939.

34. January 22, 1940.

35. Albert Spalding, in *Tributes of the American Academy* (New York: American Academy of Arts and Letters, 1951), p. 127.

36. Michel Mok, "Meet the Maestros," *New York Post*, November 11, 1938.

37. Academy files, Train's statement, December 1939.

38. Academy notes; Cowley, " 'Sir: I Have the Honor.' "

39. Academy notes.

40. Statement at Academy meeting of November 14, 1940.

41. June 8, 1940.

42. October 20, 1940. Damrosch then voices what seems to be an old grudge: "Archer Huntington in return for his election as an Academician has already burdened us with an entirely useless building which is used by less than one-half of our members only once a year. Its grandeur is oppressive and its location too far away to be of any real service."

43. Minutes, Academy board of directors meeting, November 29, 1940.

44. Poem dated September 13, 1939.

45. Minutes, Academy board of directors meeting, November 29, 1940.

46. December 11, 1940.

47. December 21, 1940. Writing to Judge Grant on February 9, 1940, Damrosch cited Gibson's report of a fit of Huntington petulance: "He said he had never seen a worse exhibition of ill-temper and general disagreeable manners as those exhibited by Messrs. Huntington and Butler towards you." A more genial glimpse of Huntington's manners is provided in Damrosch's letter of November 20, 1940 to William Lyon Phelps: "After our meeting last Thursday, Huntington came to where I was sitting and in answer to his smile I asked, 'Are we friends?,' and he answered, 'Of course we are,' and gave me both of his hands."

48. Hellman, "Some Splendid and Admirable People," p. 74.

49. January 28, 1941.

50. Ceremonial program, January 18, 1941.

51. Minutes, Academy board of directors meeting, April 7, 1941. Proposal to assist British artists originally presented by Barry Faulkner at Institute meeting on April 2, 1941.

52. To Institute secretary, January 13, 1940.

53. Academy board of directors meeting, November 14, 1941.

54. Ferber to Arthur Train, April 18, 1941; Mason to Train, April 18, 1941; James Truslow Adams to Walter Damrosch, April 4, 1941; Lewis Mumford, "Memorandum of the Purposes and Policies of the NIAL" (undated); Sinclair Lewis to Train, April 18, 1941; Strong to Train, May 2, 1941; Lewis to Train; Peattie to Train, April 14, 1941; Harper to Train, April 12, 1941; Becker to Train, April 11, 1941.

55. *Aims and Purposes of the Institute* (New York: American Academy of Arts and Letters, May 15, 1941), p. 5.

56. Minutes of meeting.

57. Such was the view of the playwright and drama critic Clayton Hamilton, who went on to outline, in considerable detail, a radio program, "half an hour in length, once a week," that would further the Institute's "fixed purpose of establishing, sustaining, and propagating the highest standards of artistic taste" (to Train, April 3, 1941).

58. To Canby, January 16, 1940.

59. Reported in Aiken to Geffen, August 23, 1954.

60. December 27, 1941.

61. Telegram, January 1949.

62. December 26, 1945.

63. To Canby, December 22, 1946.

64. Hellman unpublished pages.

65. April 18, 1941.

66. To Canby, May 10, 1942.

67. To Canby, April 24, 1943.

68. To the members of the National Institute of Arts and Letters, April 5, 1943.

69. 1944.

70. Hellman, "Some Splendid and Admirable People," p. 76.

71. January 27, 1939; January 30, 1939; April 13, 1939.

72. March 16, 1942.

73. Institute council minutes, October 9, 1969. Diederich's name is now on the list at the back of this volume.

74. Undated.

75. March 11, 1938.

76. March 12, 1938.

77. To Vanamee, March 21, 1938.

78. March 14, 1938.

79. April 22, 1941.

80. June 24, 1941.

81. February 25, 1843.

82. February 25, 1943.

83. March 11, 1943.

84. March 25, 1943.

85. M. M. Marberry, "National Institute Members Protest Board's Refusal to Drop Ezra Pound," *PM*, March 14, 1944.

86. March 15, 1944.

87. Marberry, "National Institute Members."

88. Quoted in Hellman, "Some Splendid and Admirable People," 61.

89. Ibid.

90. *New York Herald Tribune*, May 13, 1943.

91. May 18, 1943.

92. May 13, 1943.

93. To Geffen, January 24, 1942; memorandum to Damrosch, December 4, 1941.

94. Academy notes, "World War II."

95. Quoted in Richard Lingeman, *Theodore Dreiser: An American Journey* (New York: Putnam's 1986), 2:445.

96. Academy files, Ceremonial program.

97. Undated address.

98. Ibid.

99. Walter Damrosch's presentation of the Howells Medal to Booth Tarkington, May 18, 1945.

100. Quoted in *New York Times*, May 18, 1946.

101. May 25, 1946.

102. *Continual Lessons: The Journals of Glenway Wescott, 1937–1955* edited by Robert Phelps with Jerry Rosco. Copyright © 1990 by Anatole Pohorilenko. Reprinted by permission of Farrar, Straus & Giroux, Inc. A note of disarticulation was also struck by the acceptance speech, for the Institute Award for Distinguished Achievement, of Arnold Schoenberg, who not quite intelligibly recalled his artistic struggles as "a pell-mell of incoherent details . . . an ocean of boiling water and not knowing to swim."

103. See, for entire paragraph, Matthew Baigell, *The American Scene* (New York: Praeger, 1974).

104. Hellman, "Some Splendid and Admirable People"; and Academy yearbook.

105. H. Wiley Hitchcock, *Music in the United States*, 3d ed. (Englewood Cliffs, N.J.: Prentice-Hall, 1988), p. 223.

106. Ibid., p. 223.

107. Academy bylaws.

CHAPTER SIX

1948–1957

THE TESTIMONY OF TWO ARTISTS
Richard Lippold and Wolf Kahn

WITH ITS INTERNAL STRUCTURE and priorities clarified by the Row, the Academy-Institute sought its place in a postwar America politically dominated by opposition to Communism. On the domestic front, anti-Communist zeal emanating from Washington threatened a "curtailment," Institute president Douglas Moore told a meeting in late 1947, "of free speech and civil liberties."[1] The Committee on Un-American Activities of the House of Representatives, headed by Congressman J. Parnell Thomas of New Jersey, was busy ferreting out Communists and fellow travelers in the ranks of Hollywood; in response, ten directors and scriptwriters were blacklisted by the industry itself. A resolution protesting the activities of the Thomas committee was submitted to the Academy-Institute's membership for approval and, with some modifications that took various objections into account, was passed at a stormy dinner meeting of February 1948. Conceding that Congress properly had "the power to inquire into activities dangerous to the people and government of the United States" yet calling the methods of the Parnell Thomas committee "a subversion of the traditional American sense of fair play and human decency," a letter was sent to the Speaker of the House of Representatives over the signatures of 123 members.[2] A group of forty, among them the architect Gilmore D. Clarke and the writers John Erskine and Charles Warren, signed a dissenting statement, on the grounds that "the Institute should not take action in a collective manner . . . on a matter which [the signers] consider to be outside of the area related to 'the furtherance of the interests of literature and the fine arts.' "[3]

The debate caught the attention of the New York press. The *Times* commented that "a greater number of members had taken sides pro or con than on any previous matter that has arisen in the organization's fifty years of existence." The *Journal American* called for an investigation of the Institute, stating

✄ *Carl Van Vechten, author (elected 1961), and photographer, in 1962 gave the Academy 110 portraits of personalities in the worlds of art, literature, and theater. This group of photographs is reprinted through the courtesy of Joseph Solomon, executor of the Van Vechten estate.*

Truman Capote, March 30, 1948. —*Carl Van Vechten*

Tennessee Williams, November 14, 1948.   —*Carl Van Vechten*

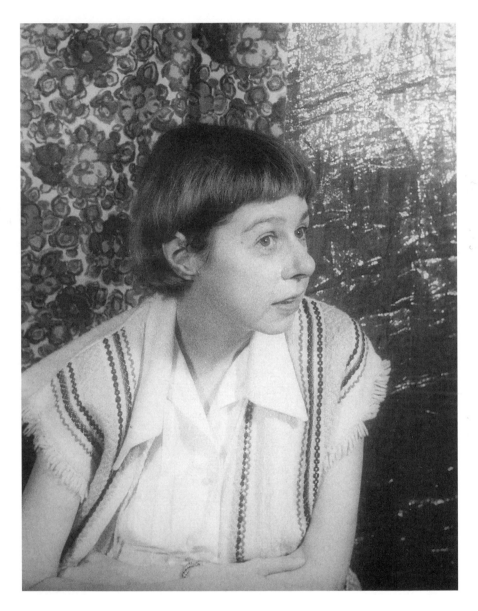

Carson McCullers, July 21, 1959.   —*Carl Van Vechten*

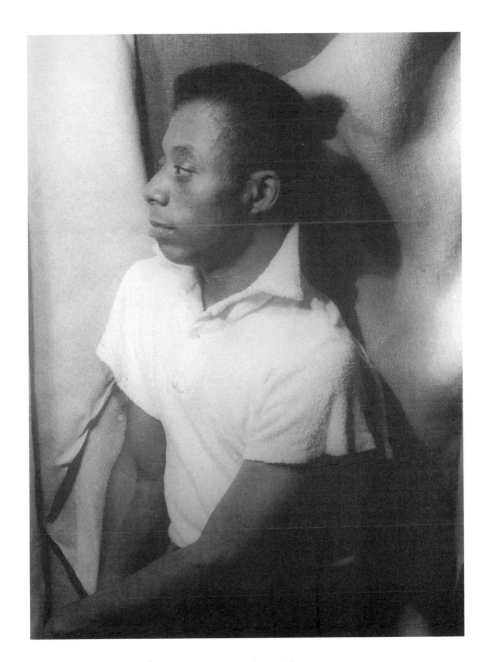

James Baldwin, September 13, 1955.   —*Carl Van Vechten*

Philip Johnson, January 18, 1933.   —*Carl Van Vechten*

Christopher Isherwood, February 6, 1939.   —*Carl Van Vechten*

Leonard Bernstein, May 24, 1944.   —*Carl Van Vechten*

of the anti-House Committee letter that "no matter what *the intentions* of the signers may have been, *their achievement* has been to give 'aid and comfort' to the Communist Party."[4] By the end of 1948 the National Institute of Arts and Letters appeared on the list of "Citations by Official Government Agencies of Organizations and Publications Found to be Communist or Communist Fronts" as a "Communist Front for writers, artists, and musicians."[5] The allegation persisted: Congressman George A. Dondero of Michigan, speaking in the House on June 14, 1956, called the Institute "formerly a respected honor society now infiltrated by brainwashed Marxists" and proclaimed that "the disgrace and degradation of this organization by Red infiltration should be a warning to other tax-free organizations bearing the word 'National' in their titles."[6] Leon Kroll, Paul Manship, Ben Shahn, and Malcolm Cowley were members frequently cited as Communist sympathizers.

However, a legal threat in 1951, when Representative E. E. Cox of Georgia called for an investigation of tax-exempt organizations, came to nothing, though President Moore saw fit to retain counsel and to write members, in June 1952, a letter expressing his belief that "any fair investigation will disclose that there never has been the slightest evidence of any communist or other insidious influences operating in our organization at any time in its long history."[7] On advice of counsel, however, the Academy abandoned plans to hold an exhibition, in 1952, of art works by its honorary members, because one of those slated for the show was the radical Mexican artist Diego Rivera.

In the wake of the bitter 1949 debate, Moore appointed the so-called Committee of Six, consisting of William Ernest Hocking, Walter Lippmann, Allan Nevins, Deems Taylor, Mark Van Doren, and William Adams Delano, to draw up an Institute policy on public statements. The policy carefully formulated was so stringent that few statements have been issued since. The committee submitted its report in January 1950; it allowed that the Institute charter committed it to "the furtherance of the interests of literature and the fine arts" and that when these interests were threatened by a curtailment of liberty, "it ought not to be impossible for the Institute" to speak out in protest.[8] An eight-step procedure was recommended; it entailed a complaint in writing by a member over a perceived threat to artistic freedom, the appointment by the ruling council of a five-member ad hoc committee, including the author of the complaint, and the submission of any complaint approved by three committee members to the full Institute membership, who then had to approve it by an affirmative vote of three-quarters before the president could issue a statement in the name of the organization. In the summer of 1953, Archibald MacLeish, president of the Academy, telegraphed Marc Connelly, president of the Institute, calling for a protest against the announced State Department plan to exclude hundreds of books from its overseas libraries, on the basis not of content but of their authors' political opinions. By the time the matter had passed through the procedural channels, President Eisenhower had denounced and annulled the plan, and the Institute confined itself to a letter expressing to the president "our deep satisfaction" in his decision and quoting Eisenhower himself: "Freedom cannot be served by the devices of the tyrant."[9]

The political paradox of the era—the tendency of a totalitarian enemy to induce totalitarian tactics in opposition—was paralleled within the Academy-Institute: there was resistance to anything that looked like official censorship and yet a ready faith that government should be involved in the arts. From 1946 on, the Institute supported the newly formed UNESCO (the United Nations Educational, Scientific, and Cultural Organization). The Institute files contain a 1946 letter addressed to Marshal Joseph V. Stalin in the Kremlin, urging his support of UNESCO "in the name of art, of literature, and of music which we jointly serve."[10] Glenway Wescott, an especially enthusiastic supporter, urged a 1949 UNESCO conference to activate the "C"—the cultural component—and asked the State Department to de-emphasize material well-being and "exporting the questionable American way of life."[11]

In the late 1940s twelve national arts organizations formed the Committee on Government and Art, which wished to revive the interaction between the arts and government that had ended when the WPA (the Works Projects Administration) was disbanded in 1943. The Institute sent delegates to the meetings of the Committee and issued resolutions of support, but nothing concrete came of it. When in 1956 the Committee proposed a bill to create a Federal Advisory Commission on the Arts "to undertake studies of and to make recommendations relating to appropriate methods for encouragement of creative activity in the performance and practice of the arts and of participation in appreciation of the arts," the Institute was advised by its attorneys that any attempt on its part to influence legislation would risk forfeiture of its tax-exempt status. No action in support of the bill was taken.[12]

Within the Academy-Institute, many committees distributed prizes, including a Medal for Good Speech to Edward R. Murrow, and administered new awards, such as the Rome Fellowship in Literature, the Richard and Hinda Rosenthal Foundation Award, and the Arnold W. Brunner Award in Architecture. The 1948 award in history and biography to Charles A. Beard caused Lewis Mumford to resign, not for the last time. In the department of literature, a number of women were elected—Carson McCullers, Eudora Welty, Margaret Mead, Phyllis McGinley, Edith Hamilton, Marchette Chute—but the painter Isabel Bishop, unanimously put forward by the nominating committee for president in 1956, withdrew upon learning that "my feeling of the unsuitability of the nomination is shared."[13] A lively discussion at the Knickerbocker Club, where the Institute met courtesy of the member Harrie Lindeberg, produced some soul-searching and the election of Malcolm Cowley. Not until 1979 would a woman—the historian Barbara Tuchman—be elected president.

Fledgling television made several overtures to the artistic elders; an offer for a television series featuring dramatizations of works by members, on the lines of the *Hallmark Hall of Fame*, was dismissed without much consideration, and the Institute declined to become involved in the National Citizens Committee for Educational Television. An offer from Lincoln Center of space for a new building was discussed, but as usual Archer Huntington's palace on West 155th Street proved, on reflection, impossible to leave. A bequest of paintings by Elihu Vedder was declared unsalable and distributed to museums. An official gown and hood, costing $35 per member, was designed, proposed, and rejected. Throughout this period Felicia Geffen capably maintained administrative order; in 1951 her annual salary was increased from $7,500 to $10,000. Within the building, a dangerous old elevator was replaced, the Hassam Room was created, the bronze doors on 156th Street were struck by a car and repaired, the heating system was converted from coal to oil, the library was revamped, and a lifetime pension plan was put into effect for employees who had served at least ten years, with, in 1950, a special directive to the treasurer to provide "generously and properly" for the eighty-three-year-old night watchman, Stephen Culhane, when he was no longer able to work.

Although the decade 1948–1957 now appears to have been a lively one for literature, coming before television distracted millions of potential readers and before French

Playwright Austin Strong proposed in 1950 that members wear robes to "add dignity and conformity" to the annual Ceremonial. The results of the postcard ballot sent to members were fifty-seven for, eighty-three against, four doubtful, and one not voting. A number of members annotated their votes. Artist Mahonri M. Young: "I wouldn't think of wearing such a disguise." Painter John Sloane: "I DREAD IT! I DISLIKE IT!" Writer Matthew Josephson: "I do not approve but wish to have a uniform brocaded in gold, with a sword!" Writer Van Wyck Brooks: "I think the gown looks rather cheap and undistinguished. It will turn our ceremony into a county college commencement, quite a mistake, I think." Writer Robert Nathan: "Sure! Anything to keep us from being the most anonymous group in the world."

criticism and political pressures had undermined the concept of pure literature, the committee for the Howells Medal reported in 1954: "The committee found it very hard to name one, or indeed any, truly outstanding novel of the last five years. The period has not been rich in outstanding novels."[14] Passing over Nelson Algren's *Man with the Golden Arm* (1949), J. D. Salinger's *The Catcher in the Rye* (1951), Ralph Ellison's *Invisible Man* (1952), Saul Bellow's *The Adventures of Augie March* (1953), and James Baldwin's *Go Tell It on the Mountain* (1953), the committee settled on Eudora Welty's *The Ponder Heart* (1954), taken along with "the general distinction of her work in fiction."

In retrospect this decade appears, above all, as the one in which the visual arts in America, long a provincial cousin of the art of Europe, became the global trendsetter. Centered in New York City, the school of abstraction and gestural painting swept all before it; the great canvases of Jackson Pollock, Mark Rothko, Willem de Kooning, Franz Kline, Clyfford Still, Robert Motherwell, Barnett Newman, Helen Frankenthaler, and others became, in association with the Rockefeller-patronized Museum of Modern Art, an electrifying proclamation of American freedom and creativity at a time when the Communist world was issuing pictorial propaganda in a conservative illustrational style. Rapidly dispersed into popular imagery, abstract expressionism and its sculptural adjuncts marked a historical divide; our expecta-

tions of art, and our sense of art's limits, would never again be the same. It seemed fitting, then, that an artist should write the chapter on this decade. The first to volunteer, the sculptor Richard Lippold, was unfortunately unable, for reasons of health, to carry his beyond the succinct and personal paragraphs that follow; the painter Wolf Kahn kindly consented to carry on, with an essay less on the Academy-Institute than on art as he saw and experienced it in this decade of international tension and spectacular artistic ferment.　　—J. U.

Felicia Geffen, executive director from 1941 to 1973, with Erskine Caldwell (elected 1942) at the 1973 Ceremonial.

Richard Lippold

The decade from 1948 to 1957 was of especial significance in American art inasmuch as it continued the postwar emergence of the United States as the leader of new attitudes and forms of expression. Most of the perpetrators of these new forms were eventually inducted into the Institute and Academy.

Symbolic of this emergence was the summer of 1948, when a group of artists in various disciplines was invited by Josef Albers to spend several months at Black Mountain College, in North Carolina, where he was teaching as the sole member of the art department. Most of us there were quite unknown, except by a few cognoscenti. At the beginnings of our careers, we shared the exuberance of that exceptional ambience, nestled in the isolation and grandeur of the Appalachians, partaking freely of one another's concepts, as well as persons. We were Bill and Elaine de Kooning; the sculptors Peter Grippe and myself; the composer John Cage; the dancers Merce Cunningham and his company, including my wife, Louise; Buckminster Fuller; the poet-potter M. C. Richards; the photographer-curators Nancy and Beaumont Newhall; the

Fiftieth anniversary of the founding of the Academy, 1954. First row, left to right: *Leon Kroll, Robert E. Sherwood, William Adams Delano, Carl Sandburg, Van Wyck Brooks, and Mark Van Doren.* Second row, left to right: *Deems Taylor, Roger Sessions, Douglas Moore, Henry R. Shepley, Gilmore D. Clarke, Paul Manship, Thornton Wilder.* Third row, left to right: *Charles Hopkinson, Archibald MacLeish, John Dos Passos, Mahonri Young, Barry Faulkner.* (Jim Rosenberg)

architecture critic Edgar Kaufman, Jr., heir to his father's Frank Lloyd Wright house Fallingwater; and, among the students, Robert Rauschenberg, Ray Johnson, and the writer James Leo Herlihy, whose successful later play, *Blue Denim*, may well have launched the continuing passion for tight jeans. Besides our presentations of our own efforts, John Cage produced all the works of Eric Satie, including his strange play, *The Mask of Medusa*; it was a festive summer.

Back in Manhattan, the Black Mountain group enlarged to include other members of the creative community. We met at one another's apartments or lofts or at inexpensive restaurants like Wah Kee's in Chinatown, or Sloppy Louis's, or one of the first Japanese restaurants, on Fifty-sixth Street, discovered by Virgil Thomson.

We were too busy looking at or listening to one another's works to be more than casually aware of the National Institute of Arts and Letters or the American Academy of the same. Thus we were, if not waiting in the wings, at least standing there for them to recognize us. In any event, we were, like most artists, quite anti-establishment, although recognition from these august bodies came fairly soon to some of us. Philip Guston, the painter, for instance, received an award in 1948, although he was not elected to the Institute until 1972. Also in 1948 the composers Henry Cowell and Lou Harrison received awards; Cowell was elected to the Institute in 1951, and Lou Harrison in 1973. Virgil Thomson was elected to the Institute in 1948 and to the Academy in 1959, and he delivered the Blashfield address in 1960.

John Cage received an award in 1949 but was not elected to the Institute until 1968 and to the Academy in 1988. Stefan Wolpe, the composer, also received an award in 1949 and became a member of the Institute in 1966. Joseph Campbell, the writer who introduced us all to the *I Ching*, the ancient "Book of Changes" without which many of us made no major career or life decisions, received an award in 1949 and was elected to the Institute in 1973 and to the Academy in 1987, the year he died. In 1950 the writer Paul Bowles received an award; he joined the Institute in 1981.

A number of composers were honored. Ben Weber received an award in 1950 and was elected to the Institute in 1971. In 1951 Alan Hovhannes got an award, with election to the Institute following in 1977. Peggy Glanville-Hicks won an award in 1953, and Edgar Varèse was elected to the Institute in 1955.

John Heliker, the painter, received an award in 1957, election to the Institute in 1969, and an Award of Merit in 1967. Bill de Kooning was elected to the Institute in 1960, as was Marcel Duchamp, with whom John Cage played chess until Marcel's death. De Kooning received a Gold Medal in 1975 and was elected to the Academy in 1978. He was astonished when one of his paintings sold, at about that time, for one million dollars. "Cheese," he said. "Imagine dot!"

I myself was elected to the Institute in 1963, much against the wishes of the elderly sculptor Paul Manship, who felt, I suppose, that I was a young upstart. This was curious to me, because as a young student I had held some admiration for his work, particularly as it related to architecture, an interest that eventually led to my nearly total involvement in that area. Buckminster Fuller (our "Bucky") was also elected to the Institute in 1963 and to the Academy in 1979.

Morton Feldman, our composer friend, received an award in 1970, as did composer Earle Brown in 1972. His wife, Caroline, was the beautiful dancer "star" in Merce Cunningham's young company. Merce himself was elected an honorary member in 1984. A disciple of Cage's, Christian Wolff, got an award in 1975. Our poet friend John Malcolm Brinnin became a member of the Institute in 1978.

Among the students from Black Mountain, Rob Rauschenberg was elected to the Institute in 1978, and the painter Cy Twombly in 1987. Another friend of Rauschenberg's, Jasper Johns, entered the Institute in 1973 and the Academy in 1988. Ray Johnson, painter of…"Correspondance [sic] School" fame, got an award in 1966. Our composer friend from Germany, Karlheinz Stockhausen, became a Foreign Honorary Member in 1979.

So, in this and the next several decades we started our fossilization process

Reception on the terrace following the 1951 Ceremonial. This annual event is now held within a tent, following the ceremony in the auditorium.

in the warm comfort of the Institute and the Academy. My own pleasure, at least, in the company of fellow members was to discover the absence of rivalry among them. There were—are—no "stars" in our gorgeous mausoleum on West 155th Street. I recall only the poet Robert Lowell, in his cups from too much of the excellent wines at our sumptuous dinners for ourselves, standing up and yelling at everyone and everything—including us—from what seemed his lonely superiority. After he was pulled back to his seat, our peaceful confraternity continued until we kissed and said good-bye. What we felt—feel— about others outside our marble sanctuary we do not let invade our assembling there. For me, it is one of the chief glories of membership.

Now, in the nineties, it grieves me to see the names of many of "our" circle among the deceased members. I'm not sure I want my own name so listed. Creators' lives are largely a mystery, or partly so, even to themselves. As an old writer answered recently when asked the meaning of his life, "It was a happy disaster." Like the Greek Mesomedes' "Hymn to the Sun," the architect Maitani's splendid medieval Duomo of Orvieto, or Emily Dickinson's "A Narrow Fellow in the Grass" (isn't each of us?), I'd prefer that my work bring joy to what will be left of future humanity on this increasingly fragile planet.

Wolf Kahn

"We are born originals and we die copies."
EDWARD YOUNG (1683–1765)

For those of us who are not historians by profession it is invariably true that in the overview of any decade the personal will outweigh the general. On the occasion of V-J Day we are far more likely to recall where we were at the time the news hit us than the terms of surrender signed by MacArthur and Shigemitsu. The decade comprising the years 1948 to 1957 was filled with political drama—the Korean War, the Suez Crisis, the McCarthy and House Un-American Committee Hearings, blacklists, loyalty oaths—but what I most remember is the endless hitchhiking I did in those years, the cool breeze along Lake Michigan when I took walks away from the University of Chicago campus, and the nervous excitement, later on, with which I awaited those issues of the *Times* and the *Art News* that included reviews of my first New York gallery exhibitions. It was the decade when Japan and Germany began their economic revival, but more importantly to me it was the decade in which I moved from a tiny cold-water flat on the Lower East Side of New York to a top-floor loft on Broadway that even had a skylight! Talk about an economic miracle! It was also the decade in which the abstract expressionists came to general attention, at the same time that I moved from being a callow art student hanging on the teacher's every word to having a full-page color reproduction in *Time* magazine. Even closer to home, it was the time when I progressed from a teenager's eager but inept attempts at love to being married, in 1957, at the Venice *municipio*. The ceremony was performed by the municipal elevator operator, who put on a tricolor sash as a sign of his high office.

Even historians understand that the true meaning of any decade is to be found in those records that document the inner *life* of its participants. Thus I, not being a historian at all but a painter of landscapes, choose simply to bring yet another personal document to the huge pile already in place. Not many late-twentieth-century landscape painters have written on the subject of their inner lives; none, as far as I can tell, have told of the tensions brought about in a young painter's development by the idea of "originality," as I will now try to do.

In 1947 I was a nineteen-year-old art student in the Hans Hofmann School of Fine Arts. I had studied at the New School of Social Research the previous semester, working under Stuart Davis (elected 1956). Davis was a famous painter, but his salad days as a teacher had long since passed: during class he would discuss baseball and jazz with longtime cronies, and one evening he went so far as to announce, at the end of class, "Let's close the magic portals, children. We've conjured up enough art atmosphere for one evening." This was not the milieu I had hoped for and as soon as practicable I transferred to the Hofmann School, which had the reputation of being the only real game in town. I was not disappointed.

As a teacher, Hofmann (elected 1964) never directly encouraged his students to be original. He well understood that it was not helpful. Did we not wish to become artists because we were enthusiastic about somebody else's work? Do we not learn by imitating? There was the example of Arshile Gorky, who spent a fair number of his early years imitating first Cézanne, then Picasso, and finally Miró (elected a Foreign Honorary Member in 1960), so as to understand as intimately as possible the ideas that guided them. But this and other similar facts were little known to students. Much more in relief were the strident dicta of greats like Ezra Pound ("Make it new!"), Paul Klee ("I want to be as though new born, knowing nothing"), and Albert Pinkham Ryder ("The least of a man's original emanation is better than the best of a borrowed thought"). And what was a student to make of Rimbaud's command "Il faut être absolument moderne"? The world, it seemed, was filled with free-floating fiats. And free-floating anxiety. Hofmann was elusive. He clearly admired those among the students whose work showed evidence of eccentricity. Was that where originality lay? I carefully observed these favored individuals. Jean Follet, whose drawings from the model invariably had a fish eye in them, wore a daily uniform to school made up of a black corduroy suit over a buttoned-to-the-top white men's shirt. To set off this severe contrast she regularly wore a thick layer of dark-red lipstick that got smudged and mixed with charcoal in the course of a long day's work. Al Israel, another favorite, subsisted on an exclusive diet of carrots and bananas.

Compared to them, my group of friends were dull and normal, almost ordinary. We were a bit overintense, inclined to take our work too seriously, but no one at the time would have called Jan Muller, Paul Resika (elected 1994), Jane Freilicher (elected 1989), Larry Rivers (elected 1979), Joan Mitchell, George Segal (elected 1981), or Allen Kaprow outrageous. And Hofmann himself seemed pretty normal, too, and while we had enormous respect for him as a teacher and as a person, the consensus in the school was that he was a great teacher but not as great a painter. Yes, he was ahead of the time in his appreciation of the work of his contemporaries (on Clyfford Still [elected 1978]: "Go to see his show, but I will tell you that it'll take you years to understand those paintings!"), but he always spoke highly of the Old Masters ("You must learn to see the beauty, in a Rembrandt, of the empty spaces"). And in his own work he was clearly influenced. He spoke constantly of Mondrian and Matisse (elected a Foreign Honorary Member in 1950) and of the cubists, less often of the German expressionists to whom, it seemed to his students, he owed the most. In retrospect, I understand why they would not be a part of his pantheon. Hofmann's system of teaching was directed toward giving the student formal control through a fuller understanding of the structural meaning of every move. The German expressionists were primarily interested in heightened expression and were thus quite willing to overlook compositional values in their search for great intensity. Hofmann spoke of the necessity of "plastic ideas" or of seeing things in "painterly terms," but he never called for originality, nor did I ever hear him use that awful suburban word *creativity*.

One of my fellow students was Robert Goodnough, clearly one of the stars in the school. He was never seen there except on the day of the weekly "crit." On such days he was likely to appear with a sizable pile of canvases large and small. As a school monitor it was my job to choose which pictures were shown at one time on the dozen or so easels set up for Hofmann's consideration. I placed all the canvases Goodnough brought in one such group. Hofmann peered at them with a certain amount of pleasure. "Who made this good picture?" he asked regarding a cubist landscape. "Goodnough." "And this one?" pointing to a Mondrian-like abstraction. "Goodnough." And this, and this, regarding the rest of the pictures, each in a different style. "Ah," Hofmann finally stated. "That is very good. You are recapitulating the history of modern art."

Another of my fellow students was Allen Kaprow. He was a restless spirit who later gained a measure of fame by inventing "happenings." The summer of 1948 he spent in Woodstock, New York; there he fell under the influence of the composer Stefan Wolpe (elected 1966). On his return he was full of argument. "I am tired of painting. I know where each of my brushstrokes comes from. This one from Bonnard, that one from Kandinsky, the other from de Kooning. There is no possibility of doing anything original as a painter. Painting is dead!"

We had long and bitter disagreements as I continued in my stubborn faith that painting was as direct and fundamental in art as singing was in music.

But the obligation to become original had lost none of its strength for me. I searched for ways in which traditional modernism might accommodate originality. How about trying to follow the impressionists' ambition of the 1860s to paint modern life? Surely modern life had changed sufficiently in the interim to allow for a slew of originality? But I could discover nothing as painterly as Manet's top hats and décolletages in present-day dress. As for present-day activity, if I painted a person, what could that person be doing that hasn't been done before? Turning on the radio? Climbing into an airplane? Maybe still life allowed for a typically contemporary expression. Cereal boxes? Not painterly. Flowers? Done to death by earlier artists. Was there a more modern way to paint fish than Soutine's? Perhaps, but it had to be ignored as belonging to retrograde, provincial American modernism or, God forbid, American Scene painting. Whole sections of recent art were beyond the pale because they couldn't stand up in their freedom of execution to European modernism or abstract expressionism. We were free to ignore Hartley, Dove, Sheeler (elected 1963), Marin (elected 1942), and we actually felt contempt toward the artists who took up the main galleries of the Whitney in the late forties: Kuniyoshi (elected 1949), Rattner (elected 1958), Speicher (elected 1930), Kroll (elected 1930), Curry (elected 1942), and Grant Wood. We were excited by Kline and de Kooning (elected 1960) and argued whether Pollock was a decorative painter; it took years for a student to discover that he was but a later incarnation of expressionism. All these were abstract painters, but Hofmann added to the weight of unanswered questions by stating that "modern art lacks human content."

Burdened by these concerns, I made a painting of a large and disintegrating wicker armchair that stood in my studio. Here was an object I knew well. It also posed a formal challenge: how to express the empty volume in a chair, which would usually be occupied by the sitter. The picture ended up as a hybrid, located somewhere between the German expressionists and Bonnard. I felt keenly dissatisfied with this and the other paintings I made at the time. Great changes were taking place on all sides, but I felt excluded from them, because I felt that I had no originality.

I tried to define myself politically. Like all young people around me, I felt no attachment to the American political mainstream. Across the hall in my tenement on Sixth Street and Avenue B lived a talented artist, Lester Johnson, who was ten years older than I. I was in the habit of looking to him for guidance and example. He had been a conscientious objector, during the war, and many of his friends and out-of-town visitors had been pacifists of various religious backgrounds. I was not religious but found the accounts of the sacrifices they had been forced to make heroic. They had been in and out of jail, dumped on lonely country roads while trying to hitchhike, and misled by the U.S. government into volunteering for experiments that were seen, too late, to have military applications. I was filled with indignation and came to see that pacifism made sense. Thinking to become a pacifist, I began by signing out of the U.S. Naval Reserve, in which I had enlisted at the time of my discharge from the service in 1946. Then I consulted Hofmann, whose school I was still attending sporadically. "Be careful," he said. "Being an artist is a full-time job, and being a pacifist can also be a full-time job."

In spite of moral reinforcement my work was not going well. I thought that it was necessary to start all over again and decided to seek guidance earlier in the history of Western art. I discovered Rembrandt's landscape drawings; I took long walks to the East River and subway rides to outer suburbs to find Holland in New York. I made tiny, crabbed pen-and-ink drawings from nature. Sometimes my friend Larry Rivers (elected 1979) came with me. One day we looked up a street in the Bronx toward a white house surrounded by very dark trees. "You know, if we could understand the meaning of the white and black up there," he said, "we'd be halfway home as artists." We were talking Kant without knowing it. We certainly understood each other at that moment, a moment that still resonates. And, surrounded as we were then by talented abstract painters, the coincidence of his aims and my own more confused ones was very helpful.

In the spring of 1949 I had enough. My neighbor Lester Johnson was undergoing psychoanalysis, other friends were questioning their own commitment, and I determined that I needed a new set of concerns and surroundings. My application to the University of Chicago having been accepted, that fall began what I thought would be a new life.

The new environment did not disappoint me. The university was an intellectually challenging institution, with a brilliant faculty. The campus at that time was divided into two extreme camps, with Richard McKeon leading the Neoplatonists and Rudolph Karnap heading the logical positivists. The first group was immersed in metaphysical speculations, while the opposition sneered at questions whose answers were not demonstrable. Friendships were strained over these divisions; arguments went on past midnight in the dorms. As an art student, I had devoted the recent past to chasing chimeras and obscure hints and had gained an appetite for unanswerable questions. I was therefore firmly on the side of metaphysics. I developed a special taste for Kant, who seemed to me to provide a firm grounding to the formal absolutism for which I had gained a taste from Hofmann. Was the idea of Beauty, or Formal Coherence as I would have said, a preexisting category of the mind or simply the residue of conventions and habits? It seemed more likely that the beauty of works like Sung landscapes or African totems appealed to innate ideals, given that they are exotic and no conventions and habits regarding these works are readily available to the

Western mind. Walking along the lake shore as I thought about these abstruse issues, I was pleased to find out a surprising thing: these larger speculations crowded out my usual, more personal worries. I took an honors course given by Kenneth Burke (elected 1951), on works by Shakespeare, Henry James, and Conrad. Between classes I walked over to Grant Park, along Lake Michigan, armed with pastels and a sketchbook. I drew solitary sailboats on the horizon and lampposts silhouetted against the brightness of the sky. I was getting ready, I thought, to regard art as a hobby, if an intense one.

In the world at large, the cold war was gathering steam, but in the intellectual enclave in which I was recuperating from the Hofmann experience—or, better, trying to digest it—there was hardly any discussion of current events: we spoke about Plato and Kant, Hume and Comte. The demands that scholarship presented seemed light compared to the shifting demands of art making. Conceptual clarity, I was beginning to understand, was different from artistic clarity; the first had to do with headings and subheadings, the other with uncertain sets of hierarchies that were simpler and more complicated at the same time.

This was in 1950. That summer, after graduating from the College, I was broke. To recoup my fortunes I hitchhiked across the continent, ending up in the Oregon forest, where I worked as a logger. The contrast between the wordy atmosphere of Chicago and the thick, damp, mossy, silence-soaked feeling of the woods of the Oregon Coastal Range was drastic. I reconnected to my earlier concerns, spending all my free time drawing. I drew the trees, the mill, the lumber trucks being loaded with the orange-colored new-sawn lumber. Late in that summer a letter arrived at the logging camp informing me that the University of Chicago had granted me a scholarship to the School of Humanities, along with a living stipend. I looked at that letter as though it had come from another planet. I was being urged to use all the confidence I had laboriously gained the previous year to go back to school! It didn't take long to decide to resume my career as a painter, and by November I was back in New York looking for a studio.

It was a wonderful time to be a young artist. The abstract expressionists—Hofmann's generation—were beginning to be celebrated by the larger world. New York was feeling itself to be an art center on a par with Paris. American museums were focused on American contemporary art, organizing large shows such as the Museum of Modern Art's "15 Americans" in 1952. As Hofmann students we used to regard ourselves as marginal types, hugging to our bosoms ideas that had been ignored for being too esoteric, too Europe-derived, too unrelated to American life. In one year, while I was away, it appeared that the whole world had begun to embrace those very ideas. A philosophy was at hand to provide a sound basis for what we had been doing naturally. It was called existentialism, and it proclaimed that all generalities were suspect, apart from those limited truths that arise from a perception of the unique instance. This was an idea made to order for the way we all painted and lived. Down with security and predictability! Instead, we looked for that precise moment when, on the canvas, all the elements meshed, when everything "worked." De Kooning, especially, as we sat in the famous Cedar Bar, talked constantly of the need for "disequilibrium" while working, the need not to know ahead of time what the final result might eventually look like. One had to be, instead, in a constant state of alertness, looking to be *surprised* by what took place before one's eyes. Previous generations of art students had been taught a very different process. They were told to make preparatory sketches and encouraged to follow a predictable set of procedures starting with underpainting, where large brushes were used to lay in broad areas of tone, and then, with each subsequent stage, to allow smaller and smaller impulses to lead to a final "finish." In abstract expressionism the idea was that the strength and energy of the initial impulse should be equally available in the final stage of painting. It was a grand idea—that there should be no letup, no flagging of the initial energy throughout the whole process of the work—and when carried out by the largest spirits among the painters it led to exhilarating art. (Although it was discovered later on that no less a talent than Franz Kline had been in the habit of filling pages of old telephone books with black ink drawings that he often enlarged to make his heroic-sized abstractions. A few years later Motherwell (elected 1970) also diluted the brew, by painting images in series. It turned out to be awfully difficult to reinvent the wheel every time.)

Abstraction had triumphed. While I had painted a couple of near abstractions as a student, it seemed perverse to give up entirely what had defined me as an artist hitherto: my love of drawing from the direct observation of nature. I was well aware that representation and, certainly, exact description acted as a constraint on the untrammeled practice of action painting, as this mode came to be known. Here the example of some European modernists was helpful. Van Gogh and, later, Soutine could be thought of as artists who combined an intense preoccupation with paint handling with a love of everyday subject matter. Bonnard and Matisse used heightened color to keep alive elements of unpredictability and surprise. Matisse especially, when writing about the *structural* use of color, indicated a way whereby the painter is constantly questioning his painting. Enough disequilibrium to keep us all happy! Thus reinforced, a group of us varying in age from twenty-five to thirty-five, including Jane Wilson (elected 1991) and Alex Katz (elected 1988), started small co-op galleries and began to exhibit painting that tried to marry the freedom of the abstract-expressionist process with traditional strategies of description. We were trying to correct what Hofmann had stated earlier as a danger in modern art: its lack of "human content." In our search we had a great advantage that had been lacking to the first generation of the abstract expressionists: we had their active help and encouragement, whereas their relation with their own predecessors, the American Scene painters, was one of mutual incomprehension and contempt. (Although the abstract expressionists also contained in their ranks purists who saw any deviation from abstraction as a threat. I remember having an argument with Jack Tworkov (elected 1981) when I said, somewhat carelessly, that painting representational subject matter added "fun" to the enterprise. Tworkov was not convinced. "What does fun have to do with it?" he fumed.)

We turned our backs on much current and recent art. "Everyone tries to paint what he thinks is most important in art" was Hofmann's dictum. We had grown up as modernists, and we had little patience with earlier artists' struggles to appropriate European modernism to their own work. We dismissed the geometric abstractionists as being fussy and narrow, as well as the whole school of earlier American modernists: Hartley, Dove, Marin, O'Keeffe (elected 1949), Sheeler. They were not "free" enough, and not *abrasive* enough. I remember one evening in the early fifties when we went to a performance by the American Composers' Orchestra of new compositions. Before and after each piece the conductor spoke to the audience. After a particularly thorny piece by Edgard Varèse (elected 1955), he said, "I know not many of you like this piece, but now we will play a piece you will all like, by Aaron Copland!" One of our group, the painter Grace Hartigan, got up and shouted, "I want to hear another piece we *won't* like!"

Nothing stands still for long; rifts were already appearing in our very group. About that time Larry Rivers, who had been painting in the style of Bonnard, went to France. When he returned, less than a year later, he was a changed man. What had he learned? I asked. "Well," he said, "I found out that I wasn't a Frenchman." The importance of nationality as a contribution toward originality had not previously interested me, though it had its effect on those of the previous generation whom we were in the habit of considering "old hat"— such as Benton (elected 1942; resigned 1965; reinstated 1966) and Wood—and it also affected another group, led by Ben Shahn (elected 1956) in painting and by Copland (elected 1942) in music, that shared a generally populist, left-wing attitude that we considered sentimental. To hear Larry abjure the cosmopolitanism that had been taken for granted not only by Hofmann's disciples but by the advanced New York art world in general: this was a serious breach. I put it aside, but later on it became clear to me that it was the first hint that there would be a dividing of the ways between those of us who believed in so-called formalist art and the artists who were heading toward pop art.

Yet art never divides neatly; we are always breathing the same air. Robert de Niro, Sr., the one among us most deeply influenced by French painting, at that time began to work from movie-still photographs; De Kooning pasted a reproduction of a photo of Marilyn Monroe's head on one of his "Woman" series; Grace Hartigan painted Lower East Side shop windows dressed in the "ab ex" look. Lester Johnson, having moved to the Bowery, painted bums, and I painted near-abstract interiors of my studio. In that way the climate formed by the group of which I was a member (later called the New York School—Second Generation) prepared the way, whether we knew it or not, for the pop sensibility.

In 1953 and 1954 I had my first one-man shows. In retrospect, I see that they were extraordinarily well received, but at the time it seemed a slap in the face that the reviews never failed to mention Soutine and the impressionists as influences on my work: "His works are derived, sometimes too directly, from Van Gogh and Soutine" (Otis Gage, in *Arts and Architecture*, March 1955); "imitative of the manner but not the feeling of Soutine" (Fairfield Porter, in *Art News*, November 1953). These comments branded me, in my own eyes, as a retrograde, ultraconservative painter who had not achieved any artistic maturity. The judgment of the painters around me was more helpful, however. In one way or another they were, each and every one, engaged in the same struggle to develop their art into an "original" statement. We had the examples of our predecessors, each one of whom had a special "look" that declared itself the instant one saw one of their pictures. Was this the result of their conscious efforts to separate themselves from the herd or a natural manifestation of individual extreme cases? I had not the ability at the time to separate the subjective from the objective element in this conundrum. Seen from the outside, every painter is a person who makes a product: paintings. The "art world"—galleries, critics, museums—is primarily concerned with placing this product in a category, assigning it a kind of trademark. When an artist's work achieves this "trademark" recognition, pressures exist to stay within the narrow range of output that most clearly identifies the work as his or her own. Subjectively, however, the requirements an artist feels inside differ greatly from those the art world assigns. The work has its own dynamic, and the artistic issues that slowly identify themselves need time and space for their natural development and their eventual clarification. My work had been assigned a trademark status very quickly, and I was encouraged to continue in my derivative ways. Others might see originality in my work of the fifties, but I was the last to recognize it.

As good luck would have it, at that very moment I had to leave New York to join my future wife in Venice, where she had a Fulbright scholarship. Totally unknown in Italy, I was suddenly freed from the expectations of the outside world and allowed to let my work go in the directions it naturally sought. We were living on the Giudecca in Venice. On one end of our huge studio was a set of big windows overlooking a large body of water, the Marittima. At its horizon sparkled the city itself, with the Ducal Palace, the Salute, the palazzi of

the Zaterre and the island of San Giorgio off on one side. My immediate surroundings have always had a strong bearing on the scale, light, and color of my
work, and they have made me particularly susceptible to influences from other
artists as well. The peculiar light of Italy caused me to become entranced with
the paintings of Giorgio Morandi, who better than any other contemporary
artist understood Italian light. Slowly, as I lived in Venice over a two-year
period, my paintings turned from being bright in color to becoming milky and
pastellish. And, unexpectedly, another artist started to loom large in my consciousness, an artist whose work I had often seen in New York and whom I
even knew personally. That summer, in 1958, the American pavilion at the
Biennale was given over to the work of Mark Rothko (elected 1968), and for
the first time I was able to see it isolated from the larger circle of which he was
a part. I was ready for the experience. Here was a whole new scale of concerns.
Nothing happened in these paintings except radiance. All incident and as much
form as possible were eliminated for the sake of color and light.

I sent my radically changed work back to New York with the predictable
result: my dealer sent me a letter expressing regret that I was not painting as
before and preparing me for scant future sales. (Later in my history I was congratulated for having had the courage to give up a successful mode in order
to experiment.) But though the contemporary obligation to be original
caused me much discomfort, recent art history held numerous examples of
artists who had successfully changed their styles over the course of their development—Picasso, for one, that paragon of modernists. I also read an essay
about Melville that devoted special praise for the author's penchant for changing his style completely depending on the genre of book he was working on
at the time. But I wasn't Picasso or Melville, and it amazes me now that I continued to work with so much conviction in the face of all these worries. I
knew that I was still half-baked and had hardly begun to shed influences in
spite of having achieved a bit of outward success. There seemed no way of ever
shedding them. Would I ever achieve artistic maturity? I can see now that
these must have been my night thoughts at the time, because in the daylight
I painted unabatedly, constantly responding to new influences and incorporating them in my work. Perhaps I was beginning to be larcenous in the way
T. S. Eliot imputed to poets when he wrote, "Immature poets imitate, mature
poets steal."

The idea of *radiance* continued to consume me until my painting became
nearly all white. Standing one day on our balcony on the Giudecca I watched
an all-white Mediterranean cruise ship plow its light-filled way through the
milky summer haze of the Venice Marittima. I tried to paint this image, never
quite successfully, but in different ways I might be said to be still painting
images like it. I learned then to experience in actual practice what existentialism had earlier hinted at: useful work can be done if one is alert to the

truths offered by the intense apprehension of the *unique instance*. This has become my artistic credo. I slowly learned that the whole issue of originality is a false one. There are better catchwords available. How about "appropriateness"? What is the appropriate scale for any specific expression? Too big an area with too little in it results in a feeling of emptiness. Too many small details (usually but not necessarily serving a descriptive function) make a work seem fussy. How about "proper concern"? Not to walk away from the work too early nor to work on it too long. And finally, "self-assurance." We learn to trust ourselves as entities, learning thereby to be confident that any work from our hand will reflect our deepest values, the striving for internal coherence and understanding, a love of order tinged by those touches of chaos and spontaneity that are equally a part of life. "Art is a collaboration between God and the artist, and the less the artist does the better," said André Gide.

Over time one learns to distrust the orthodoxies of the outside world, even one's own overly conscious intentions. As Goethe observed:

> We are indeed born with faculties but we owe our development to a thousand influences of the great world, from which we appropriate to ourselves what we can and what is suitable to us. I owe much to the Greeks and the French, I am infinitely indebted to Shakespeare, Sterne, and Goldsmith but in saying this I do not exhaust the sources of my culture, that would be an endless as well as an unnecessary task. People are always talking about originality but what do they mean? As soon as we are born the world begins to work upon us and this goes on to the end. And after all, what can we call our own except energy, strength, and will. If I could give an account of all that I owe to great predecessors and contemporaries there would be but a small balance in my favor.

These were not ideas to stir up the young of 1957, although I have no doubt that more mature artists, then as now, understood them well. Every artist eventually must paint something that has not been seen before, but I have since found out that a headlong pursuit of originality may be the hardest way to get there. Like happiness, originality is best achieved by walking like a crab: look forward, but go sideways.

NOTES

All archival materials are in the Academy files unless otherwise specified.

1. Minutes of December 17, 1947, annual meeting of the members of the Institute, held at the Knickerbocker Club.
2. February 12, 1948.
3. February 13, 1948.
4. "Institute Splits on Thomas Attack," *New York Times*, February 14, 1948; "Worth Investigating," *New York Journal American*, March 2, 1948.

5. Mentioned in a letter from Gilmore D. Clarke to Dr. Douglas Moore, May 19, 1939. The Academy was cited on p. 73 of the "Citations" prepared by the Committee on Un-American Activities, December 18, 1948.

6. *Congressional Record: Proceedings and Debates of the 84th Congress, Second Session.*

7. June 4, 1952.

8. Report submitted at the annual meeting of the Institute, held at the Knickerbocker Club on January 17, 1950.

9. Undated.

10. May 25, 1946.

11. March 31, 1949.

12. Cited in minutes of Institute council meeting, January 30, 1956.

13. To Douglas Moore, January 15, 1956.

14. Malcolm Cowley to Felicia Geffen, November 29, 1954.

CHAPTER SEVEN

1958–1967

ROUNDING CAMELOT

Norman Mailer

IF THE EARLIEST ROSTER of the Institute can present such luminaries as Mark Twain, Henry and William James, Henry Adams, William Dean Howells, Edward MacDowell, and Augustus Saint-Gaudens, as well as Admiral Mahan, Theodore Roosevelt, and Woodrow Wilson, let us not be overcome by the short list of our immortals. The Institute, and by 1904 the Academy, was indeed seeded with these notable exceptions, but in large part the organization was not much more than another turn-of-the-century gentlemen's club, our collective panache not lacking in sideburns, cigars, and a vocation of sorts for the arts. We were, in short, a society that had been planned and planted to keep the riffraff out. The comments of Robert Underwood Johnson, Permanent Secretary for the first three decades, make the point: "The first step is to uphold . . . the dignity and distinction [of membership] and always to show undaunted faith in the civilizing mission of literature and the arts.[1]

Six decades later, the caliber of our members would have upset Robert Underwood Johnson (Henry Miller does come to mind), but we were still by our charter and its manacles (a.k.a. the bylaws) all but wholly incapable of any kind of effective social or political action.

That is the subtext to our endeavors in the decade 1958–1967. A period like others, rich with episode and anecdote, the sixties was also a political decade, and even if the Academy and Institute were less affected than our universities and government institutions (Congress and the Pentagon for two!) the Cold War was on full bore, and Washington had taken note of Soviet techniques in worldwide propaganda. So, from the Eisenhower through the Johnson administrations, overtures were made to the Academy-Institute. In part, the interest was cynical—national attention to the arts might be useful for constructing a facade to counter Soviet maneuvers in the arts—on the other hand, John and

Jacqueline Kennedy had begun to take a real interest in our existence by 1961. It is certain that the question of a new relationship of the Academy to the federal government developed. In the years following JFK's death, there was even a remarkably well articulated conference in 1966 to explore the possibilities of future relations between the federal government (the National Council on the Arts) and the Academy-Institute.

All the while, through the decade, we will find no dearth of interesting personalities, fine remarks, intriguing contretemps, subtle strainings of conscience, as well as Lewis Mumford's extraordinary, passionate, and excoriating condemnation of the war in Vietnam during the Joint Ceremonial gathering on May 19, 1965. There was also a remarkable amount of good writing for the Ceremonial and dinner addresses. Such pro bono prose is all but equaled by the exceptional dedication of the Academy and Institute presidents of those years: Glenway Wescott, Douglas Moore, Lewis Mumford, George Kennan, Malcolm Cowley, Allen Nevins, and their secretary, the redoubtable Felicia Geffen. Their letters to one another engender respect for the concept of an American Academy; it would be improper not to quote copiously from them. The finest hours of the organization are to be found in its words rather than its deeds.

1958 and 1959

The formal content of 1958 is, however, not remarkable. A. Whitney Griswold gave the Blashfield address at the Ceremonial; worthy in sentiment, it was quintessentially soporific: "The security of the United States depends as much upon the degree to which our culture and our way of life command the respect of the free nations and hold out hope to the people of the unfree, as it does upon our ability to overawe and impress either by military prowess and races in interstellar space."[2]

Earlier, at the first dinner meeting of the year, Glenway Wescott gave a beautifully written speech, "Never do I go to the oracle of Yeats in vain," and balanced such aesthetic bliss with the comment, "The remainder of the twentieth century may turn out to be a worse world than anything the human species has experienced to date," but then Wescott, like everyone around him in 1958, was living under the sword of nuclear war. "Not long ago," he remarked, "Bertrand Russell told his biographer that the secret of happiness is to face the fact that life is horrible, horrible, *horrible*. 'You must feel it deeply,' he said, 'and not brush it aside. You must feel it right in here,' and he beat his breast (or should one say) his chest—'and then you can start being happy.' "[3]

Still, it was a year in which the ranks of the Institute's literary members were swelled by none less than Saul Bellow, Kay Boyle, Arthur Miller, and

S. J. Perelman. At the dinner meeting on April 14, all the new inductees having been asked to offer a few remarks, Kay Boyle made an interesting point:

> It occurred to me not long ago that when writers, painters, musicians in the nineteen-twenties were honored by election to the National Institute of Arts and Letters, many of them would have been permanently settled in foreign countries and would not have been able to be here as we are tonight. That we are able to be here may be evidence that the creative American no longer needs to find a place, an atmosphere, outside of America, before he can produce his finest work. [Perhaps] there is place enough in the United States, as Gertrude Stein put it, to get away from home. Perhaps there is in the artist himself an awareness that his presence is essential here.[4]

In the minutes of the Academy board of directors meeting of December 5, 1958, a new note is sounded: "Secretary Allen Nevins reports that a communication has been received from the White House asking for our thoughts and recommendations regarding legislation setting up a Cultural Center in Washington DC, and asking the Academy to nominate a member to join the Advisory Committee on the Arts." A cultural front! But all that was still far away. The most intense discussion of 1959 would revolve around a censor's attack on John O'Hara, and it served to underline the essential paradox of the Academy and Institute.

O'Hara had for years been irked at not being voted into the Institute. In 1954, passed over once again for membership, he wrote in his column in the *Trenton Times-Advertiser*:

> I am, I think, All Boy, and yet I began to understand how a town girl feels: I was all right to play around with during the school year, but at Commencement the Yale Fellows always had a date with Thurber. . . .
>
> I have had much the same experience with a secret society called the National Institute of Arts & Letters.[5]

A little more than two years later, he was at last chosen by the Institute and immediately sent a letter off to Deems Taylor:

> *Dear Smeed:*
> . . . I plan to spend the afternoon with a razor blade, slitting the stitching in my lapel buttonholes to make way for the rosette. (Ready made clothes, you know.) . . .[6]

The American novel has probably never had as talented an author so preoccupied with clubs and clothes. O'Hara was therefore horrified when in the following year he came under a censor's attack. Immediately he dispatched the following letter to Malcolm Cowley, President of the Institute.

17 DEC. '57

Dear Malcolm:
I have been informed by counsel that my presence in New York makes me liable to service of papers compelling my appearance in Albany to answer charges of obscenity made against my novel, *Ten North Frederick.* I have been indicted on this charge, can be arrested, and held in prison until bail is found.

I had intended to go to tonight's dinner, and came to New York for that purpose. But I have been informed that the longer I stay in New York, the greater the risk, and I am therefore returning to Princeton and missing the dinner.

I am hopeful that I can count on the moral support of the Academy and the Institute. This is a dangerous action affecting not me alone.

Cordially,
John O'Hara

Cowley was away at the time, and O'Hara subsequently gave an interview to Publisher's Weekly in which he attacked the Authors' Guild, the Civil Liberties Union, and the Institute for failing to come to his aid. Cowley then responded with a long letter on November 26, 1958, almost a year after O'Hara's letter to him.

Dear John,
About that interview you gave to Publishers' Weekly—
You are absolutely right that the Institute should have done something about that indictment against one of its members, and about the danger of your being jailed for having written an honest book that added to the scope and richness of American literature. We didn't do anything publicly, and that is something I deeply regret. I was in Rome at the time but my absence can't be offered as an excuse. We couldn't have done anything quickly in any case, such as drafting a statement at the dinner meeting you couldn't attend, because the Institute has to go through a long procedure before issuing any public statement whatsoever. . . .

The rule was and is that none can be issued until (1) a complaint is submitted to the Council in writing; (2) the Council appoints an ad-hoc committee from a panel of 25; (3) the committee drafts a statement and submits it to the Council; (4) the Council approves the statement and submits it to the membership; and (5) the membership approves it by a majority of three-fourths of those voting.

Since the adoption of that rule in 1950, the Institute hasn't issued a single public statement. [I agree that] we should have gotten behind you with speed. But it's quite a job changing the rules of an institute, or institutions, and there would have to be a lot of members supporting the change. You ought to come to some more dinner meetings, and see how things work, and raise your voice. . . .

O'Hara responded on December 1. After thanking Cowley "for your good letter," he went on to say:

> Machinery should be available whereby in an emergency such as mine, with prison a very real threat, the Institute can state its support of the artist. Either a separate committee should be established for just such purposes, or the trustees should be empowered to speak for the organization after having been polled by telephone.
>
> I never intended to go to Albany. I did not retain counsel. The case, I strongly felt, was for the Guild, the Civil Liberties Union, and, if possible, the Institute to fight immediately, spontaneously, and thoroughly. . . . Whatever the reasons for the aloofness of the three organizations, the big fact on the record is that they did nothing.
>
> It may turn out to be a very unwise decision for American literature, and as though Pearl Harbor had been allowed to pass unnoticed. . . . Instead of staying out of these things the Institute should be the first to come to the defense of a member . . . if only to say to the world that membership carries distinction.

The case of John O'Hara (even if it was dismissed on a legal technicality and never quite became a case) occasioned a good deal of discussion at an Institute council meeting on February 3, 1959. Papers concerning the question of censorship were read by Glenway Wescott, Mark Van Doren, Malcolm Cowley, and Robert Penn Warren.

Wescott:

> The Institute is idealistic in other ways: dedicated to excellence, to strength of expression, to beauty of form. . . .
>
> So it behooves us—in the event of repressiveness toward our independent productive life, or toward particular creative products—not to seem aloof or indifferent.

Mark Van Doren:

> The Academy and the Institute . . . might take this single position: that censorship is in all cases undesirable because it does more damage to society than any work of art could do.

Cowley:

> Of course we should oppose the censors in nine out of ten cases that arise. But [we] shouldn't, for example, make a ringing declaration that would

commit us to the defense of someone who had written a handbook of abortion, or directions for robbing banks with case histories of successful robberies, or had argued for the assassination of the President. . . . I can think of dozens of instances where censorship is justified.

Robert Penn Warren:

To quote Thomas Hardy: "A novel which does moral injury to a dozen imbeciles and has bracing results upon intellects of normal vigor, can justify its existence; and possibly a novel never was written by the purest-minded author for which there could not be found some moral invalid or other whom it was capable of harming." He specifies that . . . it is not our duty to consider too closely the effect it may have on weak minds.

. . . Public agencies having to do with the arts should be under constant scrutiny and attack. The life of anyone who sets up as a censor should not be allowed to become a happy one.[7]

Of course, none of this could engage the bureaucratic problem of how the Academy or the Institute or both at once could act quickly. Cowley, before the meeting on February 3, had drafted a recommendation that the Council saw as too "complicated" and so authorized Wescott to appoint Van Doren, Cowley, Penn Warren, Gilmore D. Clarke, and Douglas Moore to prepare a statement on censorship for the dinner meeting.

A full year later, in February 1960 at the annual dinner meeting, the matter was more or less concluded: "a single statement of principle has not been decided upon; but the members have submitted to one another several excellent individual texts." In April the texts were sent to the Publications Committee and eventually appeared in the *Proceedings of the Academy and Institute* published in 1961, a few months before the censorship committee was disbanded. The ratiocinations of good men trapped in the legalisms of their forbears makes for a wistful denouement.

Let us not leave 1959 without some idea of the expressions of the membership on celebratory occasions. An invitation to give the annual Blashfield address had been sent to Adlai Stevenson, and he declined with a letter that improbably but definitively suffers from an excess of charm.

FEB. 12, 1959

Dear Mr. Van Doren:
I have thought long and anxiously about your letter of January 30. Surely no greater compliment has befallen me and I wish my gross vanity did not leave me in such disorder. But reason has prevailed at last and I must sensibly and promptly decline. I have been in austere company

before, but this is too much. Some time I hope I can tell you about the time I dined at Oxford with the Warden of St. Anthony, the Master of All Souls and the Principal of Jesus!

Anyway I enjoyed the flirtation with your letter.

Thank you, Sir, and I would like to come—and will—just to listen on May 20 if I can make it.

> *Cordially yours,*
> *Adlai E. Stevenson*

In Stevenson's absence, Meyer Schapiro was chosen to give the address, and it was exceptional in its brilliance. But then these were the years when Meyer Schapiro could not make a remark that failed to attain to the extraordinary. He had the rarest of minds: he could peer into the poetic relations of matters that appeared not to be related to each other or to poetry, and in this case, open our understanding of Abstract Expressionism:

> An abstract painter entering a room where a mathematician has demonstrated a theorem on the blackboard is charmed by the diagrams and formulas. He scarcely understands what they represent; the correctness or falsity of the argument doesn't concern him. But the geometrical figures and writing in white on black appeal to him as surprising forms—they issue from an individual hand and announce in their sureness and flow the elation of advancing thought. For the mathematician, his diagram is merely a practical aid, an illustration of concepts; it doesn't matter to him whether it is done in white or yellow chalk, whether the lines are thick or thin, perfectly smooth or broken, whether the whole is large or small, at the side or center of the board—all that is accidental and the meaning would be the same if the diagram were upside down or drawn by another hand. But for the artist, it is precisely these qualities that count; small changes in the inflection of a line would produce as significant an effect for his eye as the change in a phrase in the statement of a theorem would produce in the logical argument of its proof.[8]

Aldous Huxley was presented the Award of Merit for the novel on the same occasion and gave pleasure to everyone present who did not have a long neck:

> Enormous aspirations are not to be realized except by enormous power, and enormous power is something that has been denied me. Balzac, who was a veritable monster of power, maintained that all men of genius had short necks. How could it be otherwise? Genius, after all, is an alliance of head with heart, and the shorter the neck, the closer the alliance. So perhaps it all boils down to the fact that (unlike Balzac who had one of the shortest necks on record) I am the wrong shape. The thought, I find, is mildly consoling.[9]

Arthur Miller was given the Gold Medal for Drama at this Ceremonial, and if the award was certainly deserved, the speech was dependable. Miller, on occasion, managed to be witty when he spoke, but you could always count on him to be pious in the last sentence of the first paragraph: "[An] honor which [the artist] perhaps would not part with, but never truly takes as his own, because labor freely given and the joyful misery of creating cannot be translated into a prize."[10] Nonetheless, his presence was an event: Marilyn Monroe, then his wife, was in the audience.

At the annual dinner meeting on December 4 of that year, Douglas Moore gave a tribute to Ernest Bloch who had died recently: "There was an impish irreverence about him which made for unpredictability in public. I remember when a reporter, meeting him at the boat upon his return from Europe, asked him whether in his latest work he had used any new or unusual instruments. 'Yes,' he replied, 'the *crying child*. We have a child in the orchestra and when we come to the place in the score, we pinch him.' "[11]

Living with such an abundance of good names, it is also worth remarking how on December 15, 1959, at a joint meeting of the Academy board of directors and the Institute council, there were six candidacies filled for the honorary membership of foreign artists. Not chosen, however, were Samuel Beckett, Albert Camus, Henry Moore, and Frank O'Connor. The august wisdom of academies and institutes is obviously intermittent.

In compensation, Dorothy Parker was made a member of the Institute, and she sent a letter whose typing is replete with the bruises that come after a misspelling is pummeled by a correction:

> *Dear Miss Geffen,*
> my typewriter trembles to try to tell you how truly elated I am that I am to be a member of the National Institute of Arts and Letters. I didn't think this could ever happen to me. Now that it has—there is no living with me.
>   Miss Geffen, I can only say, in older words—I will try to be a good queen.
>
>

> *With gratitude,*
> *Dorothy Parker*[12]
>

Felicia Geffen was at her gracious best:

FEBRUARY 18, 1959

> *Dear Miss Parker:*
> What a priceless letter you wrote me!

1960 and 1961

In May 1960 a request came from Senator Case of South Dakota. He was looking for support of a bill that would provide for a National Academy of Culture.

Glenway Wescott wrote in answer that the proposal "somewhat unpleasantly surprises us."[13]

There were two obstacles. The proposed National Academy of Culture would have functions that would obviously overlap with the Academy; moreover, it appeared to be a *performing* arts center, the already appointed members being "a radio and TV personality, a band leader, and a football expert."[14] Nonetheless, by December 2 of 1960 (less than a month after President Kennedy was elected), the decision was taken to support the concept in order "to lend our influence . . . particularly with the coming of a new administration."[15]

The year 1960, however, is best distinguished by the remarks made on ceremonial occasions. On February 2, W. H. Auden delivered at the dinner meeting a remarkable set of aperçus on the meaning of love. The prose verse quoted is the thirty-eighth of a set of stunning perceptions:

> Do I love You? I could answer *No* with a certainty that I was speaking the truth on condition that you were someone in whom I took so little interest that it would never occur to me to ask myself the question; but there is no condition which would allow me to answer *Yes* with certainty. Indeed, I am inclined to believe that the more closely my feelings might approximate to the feelings which would make *Yes* the true answer, the more doubtful I should become. (Were you to ask, "Do you love me?" I should be readier, I believe, to answer *Yes*, if I knew this to be a lie.)[16]

At the Joint Ceremonial on May 25, E. B. White (who was probably most responsible for creating the tone of the old Harold Ross and William Shawn *New Yorker*) received the Gold Medal for Essays and Criticism. White's style—and his response here is a fair sample—may not wear well into the next century, for his wit can seem cloying:

> I do not know what charges you have levelled against me today, but I deny everything. I assume that I have been presented as a man of letters. A glance at the shelf of my published works leaves me wondering whether I am simply a man of indecision, a butterfly who has skipped from flower to flower to try the newest taste. My shelf begins with a thin volume of poems which, even allowing for my youth, are too weak for public recognition, and it ends with a thin book of rules which are so strong as to be presumptuous. In between are two works of fiction addressed to children, who, as you know, will put up with almost anything.[17]

Charles E. Burchfield, on being awarded the Gold Medal for Painting, gave a straightforward address, warm in its simplicity:

> There comes to mind the early days when I was just beginning my life's work. It was my custom then to walk to the spot where I wanted to paint. . . . Often I walked five or ten miles, and on many occasions I

would walk home in a driving rain with no protection other than ordinary clothes. My chief concern was that somehow the sketches of the day might be kept dry. . . .

If anyone had told me then that I would someday be the recipient of a gold medal from a group of distinguished artists drawn from all fields, as I am now, I would not have believed them, but I am sure I would have liked the idea.[18]

For the Blashfield address, Virgil Thomson delivered a set of refreshing if trenchant remarks:

There is far too much music in the world.

I do not feel this because I get tired of musical sound itself. Musical sounds are always a pleasure. It is unmusical sounds masquerading as musical ones that wear you down, and the commercializing of musical distribution has given us a great many of these as a cross to bear. It has also given such currency to our classics that even these the mind grows weary of. Because though musical sound is ever a delight, musical meaning, like any other meaning, grows stale from being repeated. Perhaps that is why so many of our contemporary composers feel safer hiding it.[19]

By 1961 it was evident that the election of John F. Kennedy would generate new attitudes and expectations in the Academy and Institute. An invitation was therefore extended to the President and First Lady to attend the Joint Ceremonial on May 24. Arthur Schlesinger, Jr., soon to be elected to the Institute, declined for them on February 11, in his capacity as Special Assistant to the President,

Dear Mr. Wescott:
Unfortunately the President and Mrs. Kennedy cannot attend the ceremonies in person; but both of them wish me to assure you of their pleasure over the invitation and their interests in the Institute. Both of them are eager to restore a sense of national dignity to the arts and letters.

At an Institute council meeting on April 11, Glenway Wescott noted that the Academy-Institute would do well to continue their objections to a new cultural center in Washington, despite the Kennedy administration's declared openness to the arts. It would be, in effect, a rival academy, and its public monies would be spent in the main on the performing arts whereas the Academy-Institute would prefer pensions to be established for some of their more indigent older members. Wescott's remarks are still pertinent:

Douglas Moore and I expressed our disappointment in the planning of the Cultural Center [inasmuch as] the visual arts and non-dramatic literature are not to be included in the activities. . . .

The Institute and the Academy conjointly are the one and only organization in the country, with a democratic unison of all the creative arts dedicated to the one purpose of upholding standards of literary and artistic excellence and of furthering creative interests, with national charters to that effect. . . .

The greatest American cultural problem is the poor remuneration of the lifework of so many creative men and women, even famous ones, including members of this Institute.

If a study of the present cultural situation by the federal and/or state governments ever is undertaken, one of its first concerns ought to be a detailed and realistic examination of the economics of literature and the arts; it would shock people. In the professions and in the sciences, in this country, good reputation and success go hand in hand for the most part, and success means prosperity. In the arts it is not so. Only a few authors are successful playwrights. Even novelists rarely make a living by their mere royalties. . . . Only a few visual artists are in fashion, with strong dealer support, at any given time. There is not a living in musical composition, unless it be musical comedies or sound tracks; composers all have to teach. . . .

Even at the height of our reputations, at the peak of our abilities, a great many of us must hold two jobs to support ourselves. . . . We wish that upon election to this Institute the meritorious, mature, and productive men and women of letters and the arts whom we elect could be given a modest pension, with a provision for its increase to a livelihood at a certain advanced age or in the event of incapacitating illness. [For] if we could invest just one half of the sum that is to be spent on the National Cultural Center building alone . . . it would provide a pension of $4,000 a year for our two hundred and fifty writers and artists and composers in perpetuity, and for our honorary foreign members besides; and also three annual international prizes larger than the Nobel Prize. [And if] the subsidy of ten million dollars that has been proposed for touring actors and ballet dancers were to be foregone for just one year, and given to us instead, in the way of capital investment, it would yield an income of about four hundred thousand dollars, with which we could do brilliant, useful things.[20]

Glenway Wescott was a tall, spare, distinguished, and handsome man with fine white hair and a youthful face; it is painful to think of how intensely he desired an American nation imbued with literary arts. Few presidents of the Institute could have given as much of themselves as he did, yet with it all he was a profoundly divided man, radical to the core, yet always overaccommodating to the traditions of the Institute.

An interesting example of Wescott in action can be gleaned from his passing relations with Robert Frost, who gave a dinner talk on the same day as Institute council meeting where Wescott had spoken.

Frost, in his later years, was dependably as pleased with himself as any American author has ever been. Indeed, Robert Frost's infatuation with Robert Frost may be the American romance of the century, and a minnow from this bottomless love for himself can be fished out of his remarks on April 11:

> The first thing I want to talk about is the government's interest in the arts, and what's been going on in Washington. I'd like to hear what the Academy and the Institute want, because I think I'm going to have some say about it. . . .
>
> I went down to Washington first to be at the Library of Congress as one of the poets who have tenure there as Consultant in Poetry. I made a complaint about that right away. I had a press conference and I told them that I had come down on a misunderstanding. I thought that I was to be consulted, as a poet, about everything. "But," I told them, "it appears by the sign on my door that I'm only to be consulted about poetry, and I've a good mind to go home." They said, "You needn't be limited to poetry any more," and they made me a consultant in the humanities.[21]

Frost then invited Glenway Wescott to meet with him in Washington. Frost was—he would let you know—in possession of the President's ear.

Here are excerpts from Wescott's letter to Douglas Moore concerning his visit. The date is May 3:

> You will recall the background of this matter: Mr. Frost's . . . insistence on his determination to do something in Washington, no matter what, for the recognition and support of the creative arts, and with expressions of extraordinary optimism about the influence he might have.
>
> I told him I was going to be in Washington on May 1, summoned by the advisory committee on the arts for the National Cultural Center. He then asked his friend, Mr. Udall, Secretary of Interior, to invite me to an evening with him in the State Department Auditorium the same night. . . .
>
> With a naivete not uncharacteristic of me, I thought that the evening with Frost would be, in some sense, a party, with a receiving line and a chance to talk. It was, in fact, only Frost's usual brilliant public performance, the great lyrics and the important sententiousness, introduced by the Secretary of the Treasury, to an audience not quite as sensitive as that at the YMHA, but wonderfully handsome and impressive. Justices of the Supreme Court, diplomats, senators, and all the youngish administration personnel. (As it was one of the nights of crisis about Laos, the White

House seats were empty.) [Afterward] I was *not* invited to a supper party by a great lady named (I believe) Mrs. Mahoney; I wandered around and around the State Department in a drenching rain, unable to find a taxi, and went to bed hungry and cross, feeling that it had been a waste of my time and energy, and of the Institute's travelling expenses.

But the next morning, [Mrs. Morrison], Mr. Frost's secretary . . . informed me that Mr. Frost was taking me to lunch with the Secretary of the Interior in the dining room attached to his office; [and that Frost had] asked me to come up to his room for an hour's conversation with him as soon as he got up.

That conversation was thrilling, really more like Benjamin Franklin than like Emerson, I thought, but *sui generis*—no deafness at all, and none of that rather stylized mumbling that he uses in his lectures; continuous early morning wit and anecdote and affection and good will— the tragic youthful romance of one of our poetesses; the kindness of A. MacLeish; the youthful Marxism of our great painter; what ought to be done about Cuba; Keats; and a great deal about our two organizations and the government. I found him not uninfluenceable, but really determined to get us affiliated with Washington in some way, kill or cure!

The philosophy of all this is of great interest—the "divine right" of the elected chief of state, embracing and using and assisting all the components of civilization, the arts as well as science and philosophy and military power, etc [but] let me say, with due respect and with love, that I took a somewhat negative line about some things he is proposing. He still wants a Secretary of the Arts in the Cabinet, or at least an under-secretary. . . .

When we arrived at the Department of the Interior, [the] luncheon was as agreeable as possible. . . . Partly for the humor of it, I began by telling Mr. Udall that we creative men would like to be dealt with in the Department of Interior . . . because we like to think of ourselves as a "natural resource," like water and parks and indeed oil; for example, as to our unfair tax situation, which the President is on record as hoping to ameliorate, we feel entitled to some equivalent of the "depletion allowance"; also sometimes we want to be regarded as wards or charges of the state, like the Indians. This amused them [although] I don't think anyone except Mr. Frost wanted a Cabinet post for the arts.

We all offered Mr. Frost the job, but wondered who would be competent to fill it in successive administrations.

Affectionately,
Glenway

On May 24, at the Joint Ceremonial, Douglas Moore opened with a surprise for many in the audience:

I am very fortunate this afternoon that instead of greeting you myself I can bring you a greeting from the President of the United States. We have received the following telegram addressed to Mr. Wescott and myself:

I WANT TO EXTEND TO THE NATIONAL INSTITUTE OF ARTS AND LETTERS AND TO THE AMERICAN ACADEMY OF ARTS AND LETTERS MY WARMEST GOOD WISHES AS YOU GATHER FOR YOUR ANNUAL CEREMONIAL MEETING. THIS HAS SURELY BECOME ONE OF THE MOST SIGNIFICANT DAYS IN OUR NATIONAL CULTURAL LIFE. YOUR MEMBERSHIP AND YOUR MEETING TODAY RENEW OUR NATIONAL DEDICATION TO THE VALUES OF THE FINE ARTS AND LITERATURE. . . .

MRS. KENNEDY JOINS ME IN SENDING BEST WISHES.

JOHN F. KENNEDY[22]

On that day, the Joint Ceremonial was also aided by Robert Graves, who gave perhaps the finest Blashfield address of the decade. Needless to say it had very little in common with government support for the arts.

An Arab village woman will prize the dented brass cooking pot that has done service for a generation or more, as having *baraka* and producing far tastier food than the brightest spun-aluminum saucepan in the bazaar. In the United States and England, a pair of blue jeans so often washed that they have faded almost white, or a well-worn gardening jacket, can equally possess *baraka*; and a wife's failure to recognize this while spring cleaning often causes a deal of trouble.

The West Village, the small district of Greenwich Village where I almost always stay when I come to New York, has *baraka* in abundance. Now of course the city planning authorities threaten to pull it down and rehouse the inhabitants in soulless sanitary residential apartments elsewhere—which seems to me a crazy project. [But we] are up against the Demon of Expendability [which dictates that when] a new appliance proves to have an uneconomically long life, it must be replaced by a shorter-lived substitute. . . . That these practices keep the wheels of industry turning, and salesmen busy, cannot be denied; but when nothing lasts long enough to become an integral part of a man's life, the principles of artificial obsolescence affect his friendships, loyalties, loves and his tastes in literature and art.

Anything made by hand has a certain glow of life. Factory-made objects are born dead—however apt their design, however sound their construction—and must have life breathed into them by affectionate use. . . . Scientists cannot explain such phenomena and therefore dispute the facts. Let them! *Baraka* will never be a scientific term [for it is] the quality of life in poems, or stories, or paintings, or sculptures or music [and] is never granted to a man more concerned with selling than with making.[23]

Nor were ironies absent. Mies van der Rohe, who would receive the Gold Medal for Architecture in 1963, was inducted (with high praise) into the Institute on the same day that Graves spoke, and Mies van der Rohe's citation read: "[He] has influenced more profoundly, perhaps, than any other man, the architecture of our time. He has sought from the beginning, with conviction and without compromise, to realize in the potentialities of modern materials and techniques and for the uses of the age an essential unity of architecture and structure, and his buildings in their austerity of structure and refinement of proportion achieve a classic authority and harmony."

This lapdog adulation for the elegance of Mies van der Rohe's designs hardly took into account how deadening would be the architectural progeny that would follow his "austerity of structure." We have the epigones to thank in large part for those faceless office buildings that ring our cities, those ethic-stripped insensate monoliths of the corporation that have by now ravaged every great cityscape of the world. What characterizes mid- and late-twentieth-century architecture is how majestic and self-vaunting are the sentiments of the architects and how void is the product. Proportion and scale, sun and shadow react upon the eye with all the verve of a Kleenex box fifty stories high.

During this same day of striking contrasts, Van Wyck Brooks presented to Fredric March the Medal for Good Speech on the Stage:

> From Walter Hampden to Katharine Cornell . . . it has signalized, though by no means every year, the most exemplary artists in our tortured American speech. I say tortured, for too many of the voices that reach us over the radio might be the voices of mud-turtles, endowed with the gift of language. They blur every syllable, they seem to speak with mud in the mouth, so that the novelist Howells said, "Who can defend the American accent which is not so much an accent as a whiffle, a snuffle, a twang?"
>
> So much more we rejoice in the men and women of the stage who belong to the royal family of fine speakers, one of whom is Fredric March.[24]

How can one not remark that another fine speaker was Van Wyck Brooks? Earlier that year, on February 16, Lewis Mumford was the keynote speaker in an evening of homage to Brooks at the dinner meeting:

> After first looking at our country with the severest eyes, with unsparing and remorseless scrutiny, showing the thinness even of Emerson, the vulgarity even of Whitman, after showing us America at its worst—he restored America to us. He made it a brave country we could associate ourselves with. He showed that there were unsuspected riches that we

had left lying around without bothering to pick them up. He discovered a phrase for all of this. He said there was a need for a "usable past." And who among us has given us more of that past than Brooks has done in the long succession of his works?[25]

To which Van Wyck Brooks responded: "I've always thought of artists and writers as the chosen people, and it's wonderful for me to think that some of them are fond of me as I am very fond of them."[26] He was responding not only to Lewis Mumford but to John Hall Wheelock, Mark Van Doren, his publisher Elliott Macrae, Matthew Josephson, Elizabeth Bishop, Louis Untermeyer, Maxwell Geismar, Glenway Wescott, Malcolm Cowley, Philip Evergood, Francis Hackett, Clare Leighton, Archibald MacLeish, William McFee, Allan Nevins, and Allen Tate—all present. Other messages arrived that night from Newton Arvin, Mr. and Mrs. Roger Baldwin, Hamilton Basso, Thomas Benton, Mr. and Mrs. Stuart Chase, Mrs. Frank I. Cobb, E. E. Cummings, John Dos Passos, Will Durant, James T. Farrell, Barry Faulkner, Hermann Hagedorn, Lillian Hellman, Alfred Kreymborg, Mr. and Mrs. Fredric March, Carson McCullers, Marianne Moore, Harry Murray, Walter Piston, Katherine Anne Porter, Carl Ruggles, Rudolph Ruzicka, John Saltonstall, William Carlos Williams, and Edmund Wilson, a representative roll call of our literary establishment in the early sixties.

If ever there was a time in the history of the Republic when the dream of our artists—that we might have some important influence on the mass of Americans—seemed possible of fulfillment, it was in the thousand days of Kennedy's presidency:

SEPTEMBER 8, 1961

Dear Mr. Wescott:

Miss Kay Halle turned over to me a few days ago two albums filled with letters from the writers and artists who were invited to the Inauguration ceremonies. Mrs. Kennedy and I have had extraordinary pleasure in going through these volumes. . . .

I am hopeful that this collaboration between government and the arts will continue and prosper. Mrs. Kennedy and I would be particularly interested in any suggestions you may have in the future about the possible contributions the national government might make to the arts in America. . . .

Sincerely,
John Kennedy

Another note was sounded, however, on December 1, 1961, at the annual meeting of the Academy:

Douglas Moore reports that "I attended a meeting of the Advisory Council for the National Cultural Center." President Kennedy spoke, urging that funds be raised for the erection of the Center as the first step in bringing about the realization of the larger plan. Moore continued, "Both Mr. Wescott and I think it grotesque to call it the National Cultural Center if it is to be used only for the performing arts and believe it might better be named the National Center for the Performing Arts." It was suggested that the Council of the Institute study the matter and through Arthur Schlesinger, Jr. find out if the President of the United States could be interested in the Academy–Institute's views.[27]

Yes, even in a period of optimism and real expectation, motions to raise the level of culture always began with raising the building. (And the building was usually arid enough in conception to depress the level of culture.) Meanwhile, insufficiently heralded artists, dying for a stipend, did just that—died.

1962

Early in the year, at the dinner meeting, Glenway Wescott stepped down as president of the Institute, and Malcolm Cowley was elected. His first act in office was to say that as he saw it, "There were three prerequisites for the presidency: willingness to preside over meetings; proximity to New York; and not too great an eagerness for the job." Cowley added that in his belief he possessed all three qualifications.[28]

By April he was busy with matters concerning the Institute's Audubon collection. In a letter to Hannah Josephson on April 7, he remarked:

> First, we don't *have* to give the collection to the Library [of Congress]. If it is indeed extremely valuable, it might be our duty to sell it and devote the proceeds to cultural purposes. But we ought to show consideration for the donor by (1) keeping the collection intact and (2) seeing that it passed into the hands of some other cultural institution. . . .
>
> The Elephant Folio of Audubon's "Birds" is pretty nearly the Mona Lisa of the book world. God knows how much it would bring, especially in combination with the "Quadrupeds." We don't have to be in a hurry to sell.

At a board of directors meeting on May 23, it was agreed that the collection should not be given to the Library of Congress. Allan Nevins remarked that would be equal to "throwing a bucket of water into the Atlantic Ocean."[29] The Elephant Folio was eventually sold in 1966 for the then record but now modest price of $60,000.

One author who was legendary for the distance he had placed between himself and practical matters in the literary world was honored by Eudora

Welty in the Ceremonial on May 24, 1962: "Mr. Faulkner, your work and our love for it have both been alive for a long time now, as your work will be after we are not. A medal may not last nearly so long, yet its worth is that it . . . can be held in the hand, taken by some appointed hand and put in the hand it belongs to." William Faulkner's speech of acceptance was given in a quiet voice and at a great rate. Few who were there could hear him, but his appearance was an event. Invited to the White House for dinner but a few weeks before, he had declined on the nineteenth-century premise that one should not travel one hundred miles for dinner. Yet here he had come from Chancellorsville, in Virginia, all the way to New York, a good three hundred miles. He said:

> I think that those gold medals, royal and unique above the myriad spawn of their progeny which were the shining ribbons fluttering and flashing among the booths and stalls of forgotten county fairs in recognition and accolade of a piece of tatting or an apple pie, did much more than record a victory. They affirmed the premise that there are no degrees of best; that one man's best is the equal of any other best, no matter how asunder in time or space or comparison, and should be honored as such.
>
> We should keep that quantity, more than ever now, when roads get shorter and easier between aim and gain and goals become less demanding and more easily attained.[30]

By 1962 the Joint Ceremonial, building now on the growing sense of importance provided by the overtures of the Kennedy administration, had become a prestigious affair. Three Nobel Prize winners—Pearl Buck, William Faulkner, and Alexis Léger—were on the platform, and another telegram came from President Kennedy. Allan Nevins gave the Gold Medal for History to Samuel E. Morison, and Aldous Huxley flew in from Los Angeles to offer the Blashfield address. I. A. Richards accepted the Loines Award, and Julie Harris was given the Medal for Good Speech on the Stage, yet some brief remarks by Alan Dugan attracted the greatest attention in the *New York Times* the next day. We will need background for that curious event.

On May 23, 1962, the Academy-Institute offered these comments on a contretemps in Rome:

> In 1951 the Board of Directors authorized a fellowship in literature to be conferred on a young American writer for a year's residence at the American Academy in Rome, the procedure being that the grant committee name two or three candidates in order of preference, subject to the approval of the Rome Academy. Up to this year the system worked smoothly; all the first choices had been accepted.
>
> This year the first choice was John Williams, "a Negro novelist." As had been done previously, Williams was asked if he would accept the fellowship if it were offered; through Williams' publisher it was ascer-

tained that he would be free to go. Douglas Moore then wrote to Williams, informing him of the award, but stating that it was subject to the approval of the American Academy in Rome.

Mr. Kimball, the new director of the Rome Academy, interviewed Williams and recommended to the Executive Board of the American Academy in Rome that Williams should not be elected a fellow, basing his rejection on the impression that Williams would not be a suitable member of the "Academy family."

The Rome Academy was then given the name of this Academy's second choice, Alan Dugan, who was accepted by them.

Kimball informed Felicia Geffen of this by phone and told her that he would write to Williams, explaining why he had been rejected. Geffen was then authorized to write Williams informing him that the Institute was now free to award him one of the arts and letters grants. . . . Williams signified that he would accept the grant and as a result his name was printed on the invitation and the program for the ceremonial. On May 7, however, Williams wrote to Douglas Moore that he had reconsidered.

Dear Mr. Moore:

. . . I am delighted that the Institute has thought me worthy of so high an honor, but the events leading up to the granting of that award are of such an ambiguous nature that I have come to the conclusion that I cannot in good conscience accept the grant. . . .

> *Sincerely yours,*
> *John A. Williams*

Douglas Moore then received a letter from Malcolm Cowley:

MAY 10, 1962

Dear Douglas,

Having examined the correspondence and clippings concerning the Williams affair, I am more than ever distressed. . . . The general misconception that prevails in literary circles is (1) that Williams was rejected by the Academy in Rome because he was a Negro; (2) that [we] took the rejection tamely, without any sort of protest; and (3) that the American Academy of Arts and Letters is also affected with racial bias, being—as some of the newspapers put it—the "parent body" of the American Academy in Rome."[31]

Cowley suggested that the arrangement with the Rome Academy be terminated. The board of directors concurred. There was a further complication, however. After Cowley, as a mark of respect, had read at the Joint Ceremonial the citation for the award that John Williams had declined, he was obliged to add: "On account of the confusion about the Prix de Rome fellowship, Mr. Dugan has asked to say a few words."

Dugan did. A lean Irishman with dark hair, a saturnine manner, and a glowering disposition—his mien was as hard-bitten as eight-penny nails—Dugan spoke out as soon as his citation was read:

> I want to make a brief statement on this award. . . .
>
> 1. If the jury of the American Academy of Arts and Letters and the Institute had been firmer in their dealings with the American Academy in Rome this painful situation would not have happened.
> 2. . . . The American Academy of Arts and Letters should define its relation with the American Academy in Rome. . . .
> 3. My personal position is: I will take the money from the Academy during this confusion and I will go to Rome in the hope that they will behave better in their future awards.[32]

Gone was all the éclat of the Nobel Prize winners, gone the plaudits awarded that afternoon to William Faulkner, Aldous Huxley, I. A. Richards, Julie Harris, Samuel E. Morison. The *New York Times* gave almost all of their account of the proceedings over to Dugan's short acceptance speech, and Cowley was sufficiently exercised to write a two-page single-spaced complaint on May 27 to Orvile Dryfoos, the president of the *Times*. Unfair is unfair! went the tenor of his letter. (As if the *New York Times* would be quick to feel shame!) But then, the day before, Cowley had received a nice letter from a lady in New Rochelle named Mrs. Horst W. Jansen, and even that may not have improved his mood.

MAY 25, 1962

Dear Mr. Cowley:
Unable to attend the awards meeting at the Academy yesterday, the report was the first thing that I looked for in this morning's "Times." My hair is standing on end! . . .

Over the past 10 years [my husband and I] have been privileged to stay at the Academy in Rome as guests—the last time as "in-residents" in 1960—three times, and are very much attached to it. . . . That some talented people (by no means all!) can be a pain in the neck hardly comes under the heading of news: 'twas ever thus.

That Mr. Kimball was made director with some kind of mandate to "clean up the mess" was evident from the start of his tenure. I have nothing against Mr. Kimball, but whatever faction had put him into the office had better take him out again. He has, in pursuit of the aims of stiffening the moral tone of the Academy and making it into a homogeneous community, been going about it as though it were a tony prep school. While we were there everyone had a good laugh over an announcement on the bulletin board that "the improper entertainment of persons of the opposite sex" in the rooms would not be countenanced. There is nothing in the least wrong with such a ruling, but as Mr. Broughton immediately pointed out to him, one cannot deal with the problem in this manner even with students at college level, let alone a bunch of adults. Within a half hour of its posting, someone had scribbled, "How about the same sex?" on the margin, and it thereupon disappeared. . . .

Now, along comes this very adverse piece of publicity. . . .

Dora Jane Jansen

On September 24, 1962, the board of directors of the Academy passed a resolution that the American Academy of Arts and Letters Fellowship to the American Academy in Rome be discontinued.[33] Following the announcement of this ruling in the press, John Williams accepted the Grant in Literature from the Institute that had been awarded to him in May.

Robert Lowell's tribute to Marianne Moore is worth noting. At a dinner meeting on November 15, he said: "Miss Moore staggers me. In one of her poems, she says, 'it takes a curious hand to describe grace.' I fear I can only bring a crude hand to describe her grace."[34]

Let us conclude this year with Henry Cowell's tribute to Charles Ives:

He once told me, "Henry, you know, people in congregations don't sing on account of the music. They sing to express their religious feeling," and he should have known because he played a church organ, you see, for Heaven knows how long. He went on, "Of course, there are always some people who play or sing the notes exactly as they are written. Those are people who have a good sense of pitch, and they're more musical. But," he added, "if you are very enthusiastic about religion, you are almost sure to sharp. And on the other hand, if you are a backslider, you'll flat."[35]

1963

Since good writers take pride in their aristocratic superiority to self-interest (and hope in private that this is true) there are only subtle indications of how much optimism was being generated in Academy and Institute circles by the presence of Camelot. One indication, however, may appear in the Joint Ceremonial of May 22, 1963. In most years, the opening remarks rise rarely above the genteel note of institutional welcome. On this occasion, however, Lewis Mumford, now president of the Academy, was having a vision!

I bid you welcome to our annual spring ceremonial. This festive civic occasion, magnified by your presence, resembles—though, of course, in a somewhat muted way—such a grand ushering in of the spring as used to take place in fifth-century Athens at the festival of Dionysus. During the Great Dionysia, for three days, other duties were laid aside so that all citizens might give themselves unreservedly to the purgative rituals of the season, saturating themselves in the day-long performance of tragic and comic dramas, accompanied by music and dance.

Before the presidential claims of office curbed such fantasies, I used to dream of our society's following the Athenian precedent, by devoting the better part of a week to such spring celebration: one day perhaps for the recitation of poems, another for the performance of new musical compositions, a third for reading works in progress, interleaved by fresh literary criticism, and still another day for the critical appreciation of new works of painting, sculpture and art.

Today those of us who love the arts feel cheated by the poor scraps and morsels that are thrown to us by radio, television, and journalism. We often long for the opportunity to respond to works of art and literature with our full energies and our undivided minds, in the spirit of those who created them, free from interruptions and extraneous pressures [but] as you know, our whole economy is a far-reaching conspiracy to prevent our inner life, or indeed any kind of life, from flourishing unless it fits obediently into our bureaucratic routines and can be profitably channeled into a machine or an electronic device. . . .

Our over-aggressive effort to conquer nature is now enslaving man to his scientific and technological liberators [and] our formless megalopolises have turned out to be anti-cities; our growing masses of scientific knowledge function increasingly as anti-knowledge; our random pollution of the habitat by pesticides and poisonous wastes expresses our prevalent anti-organic bias. And finally, what is our demoralized commitment to collective nuclear and bacterial extermination but a colossal expression of anti-humanity? . . .

Do not think that I am violating the Dionysian spirit of this occasion by dwelling for a moment on the dark side of our culture; one must recognize Bacchus's death before his resurrection can take place. The spring festival at Athens, although it celebrated the rising sap of life, was equally dedicated to facing life's tragic moments: its vulnerability to malign chance, to purpose-defeating disorder, to the grim Fates and the sadistic Furies, to both premature and eventual death. Only by consciously facing these threats can we summon forth from our own interiors the spiritual energy that will bring about our own renewal. . . . As writers and artists [we dedicate ourselves to] the increase of human consciousness. . . that passion is our life.

I now invoke the spirit of Dionysus, god of bread and wine, of procreation and passionate love, of ecstasy and insurgence, he who triumphs over death and replenishes life, to preside over this ceremonial.[36]

In 1963, one could still hope that America would yet come of age and artists would take their rightful place at the center of our culture. American life might even be enriched sufficiently to fill a few of those empty places in our American soul. Mumford might have done better to propitiate the spirit of Thanatos. This is the year in which John F. Kennedy will meet the bullet of his assassin.

The beginning of 1963 had been quiet for the Academy-Institute. Irked by the fiasco with John Williams, the Academy had decided to establish its own traveling fellowship for Europe. Early in the year, it was awarded to Anne Sexton.

FEB. 6TH, 1963

Dear Miss Geffen:
I cannot tell you how happy I am to accept. . . . I feel quite sure that it will have a powerful and much needed impact upon my work. I tend to get a lot out of a new experience and I am tremendously excited about the prospect of this one. . . . I have already pasted a large map of Europe onto my kitchen wall. . . .

I am really thrilled!

Most sincerely yours,
Anne Sexton

FEBRUARY 11, 1963

Dear Miss Sexton:
Thanks for your happy letter and the lovely account of your plans. . . .

Very sincerely yours,
Felicia Geffen

NOV. 5TH, 1963
ANNE SEXTON
40 CLEARWATER RD.
NEWTON LOWER FALLS, MASS. 02162

Dear Miss Geffen and Dear American Academy, etc—
This is a letter of failure. If you can bear with me I will try to explain why I am "home" and not in Europe. I could, I am aware, just tell you that I am home under doctor's care and that he forbids any further extensive travel.

And yet I think there is a point to my failure. As the salmon fight upstream to spawn I fought to stay in Europe. Everywhere my eyes and senses were stimulated and excited. But I began to feel smaller and smaller—unreal. There is more to it than that. It is called in psychiatric terms "impoverishment of the ego." . . . For someone with my "history" staying was becoming an endurance test, and in the doctor's word a "luxury," a "skating on thin ice."

You, I know, did not intend the trip to be that way. Even when I said "yes" I knew I'd have trouble (but I have trouble at home) but I wanted to see, to know, to find out with my own eyes.

Perhaps now I have learned only one thing, a very American thing— that to fail (the endurance shattered, broken into small unimportant pieces) is the ultimate humiliation. How does one muddy oneself with failure in this "literary marketplace" and survive? There is something about it that is not respectable ... to crawl home, shrunken, hardly a wife,

Ceremonial, 1963. Anne Sexton, winner of the traveling fellowship, being congratulated by Malcolm Cowley. (Budd Photograph)

hardly a mother—and even the writer has fled. I left suddenly, the thin ice breaking under me . . . left clothes and books and my car in Rome.

I was most honored by your award to me—and have still no wish to dishonor it. That is why I write you now, although I am still incoherent—because I felt you deserved to know first—not via the grapevine "Sexton cracked up" and all that. . . .

Damn! It is hard to send you this. A bludgeon to my pride and even worse, to hope and to that bright place, "a year abroad."

I know this letter isn't very official in tone. I could not. Drowning is not so pityful [*sic*] as the attempt to rise.

> *With sincerity,*
> *Anne Sexton*[37]

In the sad state of her return to America, in the depths of her breakdown—or, what may be worse, her semibreakdown—she finds the creative means to give the best explanation of the odd dislocated turmoil so many Americans feel in Europe; she gets right down to the secret of it and gives us a penetrating insight: Going to Europe for the first time leaches out the very salts of one's ego. A sojourn on the Continent is equal to a crisis in one's identity; the artist discovers (and it is the woe to be avoided beyond all others—since of all professions, ours has the most perishable construction of ego) that we are a lot less than we thought we were.

Not all communications to Miss Geffen are so sad. Here, for example, is a letter from John Steinbeck:

APRIL 25, 1963

Dear Miss Geffen:
You must admit that our communications are seldom, but unusual. This one is screwy, also.

A number of years ago, when my oldest son was a little boy, he wore the little winged horse of the Academy to school and lost it. Maybe he sold it or melted it down or threw it away. Anyway, he said he lost it and since he lost everything else, perhaps he did. Ever since I have wanted to ask you whether it can be replaced. I would be very happy to pay for the replacement. Can it be done?

> *Yours very sincerely,*
> *John Steinbeck*

APRIL 26, 1963

Dear Mr. Steinbeck:
It is always good to hear from you, even though the last time it was about a lost button and this time about a lost horse! Your little boy was playing

with a very expensive toy because the replacement of the Academy medallion will cost in the neighborhood of $60.00, since it is 14 carat gold. Are you willing to pay this much for its replacement?

27 APRIL 1963

Dear Felicia Geffen:
Thank you for your letter of yesterday. I was well aware of the metallic value of the little horse and am quite willing to pay for its replacement. My boy always had a sense of values. For example, he never lost a Commonwealth Club gold medal which was so thinly plated that I could not trade it for ten pounds of dried beans when I needed them. Just tell me the amount and I will send you a check for the replacement. . . .

At the Joint Ceremonial on May 22, Robert Penn Warren posthumously presented the Gold Medal for Poetry to William Carlos Williams and delivered a tribute to Williams at the dinner meeting in November. To capture Williams' primal connection to the act of writing poetry, Penn Warren quotes from an anecdote related by the poet:

"In Uncle Billy Abbott's class at Horace Mann we read a book of Robert Louis Stevenson's—a travel book I think it was. There was a young man and an upset canoe and a line that said, 'I never let go of that paddle.' I was crazy about that line. I'd say it over and over to myself."

He, apparently, kept saying it over and over to himself all his life. And the world is richer for the fact that he never let go his paddle.[38]

The minutes of October 21, 1963, are the comic tempest before the upheaval that visited America on November 22, 1963:

Joint Meeting of the Board of the Academy and the Council of the Institute—Lillian Hellman noted that the Ceremonials seemed endless to her and lacked theatrical form. Virgil Thomson reacted by saying that tickets for these events had always been at a premium and that hundreds of people were turned away each year. He maintained that this was not intended to be a theatrical performance and that what was of prime importance was the quality of the award winners and the eminence of the speakers. A committee was appointed to study the problems having to do with the Ceremonial: Lillian Hellman, Virgil Thomson and Henry Cowell.[39]

On December 7, 1963, twenty-two years after Pearl Harbor, a press release from the Academy gives its echo of the national disaster two weeks earlier. In his letter of condolence to Mrs. Kennedy, Lewis Mumford wrote: "He gave our vocations a place of dignity and honor in the national life as no other president has done before him. Our gratitude for his generous initiatives on behalf of the arts extends in equal measure to you, as his companion and helper in the effort."[40]

1964 and 1965

In the gloom of January 1964 there was a meeting of all the museum directors of Audubon Terrace; common concerns were discussed, most specifically, building security. The minutes relate: "The problem has become very difficult in recent years because of the decaying neighborhood. Teenagers climb or slip through the gates after they are closed, and the terrace is said to be a place where addicts congregate to obtain drugs."[41] All agreed that the present security arrangements were not sufficient. The first tolling of the bell is heard in the Academy. We are going around the turn in the American Century from Empire to acromegaly. The megalomania of Vietnam is close upon us.

There are few signs of this, however, at the dinner meeting on April 1, where newly inducted members were asked to speak:

MR. COWLEY: ... I should like to call upon Mr. John Updike as the youngest member elected to this body in many years, perhaps from the beginning.

Academy meeting, December 6, 1963. Left to right: *Mark Van Doren, W. H. Auden, and Marianne Moore.*

JOHN UPDIKE: Thank you. I feel in this company like hiding behind the dictum that children should be seen and not heard.

I have prepared no real address. I have just one slip of paper in my pocket. In writing fiction, you tend to wonder why you do it and why people care so much about it—because people do care. They care quite intensely, negatively and positively. Once in a great while I hear from people who seem to care about me almost more than I do myself—who feel, that is, very keenly, the importance of fiction, which this Institute, among other arts, honors.

Recently I was sent . . . a little paragraph from Pascal that I had not read and maybe some of you haven't. I don't know what number Pensée it is. It goes: "When a natural discourse paints a passion or an effect, one feels within oneself the truth of what one reads, which was there before, although one did not know it. Hence one is inclined to love him who makes us feel it, for he has not shown his own riches, but ours."

These are rather strong terms perhaps, but I think it is a nice idea that, in trying to write, you are attempting to disclose to people riches that are not your own but theirs; and indeed, it is a good way to conceive of all human intercourse.

Academy meeting, 1964. Seated, left to right: *Leon Kroll, Malcolm Cowley, Marianne Moore, Lewis Mumford, Lillian Hellman, and Allen Tate.* Standing, left to right: *Douglas Moore, Peter Blume, Glenway Wescott, Gilmore D. Clarke, Edward Hopper, John Hersey, Edwin Dickinson, Jacques Lipchitz, Barry Faulkner, Paul Manship, and Robert Lowell.*

A moving talk, indeed, under the pressure of the occasion, and Updike's presentation was nicely followed by Ralph Ellison:

RALPH ELLISON: ...As a kid in Oklahoma I read some of you. I listened to some of your music. Indeed, I might possibly have seen some of your art reproduced in *Vogue* and *Vanity Fair* and *Harper's* and so on. You could not possibly have known of my existence because even with all of the more obvious reasons discounted there remained the fact that I come from one of the lesser explored areas of American life. Nevertheless, I knew of you, and across the whirling chaos of our society you spoke to me and contributed to that creative restlessness that sends young people away from the provinces in search of the world of art and the artist.[42]

At the Joint Ceremonial on May 20, 1964, the Award of Merit for the Novel was given to John O'Hara, who said in his acceptance: "The first author to receive [this] Award of Merit was Theodore Dreiser, an author with whom I have much in common. The second was Thomas Mann, whose work I admired. The third was Ernest Hemingway, who was a friend of mine, and as some of you may recall, the author of a book which I reviewed favorably, and in so doing may have set back the cause of favorable reviews a couple of decades."[43]

It was probably the most favorable review of the American century. Appearing on September 10, 1950, in of the *New York Times* Sunday book section, page one, it showered encomiums on *Across the River and into the Trees* (which may have been Hemingway's weakest work), calling Hemingway "the outstanding author since the death of Shakespeare ... the most important, the outstanding author out of the millions of writers who have lived since 1616."

Early in 1965 President Johnson, hard at work on two opposed projects—beefing up the war in Viet-

Ceremonial, 1964. Lewis Mumford, Academy president, at the reception on the terrace. (Budd Photograph)

nam, and building his Great Society—was, in the course of the second, making overtures to the artistic community. He proposed a "national foundation of the arts" to "help promote and honor creative achievements."[44] Since Johnson did not seem aware of the Academy or the Institute, George Kennan, new president of the Institute, wrote to McGeorge Bundy in January to inform him of their existence:

> "I do think it essential . . . that anything done in this field take full account of the Institute's . . . interest in the furtherance of the arts; I feel sure that the President would wish to consult its experience before taking steps toward the establishment of any sort of new foundation."
>
> At a Joint Meeting of the Board of the Academy and the Council of the Institute on February 13 . . . Lewis Mumford remarked that he would be very glad to go to Washington with Kennan should they be invited to discuss the matter further.[45]

It is interesting that this is only four months before Mumford will make his unforgettable speech about Vietnam at the Ceremonial on May 19. On February 1, he is, however, still interested in going to Washington. The desire of the artist and the intellectual to have an impact on the political process can approach the intensity of thirst. To possess power in one's mind to see further than others and have no access to those who change the shape of society is equal to a parching of the spirit. Mumford wished to go to Washington. By May 19, 1965, however, the buildup in Vietnam was undeniable. The legitimate desire to obtain some national influence (who indeed had thought more intensely and more consecutively than Lewis Mumford on many a relevant national matter?) would now suffer. He could not in good conscience approach a government whose military policies he abominated. So, at the Joint Ceremonial, his welcoming address was aimed at the war; he broke, thereby, one of the basic rules of the Academy and the Institute: no open political discussion is appropriate on celebratory occasions. While his audience listened in bewilderment, rapt silence, joy, and audible displeasure—the president of the most august literary society in the nation was attacking the nation!—Mumford gave a splendidly prescient and daring speech. To attack the war in Vietnam this early was shocking even to the majority of his audience, presumably liberal.

> Traditionally, this ceremony, with its bestowal of honors, prizes, and awards, has an air as festive as the spring itself [and] should not be marred by any somber or discordant note.
>
> But as the ancient Greeks well knew, one cannot escape the Fates or the evil Furies when they are pursuing a man or a people. And I cannot artificially manufacture an atmosphere of joy for this meeting, when under the surface of our ritual a rising tide of public shame and

private anger speaks louder than my words as we contemplate the moral outrages to which our government, with increasing abandon, has committed our country.

Last year when we met here, the pain of unhealed grief, occasioned by the assassination of President Kennedy, still gnawed at our hearts. And this year an equally ominous black cloud, also the symbol of unpredictable and irrational violence, hangs over our own land and people, even as it hangs over the peoples of Vietnam and the rest of Asia, threatening the lives and prospects of our own younger generation, staining the good name of our country, and violating the peace of the world.

Now, on such grave national issues, institutions like ours have no special license to express an opinion, even if we had any mechanism for formulating a common judgment and recording our reasoned convictions. So, in what I say to you now, I speak on my own initiative alone, without consulting a single other member, addressing you and my colleagues not as President of the American Academy of Arts and Letters, but as a private citizen, appealing to our common love for our country. . . .

At this moment I would be untrue to the best traditions of our country, the proud home of a Jefferson, an Emerson, a Thoreau, a William James, if I remained discreetly silent and encouraged you, too, to close your eyes and your ears to the realities we must now face. By what legal or moral code has the United States a right to exercise political authority or military coercion on a distant foreign country like Vietnam? Obviously we have no more reason to have our will prevail in Vietnam than Soviet Russia had to establish rocket bases in Cuba; and if Russia could liquidate that blunder and withdraw under pressure, our own country can do the same in Vietnam—and all the better if the pressure come, not from an outside power, but from our own citizens. . . .

Twenty years ago, our country reached the height of its authority and influence by generous acts of succor to the starving wartorn countries of the world. . . . Instead of building on that massive foundation of good will, foolish men allowed the invention and exploitation of nuclear weapons to foment delusions of grandeur based on absolute power; and as a result of our growing preoccupation with this kind of power, a vast network of secret agencies, armed with secret weapons, prepared with secret plans, have committed our country to a strategy and a policy whose dehumanizing effects, though visible from the beginning, are now being nakedly exposed. As a result, from the heights of effective power that our country had achieved, by evoking the admiration and gratitude and even love of other nations, we have now descended to the depths of political and military impotence; and still more sinister depths of demoralization already yawn beneath us.

The whole world has reason to fear such leadership and unite against it; and our own citizens have perhaps even more to fear, for this is the first time in our history that a victorious presidential candidate has dared to carry out the odious policy that caused his rival to be rejected. One may well question the value of a democratic election when confronted by such totalitarian outcome.[46]

Mumford's speech had its instant repercussion. The painter Thomas Hart Benton, writhing in his seat on the stage, soon shocked the four-score luminaries assembled up there with him by declaring, "I'm not going to listen to this shit!"[47] and storming off the platform. Ten days later, Benton sent in a letter of resignation and gave an interview to Leonard Lyons of the *New York Post*. "It's all a lot of artistic snobbery anyway, the Academy. . . . Most of the members came under Marxist influence in their youth. It's impossible now for a Midwesterner to get in. It's corrupt, like the French Academy."[48]

Not a year later, in March 1966, Benton was reinstated, and Mumford resigned. There is no doubt that he was bitter. From a letter to Babette Deutsch on May 4, 1966: "I celebrated my 72nd birthday by resigning from the American Academy when I found out, by accident, that they had lost no time after I had stept [*sic*] down from the Presidency in bringing Benton back again. . . . Without an apology for his conduct, they were in fact repudiating me—as they probably wanted to do, but lacked the courage—while I was still President,—well, that's over, and I feel definitely relieved."

Conceivably, his decision to resign was in part the product of a letter from George Kennan:

BELLAGIO, LAKE COMO, ITALY
JUNE 5, 1965

Dear Mumford:
. . . I understand and respect the anguish of spirit that moved you to make this statement. It is an anguish which, in large measure, I share. Nevertheless, the use of the recent ceremony as an occasion for giving expression to it was, as I see it, something which, in the interests of the Academy itself and the purposes to which it is dedicated, had been better omitted. . . .

In taking this position, I am very much aware that questions of this nature are ones of conscience. . . . My conscience would have dictated a different answer; but . . . however the matter develops, you may be sure that I shall not be unmindful either of your great services to American thought and letters generally or of the extent to which I personally am indebted to you for the enrichment of my own understanding of the trends of history and the problems of our own time.

It would not do to quit 1965 without a mention of John Cheever's acceptance speech on receiving the Howells Medal for Fiction: "When *The Wapshot Scandal* was completed my first instinct was to commit suicide. I thought I might cure my melancholy if I destroyed the novel and I said as much to my wife. She said that it was, after all, my novel, and I could do as I pleased, but how could she explain to the children what it was I had been doing for the last four years?"[49]

1966

On May 25, the day of the Joint Ceremonial, Edward Albee, John Kenneth Galbraith, Francis Steegmuller, and William Styron were inducted into the Institute, as were David Diamond, Moses Sayer, and Jose Luis Sert. The new honorary members were, among others, Isaiah Berlin, Pierre Boulez, C. Day-Lewis, and Herbert Read. J. Bronowski gave the Blashfield address and Romare Bearden, Ezio Martinelli, William Alfred, John Barth, James Dickey, Shirley Hazzard, Josephine Herbst (honored at last!), and Gary Snyder were among

Ceremonial, 1965. John Cheever receiving the William Dean Howells Medal from Ralph Ellison. The medal, given for the best novel from 1960 to 1964, was awarded to Cheever for The Wapshot Scandal. (United Press International)

Ceremonial, 1965. Left to right: Kevin Roche, winner of the Brunner Prize in Architecture, with Institute president George F. Kennan and Walter Gropius, who presented the award.

those receiving awards. The Loines Award for Poetry went to William Meredith, and the Gold Medals for Sculpture and for Music were given respectively to Jacques Lipchitz and Virgil Thomson.

Yet all of this was dwarfed next day by the Conference on Government Participation in the Arts and Humanities, attended, among others, by Milton Babbitt, Peggy Bacon, Jacques Barzun, George Biddle, Isabel Bishop, Peter Blume, Catherine Drinker Bowen, Bruce Catton, Stuart Chase, Marchette Chute, Malcolm Cowley, John Dos Passos, Richard Eberhart, Leon Edel, Ralph Ellison, Francis Fergusson, Chaim Gross, John Hersey, George F. Kennan (presiding), Harry Levin, Walter Lippmann, Jacques Lipchitz, William Maxwell, Allan Nevins (new president of the Academy, also presiding), I. M. Pei, Elmer Rice, Arthur M. Schlesinger, Jr., Glenway Wescott, John Hall Wheelock, and Felicia Geffen. Guests from the National Council of the Arts or with experience in the interplay of government with the arts were John B. Gardner, August Heckscher, John B. Hightower, Harry Starr, Roger L. Stevens, and Howard Taubman.

The conference took a morning and a long afternoon session; more than half of those present spoke, and the theme—what should the relation of the Academy and Institute be to a government body like the National Council on the Arts—was discussed back and forth, to and fro, until it was impossible, as George Kennan said at the end, to summarize what was said. It was certainly the most important and eloquent meeting of this ten-year period from 1958 to 1967, and no summary is going to do justice to the nuances and explorations of the occasion because there cannot have been many such events in the history of the nation as well written and as well spoken.

Let us now offer a surgical abridgement of the proceedings.

The morning commenced with a paper written by Henry Steele Commager that was read in his absence by Glenway Wescott:

> The fact is that we must learn to live with and manage danger. We must learn to sterilize financial support, whether from local, state, national or international sources—whether private or foundation or public. This is not a new lesson. We have learned it in the realm of justice—supported, I remind you, by the state. We have learned it in the realm of religion—indirectly supported through tax exemption. We have learned it for the most part in higher education. Our task is not to bewail the dangers from government (which is us, of course) but to educate governments at all levels in their proper operation, and to perfect techniques which will frustrate dangerous or improper intervention.
>
> I say this is the real problem, the only one that rises to the dignity of an intellectual problem. For government intervention is not a prospect, it is not a theory—it is a fact. It is a fact at almost every level and in almost

every realm—in the realm of education at the higher as at the lower levels; in the realm of science and public health; somewhat more tentatively in the realm of museums and music. It is with us, and with us to stay. It will in all probability grow quantitatively and spread into new areas. Let us see to it that what it does, it does wisely. That is our job as citizens. That is your job as artists.

Art is by its very nature cosmopolitan or universal. Throughout history it has played the benevolent role of appealing across the boundaries of people, race, nation, faith, and even of time, bringing together in common intellectual and moral experience peoples separated by languages, religions, ideologies, by centuries and millennia. As such, art takes its place alongside those other affluent institutions that serve to knit mankind together rather than separate and fragment it.[50]

Under the twenty mattresses of Commager's certainty, lies the pea that will destroy sleep. It is the sentence: "Our task is not to bewail the dangers of government . . . but to educate governments at all levels in their proper operation. . . ." He is saying this in 1966 in the shadow of the vast buildup in Vietnam, saying it to the membership in the aftergloom of Lewis Mumford's remarks a year earlier; yes, our task is to "educate governments at all levels in their proper operation." Good luck, Commager, one thinks, and Godspeed! Unwittingly, he must have touched the core of distrust in many of the assembled. Does the Academy-Institute dare to have anything real to do with the government, especially when its superior critical faculties of choice and appreciation of artistic merit are equaled on the negative side by its history of political inanition?

To support Commager, Roger Stevens, who was chairman of the National Council on the Arts, read from the Declaration of Purpose he was given by the government:

It declares that the encouragement and support of the arts, while primarily a matter for private and local initiative, is also an appropriate matter for concern for the federal government. A high civilization, it notes, must give full value to man's scholarly and cultural activity, for democracy demands wisdom and vision in its citizens.

It concludes by asserting, and I quote: ". . . that the world leadership which has come to the United States cannot rest solely upon superior power, wealth, and technology, but must be solidly founded upon worldwide respect and admiration for the Nation's high qualities as a leader in the realm of ideas and the spirit. . . ."

After painting so broad a brush stroke, we then find that we are expected to foster and stimulate the arts throughout the United States . . . with less than $10 million a year. . . .

I do not wish to excuse the Council from its responsibility. However, it is necessary to emphasize the fact that we have little money but great hopes.[51]

The noble language of the Declaration of Purpose and the paltry government sums allocated give the likelihood of the game away. The arts will become one more weapon in the cold war on a par perhaps with the Congress for Cultural Freedom but certainly not equal to the importance of Olympic athletes.

Later in the day, Leon Edel aided Stevens with some well-chosen words: "We *know*. And we must say what we know. If we do not speak out of our wealth of creativity, the pastiche-makers, the commercializers, the advertisers will speak for us, and we will be relegated to the sedate and innocuous antiquarianism which has been the fate of so many old academies. This is our danger at this moment —when modern government at long last has gone in search of the artist. Let us make sure that it finds him, not his counterfeit."[52]

Earlier, Arthur Schlesinger, Jr., had also come to Roger Steven's support:

I would like to suggest only two points. . . .

The first is that the undertaking . . . does not enjoy the advantage of a long tradition and of clear precedents in our society. Therefore, it is bound for a time, and perhaps for a very long time, to be an *experiment* in which a number of things will be tried, and one can never tell in advance what will work and what won't work. . . .

The tremendous difficulties . . . inherent both in the novelty of the undertaking and in the political environment—suggest that criticism might well be accompanied by a measure of forbearance and sympathy for those on the firing line.[53]

These defenses of Stevens's point of view had come in answer to a paper by Jacques Barzun that may have been the most salient presentation of the afternoon, for it cut to the bone beneath the meat of the day's polemics. Barzun's point was that half the good artists in America were secessionists:

They want nothing to do with this world; for them art is another world which provides the meaning and comfort that they seek, and indeed demand. . . .

Secessionism is highly significant, because [it says that] politics, law, public service, and particularly trade are to be despised. The upshot is that when we are supporting the arts in this day and age we are really supporting something that is an alternative to society and not a functional part of it.

We are also, as it were, casting a vote against science, urbanization, technology, and the life that they impose upon man. Art—and maybe that is why everybody is so much excited about it—art nowadays seems to confer the benefits of detachment, of disinterestedness from commercial or other profits, [and offers] the value of pure sensation, sensation without thought. . . .

We respond to this doctrine. We find ourselves especially keen about the . . . arts that suggest or permit fantasy, madness, and the unexpected. . . .

If all this is true, what is it that we are supporting when we say we are supporting art or the arts? There is a wide range here.[54]

Mr. Kennan:

Mr. Barzun [presents] a very real problem in the relationships between the government on the one hand and art on the other. . . . While a great deal can be expected of the government in the way of tolerance, it would be going pretty far to ask it to support financially and morally a rebellion against itself.[55]

From George Kennan's point of view, there might be enemies to art far more profound than the government. He went on to say:

I have had the experience of coming home to live in this country after the last war, after some twenty-five years abroad, and being really appalled and alarmed to see what had happened here in the field of the mass media, to note the cacophony in the midst of which real art is obliged to live in this country, to realize how hard one has to scream to make oneself heard in any field of aesthetics. And this continues to worry me very greatly to this day. I have never said this publicly, but I must say that I have asked myself several times a week what is wrong with a society that on the one hand recognizes education is a public responsibility and sets up schools for it which are normally under public control, and then, for example, turns over the financing of literature plus the enormous educational medium of television to the good graces of the advertisers, who have no commitment and no natural interest either in the educational process or anything else but their own commercial advantage . . . and their domination of the means of communication in our country. . . .

One thing that struck me very much in the years that I lived in Russia was the extraordinary freshness of perception on the part of young people, and indeed even of workers and simple people all over Russia. I have seen young people sit on benches in parks on a summer evening with nothing else to do . . . and if you had a discussion with them, you found their minds were fresh and joyous and endlessly thirsty; thirsty for ideas. I have seen workmen coming from their factories, standing in great heavy greasy fur coats in the aisle of a hot overheated classroom of the

Moscow University, listening motionless for hours to the reading of poetry, where this would have caused many of us to faint.

Now this is partly because, as I see it, their senses were not bombarded all through their youth with an unremitting deluge of advertising impressions which attacks us from every side through the loud speakers, on the pages of every newspaper. . . .

These things worry me very much. . . . Before we can really do what we ought to do to preserve the quality of the arts, we must find some means of coping with this fearful competition.[56]

Performing his function as co-host and president of the Institute, he would sum up the long day with these remarks:

It seems to me that we face here two dangers. The artistic community has, so to speak, one foot in the good order of society and a well-behaved participation in the life of the community, but it always has, by definition and unavoidability, another foot in chaos, in madness and mayhem.

And we have to deal with both of those tendencies. You can't expect the government, for example, to embrace them both. On the other hand, the government comes to us also in a varied form. It is not a single personality. At one end there is a great deal of provincialism, a great deal of lack of understanding of art; on the other hand we have now a situation (perhaps for the first time since Jefferson) where a great many people in the government have a serious understanding of the importance of art and a serious interest in it, recognize its place in our culture, in our national life, and would like to do what they can for it.

What seems to me to be our task—our common task between the Council on the Arts and our Academy and Institute—is to hold together the two wings of these two great camps which do fit together, without trying to force into this union those wings which don't belong in it.[57]

The life of the literary artist is the reverse of the objective law that it is the actions of men and women, and not their sentiments, that make history. Writers make little history but enjoy large sentiments. So the results of this extraordinary day of discussion were moderate. Roger Stevens, working out of his limited budget, succeeded, with the aid of the Institute, in choosing fifty candidates in literature, arts, and music to receive sabbaticals of $7,500 each. Six years after Robert Frost came to the Academy and Institute with his notion of an imperial collaboration between government and the arts, a first accommodation had been found, a process had begun. As Jacques Barzun had foreseen (and George Kennan), it was more than vulnerable to a curious outcome or two. We need only think of congressmen in need of a cheap political meal face to face with the top sirloin of Robert Mapplethorpe and Karen Findlay.

1967

At the Joint Ceremonial on May 24, Lillian Hellman gave a tribute to Dorothy Parker: "She once told me she wanted written on her gravestone, 'If you can read this, you've come too close.' " Truman Capote gave his tribute to Carson McCullers: "I remember that the first time I saw her—a tall slender wand of a girl, slightly stooped and with a fascinating face that was simultaneously merry and melancholy—I remember thinking how beautiful her eyes were: the color of good, clear coffee, or of a dark ale held to the firelight to warm. Her voice had the same quality, the same gentle heat, like a blissful summer afternoon that is slow but not sleepy." And Mark Van Doren gave his to Carl Sandburg: "This poet has seen the faces of those who go forth early in the morning / Tired of wishes, / Empty of dreams." Andrew Wyeth paid tribute to Edward Hopper: "The profound silences of his work will ever be a source of strength." Of course, the silences in a Wyeth can bear comparison to a Hopper. Whenever one artist praises another, we do well to look for the subtle leg up he may be offering himself.[58]

Speaking of a leg up, we can note that on this same Ceremonial day, George Kennan made reference to a writer whom one would hope that readers know well:

> Norman Mailer has a professional engagement this evening at one of the universities in Texas. However, he did write us a letter which I read to you because he himself suggested that I do so. It is a characteristic letter. It is not the first of this sort that I have seen. I think many of our members—some of our most valued ones and some who most value their membership—wrote similar letters when they were elected. Let me read it to you:
>
> "You will perhaps forgive the reluctance with which I accepted the invitation from the Institute, but it was a matter which required much serious thought. I have been offended in the past, you see, by the election of a few contemporaries and men younger than myself who were not, I felt, writers necessarily in the same category as my own. On the other hand, novelists as distinguished as Henry Miller, Nelson Algren, James Jones and William Burroughs, had never been elected.
>
> "So it seemed more a mark of honor not to belong to the Institute. When I decided finally to accept the invitation, it was because I thought it would be ungracious to those people kind enough to nominate me and pass on my membership. It also occurred to me that the best way to rectify the absence of such writers as the ones I have named might be as a member of the Institute. Therefore, I accepted. I look forward to the day Allen Ginsberg becomes a member."

After being told that Mr. Miller was a member, Mailer wrote a second letter: "Henry Miller—oops. Well, any Institute which elects Henry Miller can't be all bad."[59]

Let us conclude with an intimate letter from Dorothy Van Doren:

FALLS VILLAGE, CONNECTICUT
MAY 28, 1967

Dear Felicia:

I am afraid I jumped you the other day at a bad time, after a long hard day, and I am sorry. I did not mean to complain of the amplifying system; the sound is all right, [but] couldn't there be smaller lights on each side of the rostrum? Then even with a strange accent, the speaker's lips could be read. . . .

I also wish members could be prevailed upon not to go to sleep so publicly while the ceremonies are going on, but this is something that no amplifying system can correct. Mark said that he spent a good part of the afternoon shaking the feet and pinching the legs of at least two Academicians who shall be nameless—at their own request, too.

Well, anyway, I always love to be there to see old friends and eat a wonderful lunch.

Fondest greetings,
Dorothy Van D.

NOTES

All archival materials are in the Academy files unless otherwise specified.

1. 1915.
2. *Proceedings of the American Academy of Arts and Letters and the National Institute of Arts and Letters*, 2d ser., no. 9 (1959): 252.
3. Ibid., p. 284.
4. Minutes, Academy dinner meeting, April 14, 1958.
5. John O'Hara, "Sweet and Sour," *Trenton, N.J., Times-Advertiser*, March 14, 1954.
6. January 25, 1957.
7. *Proceedings*, 2d ser., no. 11 (1961): 72, 76, 75, 79.
8. *Proceedings*, 2d ser., no. 10 (1960): 318–19.
9. Ibid., p. 335.
10. Ibid., p. 340.
11. Ibid., p. 380.
12. Undated.
13. To the Honorable Lester Hill, chairman, Committee on Labor and Public Welfare, U.S. Senate, May 20, 1960.
14. Minutes, Institute dinner meeting, November 1, 1960.

15. Minutes, annual meeting of the members of the Academy, December 2, 1960.

16. "Dichtung und Wahrheit (An Unwritten Poem)," *Proceedings*, 2d ser., no. 11 (1961): 57.

17. *Proceedings*, 2d ser., no. 11 (1961): 28.

18. Ibid., 25–26.

19. "Music Now," ibid., p. 23.

20. *Proceedings*, 2d ser., no. 12 (1962): 173–79 passim.

21. "Playful Talk," given at the dinner meeting of the Institute, April 11, 1961, reprinted in *Proceedings*, 2d ser., no. 12 (1962): 180, 182.

22. *Proceedings*, 2d ser., no. 12 (1962): 97.

23. Ibid., pp. 106–8.

24. Ibid., p. 132.

25. Ibid., pp. 150–51.

26. Ibid., p. 162.

27. Minutes, annual meeting of the Academy, December 1, 1961.

28. Minutes, annual dinner meeting of the National Institute of Arts and Letters, January 24, 1962.

29. Minutes, Academy board of directors meeting, May 24, 1962.

30. *Proceedings*, 2d ser., no. 13 (1963): 225–27.

31. Minutes, special meeting of the Academy, May 23, 1962.

32. *Proceedings*, 2d ser., no. 13 (1963): 243.

33. The fellowship was renewed in 1976.

34. "Homage to Marianne Moore on Her Seventy-fifth Birthday at the Dinner Meeting of the Institute, November 15, 1962," cited in *Proceedings*, 2d ser., no. 13 (1963): 277.

35. "Homage to Charles Ives by Henry Cowell of the Institute," *Proceedings*, 2d ser., no. 13 (1963): 266.

36. *Proceedings*, 2d ser., no. 14 (1964): 311–16.

37. *Anne Sexton, Letters*. Reprinted courtesy of Linda Gray Sexton.

38. *Proceedings*, 2d ser., no. 14 (1964): p. 386.

39. Minutes, joint meeting of the Academy board and the Institute council, November 22, 1963.

40. December 7, 1963.

41. Academy minutes, January 9, 1964.

42. "To Greet New Members," *Proceedings*, 2d ser., no. 15 (1965): 449–50, 453.

43. Ibid., p. 428.

44. Minutes, meeting of the Academy board and the Institute council, February 1, 1965.

45. Ibid.

46. *Proceedings*, 2d ser., no. 16 (1966): 9–15 passim.

47. Geoffrey T. Hellman, "Some Splendid and Admirable People," *The New Yorker*, February 25, 1976, p. 68.

48. Leonard Lyons, "The Lyons Den," *New York Post*, September 9, 1965, p. 29.

49. *Proceedings*, 2d ser., no. 16 (1966): 45.

50. *Proceedings*, 2d ser., no. 17 (1967): 114.

51. Ibid., p. 122.

52. Ibid., p. 176.

53. Ibid., p. 144.

54. Ibid., p. 142.

55. Ibid., pp. 143–44.

56. Ibid., pp. 177–78.

57. Ibid., pp. 196.

58. *Proceedings*, 2d ser., no. 18 (1968): 122, 111, 107, 104.

59. Ibid., pp. 51–52.

CHAPTER EIGHT

1968–1977

HOUSEKEEPING IN A MESSY WORLD

Jack Beeson

IT IS FORTUNATE FOR THE WRITERS and readers of these chapters that the founding of the Institute in 1898 prevents any neat parceling of our century into the usually nicknamed decades, from the Gay Nineties through the Gay Eighties. Straddling two of "our" decades, the previous chapter and this one, was the bloody decennium beginning with the Tonkin Resolution of 1964 and the intervention of the United States in Southeast Asia and ending with the peace agreement in 1973—the beginning and the end both blurred.

Lewis Mumford's address as president at the Joint Ceremonial in May 1965, early in the Vietnam engagement, as already recounted, led to wide press coverage and the resignation of Thomas Hart Benton, whose subsequent reentry into the Academy led to Mumford's resignation from that body (but *not* from the Institute). That Mumford was still angry three years later is clear from his letter to Babette Deutsch: "As for missing me at the Institute meetings, do you not know that I resigned, for good reason, from the Academy, and have no intention of ever 'darkening the door,' as my old Irish nurse used to say, of 155th street, lest I rub shoulders by accident with people I do not care to meet."[1]

In 1969 he was awarded the Gold Medal for Belles-Lettres and in his response referred to his 1965 speech: "It took a little courage on the part of the Academy, I would say, to give me the medal and to ask me to appear again on this platform, when the affairs of the world have grown much grimmer, much more horrible, much more atrocious. We are all of us involved in atrocities that have been committed in our name by the government and by the military arm of this country. We have taken part in this moral debacle and by our silence, insofar as we have been silent, we have sanctioned it."[2]

The Mumford–Benton encounter may have been paralleled by other personal hostilities; if so, they do not appear in the record. Such divisions of opinion may have been expressed at dinner meetings, but one is reminded that at the height of the Dreyfus Affair (in 1898, as it happens) Parisians were invited to dinner on condition that *l'affaire* not be discussed; at the height of the Vietnam buildup the parents and grandparents of draft-age men may have kept their fears to themselves. It is remarkable, given the large number of members who were also professors, that there is no mention in the files of campus turmoil: the Berkeley Free Speech Movement followed in 1968 by the Columbia riots and a year later by those at Harvard—not to mention the Kent State killings in 1970.

Thirty-nine blocks south of "The Temple" is Columbia University, designed by McKim, Mead & White, two of them Academicians (White having been murdered before he could be elected). Over their handsome chef-d'oeuvre, representing the highest aspirations of the Academy in its first decade, presides the large bronze Alma Mater by Daniel Chester French, who was in the entering class of the Institute and promoted to the Academy in 1905. During the night of May 15, 1970—student unrest is always at its most ardent in the spring—a bomb exploded next to the right buttock of Alma, quite unsettling her in her ceremonial throne. When, after extensive recasting and regilding, she was returned to her place of honor, the university said little about the bombing and about the Vietnam protests that had led to it. Institutional reticence was as highly developed on 116th Street as on 155th Street.

Although there were no other resignations for political reasons during these years, there was an unexpected salvo from that expert on matters of loyalty and disloyalty, Graham Greene, who had been elected a Foreign Honorary Member in 1961.

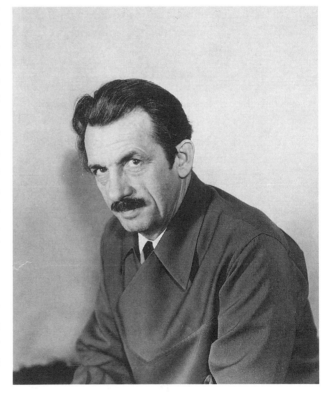

Sir,
With regret I ask you to accept my resignation. . . . My reason—that the Academy has failed to take any position at all in relation to the undeclared war in Vietnam.

Thomas Hart Benton, circa 1940. Elected to the Institute in 1942 and to the Academy in 1962, he resigned in 1965 over Lewis Mumford's Ceremonial speech denouncing American involvement in Vietnam. He was reinstated in 1966.

I have been in contact with all your foreign members in the hope of organising a mass resignation. A few have given me immediate support; two supported American action in Vietnam; a number considered that the war was not an affair with which a cultural body need concern itself; some were prepared to resign if a majority of honorary members were of the same opinion. I have small respect for those who wish to protect themselves by a majority opinion, and I disagree profoundly with the idea that the Academy is not concerned. I have tried to put myself in the position of a foreign honorary member of a German Academy of Arts and Letters at the time when Hitler was democratically elected Chancellor. Could I have continued to consider as an honour a membership conferred in happier days?[3]

George Kennan agreed to accept the resignation: "The chartered commitment of these organizations is to the furtherance of the arts and letters, and it is to this purpose that their efforts . . . have been directed. Many, including myself, have voiced opinions on political subjects outside this organizational framework. . . . It would be unfair to our members—and particularly in the present instance—to interpret this forbearance as the evidence of support for any particular governmental policy and to hold them, by implication, responsible for that policy."[4]

Kennan's measured response reflects other official and semiofficial statements of the Academy-Institute's policy concerning the taking of institutional political positions. That policy, set down in 1950, prohibited the issuance of any statement on a controversial subject without an affirmative vote of at least 75 percent of the members. There was, naturally, some sentiment for a change in this policy or for letting it be more widely known why the Academy and Institute were issuing no statements when everyone else was. A letter to William Maxwell, president of the Institute, from the poet John Ciardi probably reflected the perturbations of the members at large:

I don't know whether Miss Paley [Grace Paley] had previous permission to circulate her petition or to make her anti-war statement. In all but finical detail I share her position. . . . I am afraid that political issues could rip up the Institute and keep it from doing the particular good work only it can do. . . . I feel that the Institute-Academy is full of finely spiny individuals, all of whom feel strongly, almost all of whom have ways of making clear how they, as individuals, stand. I should be sorry to see politics get all those spines up. I submit that we will function best in formal neutrality. This is the saloon above all others in town where we should park our guns at the door. . . . Were the Institute to be polled on its stand on the Viet Namese war and were the results of the poll—so many pro and so many con—to be made public as a declaration of commitment, that might be a good thing. . . . Should we preserve a careful formal neutrality on public issues (as an Institute, never as individuals)? If so, shouldn't we phrase and make public the principles of that neutrality?[5]

As the casualty lists from Asia lengthened, there were ever more ingenious attempts to evade the stern 1950 policy. It was pointed out that the admonition had been passed only by the Institute and that the Academy could do as it wished; the Academy declined to take advantage of the opportunity. It was suggested that a department be permitted, given a majority of its members, to issue a protest; the Institute's council replied that *any* political statement would require a majority of 75 percent of the whole membership.

And so it was that the Vietnam War came to its messy end without help or hindrance from the Institute or the Academy.

During these years, official silence concerning the war inhibited comment on other matters that could, and *should*, the departments insisted, have become part of the public discourse in "furthering of the interests of literature and the fine arts," as provided for in the charter. This silence, and other matters that had simmered for years (including four years of committee discussion concerning a merger of the two organizations) led the council to convene the standing (but more often recumbent) Committee on Progress. Its membership (the council officers and strong representation from the departments) invited the Academy officers to join, an unprecedented gesture. There were two lengthy meetings in May and October 1974 and a subcommittee meeting sandwiched between. Nine topics were listed for discussion, but to no one's surprise in a too-large committee of twenty-two, these proliferated into a welter of aspirations and muted exasperations. The chairman, Jacques Barzun, was nevertheless able to summarize in a memorandum to the council numerous suggestions for change and a motion "voted favorably, that for the sake of creating a clearer public image and simplifying regular activities . . . the Academy and the Institute should amalgamate into a single body."[6]

Outsiders even dimly aware of the action taken by a committee in one of the buildings on Audubon Terrace would have thought it merely the housekeeping equivalent of removing a partition between a large and small room, permitting access by the whole family to the quarters of the elderly. But to its inhabitants the motion sparked both hope and fear: there were those among the two hundred and fifty of the Institute who had so far vainly hoped to be promoted, as well as those, more generous, who believed amalgamation best for everyone; and there were those among the fifty Academicians who feared that their prerogatives would be lost (their travel expenses to meetings, for instance) and that their high status would be diluted among the hoi polloi.

Barzun, an Institute member since 1952 (who was to decline membership in the Academy in 1982), while presiding with an even hand at the meetings, confided to Margaret Mills: "We [members of the Institute] were there first, and at Saratoga besides, which establishes the Americanness of the *institution* later split and misnomered. For an important point to remember is that we are not two bodies forced to live together in one house, but *one* body, of which the hinder (I mean later) part just wanted to sit and be admired by the rest as well as by itself."[7]

His confidante was the executive director at the time. When she retired in 1990 there had been but three (Vanamee, Geffen, and Mills) in charge of day-to-day management for almost three-quarters of a century. She was as adept in coping with cantankerous members as her predecessors. Her gray, then white, hair was as square-cut as her shoulders; her clipped British accent lent as much class to the establishment as her fluent Portuguese and Spanish astonished and pleased the local neighborhood, in which each year less English was spoken. Though she refused to be addressed as "Ms." and resisted using the abbreviation on dinner place cards, she did her best to convince members that they should not restrict their nominations to names in their Rolodexes but seek out talent among women and minorities.

The committed and the cantankerous reacted to the looming possibility of amalgamation:

The painter Peter Blume at an Academy meeting said that he "felt that the question of amalgamation emanated from the Institute whose members could never understand how some became Academicians and how others had to be satisfied to be members of the Institute. [He said that] perhaps half of us shouldn't be here, but then perhaps half of the members of the Institute should not be there either. The Institute provides the strength and muscle and fresh ideas and the Academy has the experience and the memory."[8]

Allan Tate wrote to Blume in the same vein: "I have just read with complete approval the statement you and Leon Edel made concerning amalgamation. If you wish to use my name to extend your minority group please do so. . . . If amalgamation takes place and the members of the Academy are reduced I think I will just resign from the whole shebang."[9]

Babette Deutsch asked Miss Mills to circulate to all Academicians a long letter with serious reservations: "One of the most persuasive reasons for amalgamation is economy—a good in most circumstances and a noteworthy element, as we all know, of noteworthy art. But economy is worthless without discrimination, a chief feature of all the arts and their practitioners. For that reason alone there should continue to be a clear distinction between the Institute, by whatever name, and the Academy by no other name. Its superiority should not be obliterated or weakened."[10]

New to the fray, Barbara Tuchman expressed herself to Richard Wilbur: "Clearly the Academy fails in its purpose and function, and in public esteem, because it doesn't do anything; it doesn't speak as an institution; it has no voice. This inadequacy or debility will certainly not be remedied, as Archie [Archibald MacLeish] points out, by enlarging—which is to say, weakening the criteria for—membership."[11]

Katherine Anne Porter (elected to the Institute in 1941 and to the Academy in 1966) wrote to William Meredith, secretary of the Institute, betraying some confusion about the two organizations and their relationship: "To an artist, the real reward of his life is the acknowledgement of his use to the art he serves and being honored by his peers and friends. I have guarded as a treasure the gold medal [for fiction, in 1967]. . . . Its real meaning is vested in my membership in the Academy, as distinguished from the Institute . . . but if we are to lose our identity, invalidate our medals, and be merged into another society, I suggest that we simply abolish the Academy and forget it and I will very unhappily return my medal."[12]

All of the above excerpts, except for that by Blume, were from writer-members. One of their number engaged a well-known law firm to represent the core of dissidents, but, when chastised by his board for such a lapse in decorum, he dropped whatever action he had in mind. I include no comments by Institute members because there are none in the files.

It was, after all, the Institute that had engendered the Academy, as R. W. B. Lewis has already explained. The formation of an elite within an elite surely could only have been applauded in the early 1900s, by both the Institute and the country at large, for the word *elite*—except in trust-busting and socialist circles—then had only the most honorable and respectable connotations. But by the sixties and seventies, in a more would-be egalitarian society, the words *elite*, *elitism*, and *elitist* were becoming tarnished. (By 1995 the *Cambridge International Dictionary* was listing all three words as "especially disapproving.") That Leon Edel was ruefully aware of this verbal and societal change is reflected in his comment to Malcolm Cowley: "I feel strongly that the impulse to reorganize seems also to be an impulse to false and hypocritical democratization."[13] Democratization, hypocritical or not, was certainly in the air, but it is difficult to believe that being one in an elite of two hundred fifty members of the Institute in a U.S. population of over two hundred million was much less significant than being one of fifty. By late 1990 each member of the Academy-Institute was one in a million, not that—to be sure—every U.S. citizen was a writer, artist, or composer qualified for admission.

Awaiting the end of disputation were votes in both bodies on the motion by the Committee on Progress. Appended to Barzun's motion proposing amalgamation were many qualifications intended to promote discussion and allay fears. Both organizations appointed ad hoc committees to consider these secondary matters. It is often the case that committees are formed to delay or to prevent action; the Institute committee quickly formulated recommendations to its membership and became annoyed by the lack of progress by the

Academy committee, which wished to ensure in any amalgamation the special status of Academicians: perhaps they could become Deans, Senators, Fellows, or Charter Members?

Everyone, in fact, was playing word games. Especially popular was Anagrams played with seven words instead of twenty-six letters: *academy, American, arts, institute, letters, of,* and *the.* The winner, The American Academy and Institute of Arts and Letters, was announced on December 30, 1976, together with the results of the votes on the 1974 motion: 28 to 5 in the Academy; 121 to 16 in the Institute. Clearly, many had not troubled to cast a vote one way or the other.

To outsiders, little seemed to have changed; the new name was as confusing to everyone—especially the press—as the old one. But inside, though the partition still stood, there was a wider door and an invitation to wider intercourse. William Meredith spoke warmly and amusingly to dinner guests at the time:

> This is the last meeting of the NIAL before our somewhat morganatic, not to say shot-gun marriage with the AAAL. The papers were drawn up, as is customary in morganatic marriages, to safeguard hereditary differences but to allow for love. The two parties are now free to cohabit lovingly, and are, I think, determined to do so. The life that we make together could be a new life. . . . If we start to work together on practical proposals—on considered statements which are moderate enough to win support from 250 vocal minorities among us—will we not change the nature of our organization into what it really is, something appropriate to ourselves and our moment in the culture?[14]

The two organizations, each a not-for-profit corporation, had become one corporation (still chartered by Congress) presided over by a quintet (a chancellor, three vice-chancellors, and a secretary, elected by the Academy) and a quartet (a president, two vice-presidents, and a secretary, elected by the Institute). Each ensemble served its own public as well as performing with the other for the benefit of *all* members. This arrangement was to endure through 1992, after which the Institute, having been invited to join the Academy, was dropped from the name, and into such histories as this.

Significantly, there was but one treasurer, elected by the Institute membership; happily, there were only murmurs against pooling the larger assets of the Academy with those of the Institute. Somewhat earlier, Malcolm Cowley had remarked that for the Institute to invite the Academy "which had the money . . . was similar to an invitation to a duck dinner in which the guest would be asked to bring the duck."[15] As recounted in the first chapter, the worldly composer Edward MacDowell suggested that the formation of a smaller group, its members chosen in part for their fund-raising abilities, might make possible the carrying-out of ambitious and expensive plans then in the making. It wasn't long before the Academy took title to the real estate, then the buildings, and began to receive large endowments. It was to the Institute, however, that donors tended to make those gifts to be used in making grants to accomplished nonmembers in one field or the other. To the common pot the Academy contributed (in round figures) $1,200,000 in real estate ($3,120,000 in 1996 dollars) and $7,700,000 in endowments ($20,020,000); the Institute contributed $830,000 in endowments ($2,158,000). Given this disparity it is not surprising that the richer Academy had been turning over to the Institute $20,000 to $25,000 annually for housekeeping expenses.

The Academy-Institute, as it now came to be called by itself and others, appointed a small committee optimistically called the Committee of the Future. All eminences, its members included Richard Wilbur, Harrison Salisbury (president of the Institute, historian, and former editor at the *New York Times*), Milton Babbitt, Jacques Barzun, Helen Frankenthaler, Philip Johnson, George Kennan (historian and former ambassador to the Soviet Union and Yugoslavia), William Schuman (composer and president emeritus of Lincoln Center), and Hugo Weisgall. Salisbury, Kennan, and Schuman were naturally disposed toward a much stronger relationship between the Academy-Institute and the world outside and worked energetically to bring it about.

The following mélange of excerpts and summaries from the extensive minutes of two of the new committee's meetings suggest the matters discussed, the actions to be taken, and a new mood and style.[16]

Mr. Kennan stated that although the country had changed tremendously . . . since 1898, our organization as a whole had not. . . . He said that he was constantly surprised that so few people in Washington . . . knew of the Academy-Institute. . . . Mr. Schuman suggested that we make ourselves available for consultation on cultural affairs, not only by the Endowment [for the Arts] but by the government. Salisbury reminded the others that during the recent Academy-Institute imbroglio he had lunched with the officers of the NEA and NEH, the Smithsonian, the Library of Congress, and the Bureau of Education and Cultural Affairs, but that the contacts thus established had not been vigorously pursued. . . . Schuman suggested that Miss Hanks [of the NEA] would be an appropriate recipient of the Distinguished Service to the Arts Award . . . and that she would accept the Award in person . . . and give us the opportunity to discuss with her the role which the Academy-Institute might fill. . . . [We are] blessed with sufficient funds . . . and could go to the government to offer assistance instead of requiring favors, like almost all other organized groups in the country. [Hanks was nominated, but not elected; in the next eight years half of the medallists were important political figures friendly to the arts.]

Salisbury reminded the Committee that at the Washington luncheon already mentioned he learned that Ronald Berman, Chairman of the NEH, had never even heard of the Academy-Institute.

[Barzun suggested that] we send our printed materials and programs to members of congressional committees that deal with the Endowments and with education.

Would it be desirable to be associated with the Smithsonian? . . . a meeting with Mr. Dillon? . . . Barzun remarked that a friendly talk with Mr. Boorstin of the Library of Congress might be useful. . . . The members thought that the Academy-Institute should be able to make public statements pertaining to the arts. . . . An invaluable opportunity has been lost . . . in our not having taken a public stand on the new copyright law.

(In fact, Wilbur Mills, chairman of the House Ways and Means Committee, had chastised the Academy-Institute leadership for its silence during the drafting of that measure, which prevented artists, writers, and composers from donating their works to museums and libraries for a tax-deductible amount greater than the cost of materials.)

These and other matters—including a complete merger of the two bodies—were summarized and laid before the membership. One newly elected wag admitted that he already found the merger talk tiresome and offered a simple solution: let the Academicians continue as they were, with whatever prerogatives, for their lifetimes, in return for their agreeing to select no new members. He realized that this would put an intolerable burden on the last lonely survivor, who would not only have to embody all the officers but also, eventually, be responsible for accompanying the Academy into oblivion.

There was general apprehension that continued quietude would give rise to some competing organizations—even another academy or institute of arts and letters. Discreet inquiries disclosed that the National Endowments, with or without Kennedy Center leadership, had no such plans. More troubling was that organization in Cambridge, Massachusetts, with an all-too-similar name, the Academy of Arts and Sciences. Dating from 1788 and with two thousand members, it was energetically planning to construct a new building and to enlarge its small number of artists, writers, composers, and performers. Representatives from Cambridge had already visited Miss Mills in New York and now invited her to Cambridge for further consultation. It was agreed that she should find out what was going on and report back to the committee.

Fears were allayed when Barzun reported the contents of a letter from Salisbury:

I have just finished casting my annual ballot in the elections for membership in the American Academy of Arts and Sciences. There were a total of 325 candidates . . . of which only a handful will be elected. Nonetheless, I thought it interesting that of this vast number not more than 10 or 12 would have been considered for election to the AAIAL. Of these a third are foreign honoraries. . . .

...The total membership of the "rival" body ... is weighted on the order of ... 15 or 20 to 1 in favor of scientific and academic persons ... nor is there any means by which this large organization could supplant ourselves.

But ... since I've taken to wearing my rosette around the country, I have been saddened at the number who have responded "Ah yes, of course, the Academy of Arts and *Sciences*."[17]

One newish idea was broached by the architect Philip Johnson, passed in principle by the committee, and then presented at a boisterous dinner meeting: to pursue anew the sale of the 155th Street building and move to midtown, perhaps to a vacated private club, the Ceremonial and other large events to be held in rented quarters. Oddly enough, the idea was supported by the older members, who had long complained about the inaccessibility of the uptown venue—though when one came by taxi or car and was returned gratis by hired limousine, it wasn't clear to others why that mattered. The younger members, not yet sated with the handsome space and comfortable grandeur, objected. One rose to say that it was surely true that the Audubon Terrace neighborhood had deteriorated since 1923, but that one could not predict midtown's condition fifty-four years hence. The West Side was rapidly moving north and changing for the better; Columbia would surely expand, as would its medical school ten blocks uptown. If the Academy-Institute were serious about selling, he offered to form a consortium, buy the building at the then-depressed price, rent it out, and then sell it back to the Academy-Institute at a handsome profit when it became dissatisfied downtown. There being no buyer to be found, at the May meeting of the committee Salisbury suggested sensibly that "we should instead explore the possibility of revitalizing the neighborhood," and the topic was set aside for the time being.[18]

In its new desire to embrace the world, the Academy-Institute overreached when it became entangled with the National Book Awards (hereafter NBA) and the Franklin Mint. The forces of Art and Commerce are rarely clearly defined, and their battles never conclusive; the skirmish between the Academy-Institute and the other two organizations neatly portrayed in large the compromises quietly or angrily experienced by individual writers, artists, and composers in the hurly-burly of the commercial world outside. Whatever the circumstances of the members—poor, comfortable, or rich—the Academy-Institute itself was wealthy enough to uphold untrammeled high standards.

The first encounter was peaceful enough. In 1975 (i.e., one year before the amalgamation) the newly elected president of the Institute, Harrison Salisbury, met with representatives of the NBA concerning its request that the Institute take over its awards program, which was in financial trouble. Begun in 1950, the awards had been continued for a decade by the Publishers Publicity Association. Accused by writers and the public of being self-dealing and commercial, they were then handed over to the National Book Committee, which put up 90 percent of the funding and ran out of money in four years; funds for the fifth year were supplied out of his own pocket by Roger Stevens. It was suggested that if the Institute would provide quarters for Joan Cunliffe (the administrator of the program) and her small staff, juries for a half-dozen award categories, and its theater for the award ceremony—perhaps to be televised—the NBA would provide the needed funds. Because the building at that time still belonged to the Academy, its board had to approve the renovations required to provide the NBA with office space. Hit-or-miss phone calls to the board reached five of the nine, who cautiously approved, provided that their treasury not be invaded. Salisbury, accustomed as an editor at the *Times* to having his way and at the Institute eager to lead it out into the world through its neo-Renaissance facade, forged ahead. He offered, as unofficial fund-raiser for the NBA, to acquire $75,000 annually from foundations and corporations.

Because the council and several of the Academy board members were as yet uninformed about the plans afoot, special meetings were called to discuss what was rapidly becoming a fait accompli, the NBA staff having already moved into its new quarters. The council did accede unanimously to Salisbury's plans, particularly as it seemed that the Institute could establish its own standards of excellence. Nevertheless, Ralph Ellison, Lillian Hellman, and John Hersey expressed uneasiness and insisted that the membership should approve the new venture. In response, Salisbury sent out an informational letter to all members, expressing a great deal of optimism. In the meantime Kurt Vonnegut, Jr., had written to Salisbury:

> It is probably too late now . . . but I am opposed to the idea. The awards have had and will continue to have commercial overtones. They are, after all, a scheme to glamorize books, to entertain the public with the notion that there are such things as champion writers. If we endorse such preposterous champions, we endorse the notion, too. . . . We will seem to be attempting to control our literature for its own good, approving this, ignoring that. We are so pleasantly innocent and purposely ineffectual now. Can't we keep it that way?
>
> The NBAS so far have generated bitterness, low comedy and apathy. This is inevitable—because of the cockamamie idea of literary champions. As a termite exterminator said to me when he found my house on Cape Cod infested with wood-eaters: "Honest to God, I'd rather see you with a houseful of rattlesnakes."[19]

From the record it appears that during its first year the undertaking was not discussed at membership meetings. The council was spared the details of planning for the first Awards Ceremony in its theater because Salisbury formed a policy committee of six writers, then an advisory committee with two of the six, two representatives of the Association of American Publishers, a foundation executive, and other luminaries from downtown. All went well, including the awards ceremony in April 1976. The Book Awards were on the brink of becoming an integral part of its hosts when the soon-to-be-amalgamated treasurer, William Schuman, recommended that:

1. The Academy-Institute should henceforth spend no more money in any year than the income of the previous year. [Would that other organizations and government bodies could and would follow such a course!]
2. That no project would be undertaken without adequate funding in hand.[20]

His suggestions were thought sensible and became policy shortly after. They are still in effect.

Then came a meeting of the Institute council on May 26, 1976 at the Century Club:

President Salisbury, in reviewing the situation, says that in 1975 " ... many people ... felt at the time, as he had, too, that the program [of the Book Awards] was extremely important and worthwhile and should not be allowed to disappear from the scene. . . . Obviously [our] takeover had been ad hoc and perforce a helter-skelter operation at its inception because there had been no time to set up the program ... in a careful manner. . . . [He felt] there was bound to be a clashing of gears until the Award program got under way and became an integral part of the Institute's activities." Miss Mills asks for clarification: Is she to sign checks for the NBA? Is its staff to be integrated into hers? The Council thereupon advances $25,000 as a loan to the NBA, to be repaid from its next year's expected income.

Clearly the council had put itself in a bind: that year's NBA income consisted in part of a loan; there was no money in hand to cover the next year's expenses; its approval of Schuman's two proposals prohibited further collaboration between the two organizations.

But Salisbury assured his beleaguered colleagues that reinforcements were at hand: he had received a letter from the Franklin Library in Philadelphia, the publishing division of the Franklin Mint. That division had recently published, in uniform, gold-tooled, leather bindings, the series The Hundred Greatest Books of All Time and a similarly uniform set of forty-nine volumes of Pulitzer-Prize–winning fiction. It now offered to publish in 1979 a series of fiction that had won National Book Awards; given the Library's 100,000 subscribers, the NBA could expect income of at least $250,000 ($650,000 in 1996 dollars). Furthermore the Library offered in two years or so to publish a series of Academy-Institute Gold Medallists in Literature, for which, for the use of its imprimatur, the Academy-Institute would receive, also, $250,000.[21]

The council decided to consider the proposal over the summer (though it pointed out that the Gold Medal was awarded for lifetime achievement in some genre of writing, not for any book in particular). It also mailed to the members a letter by Salisbury explaining the possible collaboration, together with ballots. The results were sixty-five in favor, forty-five against, six with reservations, and many letters. Over the summer Salisbury also wrote to Miss Mills and Joan Cunliffe confiding that he was attempting—together with Arthur Tourtellot of the CBS Foundation—to raise a million dollars to underwrite the Academy-Institute's collaboration with the NBA.

Margaret Mills took umbrage and replied:

> These are indeed very important plans. . . . This being the case, may I respectfully request that our two treasurers be brought into any discussion. . . . I do feel that an error was made last year in not discussing the Institute's take-over of the Book Awards with the membership and this error will be compounded in my view if the fund-raising plans you have in mind are not openly discussed in the very near future.
>
> I am also a little disturbed by your injunction not to discuss these plans to any member or officer of either the Institute or the Academy. . . . I shall keep the contents of your private memo confidential for the moment . . . but in fairness to the two institutions I serve, I cannot give you my word that I shall continue to do so.[22]

Gold Medal of the National Institute of Arts and Letters (2 1/4 inches diameter), designed by Adolph Weinman in 1909.

Given the large number of negative votes and letters received, it was decided to convene the council, the board, and a special meeting of the members. Inasmuch as only sixteen members showed up, there was no quorum, and no action could be taken one way or the other. In the following conflation of the three meetings and correspondence, direct quotation and précis are chosen to reflect the enclave's attempt to protect its standards of excellence from downtown and Philadelphian commerce and individuals' attempts to live with both. In the discussions there were very few quiet termites and a good deal of rattlesnake rattling, as Vonnegut might have noticed had he been present.[23]

Peter De Vries, Theodor Roszak, and Hugo Weisgall asked why the Franklin Library did not proceed with the publishing venture without asking permission of the Institute given that it could go directly to the publishers and to the authors or their estates to obtain the necessary permissions, thereby saving the quarter of a million dollars they would have had to pay the Institute. "President [Salisbury] said . . . they wanted the imprimatur on both series and were prepared to pay for it." He reported that Columbia University had refused to cooperate, whereupon the Franklin Library had proceeded to publish its Pulitzer series without the university's imprimatur. Columbia had therefore received no money.[24] If the Institute refused its sponsorship of the Gold Medal series, the Mint would make a donation of $25,000 to $50,000 anyhow. Someone again pointed out that Gold Medals were awarded for a lifetime of achievement in some literary genre and not for a particular republishable book. Joseph Mitchell mentioned that Jean Stafford's Pulitzer Prize novel had not been included in the Library's series and referred to "the Institute's takeover of the NBA, which he felt had been done too quickly and without proper investigation . . . forcing the Institute to raise funds for an essentially commercial enterprise." Glenway Wescott asked "whether the Institute had ever helped anybody make money before. . . . Would the Franklin Library actually publish *all* the Gold Medallists, as some were very obscure writers? . . . Scandalous that more money should be spent on six [Book Awards] than the Institute spent on its own 36 awards." Roszak said that "he had made a study of the Franklin Library . . . a huge organization with tentacles in everything . . . masters at packaging. . . . The parent company, the Franklin Mint, had made $240,000,000 two years ago minting coins for collectors. . . . Why get involved with its Library in reissuing beautifully bound books by those who had been honored in previous years when the Institute's main business was to aid and nurture the hardworking contemporary writer?" To which Weisgall added "that in effect the Library was embalming decisions we had made, right or wrong."

Malcolm Cowley said that whatever decision the Institute made would outrage some of its members. "If we refuse the proposal . . . then some members would feel that they were being denied $14,000 to $20,000 in royalty payments." Bernard Malamud commented, "Moreover, our colleagues in art and music may be offended. . . . Those who aren't will be within their rights to suggest we also use our Imprimatur to sell paintings and sculpture reproductions by members who have received Gold Medals, and even musical recordings of compositions by Institute members whose works have been honored by the Institute. Franklin Library is a wealthy aggressive commercial enterprise. I suggest that selling or leasing our Imprimatur to them is the moral equivalent of destroying our good name."

Salisbury replied to the critics saying "that so far as he knew sculptors and artists did not object to receiving commissions from large corporations who buy and exhibit their work. The same is true of commissions to composers. He thought this was a happy marriage of commerce and art . . . Yet the fact was that the Medicis of the past had always been the supporters of artists and culture and in each generation wealth had played this role with respect to the arts—rightly or wrongly. There was nothing new about it. In our present generation it was the large corporations which filled this role. "

Salisbury later lent another note of ambiguity to the controversy in a letter to Barzun: "So far as the interests of our members are concerned I think it should not be overlooked that to my knowledge no member of the Institute has declined on any grounds to permit his works to be included in a Franklin series. The fact is that a substantial number of works by Institute members has now been published under the Franklin imprint; and many more such works are under contract to be published."[25]

In early 1977, having simplified itself by merging, the Academy-Institute turned down the Franklin Library offer. The board gratefully accepted a third motion by its treasurer, Schuman: that the Academy-Institute henceforth not involve itself in the sponsorship or administration of any profit-making organization, however acceptable otherwise.[26]

This action left dangling the fate of the National Book Awards relationship, now shorn of its promised windfall, while planning was under way for an even grander, televised Awards Ceremony in the spring. The new president, Jacques Barzun, had invited C. P. Snow to be the featured speaker; on his own, the outgoing president had extended an invitation to President Carter—or, if necessary, to Vice-President Mondale—to attend. What to do, for if Barzun refused to uninvite Lord Snow, would Carter take kindly to being lectured at by a member of the House of Lords?

Another complication arose, neatly exemplifying the difficulties experienced by individuals in weighing the demands of Art and Commerce: Marchette Chute pointed out that at least one officer was a nominee for an award. If he won, IRS regulations would prohibit his receiving the cash award; more troubling, would he have to forgo the increased royalties that would result?

All these considerations led the board to impose its plans for the Ceremony, including canceling the TV coverage and Barzun's suggestion that "if President Carter is able to attend, he can say a few words that Royal sponsors, chancellors and their kind utter at the opening of ceremonies, university convocations and the like."[27]

Not wishing to give the impression to the outside world—the press in particular—that it was abandoning its relationship with the National Book Awards as hastily as it had begun it, the Academy-Institute agreed to continue indefinitely or for another year (1978) under certain conditions that Barzun pleasantly but firmly set forth in a letter to Salisbury. The conditions were unacceptable to the Publishers Association, which thereupon received a sizable grant from the Franklin Library, and the two went off together, uninhibited by any uptown scruples.

Shortly after this divorce, Joseph Mitchell wrote Miss Mills on his *New Yorker* letterhead:

MAY 19, 1977

Dear Maggie,

Of course I am only joking but it might be possible that the recent decision of the Institute had an effect on the stock market. Please read the enclosed story from . . . the *Times*, showing that the Franklin Mint hit a new low for the year on May 18 (selling at its lowest price *since 1975*) and quoting an analyst who said that she expected the stock to show a decline in earnings for all of 1977.

Realizing that the world had been too much with it and recently having been getting and spending money for another institution, the Academy-Institute's Future Committee turned to problems of the present. During the winter Philip Johnson and Helen Frankenthaler had told their colleagues that they regretted that over the years certain important artists had not been admitted; perhaps members of the other departments might suggest candidates for election in art. This ecumenical gesture led to the more limited request that each departmental committee examine what glaring omissions existed and suggest that its members nominate and vote accordingly. This concerted effort was to pay off handsomely, if slowly, for new recruits could join only when death created openings in the ranks. Those singled out as deserving by one or the other pessimistic members must have delighted their champions at the annual welcoming dinners; such pleasant encounters, of course, had always occurred. As he said in the preceding chapter, in 1967 Norman Mailer was disappointed that Nelson Algren and William Burroughs had never been elected (Algren was to make it in 1981). Limits were being tested; barriers were falling. He looked forward to the day when Allen Ginsberg would become a member. Well, Ginsberg too was elected, in 1973, and in turn regretted certain absences when he spoke at a dinner meeting in 1977:

[He] stated that the absence of William S. Burroughs on the ballot reflected some vast misjudgment on the part of the Institute. He felt that the greater poets were being neglected while lesser lights were nominated and that none of the candidates on the ballot could be compared to Burroughs, an international genius, or Gary Snyder, who had influenced a whole generation of poets. He thought that the problem was due to the strength of an older tradition within the department which completely ignored the culture revolutions of which he believed himself to be the lone representative in the Academy-Institute.[28]

Burroughs was elected in 1983, Snyder in 1987.

Marchette Chute, ever meticulous and tactful, submitted an alphabetized and catholic selection of twenty-eight writers she thought worthy; half of those she recommended eventually became members.

In answer to a letter from Miss Mills saying that the art department had so far sent in only two nominations for six vacancies, Robert Motherwell recommended nineteen painters and sculptors, half of whom were elected during the next seven years.[29] Three years later George Rickey wrote Barzun a long letter with suggestions for improving the state of the department of art and its juries, which

> would be unnecessary if the Institute membership matched the distribution of talent and accomplishment in the U.S. There are many American artists whose achievements and influence seem to be known everywhere except inside the Institute. We tend to put up as candidates friends and acquaintances from our own parish, who are then elected faute de mieux, while many artists widely known and admired elsewhere are ignored. I recognize that this is an improper, invidious statement, disparaging some of my colleagues; I recognize also that it applies to the way I was elected. An outside observer of the fine arts might well wonder whether it was more honorific to be outside than inside.[30]

Ross Lee Finney, identified in those days with the University of Michigan and a tireless champion of wider geographical representation—particularly of the Midwest—had earlier listed eligible composers: "Because of the natural tendency for an organization to become entrenched and a little conservative, the A-I fails both in geographical and cultural representation. This fact becomes a serious limitation and more and more damaging to the nation's image. The following composers whom we might have honored in the past [with grants and prizes] might well deserve membership. . . . Even so, women and minorities are not adequately represented in this list."[31] Of the eighteen he named, ten were eventually elected, five from outside New York City.

The above sketchy account of those elected and not elected from 1968–1977, together with similar accounts in the other chapters, may well lead to the question: Well, and how *does* one get in? (Or: How do *I* get in?) Oddly enough, there are members of long standing who but vaguely understand the process, which has been altered in detail over the years, but remains today (set forth in the bylaws) very much as it was in 1953. The following is an abridged and simplified version of article 1:

> A notice inviting the Members to submit up to two nominations for vacancies, together with a report as to the number of vacancies existing, shall be sent out by the Secretary. . . . A nomination . . . must be filed by

three Members, of whom two must belong to the department for which the candidate is proposed.... In order to be eligible, the candidate's work must be essentially creative rather than interpretive....

Each of the Departmental Committees shall review the nominations for membership in its respective department to see that each of the candidates is qualified by his or her creative work and is a native or naturalized US citizen.... If the list of candidates for any department is too short or if persons highly qualified for membership have been omitted from the list, the Department Committee may make additional nominations. A ballot containing all such nominations, together with a statement of the candidates' qualifications, shall be mailed to the membership of the appropriate department.... Members of a department shall vote for only so many candidates as there are vacancies and shall return the [secret] ballot.... The names of those candidates receiving the highest number of votes shall be submitted to the entire membership for election.

The number of names in each department to be submitted is as follows: For one or two vacancies, one more than the number to be elected; for three through six, two; for seven, three; ties in a department are to be resolved by run-off elections. For election a candidate must receive a majority of the votes cast in the department for which he has been nominated; those receiving the highest number of the votes [in the general election] for the number of vacancies shall be declared elected.[32]

In the sixties and seventies, the continuing breakdown in all the arts of several generally recognized styles into many, often highly idiosyncratic, personal idioms also splintered their admirers into smaller, often combative, groups. Accordingly it became difficult, particularly in the art department, for a candidate to receive two-thirds of the vote, as had been required until 1974. In addition, although the bylaws had never mentioned negative votes, they had always been acceptable and useful only—would-be blackballers excepted—in arriving at the total vote from which the two-thirds was figured. In 1974 the negative vote was abolished, and the bylaws amended to provide for a simple majority. The art department nevertheless continued to be embarrassed by unfilled vacancies. The change helped but did not cure.

Until 1953 the problem had not existed, for each department filled its own vacancies; the members as a whole could either approve or disapprove. In the middle of the seventies there were states' righters, so to speak, who resented the power of the membership at large to influence the membership of their departments and wished to go back to the good old days. Malcolm Cowley explained:

The double vote had been instituted for a very good reason. In the past some departments had become fixed in their ways with a very high proportion of aged and conservative members. It had happened in the Department of Music and later in Art, and there was a danger of it happening now, especially since there were so few vacancies. By giving the whole membership one, two, or three candidates, the field was opened up to artists, writers, and composers who otherwise would not have been elected. The double voting system was initiated to loosen up the membership . . . and . . . it had succeeded to a very great extent.[33]

Because the states' righters continued to agitate, Margaret Mills was asked to draw up from the election results for 1973 to 1980 pairs of names, the first of which had won the department election and the second of which had won the determining general election. Examining the lists twenty years later, it does seem that Cowley was correct; those chosen by all the members were more widely known, naturally, than the often more hermetic departmental favorites. Nevertheless, thirteen of the seventeen overruled by the whole membership had been elected by 1984. Perhaps they had become better known in the interim simply because their names appeared often as departmental choices; more likely it was because, as often occurred—and occurs still—the wide coverage accorded a painting or sculpture retrospective, a striking new addition to the skyline, an important musical performance (especially of an opera), or a Pulitzer-winning novel or volume of poetry suddenly led to the election of a person who had been nominated half a dozen times.

However much the board might tinker with the bylaws in order to ensure wider representation, everyone recognized that the pre-eminent arts and letters organization must respond somehow to the growing population: presumably quality is usually a function of quantity. Jacques Barzun, with experience as a graduate dean and provost in predicting the number of applicants for studies in a prestigious university, had commented already in 1974:

> As regards the extent of our representation—250 members . . . in 1900 there were 76 million people in the United States and in 1916, when the Academy's charter was signed by President Wilson, the population was 102 million and in 1971, it was 206 million. So the original 100 members at the turn of the century were properly brought up to 250 in 1916. He added that something should follow, though exactly what he was not quite sure, since the country now had more than twice the population it had when the Academy's charter was signed.[34]

Three years later, George Rickey, long accustomed to working with high-quality materials and to judging their resistance to everyday wind and rain, wrote to Margaret Mills more elaborately. I reproduce his letter in its entirety, for it offers precision instead of hand-wringing and summarizes the solutions then much discussed and still being argued, when the U.S. population exceeds 260,000,000.

Here is some arithmetic about turnover and longevity in the Institute-Academy:

Given a total constant membership of 250, the following may be stated:

1. With average election age at 45 and death at 75, each incumbency is 30 years. Therefore the total turnover will average 8.33 per year, which would be pro-rated among the departments in accord with the total membership of each.

2. An increase of five years life expectancy, to eighty, with election at forty-five, will diminish the average turnover to 7.1 per year.

3. To increase the annual turnover to, say, ten (with possible distribution of 5-3-2 to literature, art, music), would require an average incumbency of twenty-five years; if the life expectancy is seventy-five, average age at election should by fifty; if eighty, then election fifty-five.

4. As life expectancy has increased since the founding of the Institute-Academy, with the membership fixed, the proportion elected, from among the qualified, has diminished.

5. The U.S. population since the founding has increased by 173% (1900–1970). The life expectancy at seventy has increased from 9.3 years to 11.6 years (25%); at age seventy-five it is increased from 7.1 years to 9.1, an increase of 28%. This has further diminished the I-A's recognition of talent (assuming the distribution of talent and achievement to be a constant in the population; actually the proportion has probably increased because of wider educational opportunity, larger and better educated audiences, and democratizing the media).

6. Spotcheck of thirty deceased members, Wendell to Zorach, shows average expectancy of 73.66 years. Stanford White throws it off a bit! Average incumbency of this group 19.9 years. Turnover rate is 1.4 for thirty members, i.e., about eleven for the whole 250.

7. It would be safe to say that, to carry out the original intent of the Institute-Academy to recognize and honor outstanding creative achievement, at least double the present turnover would be required. This can be done by (1) doubling the membership limit, (2) a minimum age rule for election, (3) declaring members emeritus after reaching a maximum age (e.g., 75) or a certain number of years of incumbency (e.g., 25), 4. some combination of the above.[35]

In a board discussion of Rickey's "emeritus proposal," Jack Beeson made a suggestion—only half-humorously—that may have met with secret approval but had to be dismissed out of hand: All the members of his acquaintance, at least after a drink or two, admitted that they could think of many on the outside who belonged inside and quite a few who should never have been admitted in the first place. Why not send ballots to the membership requesting that everyone list those they thought most undeserving, from one to ten? Counting the ballots could serve the purpose of electing the "most undeserving" to some new, more exalted honorary category, leaving vacancies to be filled by regular membership.

There had been many who had been insistent that the limit of two hundred fifty members be raised, even to the doubling mentioned by Rickey. But organizations chartered by governmental bodies are wary of requesting changes for fear that legislators will impose their own agendas. (The enlargement of the Foreign Honorary Members from fifty to seventy-five in 1969 had not necessitated a charter change.)

The election of Charlie Chaplin (by then Sir Charles) as a Foreign Honorary Member focused attention on the anomaly that he could not have been elected to the Institute even if he had been a U.S. citizen. As noted earlier, one's work must be "essentially creative rather than interpretive," difficult though it often is to make the distinction. Conversely, Martha Graham as a choreographer (*not* as a dancer) would be qualified for foreign membership, if only she would renounce U.S. citizenship. The subject of Charlie and Martha soon became a hot topic at meetings and dinners. Margaret Mills had observed much earlier, in 1968, "I myself gained from the discussion the impression of a general consensus that if any one of the departments had a candidate whose work was in one of these fields (photography, choreography, theatre or motion-picture direction) but who, it was thought, had made a significant and creative contribution to arts and letters generally, it could . . . propose him [or her] for membership . . . and go through the regular procedure."[36]

The department of art since its beginning had included architects, though some thought there were too many of them and the architects thought there were too few. Those who were not artists—and a few who were—believed that photographers should be included, but within the dual election system it was impossible to impose an answer to "What is Art?" on the department. The painter Robert Motherwell was heard to say that though his wife was widely recognized as an excellent photographer, he could not accept what she did as art. "In answering [Dwight] Macdonald's charge that photography was a craft, [Ted Roszak] felt that the camera should be regarded as a tool, just as a brush or a chisel was a tool and what was important was what happened [while] the tool was being used."[37]

Some of the pressure to include these new classes of members within the two hundred fifty limit was relieved in 1982, when the new category of American Honorary Members—ten in all—was established. This will be discussed in greater detail in the next chapter, but it is instructive to include here an extrapolation of Rickey's formulation: the average age of the first Honoraries when elected was eighty-one. By 1996 eight had died, five of them when in their nineties, the "low" average of eighty-seven brought about by the "early" death of Orson Welles at age seventy. Their average incumbency was not quite six years; clearly, too few were being honored too late in their lives.

If electing new members caused a good deal of soul-searching, those who declined admission or resigned were no trouble at all, for the Institute had always offered reinstatement of repenters as soon as vacancies occurred. From 1968 to 1977 no foreign members resigned except for Graham Greene, even those he had urged to do so. Samuel Beckett, Balthus, Jean Dubuffet, and Simone de Beauvoir declined admission, the first two because they were not accepting *any* memberships in honorary societies. In this country William Meredith almost declined but then "thought of all the good friends who must have busted their asses to bring about this unlikelihood" and became a very active member and officer. E. B. White said NO in 1946 but YES sixteen years later. The poet and translator W. S. Merwin accepted membership in 1972 but then changed his mind and declined; he changed his mind again in 1976 and took his place the next year. It is to be noticed that there are no American artists or composers in this listing. Perhaps writers as a group are more given to complication, to such things as tergiversation. Sinclair Lewis and William Saroyan, both members of the Institute, refused Pulitzer prizes, the latter saying that the accompanying thousand dollars would corrupt his art.

Several of the newly elected members were present at their welcoming dinner in the spring of 1976: invited were the painters Balcomb Greene, Conrad Marca-Relli, and Alice Neel; the architect Charles Gwathmey; the writers Gwendolyn Brooks, James Thomas Flexner, and Meyer Schapiro; and Jack Beeson, the only composer that year. The buzz among writers in the know was about Gore Vidal, who was said to have sent a telegram declining membership on the ground that he was already a member of the Diner's Club. Soon thereafter I learned that for a long time he had not responded at all to the invitation to join. Then he had sent a telegram, which read "THE INSTITUTE DOES ITSELF BELATED HONOR MY CONGRATULATIONS I CANNOT OF COURSE ACCEPT MEMBERSHIP BEST WISHES TO YOU."[38]

As one so often does, he had invented a wittier turndown and retailed it to friends before the date of the dinner. He did not respond to the letter of the secretary, William Meredith, asking him to reconsider. I recounted this story a short time later to a friend who had been Vidal's editor in their early days. She laughed and said, "Oh, yes, Gore once showed me a small notebook in which he had listed the honors and awards he expected to win and, in the second column, the dates by which he expected to receive them. I suppose his election to the Institute was off-schedule—'belated,' as he put it—and he was miffed."[39]

There can be few publications of its size that contain such a quantity of fine, if sometimes fugitive, prose as the *Proceedings* published annually by the American

Academy of Arts and Letters and the National Institute of Arts and Letters (once upon a time) and then, after 1976, by the American Academy and Institute of Arts and Letters, and finally, after 1992, by the American Academy of Arts and Letters. (Such a listing encapsulates a short history of the organization!) Each volume contains everything spoken at the annual Ceremonial, transcriptions of occasional after-dinner entertainments, and the commemorative tributes, some ten a year of varying length, written with warmth and care by member friends of the deceased.

The mid-May Ceremonial—sometimes known as the tent meeting—takes place in the midafternoon and is preceded by cocktails and lunch and followed by a reception attended by the whole audience: about nine hundred guests. The Blashfield address, supposedly the centerpiece of the Ceremonial—some think of it as something to be endured—was given almost every year from 1968 to 1977, four times by Foreign Honorary members: Sir Maurice Bowra, Dame Iris Murdoch, Dame Muriel Spark, and Sir Stephen Spender. All are reprinted in the *Proceedings*, as are the usually carefully wrought remarks of the president.

As the years passed, and the prize and award money increased, many who had wondered what could be the purpose of the Academy-Institute came to believe that rewarding the talent and achievement of non-members was reason enough. (In 1977 the total amount awarded was $130,000 [$338,000 in 1996 dollars]. In 1997 the amount given away was $750,000. In that year the NEA was making hardly any awards to individuals.) The president in 1974, Jacques Barzun, had this to say on the subject:

> After many years of conversation and correspondence with other philosophers all over the world, William James thought he had discovered what it was that they all wanted: it was praise. This observation was psychological, not critical or moralistic. For seeking praise is the sign of a candid and industrious nature. Praise is a good thing, a precious thing, and always in short supply. That is why the Lord had to praise his own work, as early as the fifth day, and thereafter commanded us all to praise *Him*. Even the dour temperament of Ecclesiasticus thought it right to praise famous men.
>
> Here at the Institute, each year, we follow these precepts and examples, and often go Ecclesiasticus one better; for we delight especially to praise and honor those who have not yet achieved fame—the young; and those of whatever age who have avoided fame, by luck or cunning. The distinctions that we award today to our writers, painters, musicians, and architects embody the judgment of their peers; they are not simply the echoes of indiscriminate popularity; they are—in short—praise at its purest.

In some cases, to be sure, it is reinforced by a sum of money, which is an always acceptable form of emphasis. But it is from the praise that we freely give that we—all of us—expect the great returns to which we are entitled when we praise truly, I mean: more works of the same magic charm and power as those that led us in the first instance to lift our voices in praise.[40]

Speaking of "returns," of those who received departmental awards, about one-quarter were later elected to membership.

The members' presentations of Gold Medals, the Awards for Distinguished Service to the Arts, the Award of Merit, and the Howells Medal, and the acceptance remarks by their recipients (not all of them members, by any means) are all to be found in the *Proceedings*, although, to be sure, the citations accompanying the thirty-five prizes and awards must be brief and run the risk of being almost as interchangeable as the citations for university honorary degrees. In 1969 an elegant Lillian Hellman strode to the lectern, followed by a shuffling Tennessee Williams dressed in denim, who was to be awarded the Gold Medal for Drama. Her pungent remarks about the American theater alluded to the turnabout of critics who were playing "the game of yesterday's genius" with Williams as a major victim. She hoped "that Mr. Williams will feel comforted by this medal [given] to him by the only body of men and women in this country who are his equals."

Without a script he drawled in response:

I think I'm essentially a humorist, you know, so I'm going to try to tell you something that will make you laugh. I hope it does. If it doesn't then I'm no good. Perhaps most of you know, or have at least heard of Maureen Stapleton. Well, one time, she received a phone call from a friend of hers who said that so-and-so was getting married, and Maureen said, "Who is she marrying?" And the caller said, "Why, she is marrying that man, you know he is a homosexual," and Maureen said, "Uh, uh, well, what about the bride?" And the caller said, "Well, of course we know she is a lesbian." And then the caller said, "You know they are not even being married by a real minister, they are being married by a minister who's been defrocked!" And Maureen said, "Oh," she said, "will you do me one favor, will you please invite Tennessee Williams to it?" And the caller said, "I don't know Mr. Williams, why should I invite him, Maureen?" And Maureen said, "Well, he'd say they're just plain folks."[41]

Another kind of return almost came about a little later when Williams was hoping that the Academy-Institute would administer the foundation he was setting up to aid young writers. But illness, incertitude, and death intervened.

The Gold Medal for Music for 1976 was presented to Samuel Barber by William Schuman, who began by saying:

There is an ancient saying that "two vinegar salesmen cannot be friends." In these surroundings we have nothing but exceptions to that thesis. We glory in giving awards to the young and later on medals to each other. Samuel Barber and I have been friends and colleagues since the 1930s. We were both born in the same year, but since I am five months his

Ceremonial, 1972. William Faulkner congratulates Eudora Welty on winning the Gold Medal for the Novel.

junior, it is a special joy for me today to pay my respects to an older colleague and honor him for his extraordinary achievements.

The history of the arts is filled with examples of those who expanded the means of expression. There have, however, been other artists who were content to create within established means. In music, for example, such composers would include Bach, Mozart, Mendelssohn and Brahms. Samuel Barber is in this tradition.

Barber's reply:

I have no prepared speech, but what I say will be even more brief than Mr. Schuman's. I remember the shortest speech that I ever heard was at Auden's house—in that rather rundown house in St. Mark's Place—at one of his birthday parties which I will never forget.

Edith Sitwell was there and he asked me if I would go over and speak to her. He said, "Don't call her Dame Edith, but call her Dr. Edith because she has just received a Doctorate from Oxford and she prefers to be called Doctor."

And so I went over and she was sitting on a brokendown armchair. She was about three inches from the ground and I leaned over her and said, "Dr. Edith, something, something. . . ." Well, it was impossible to talk in that position and I said, "Dr. Edith, it's really awfully difficult to talk to you in this position." And she said, "Don't."

He added a "Thank you" and sat down.[42]

It was also an inspired choice to invite the sculptor Richard Lippold, who had often collaborated with architects, to present the Gold Medal for Sculpture to Buckminster Fuller. Lippold spoke warmly of having met "Bucky" for the first time at Black Mountain College twenty-one years earlier and then added: "He delighted me with a speech scheduled to last for forty minutes which went on for four hours and which filled me with a total sense of permanent and irrevocable dudness because of its tensegrities, and dymaxions and energetic geometrics." Fuller began his response with a reference to his wife, spoken quietly at the lectern, but as his subject matter expanded—to include entropy, the second law of thermodynamics, and $E = mc^2$—he took over all the space downstage left. To the subjects Lippold remembered from the past, Fuller added a comprehensive outline of technological developments from steam power through electricity to "that great invisible reality of the electro-magnetic spectrum of 99.9% untouchables, unsmellables, and unhearables." As he became ever more excited by his visions of beckoning futures, one peroration followed another, and the audience fidgeted. Margaret Mills, aware that Fuller had already given the equivalent of two Blashfield lectures (and no doubt concerned about the caterers in the tent awaiting the thirsty multitude) made her way to the back of the theater, found some eager confederates, and began applauding enthusiastically when Fuller stopped momentarily to inhale. The audience joined the claque with deafening applause; the last audible words were, "Suddenly it will be realized that the meek have inherited the Earth and that the Earth is good. That is what the intuitions of youth seem to be trying to say." Overcome by his ovation, he stopped, open-mouthed, and took his seat in the front row.[43]

As I noted earlier, published each year in the *Proceedings* are the commemorative tributes to the recently deceased. They are presented (usually) by their writers, who read them to the members and their guests in the Members' Room, with its fine and appropriate view of the cemetery across the street. Many of the tributes are remarkable evocations of the departed, largely because their writers are chosen with such care; most have not been reprinted elsewhere. Some of these pairings from 1968 to 1977 were: Edward Hopper, by Andrew Wyeth; Dorothy Parker, by Lillian Hellman; Douglas Moore, by Virgil Thomson; Mies van der Rohe and Louis Kahn, by Philip Johnson; Duke Ellington, by Gunther Schuller; Louise Bogan, by W. H. Auden; Auden in his turn, by Stephen Spender; Hannah Arendt, by Robert Lowell; and then, fittingly, Lowell, by Peter Taylor. The following passage is by the last named:

> He turned himself, of course, into his own fictional character with a certain amount of interplay always between the fictional character and the real. It was partly this concern of his that there be no distinction between what was public and what was private in his life that led him into the Roman Church in 1940 and that led him to take the stand he did as a conscientious objector in 1943. There was always something profoundly personal about his public stance. When his draft notice arrived, he wrote to President Roosevelt as a citizen writing to the president but also as a Lowell writing to a Roosevelt: "I very much regret that I must refuse the opportunity you offer me in your communication of August 6, 1943, for service in the Armed Forces." And the letter concludes, "You will understand how painful such a decision is for an American whose family traditions, like your own, have always found their fulfillment in maintaining through responsible participation in both the civil and the military services, our country's freedom and honor."[44]

The members of the smallest department of the Academy are all magicians, or are thought to be. In most professions the tools of the trade are known to everyone. There may be some mystery as to how the users of words become transcendent novelists, poets, or playwrights, but ideas, words, and dialogue are all too ubiquitous. And if painters, sculptors, and architects can move, stun, or offend, we all know the rudiments of their games: who has not, if only as a child, sketched, watercolored, whittled, Play-Dohed, or Tinker-Toyed? But composers—to noncomposers—are magicians, for they can move, stun, or offend by means that seem as immaterial as they are evanescent. Furthermore, and suspiciously, they communicate with other musicians in code. To be sure, very many children—even these days—when they learn to play an instrument also learn the rudiments of code breaking: how to read music. A child playing Beethoven's *Für Elise* exemplifies perfectly an important difference between music and the other arts. Beethoven wrote on paper a set of instructions indicating, in some ways very imprecisely, how one was to bring the music into being; few would suggest that the music is all there on paper. And each performer will bring about a different semblance of what the composer had in mind—or in ear, or liver, or wherever. Elaborate codes—orchestral scores of the twentieth century, for instance—can be converted into performances only with difficulty by some conductors, and there are few music critics who even pretend to be able to read them.

Because the ideas of a composer become audible only when performers do more or less what they're told to do, composers resemble architects more than writers, painters, or (sometimes) sculptors. An architect's plans become a building by means of engineers and artisans following the drawings more or less, and there are not often copies of that building. A written work or a painting on a wall is the thing itself; when we are confronted with a cut version or a reproduction we usually know it. On the other hand, each performance of a piece of music is a simulacrum: a recording of a piece is not like a copy of a book; it is but a fixed *version* of the piece.

Because it erased one of the basic differences between music and the other arts, a development in the fifties may be said to have been the most revolutionary twentieth-century musical innovation. In 1952, Otto Luening (elected to the Institute that year) and Vladimir Ussachevsky (elected in 1973), later joined by Milton Babbitt, Edgard Varèse, and Mario Davidovsky (all members) began to use tape recorders and other electronic equipment as their medium. (More recently computers have taken their place.) By these means composers could short-circuit live performers, fixing their exact intentions on tape or disc, which could then be duplicated in any number of exact copies. One performance became exactly the same as another except for variations in the qualities of speakers and hall acoustics. A new parallel: the original painting or sculpture, which may change in effect with varied placement and lighting in a gallery.

Doubtless the first experience of many noncomposer-members with "electronic music" was at an after-dinner entertainment on January 16, 1974. Jacques Barzun introduced the subject cheerfully and knowledgeably, and then Ussachevsky in turn initiated the audience in some of the medium's sleight of hand. On that evening, as on earlier concerts presenting electronic music, the reactions were unequal measures of curiosity, fear, and derision. That these early electronic music composers were also expert and stylistically varied composers in conventional media doubtless weighed heavily in the departmental and general elections that had brought about their membership. They were all closely associated with the Electronic Music Center at Columbia University. They and their students, many of whom set up studios in other universities, were largely responsible for the marriage of music and electronics, the progeny of which—in the form of synthesizers and such—are to be heard at the flick of a radio or TV switch and from theater pits everywhere.

Despite the special nature of composition, there are members in other departments who have written music, or played it, or dabbled in it. The architect John Johansen writes songs, John Guare also—do you remember "Where is the devil in Evelyn? / What's it doing in Angela's eyes?" in *The House of Blue Leaves*?[45] Paul Bowles was for years a professional composer who wrote incidental music for innumerable plays, chamber music, an opera, and songs (including four delicious settings of Tennessee Williams lyrics) before he became a member as a fiction writer. Larry Rivers was a jazz clarinetist before he became a painter; Woody Allen (American Honorary Member) plays clarinet every day and gigs on Mondays; his predecessor, the Foreign Honorary Member Charlie Chaplin, composed scores for his films. When Robert Ward spoke to Arthur Miller about his wish to write an opera based on *The Crucible*, he was surprised to learn that the playwright hoped to compose his own opera on the subject. Miller then asked his friend Marc Blitzstein how long it would take for him to learn how to do so. In response, Blitzstein asked him how long it had taken him to write his first important play. Miller answered, "Twenty years." Ward acquired the rights and won a Pulitzer for his *Crucible* in 1961.

If others do not often poach in the musicians' enchanted forest, composers have never shown any such scruples. Berlioz, Schumann, and Debussy—not to mention Wagner and Boito—were writers to be reckoned with in the nineteenth century. Stephen Sondheim might just as easily have been elected as a writer; Ned Rorem has more than a dozen books to his credit; Virgil Thomson, so far our most musical and most literate music critic, could have taken his place as a writer alongside some of the literary critics. Libretto writing may be thought a kind of lowly wordsmithery, but otherwise fine writers sometimes don't acquire the knack. Gian Carlo Menotti (a Foreign Honorary Member, for he is still an Italian citizen) has written all his libretti. Both Dominick Argento and I have on occasion written our own.

Collaboration between composers and poets—whether fellow members or not—is too well known to require much comment. Generally speaking, poets are flattered when composers ask permission to set their lyrics. To be sure, the vocal line establishes *one* reading of the poetry, whereas the poet may have intended some other, or others. And while a living poet may permit lines to be cut or words repeated, his/her estate is likely to be less accommodating. Though instrumentally inclined composers have been known to belittle those composers who dally with words, singers, and the stage, music with words—in the theater or not—makes things easier for nonmusicians. Accordingly, a recital of composer-members' songs as an after-dinner entertainment in the mid-eighties met with some enthusiasm, whereas on the occasions when instrumental works have been presented, members have reacted like all audiences confronted with music new to them: with polite applause. Such concerts have not taken place for years, for *all* entertainments came to an end in the late eighties.

In fact, the sponsorship of concerts for the public at large, in Town Hall, the McMillin Theatre at Columbia, and its own theater, no longer took place after the early fifties. The Academy's fine Aeolian-Skinner organ fell into disrepair in the sixties and was only heard again after its restoration in the mid-nineties. The funds expended in earlier years for live public concerts have been spent since 1970 on issuing recordings of new music, initially on vinyl, now on CD, which are of more permanent value to their composers and can benefit more listeners than occasional live concerts. The works recorded are those of the annual music awardees, who, in addition to the $7,500 granted to all award winners, receive an additional $7,500 toward recording expenses.

In German-speaking countries there are two kinds of music—*Kunstmusik* (art music) and *Unterhaltungsmusik* (entertainment music)—and any mixture of the two is treated harshly. Here in the United States we are more permissive. We have serious, or concert, music (both unsatisfactory terms, but the best we have), i.e., what the laity call classical music, whether old or new; we have semiclassical music, light music from the start or classical music that has become widely known; and we have popular music: 95 percent of what is recorded. (We lack the balancing fourth type, semipop, for that which doesn't succeed in becoming quickly popular rarely persists.) These days various kinds of crossover music blur these neat categories, and nobody minds much.

With some of these notions in mind, it may be of interest to revisit a few musical matters that some of the authors of this volume have been too modest to delve into.

The German terms noted above are appropriately applied to the fourteen original composer-members of 1898. Eleven of them learned their craft in Germany; Walter Damrosch was born there, and Harry Rowe Shelley learned Central European musical manners from Dvořák, with whom he studied in New York City. It is odd that Arthur Bird was selected, for he had already been in Germany and Halifax for twenty years when he was elected, and he then continued his long and unproductive life in Germany. Respectability, characteristic of all the 1898 members, was represented by several composers of church music and parlor songs, as well as by Chadwick, the head of the New England Conservatory, and the first professors of music at Harvard, Yale, and

Columbia, as mentioned earlier. In retrospect, it is difficult to believe that these Central-European–styled worthies could have offended the ears of their contemporaries. The historian Francis Parkman would surely have been a charter member of the Institute had he not died a little too soon; he would then have run into John Knowles Paine, about whose department Parkman is supposed to have said at each meeting of the Harvard Corporation, "musica delenda est!" (music must be abolished!).[46]

Some of the most amusing music reviews reprinted in *The Lexicon of Musical Invective*, by Nicolas Slonimsky (an American Honorary Member from age ninety-seven to age hundred and one), were written by Henry E. Krehbiehl. He was offered membership as a writer in March 1908.

> I am too jealous of my peace of mind . . . to associate myself with any movement or body to which I cannot give my whole-hearted approval. I fear that this will not be possible in the case of the Institute which, I believe, had taken an active part in the matter of the MacDowell glo-rification which appears to me to be extremely unwise. The exagger-ated, fearfully exaggerated, estimate of the very amiable merits of Mr. MacDowell is little less, in my estimation, than a humiliation to the country and the art and an affront to other admirable and estimable American composers. It will do neither the country nor the art any good to put so small a god on so lofty a pedestal. . . . You can now understand why it might not be pleasant for some of the members of the Institute to have me among them; I can best avoid discussion of a grievous subject by keeping away from those who might unwittingly provoke it.[47]

MacDowell had died two months earlier.

Ethelbert Nevin's election coincided with the fame of his song "The Rosary," perhaps not coincidentally, and his membership was as brief as his songs and piano pieces, for he died in 1901. Of the other original members, Reginald de Koven was very well known by 1898 for a string of operettas, Americanizations of German and Austrian originals. His *Kunstmusik* operas for the Metropolitan, Chicago, and Boston are in relation to his popular works rather like his near-contemporary Sir Arthur Sullivan's foray into serious operas: forgotten.

All things considered, it is an odd group. Only three of the fourteen were members of the Century Club, which was not then hospitable to composers. The Century connection may seem irrelevant to this discussion, but one should note that more than half (72) of the artists and writers (135 in all) were thought "clubbable" by both organizations.

Having extended themselves in 1898, the Institute admitted no composers for a decade, with one forgettable exception, Arthur Whiting. In 1908 five were elected, three of them interesting choices. Victor Herbert, an Irishman, had acquired a taste for operetta while a student in Germany. In his early years he was a well-known cellist and conductor. His Institute years were his semi-classical years: thirty operettas, two of which, *Naughty Marietta* and *Sweethearts*, were later filmed. His two operas, like those of Nevin and Sullivan, were less durable. The second of the five, Daniel Gregory Mason, is unique in the annals: elected at the early age of thirty-five, he resigned two years later but then accepted re-election in 1938. He is the only composer to have resigned; no composer has declined membership. He and the third of the five, Charles Martin Loeffler, a German-speaking Alsatian, were the first composers to have studied for a time in Paris (though MacDowell—mainly German-trained—had studied a year as a classmate of Debussy in the Conservatoire, having lied about his age in order to be accepted). The other two elected in 1908 were Henry Hadley and Frederick Converse, both fine musicians who returned to America from Central Europe to share their gifts as conductor and teacher, respectively. The Metropolitan produced operas by both of them, back in the days when the Met regularly performed American works (under the directorship of an Italian, by the way).

Whether by design or inadvertence, the Institute elected only fourteen composers during the next thirty years, some of them better known as conductors even then. In so doing, the old guard managed to bypass several eligible men and at least two women. Two genial composers, John Alden Carpenter (elected 1918) and Deems Taylor (elected 1924), were trained in the United States, though the former studied briefly with Elgar in Rome. One need only to scan the titles of some of their works to imagine a musical world different from that of their elders: *Improving Songs for American Children*, *Adventures in a Perambulator*, *Gitanjali*, *Skyscrapers*, and *Krazy Kat*; *Through the Looking Glass* and two Met operas, *The King's Henchmen* and *Peter Ibbetson*. These titles represent, of course, an interest in the American vernacular, however much European models might echo in the music itself.

Another attempt at writing so-called American music, but rather short-lived, dates back to MacDowell's *Indian Suite* of 1892 and forward to the World War I years when *Azora, Daughter of Montezuma* (by Henry Hadley, another of the 1908 admissions) and *Shanewis* by Charles Wakefield Cadman (1932) were both performed by the Met; Victor Herbert's *Natoma* had been performed widely after 1911. Naturally, basing libretti on American Indian stories and quoting traditional melodies here and there led to no more of an indigenous style than did the Indian squaw singing "Hao, wari! . . . Ugh . . ." in Puccini's *Fanciulla del West*, first performed at the Met in 1910.[48] A year later MacDowell wrote: "I do not believe in 'lifting' a Navajo theme and fitting it into some kind of musical composition and calling it American music. Our problem is not so simple as that."[49] The one excellent composer who actually studied

Indian music and transmuted it into a highly personal idiom, Arthur Farwell (1872–1952), was never admitted, perhaps for that reason. It is more than likely that the Americans mentioned above were influenced as much in their choice of subject matter as in their musical language by their European contemporaries. Particularly in France, exotic Far Eastern and Near Eastern subjects for libretti, orchestral works, or whatever were a great attraction to composers avoiding the traditional. Perhaps the Great Plains and the Far West seemed sufficiently exotic to East Coast composers.

In the later twentieth century, when Indians became Native Americans, a number of composers turned again to that subject, with more interest in ethnicity than nationalism. Few of them can claim any genetic connection. One who can is this writer, whose musical contribution to the subject dates to the late thirties: an aborted opera, *Redwing*, based on the legend of an "Indian princess" supposedly buried under the main tent of his Boy Scout camp.

Toward the end of these thirty years of hit-or-miss elections both Howard Hanson and Leo Sowerby were elected in the same year; much earlier they had been awarded the Rome Prize in the same year. Given their birthplaces, in Wahoo, Nebraska, and Grand Rapids, Michigan, it is perhaps not surprising that both received their early training in the United States. Two years later, in 1937, an already internationally well-known composer was elected, the Swiss-American Ernest Bloch, who had studied in Geneva, Paris, and Brussels.

One should not read too much into this record of where composers studied abroad, for some remained only a short time and sturdy individualists were less influenced. Nevertheless, when World War I brought an end to study in Germany and a steady stream of American composers went to Paris—a few to Rome—differences in point of view and sound became apparent before long; just as those who had studied in Central Europe had returned and passed on to their students a tradition, so did those who had been in Paris bring other traditions, notably French and Russian. Bloch was in the United States as early as 1917, sharing his faith and musical points of view with young composers, several of whom later became Institute members. The number of composers who studied with Nadia Boulanger in Paris in the early twenties—and for decades thereafter—was so large that they came to be known as the Boulangerie. Marc Blitzstein (elected 1959) and Ross Lee Finney (elected 1962) both worked with her for a time and then traveled on to Berlin and Vienna, against the tide. By the forties, as the old guard disappeared, their places were taken by those who had been students in the twenties. Samuel Barber and Douglas Moore became members in 1941, Aaron Copland in 1942.

From the forties to the present the composer-members have been a remarkably varied group, ranging from the personalized traditional to what used to be called the avant-garde, from Percy Grainger and Virgil Thomson to John Cage and Edgard Varèse and to representatives of Broadway such as Jerome Kern,

Richard Rodgers, and Stephen Sondheim. Both ends of the spectrum—and ethnic and Asian-influenced music to boot—were represented by the election of Henry Cowell in 1951, a few years after his pardon and release from San Quentin. The broad-mindedness of his music department sponsors reminds one of the Ezra Pound affair. Still, had he served out his entire sentence (for a sex offense), it is doubtful that the whole membership would have voted him into the Institute the same year he was to have got out of prison.

The recrudescence of Central European influence via the Second Viennese School is represented today by Milton Babbitt and Charles Wuorinen, among others. Given the small number of vacancies, there continues to be a time lag in the representation of emergent styles, but if the maximalists are now well represented, can the minimalists be far behind? Women and African-American composers may well be underrepresented, but the qualified pools of both have enlarged only in recent decades.

It is the members of other departments who sometimes urge the composers to be more forthcoming toward jazz, just as it is members of other departments who wonder why the artists do not nominate photographers and why so many writers are dismissive of playwrights. That there were no members of any color but white for forty-six years accounts in part for the fact that no jazz musicians were nominated. But those days are long gone: Ulysses Kay was elected in 1979 and Olly Wilson in 1995. Furthermore, there is no antipathy toward jazz; the membership includes many composers who have played it, and one, Gunther Schuller, knows more about it than anyone else and taps his foot *only* when listening to it. Rather, the obstacle seems to be that real jazz implies improvisation, a tight combination of playing and inventing, and it is often difficult to separate the variation from the theme—which may be someone else's. Thus the difficulty for many is the bylaws' requirement that "the candidate's work must be essentially creative rather than interpretive." Nevertheless, Duke Ellington was elected in 1970, Dizzy Gillespie in 1993, Benny Carter in 1996, and Ornette Coleman in 1997, and Max Roach became an American Honorary Member in 1995. As already noted, the "Honorary" category was set up precisely to recognize those whose work combines creation and interpretation; jazz is just such an art. It is said that there are those who resent having been set apart from the regular members, but surely there is no department that can lay claim to being so distinguished overall as the group of ten American Honorary Members.

Most jazz and "serious" composers have in common the disadvantage that it is performing and conducting that make a living, not composing. Musical manuscripts are not ordinarily bought by collectors and speculators to be hung on walls. Nor is a piece of music as replicable as a novel without the apparatus and expensive performers for each new performance. Writers are shocked to discover that the copyrights of most musical works belong to their publishers; a composer who quotes from himself is wise to seek permission to do so, in order not to commit plagiarism. Creators tend to be complainers, but composers do have special ailments.

Because of all this, most composers teach, in numbers that only poets can match. At least thirty-eight of the present forty-seven members (in 1996) are or have been professors or teachers in universities or conservatories. When introduced during the dinner to welcome new members in 1967, Robert Ward had this to say on the subject:

> I stand halfway between a moment in which I thought I'd be spending the majority of my time as a composer and a moment when in fact I'm going to be spending most of my time for a while as a very busy administrator. And I couldn't help but think of the three newly elected composers here tonight. Mr. Schuller is going to Boston to head the New England Conservatory; Mr. Bergsma is one of our most lively young administrators out on the West Coast; and I'm going to Winston-Salem to the North Carolina School of the Arts. I don't know what this says about the state of composers in this country except that I know that ten years from now Gunther Schuller will still be turning out music, and I know that William Bergsma will be, and I hope that I will be. This is the way a composer's life goes in this country today, and it is wonderful that there is a society such as the National Institute which bolsters us in the creative side of our lives.[50]

These three administrator-composers remind one of Charles Ives, who was an insurance-executive-composer. In his earlier, productive years (roughly 1888–1921) he was so little performed that by the early twenties he published the *Concord Sonata* and *114 Songs* at his own expense, without copyright. In a statement accompanying the latter volume he wrote: "Some have written a book for money; I have not. Some for fame; I have not. Some for love; I have not. Some for kindlings; I have not. . . . In fact, I have not written a book at all—I have merely cleaned house. All that is left is out on the clothes line."[51] Until the late thirties and forties only friends and various musicians were aware of him; to a few of these Ives gave the copyrights of some pieces. He was amazed when the Institute "bolstered" the creative side of his life by electing him in 1946, at the age of seventy. It was the first and one of the few honors accorded him during his lifetime. After his death, his widow, Harmony Twitchell Ives, bequeathed all her (i.e., his) copyrights to the Institute in 1969 (those he had given away were later acquired by the Institute at the end of the first term of copyright coverage). Her will stipulated that for ten years one-half of the income be used for "the furtherance of the publication and performance" of Ives's works, and the other half be used to create scholarships for young musicians. Because the mass of manuscripts, chiefly at Yale, were left in such disorder, the Academy is still underwriting their editing, to the end that

they may be published or republished in correct and newly copyrighted editions. When the Institute received the Ives gift in 1969, the income was
$19,000, and an Ives Scholarship was duly awarded. In 1974 the annual income
had risen to $46,000, and the Institute presented "A Charles Ives Centennial
Festival, an exhibit of original manuscripts and a song recital."[52] It was
believed at the time that after the plethora of American music performed during the 1976 bicentennial the performance income would dwindle; to the
contrary, it has increased from year to year and in 1997 amounted to almost a
quarter of a million dollars. As the income has increased, the board has wisely
returned substantial sums to the endowment to ensure that there be sufficient
income in perpetuity for fellowships, for in 2004 (or in 2024, if Congress
passes amendments to the Copyright Act) Ives's music will begin to enter the
public domain. At the 1996 Ceremonial six Ives Fellowships of $7,500 each
and an Ives Fellowship of $12,500 were awarded, as well as a grant to the Ives
Society for continuing work on the manuscripts. In addition, in 1998 an Ives
Living similar to the two Strauss Livings will be awarded; by then, or a little
later, the Ives Endowment may become the largest in the Academy.

That Connecticut Yankee occasionally wrote passable verse for setting and
was partial to slant quotation of familiar material. One may hazard, in his style:

From fertile acorns sown by Charlie Ives
Have grown the golden oaks that shelter others' lives.

In 1955 Richard Rodgers, who even then had lacked neither recognition nor
awards, was delighted to find himself elected to the Institute. True, his collaborator Oscar Hammerstein II had been a member for five years, but except
for the early spate of operetta composers and Jerome Kern (1945) the Institute
had not been hospitable to those from the popular musical theater. Late in
1977 Rodgers wrote to Jacques Barzun, then president, of his intention "to
give the Academy-Institute the sum of one million dollars as a Fund, the
income of which would be used to establish 'The Richard Rodgers
Production Award.' "[53] He wished to aid young, as-yet-unknown composers
and lyricists to learn their trade by experiencing their work in productions by
not-for-profit theaters in New York City. His wishes were clearly, compre-
hensively, and loosely set forth in a document signed by both parties early in
1978. Because few members are from Broadway (on or off), from the outset it
has been necessary to add to the few theater-wise insiders experts from outside to form juries of seven. Two of those erstwhile outsiders, Stephen
Sondheim and John Guare, are now, happily, insiders.

These two large endowments in music were noticed uptown and downtown, and they made more audible the complaints of the composer-members
that they had long been underrepresented. It may be remembered that the

Committee of the Future, newly invigorated after amalgamation, had asked the three departmental committees to draw up lists of those outsiders most worthy of admission. The music department committee invited *all* the composers to consider the matter at a dinner meeting at the Century Club, which was at the time also seeking composer-members—as one Centurian said at the time, "to leaven the dough."

Almost half attended, two from the West Coast. The names of forty-eight qualified for membership were put forward, with due attention to geographical distribution, gender, and color. Of these, nineteen were elected soon or not long thereafter, and nine died before the time of testing. Also discussed was a scheme that would permit a weighted vote by composers in final elections, to overcome their fear that their nominations would be overturned by the more than two hundred writers and artists; as indicated earlier, Margaret Mills demonstrated that the fear was groundless, at least in the long term. Their discussion centered on increasing the size of their department. In his position paper to the board, Hugo Weisgall remarked:

> The Department of Music is, by far, the smallest of the three departments of the Academy-Institute. Although there may have been some historical justification for the proportions decided upon at the time of the Institute's founding, it is not altogether clear why these proportions have remained essentially unaltered up to the present time.
>
> Certainly during the past several decades the extent and the quality of musical creativity in the United States has increased greatly. If the impression remains that contemporary American music is not as widely known here and abroad as it deserves to be, the fact is different from the impression, which is a hangover from the past or the effect of a lingering sense of inferiority about American music other than popular.[54]

The board has always had the power to assign a vacancy or vacancies in one department to another, music usually being the beneficiary. The original number of 14 had grown to 40 in 1977; seven more have been added since then. One is startled to discover that of the 1,161 members of the Institute from 1898 through 1997, only 124 have been composers, just about 10 percent.

Small as it may be, the department of music is pleased to include its just proportion of prickly members. Nevertheless, as John Updike has remarked, it is the most collegial of the three. And with reason: serious composers and jazz musicians have always had in common their minority status in a musical world dominated by commercialized popular music. In addition, concert and opera composers must compete for performances with the mass of public-domain music endlessly repeated and rerecorded. Such a situation is a twentieth-century phenomenon and not duplicated in the other arts and letters.

Reacting to these circumstances, composers—like other minorities—become collegial. They organize chamber-music ensembles specializing in new music, orchestras here and there, publishing and recording outlets, and innumerable modest not-for-profit organizations that proselytize their cause. Most composers are delighted to serve on juries of these and other prize-giving organizations. Because they serve as officers and board members of so many outfits and also because as professors and teachers they are accustomed to the give-and-take of compromise, they are not often shy or bumbling at Academy meetings. In fact, at general meetings of members, composers are disproportionately present, usually making up at least a third of the gathering.

Walter Damrosch, composer-conductor-teacher, was president of the Institute for seven years and then president of the Academy for seven more, after the Row. To a conductor accustomed to leading orchestras and singers in Wagner's *Ring*, conducting the "operettas" laid in Upper Manhattaniana must have been a simple matter. He was followed to that podium by Douglas Moore, Aaron Copland, and Hugo Weisgall.

Because the Academy's investments are managed by downtown experts, it would be unfair to suggest that the solid financial state of the Academy has been maintained by composers. Nevertheless, for half a century after 1941 the Institute (with but one exception) elected as treasurers *only* composers; for eight of those years the Academy entrusted its real estate and endowments to Deems Taylor and William Schuman. George Bernard Shaw (a Foreign Honorary Member from age eighty-seven to ninety-three) might well have thought it dangerous to put financial affairs in their hands, for several of his characters claim that only the rich can afford to be honest. But our membership has decreed otherwise; it has noticed that when composers congregate, they discuss mainly publishers, copyrights, and money and that their comparative impoverishment has led, not to crime, but to thrift. The truth is that though composers do practice magic, they resemble their singers: they are just like people, only more so.

NOTES

Unless otherwise specified, all materials cited are located in the Academy files.

1. June 3, 1969.
2. *Proceedings of the American Academy of Arts and Letters and the National Institute of Arts and Letters*, 2d ser., no. 21 (1971): 37–38.
3. Graham Greene to the board, May 19, 1970.
4. George Kennan to Graham Greene, May 27, 1970.
5. Letter sent after the Ceremonial, May 26, 1970.
6. Minutes of a meeting of the board and the council, October 30, 1970.
7. February 5, 1975.
8. Minutes of the Academy, December 6, 1974.

9. September 5, 1975.

10. Babette Deutsch to Academy board members, October 30, 1975.

11. September 11, 1975.

12. October 23, 1975.

13. December 3, 1974.

14. November 1976, in a handwritten manuscript.

15. Minutes of the Committee on Progress, May 28, 1974.

16. Minutes of the Committee on the Future, December 17, 1976, and May 2, 1977.

17. February 8, 1977.

18. Minutes of the Committee on the Future, May 2, 1977.

19. June 20, 1975.

20. There exist several versions of the recommendation, one of them considered and passed as a resolution by the board of the Academy, October 13, 1976.

21. Quotation from the minutes of the Institute council, May 26, 1976.

22. June 24, 1976.

23. Minutes of the Institute council, September 10, 1976, and of the Academy board and the meeting of the members, September 13, 1976.

24. The Mint later denied that Columbia University had ever been approached (Robert Vincent O'Brien to Harrison Salisbury, December 29, 1976).

25. January 11, 1977.

26. See "Draft" for the Board meeting, January 28, 1977.

27. Memorandum, Jacques Barzun to Harrison Salisbury, January 27, 1977.

28. Minutes of the dinner meeting, November 9, 1977.

29. January 7, 1977.

30. April 3, 1974.

31. Letter to Margaret Mills, April 13, 1974.

32. Bylaws, as reproduced in *The American Academy of Arts and Letters* (New York: American Academy of Arts and Letters, 1995–96), pp. 129–32.

33. Minutes of an Academy meeting, November 9, 1977.

34. Minutes of the joint meeting of the Committee on Progress and the Academy board, May 28, 1974.

35. November 30, 1977.

36. Minutes of the Institute dinner meeting, January 29, 1968.

37. Minutes of the Institute, November 19, 1975.

38. Telegram, Gore Vidal, Rome, to William Meredith, New York City, January 16, 1976.

39. Private communication between Constance Darby Moore (1924–1996) and the author, 1976 or 1977.

40. *Proceedings*, 2d ser., no. 23 (1973): 9–10.

41. *Proceedings*, 2d ser., no. 20 (1970): 27–28.

42. *Proceedings*, 2d ser., no. 27 (1976): 26–27.

43. *Proceedings*, 2d ser., no. 19 (1969): 62–64.

44. *Proceedings*, 2d ser., no. 28 (1977): 73–74.

45. John Guare, *The House of Blue Leaves* (New York: Penguin, Plume, 1987), p. 15.

46. Gilbert Chase, *American Music*, 2d ed. (New York: McGraw-Hill, 1966), p. 336.

47. H. E. Krehbiehl to R. U. Johnson, "March, 1908."

48. Giacomo Puccini, *La Fanciulla del West* (Milan: G. Ricordi, 1910), pp. 510–11.

49. MacDowell's comment to Hamlin Garland is quoted in Chase, *American Music*, p. 363.

50. *Proceedings*, 2d ser., no. 18 (1968): 57–58.

51. Quoted in Henry Cowell and Sidney Cowell, *Charles Ives and his Music* (New York: Oxford University Press, 1955), p. 77.

52. Publication no. 294 of the Academy and Institute, October 17, 1974.

53. Letter of agreement, Richard Rodgers with Academy and Institute, March 6, 1978.

54. Attachment to the minutes of a board meeting, November 9, 1977.

CHAPTER NINE

1978–1987

HOLDING THE HIGH GROUND

Ada Louise Huxtable

THE DECADE from 1978 to 1987 is not a time that sticks in the mind. The social and sexual radicalism of the 1960s was becoming assimilated and institutionalized;[1] by the 1980s the idea of making it and flaunting it had replaced the desire to change the world. The seventies began the popular trip back to kitsch; this was a generation far enough away from its sources to invent the new-old world of retro: revivals of the styles and artifacts of the fifties that combined irony and sentimentality in an innocent and sometimes perverse revisionism surprising to those who had lived through the period with a set of values that now seemed as quaint and dated as the objects being revived. If the sixties stood for protest and passion, morality and idealism, the seventies were a transitional decade to the excesses of the eighties, which has been called the decade of greed, measured in buyout billions and the status symbols of upward mobility and marked by the celebration of the heroes of ingenious fiscal manipulation untainted by time spent in jail. Each decade's media characterizations have just enough reality to support easy generalizations. But the heritage of the self-liberated young of the sixties still reverberates in the nineties, even as the ostentatious self-indulgence of the eighties, declared passé and supposedly replaced by a new austerity—one basic Jag in the garage and a few seminal black Calvins in the closet—has resurfaced in new heights of conspicuous consumption. The hippies have given way to the baby boomers, who are now becoming their own parents, which happens to us all.

None of this happens at the Academy; values are steady and worn like comfortable old clothes, excesses of taste and style, in art or in life, do not penetrate the beaux arts facade. The course stays smooth, the bumps along the way caused only by routine jousting between the various schools and generations of art and thought that make up the membership, differences that can become impassioned but seldom reflect a rapidly changing culture or influence a larger, less privileged world. The climate of the seventies and eighties was not hospitable to bold stands or innovative ideas. The growing conservatism was particularly hostile to the arts. These were the Reagan years, when time ran backward and the country turned inward and the Administration began the process of undermining and dismantling our liberal institutions and ideals by fox-in-the-henhouse appointments that put the enemies of educational, environmental, and social welfare programs in charge. Reagan took on the "Evil Empire" with promises of "Star Wars" and presented the nation's first trillion-dollar budget. As the decade finished and Gorbachev called for glasnost and perestroika, Reagan called on Gorbachev to tear down the Berlin Wall. The cold war ended.

It was an odd, transitional period in the arts, a mix of the retrograde and the far out, a kind of backing and filling into the future. Efforts to rehabilitate history, so long spurned by modernism, coexisted with attempts to push denial of the past into frontiers of expression never broached before. In the orgy of rediscovery of the past by the young, what was new was old. The official label for all this was *postmodernism*; the name covered anything that broke with the modernist doctrine that had defined and dominated the century. Representation in art, melody in music, and respect for the past were acceptable again. A new skyline appeared in fancy dress: caricature-classical, short-attention-span buildings that made the honest banality of the flat-topped glass boxes of the sixties look good. In a sense, the failures were as important as the successes. Because postmodernism broke the rules and cleared the air, it ultimately provided the freedom that was to revitalize the arts and lead them into genuinely new creative territory.

This turn to the past found sympathetic ground in the latent conservatism that had always rejected modernism; popular taste, vindicated, rode high, celebrating the comfortable and the familiar and the virtues of a no-frills bottom-dollar mentality, which soon dominated government policy. The danger for the arts in America became clear. Government support of the arts and humanities, so long delayed and so hard-won, was attacked and politicized. Yet after some inconclusive discussion, the Academy-Institute took no stand. The elaborate machinery set up in the 1950s at the time of the McCarthy hearings had made it virtually impossible to produce a public statement on politically sensitive issues. Fear of dissension of a far more disruptive nature than the usual aesthetic rifts takes precedence over political action that might split the membership into angry, warring factions.

This cumbersome machinery has insulated the organization against importuning publishers whose books are attacked by conservative school boards or adherents of political causes that may or may not pose First Amendment threats. But the difficult and delaying process also foreclosed participation in significant events closely related to Academy-Institute interests. In 1981 the Committee on the Future, a body activated, dissolved, and reactivated over the years to study future roles, responsibilities, and substantive issues, addressed the matter of taking stands on questions of censorship, plagiarism, forgery, and literary and human rights. It reported that "most of the members . . . did not seem unduly frustrated or dissatisfied by the existing passivity . . . in face of issues of artistic and intellectual freedom."[2] The Academy-Institute remained mute.

Two incidents prompted exceptions to this cautious abstention: the Soviet condemnation and exile of the dissident Andrei Sakharov and the Ayatollah Khomeini's death sentence on Salman Rushdie, both virtually fail-safe causes. Letters expressing "profound concern for the fate of Andrei Sakharov" signed by the president and the members of the board were written to Jimmy Carter, who was nearing the end of his presidency, and to Leonid Brezhnev in the Soviet Union. Carter replied with his personal assurance that his "administration will continue at every opportunity to press for relief for Soviet dissidents."[3] There was dense silence from the Kremlin. As for the Academy's response to the *fatwa*, a statement on Salman Rushdie was released to the press, joining many others.

This tacit institutional forbearance was shattered, however momentarily, at the 1986 Ceremonial. Informed of his election, one of the newly chosen, the sculptor Mark di Suvero, sent a modest, handwritten note in which he suggested that a mistake might have been made in the elevation of "a manual laborer to your prestigious Academy and Institute," after which he gave instructions on the correct spelling of his name for the membership roster. He also asked to be "allowed to make a small ten minute speech at the formal induction." This turned out to be a statement that touched every political protest button from the Tonkin Gulf to the suppression of democracy in Chile and the "bloody and tyranical fascism" of the CIA. It may not have measured up to the political grandstanding featured on prime-time TV during some Oscar ceremonies, but it would have been a distinct shock—despite the familiarity of the litany—to the members and their guests assembled in sedate rows in the auditorium and on stage. The speech was not read at the induction ceremony but distributed by its author at the reception that followed.[4]

What interested members in the Reagan years was of a more practical nature. Letters fairly flew to elected officials and the press protesting changes in the tax laws that had eliminated artists' right to deduct for work contributed to a museum, library, or other public institution. Another bit of federal fiscal fancywork reclassified authors' books held in warehouses as taxable stored assets, like machine tools, encouraging the elimination of books in print through quick disposal as remainders or by outright destruction.

If the membership kept its powder dry on the big issues, there was no lack of passion on parochial ones. Any partisan in-fighting—and there is always enough to keep things lively—is strictly private, professional, and generational. Battle lines drawn from the beginning between the supporters of tradition and innovation have been only slightly muddied in recent years by postmodernism's radical rewriting of history; those professional animosities in which artists specialize as a matter of personality and principle have remained consistent. These divisions surface noticeably in the matter of new members and awards, sometimes escalating to open feuds. But while the verbal jabs are sharp, only once has the conflict come to something like public blows, when Jacob Druckman struck a folder out of David Diamond's hand at the 1979 Ceremonial, in protest over changes in the wording of an award citation Druckman had written. Whether the punch was meant to hit the offending person rather than the offending citation in the folder is not clear, but the incident highlighted the seriousness with which these differences of opinion are taken and brought about several months of mutual demands for apologies and resignations. Hell hath no fury like the author of a citation spurned.

The affair started routinely enough with a fairly normal panegyric of the genre, written by Druckman to accompany the award in music to be given to the composer Morton Sobotnick "for his vision as well as his oeuvre." The tribute continued, "A trailblazer aesthetically and technically, his contribution has already profoundly touched both his contemporaries and his followers." Just as routinely, the citation was sent to the chairman of the Awards Committee, David Diamond, for any correction or editing that might be necessary. What followed was not quite so routine. As edited by Diamond and delivered at the Ceremonial, the substitute wording was considerably muted. Although the revised tribute—"for his visionary works which have impressed a large public interested in contemporary music"—allowed that there was a large public interested in contemporary music and this was an audience for which the composer's work might have an appeal, in the flatness of tone lurked an implication that neither that public, nor the work, had much appeal for the citation's critic.[5]

Druckman's anger erupted when he met his censor near the stairs to the stage on the day of the Ceremonial. "He came towards me," Diamond wrote in an indignant letter to Margaret Mills, "threatening to punch me, punched my folder into the air . . . accusing me of editing his citation out of all of its original meaning." Defending the citation surgery, he added, "I cut its verbosity, crudities (oeuvre, etc.) but left the essential 'visionary' implication," adding in a later letter to the president, Barbara Tuchman, "I believe I retained the basic estimation and kept the word *visionary* which, I have always felt, should be reserved for those who have reached occult presciency in their work, rare enough in Art in our time." Not only was the folder "punched out of my hand," he continued, but being "called 'you son of a bitch' demands an apology. . . . I was publicly humiliated."[6]

Throughout the dispute the unflappable Maggie Mills directed the flow of accusations and demands for resignation and apology, until the ball finally landed in Barbara Tuchman's court. Solomon-like, she split the blame. "I have seen the copies of both the original citation and your edited version," she wrote. "While it is obvious that the original required editing from the grammatical point of view, my impression is that your version did indeed rather change the spirit and, if I may say so, was rather parsimonious of praise and somewhat cold in effect." As for an apology, she felt that this was a personal matter between the two men. She then discreetly but firmly expressed the hope that with the lapse of time it might be just as well to let the issue fade away. When it did not, she sent another letter stressing "the fairness and magnanimity" of Academy-Institute members in their dealings with one another and the undesirability of prolonging the incident by bringing it before the board. "May I ask you to reflect further on this matter," she suggested with an iron graciousness, "before advising me of your decision?" Eventually, both men were persuaded to send apologies to each other through Maggie, to be delivered simultaneously, though not, alas, at sunrise, with seconds, as the affair might have required at an earlier time in the more flamboyant European Academic tradition. Peace and reputations were restored.[7]

As a result of this incident, the procedure for writing citations was changed. The final form was no longer to be left to the Awards Committees; all texts were to go through an oversight group that was to include board members. The new system showed a fine sensibility, but the delicacy may have been exaggerated: without the uproar preceding its delivery, the citation that provoked the controversy might have gone unnoticed on a warm spring afternoon when the delivery of a seemingly endless and ever-growing number of encomiums after a luncheon featuring generous amounts of good wine (from a cellar selected for many years by Virgil Thomson) had had a predictably numbing effect. Reading the citations aloud was eventually supplanted by printing them in the Ceremonial program; but one can still admire how expertly some of them hedge.

Although the intrepid Maggie had a fielder's skill for defusing angry members and warding off threatened resignations, not all departures were avoided. Paul Horgan resigned from the Institute in 1979 "for personal reasons," which may or may not have had something to do with the poetry prize (he denied it, although admitting to a certain pique at a procedural gaffe involving the Witter Bynner Poetry Award). Taking advantage of an unwritten revolving-door policy, he was reinstated two years later. Kurt Vonnegut tried to jump ship in 1981, submitting a letter of resignation in which he made the statement that "since the sole virtue of the Academy-Institute was as a dispenser of cash and encouragement to the young" and he no longer intended to serve on awards committees, he felt it appropriate to leave. There was, however, a subtext to the letter, in which Vonnegut scored the "willy-nilly nominating and election schemes" that left deserving artists out in the cold, implying "to them and to the world," that they "are not quite topnotch." In this case, Arthur Schlesinger, Jr., intervened to persuade Vonnegut to stay, but he tried to leave again in 1987, offering this time to "retire." This led to a full-scale debate on the pros and cons of establishing an emeritus category, which was also seen as a way of enlarging the membership without compromising the immortals' exclusivity by actually increasing their number. The idea was defeated by a mail vote in 1989, while Vonnegut, who had been asked to wait for the resolution of the broader issue, presumably did not hold his breath. He stayed. In 1987 Joseph Brodsky resigned from the Institute as a protest against the election of the media-celebrated, populist Soviet poet Yevgeny Yevtushenko as a Foreign Honorary Member. His action caused surprisingly little fuss; the board seemed more miffed by the fact that Brodsky had made the announcement to the press before notifying the Academy–Institute.

But perhaps the most disturbing resignation of the decade was that offered by former president Jacques Barzun on the occasion of his election to the Academy from the Institute in 1982. Because he had so ardently championed the integration of the Academy and the Institute during the previous decade, he felt obliged not only to reject his elevation to the higher body on the grounds of the unfairness and inequity in the arbitrary nature of the selection process but also, as a matter of principle, to resign from the Institute as well. In subsequent letters, he increasingly boxed himself in through the eloquence of his arguments against the existence of the separate Academy; his position was further complicated because he was about to publish a book on William James, "in which I quote with tacit approval the comparable doubts that he expressed on declining his election (to the Academy) in 1905."[8] Cajoled and reassured, Barzun was eventually persuaded to stay.

Among those elected to membership in the Institute or elevated to the Academy in these years, some responded with personal and literary grace: Hortense Calisher wrote two heartfelt pages on the meaning of membership, and Wolf Kahn not only expressed doubt that anyone had ever rejected election to such a distinguished roster but added, "if such a graceless individual exists let him stand alone, I would not stand by his side."[9] That would have left him sitting in 1979, when his fellow artist, Frank Stella, declined. Thomas Berger declined in 1983, quoting an English paraphrase of Rilke: "It would certainly be unfair to attribute this action of the undersigned to any lack of respect; he declines simply in order to remain personally inconspicuous, as his work as an artist unconditionally obliges him to do."[10]

Leon Edel objected to the "philistine choices" that included journalists; it was generally agreed in informal discussion by the board that they were to be considered only if they had made a considerable literary contribution.[11] To this the ink-stained wretches who were subsequently elected added a few literary flourishes of their own. Russell Baker, admitted to membership in 1989 in spite of such dire warnings of intellectual decline, wrote that he accepted "with pleasure, gratitude and a suspicion that I am wading beyond my depth. Ah well, shameless immodesty is the order of the age. I thank the Academy-Institute for this opportunity to display mine."[12] Touché. When Art Buchwald's election followed, he asked where he could have his cape and sword made, in the French tradition, which allows Academicians to design their own outfits. Perhaps suspecting that such levity might be misunderstood, he added a hand-written postscript: "I officially accept."[13]

Ultimately, however, members are self-selected, a process that has its incestuous and networking aspects. There is the usual amount of rivalry, resentment, and those intricate power plays found in any group of high-profile, high-achievement, high-ego peers. Partisan electioneering for friends and colleagues reached the point where it was necessary to limit the number of seconders brought into play, and it never ceases to be popular sport to point out that some not elected have achieved more fame than those invited to membership. But artists recognize artists, and respect them; in a company not exempt from human failings, there is unanimous understanding and appreciation of the real thing.

Inevitably, however, definitions of the real thing vary wildly. Members are as sincere, if divided, about talent and achievement as they are agreed that "excellence" is the only viable standard, even at a time when excellence as an ideal—always elusive—was becoming intellectually discredited and politically incorrect. With value judgments attacked, high art has ceased to be high ground. There has been no rush to summon representatives of an egalitarian, pluralistic, popular culture through sculptor-member Adolph A. Weinman's Renaissance-inspired bronze doors at the 155th Street entrance. It had been so much simpler at the start: there was high art and low art, and the Academy was for high art; its role was to protect high art from the culturally unwashed, artistically unappreciative multitudes. Today high art and popular art coexist in an uncertain and uneasy mix. It is this crossover art, however, that has enriched and defined contemporary American culture, at the same time that it has thrown accepted attitudes and practice into disarray. And while the modernism so railed against by the Academy's founding fathers has long since been accepted, with its most distinguished practitioners seated in the Academy's noble chairs, the encroachment of an aggressive popular culture does not sit equally well.

What it comes down to is age versus youth, a constant theme in Academy-Institute affairs. The need for new versus old blood is balanced by the ever-present desire to honor overdue nominations. The artist George Rickey's perceptive comment that a list of proposed arts nominations "shows the future membership filtering through a tiny group of aged men" defined the process succinctly.[14] In this decade, concern for the age gap was extended to the low number of women and minorities, and the objective of diversity was actively pursued, if with some curious results. Member Ralph Ellison's *Invisible Man* was paralleled by the Academy-Institute's invisible woman: the election of Mary McCarthy in 1988 brought the number of women in the Academy to five; this reduced the total from seven the year before, down from eleven in 1985–86. The explanation was that "as women died, they were being replaced by men. No one could understand why this should be happening at this time."[15]

Some members have managed to maintain a qualified Olympian objectivity in the Academy-Institute culture wars. In a footnote to his nominations in 1984, George Rickey wrote, "I recognize that such a list indicates my age and bias but I do include some artists that I don't like but who I believe ought to be considered." Asked to second a nomination, another member agreed: "Not that I like him, or even his work, but I really don't believe in letting personal prejudice dictate my actions; the man has a distinguished reputation and he is able, of this there is no doubt, and he belongs in the organization."

From the late seventies through most of the eighties the art department proved particularly cantankerous, requiring the most skillful prodding and handling by the ever-patient and consistently goal-oriented Margaret Mills. Arts members displayed a rather higher than average unwillingness to serve on committees, make nominations for membership or awards, or vote in elections. This finally became a matter of official concern in 1979, when it was noted at a board meeting that "most suggestions were made by a comparatively small number of (arts) members and that proportionately more writers and composers than artists sent recommendations."[16] In 1980

Bronze doors on West 155th Street by Adolph A. Weinman (elected 1910) in memory of Mary Wilkins Freeman (elected 1926).

Isabel Bishop, the Academy's vice-chancellor for art, presented a report to the board detailing the situation in terms of statistical abstention in relation to other departments, which consistently demonstrated a more inclusive and welcoming view of their fellows. Arts vacancies were left empty; in 1981 the department was unable to fill six.[17] This response was a given even in the awards program. In one instance the executive director complained that "about one quarter of the art [awards] candidates contacted do not respond to our request for slides."[18] Whether the artists were concentrating on their work or sulking in their studios is uncertain, but as a group they are notorious loners. The generational and philosophical gap between the realists and abstract expressionists also led to some bitter exchanges. Paul Cadmus wondered angrily about one of the leading abstract expressionists, "Who, and how many, proportionately, are the artists whose work she 'despises' ... also what, and how many, of the despised feel about her work and various other self-expressionists?" his grammar apparently affected by his feelings.[19] Accusations of partisanship approached paranoia. Members suspected each other of making nominations "in batches" from their own galleries, aided and abetted by the gallery owners. Peter Blume was "shocked at the composition of the Awards Committee," feeling that "it reflected the prejudices of the 'new' Academy, and, from my point of view [was] completely scandalous. The granting of awards ... cannot be left in the hands of bigots."[20]

Meanwhile, behind the scenes, Maggie Mills worked assiduously to keep the Academy-Institute and the membership relevant and up to date, doing her best to persuade the "new" artists so disliked by the "old" artists to serve on the Awards Committee. In 1983 she wrote abstract expressionist Robert Motherwell regretting that he and Jasper Johns and Roy Lichtenstein were leaving the committee: "We could have done with at least two more years of your help."[21] The following year, she again wrote Motherwell, commenting, "I would hate to see the committee choose only figurative artists," and adding hopefully, "George Segal and Will Barnet frequently vote for artists whose work is abstract, so it may be possible to avoid a total debacle."[22]

In spite of all efforts, the age level remained high, and innovation only found its way to the classical citadel when the risk factor was gone. It was becoming increasingly obvious that the arts had outstripped and transcended the Academy-Institute's traditional categories. In 1982 the bylaws were amended to create the new category—hors de combat, so to speak, because all privileges were included except the right to vote—of American Honorary Members. This group of ten places was intended to include film makers, photographers, choreographers, and others whose work fell between the traditional categories or was hard to categorize in a more conventional way. This solution, rather than the creation of new departments, was the simplest way out of the dilemma without radical amendment of the charter. The first American Honorary Members, inducted in 1983, were Berenice Abbott, Ansel

Adams, Martha Graham, Orson Welles, and George Balanchine, who died before he could be notified. (Sometimes the Academy-Institute loses the race.) Among those elected since have been film makers Frank Capra, Reuben Mamoulian, Woody Allen, and Billy Wilder; jazz percussionist Max Roach; choreographers Agnes de Mille, Merce Cunningham, Jerome Robbins, Trisha Brown, and Twyla Tharp; dancer Paul Taylor; critic Anna Sokolow; patron Lincoln Kirstein; and photographer Harry Callahan.

The most enduring infighting has not been between the champions of tradition and those of innovation, or between one school and another; it has pitted department against department in a long-playing rivalry for the number of members and the distribution of vacancies. The board can assign vacancies to any department, at its discretion, regardless of where they occur. In the seventies and eighties, the music members made dramatic pleas for the enlargement of their department, pointing to the much greater number of artists and writers. David Diamond suggested a mild mutiny if action was not taken to correct the existing inequities. "I have decided once and for all," he wrote in 1987, "that I will not nominate anyone for membership in any other departments until our poor little Music Department . . . is augmented. Whatever the stupid technicality is (and I have never understood the mumbo jumbo about this at meetings), unless it is changed to allow more members into our department, I cannot nominate anyone in Art or Literature, in protest, I have counseled other musicians to do so too."[23] (Arts and music seem to have more difficulty with language in moments of stress than does literature, which, not surprisingly, keeps its grammatical cool.) Maggie Mills replied that the departments of art and literature had "given" the department of music eight vacancies that had occurred over the previous ten years. She added that she had also done a little research to find out how many music

Ceremonial, 1983. Kay Boyle with photographer Berenice Abbott after Abbott's induction as an American Honorary Member.

members had died in the previous decade, creating vacancies, compared with other departments, and had concluded that the problem was as much a matter of musicians' extraordinary longevity as of vacancy distribution.[24]

Earlier, Hugo Weisgall had argued persuasively that "although there may have been some justification in 1898 for limiting the size of the music department, it was very surprising that the proportion had not been changed," adding that "the extent and quality of American musical activity had multiplied enormously and that there was more musical talent in this country than in any place in the world."[25] The music department was gradually increased from thirty-seven to forty in 1974 and forty-two in 1978 and then, with three more board-assigned vacancies, was brought up to forty-five in 1984. All of the additions were made from other departments. Jacques Barzun, in his role as president and peacemaker, observed diplomatically that it would be difficult to determine a "fair" proportion in the membership "corresponding to the work being done in art, literature and music."[26]

In this game of articulate one-upmanship, the architects were a distinct, and voiceless, minority. As members of the art department, they dwelt in a kind of limbo with the artists with whom they had been in so much closer professional contact in those first golden decades when murals and statuary were an intrinsic part of the architectural product, orchestrated by the architect in charge. Men (there was no tighter male club professionally and socially in those years) like Charles Follen McKim, William Rutherford Mead, and Stanford White had created the classical White City at the 1890 World's Columbian Exposition in Chicago with the collaboration of a corps of painters, sculptors, and decorative artists; the prestige this created for the Eastern architectural establishment and the commissions that followed controlled the face of American building for the next fifty years. Cass Gilbert gave corporate America its architectural identity in the 1920s with elaborately historic skyscrapers like New York's Woolworth Building, and Carrère and Hastings's beaux arts Public Library was an extravagantly rich banquet of the allied arts. They were all not only prominent members of the art department but also leading figures in the organization.

Perhaps nothing in the arts has changed as radically as the perception and practice of architecture in the intervening years. As business, patronage, technology, and the arts themselves were transformed over the century, architecture not only no longer dominated the arts; it was sidelined. Construction, on an unprecedented scale and subject to speculative investment economics, became a business and a service rather than an exercise in patronage or civic splendor. Beaux arts training gave way to fast-track construction. Once proudly proclaimed the mother of the arts, architecture had become the stepchild. The position of the architects in the Academy-Institute reflected that reality.

There was only one prize in architecture, although the other arts overflowed with generous awards for every stage of an artist's development. The architect as artist was viewed as suspect by a public trained to believe that bottom–line building is the virtuous and responsible use of taxpayers' money and that architecture is a luxury that runs up costs and thus an unjustifiable extravagance. There seemed to be no way to resolve the architect's conflicting and unclear roles as artist and businessperson. Even the most successful practitioners rarely made enough money to adopt the role of patron with largesse to spare for gifts and prizes. Unlike musicians and writers, they had no royalties to donate, and unlike painters, their work could not be left to the Academy-Institute to be sold as it appreciated in value, with the proceeds then used for awards.

It was also proving increasingly difficult to nominate and elect architects to the art department. In the balloting, architects were in competition with painters and sculptors. This became a classic catch-22 situation: the artists were often not familiar with the architects' names and, not knowing them, did not vote for them. Arguments for a separate section for architects, although rarely made, were blocked not only by the intricacies of the charter, but by the ambiguity of the art.

Kevin Roche, an active and influential architect-member and later the Academy's president, was keenly aware of the public perception of architecture as a business rather than as an art; he had juggled this duality with skill in his career as a designer of distinguished institutional and investment structures for clients who rarely viewed architecture as something other than a status symbol or real estate investment. He argued that architects should not be separated from the artists at a time when their status as artists hung so delicately in the balance and was so publicly misunderstood. And while it was no secret that the artists, writers, and musicians, in this well-advertised community of fellows were not always well informed about each other's work except in their own fields, within the art department itself the architects generally knew more about the artists than the other way around. They frequently selected artists and worked with them on commissions for buildings or acted as advisers to client-collectors and were often collectors themselves.

Because Roche was convinced that architects should not be separated from artists, he opposed the potential power base of a separate member category in this hotbed of genteel politics. Others countered that a limited aesthetic definition of the profession misconstrued the broad and varied role of today's architect as planner, urbanist, and environmentalist and diminished the art of architecture's real scope and influence. This was not a debate that aroused the rest of the membership. No changes were made, no more awards were forthcoming, and the architects themselves showed remarkably little concern. With a few exceptions, they shared their fellow artists' lack of interest in Academy-Institute affairs. Their status, to this day, has remained resolutely quo.[27]

Eventually, and eternally, all arguments led to the question of admission to Parnassus: which members were to be elevated from the Institute to the limited membership of the Academy as the inevitable deaths occurred. All were immortals, of course, but some were considered more immortal than others, and slights and omissions, real or fancied, evoked strong feelings. To sit in those stately wooden throne-chairs with the brass plaques on the back attesting to one's immortality, formally arranged on the steps of heaven, was the ultimate stamp of superiority in a democracy of equals. It was no guarantee of enduring fame, however; some occupants have proved more mortal than others. Among the names are the once-famous and now-forgotten, a testament to changing tastes and fashion, the fallibility of choice and the fragility of cultural and political agendas and hierarchies. Richard Eberhart mounted a two-year campaign to have the announcement of Academy appointments accompanied by a list of former occupants of the chair, either in the tidy little death notices sent out with alarming regularity or in the Ceremonial program. The idea was deemed unfeasible for practical reasons: program space and printing costs. A proposal by Harrison Salisbury that Academicians should be buried together in the adjoining Trinity cemetery that shares the Academy's spectacular views led to restrained hilarity.

All this was to become moot with the elimination of the Institute by the elevation of all Institute members to Academy status in the next decade. The first legal and administrative steps necessary to form one body had been taken in 1976 with the institution of a single board of directors, but the Academy and the Institute had otherwise remained separate. Although she had previously opposed consolidation, Barbara Tuchman, as president, reopened the subject in 1979, deploring what she called the "hermaphroditic" nature of the institution. A statement sent to the membership, to be voted on by mail, received mixed responses; some, like Glenway Wescott, were ardently in favor of unification, others, like Malcolm Cowley, were just as vigorously opposed; still others, like Arthur Miller, voted first one way, then another, and finally not at all. The measure was rejected in 1980.

Not surprisingly, awards are subject to the same disagreements as the nominating process, based on the same polarized points of view. But awards have been refused even more rarely than election to membership. Edward Abbey declined an award in 1987, writing, "To tell the truth, I think that prizes are for little boys. You can give my $5000 to somebody else. I don't need it or really want it. Thanks anyhow."[28] This inspired Irving Howe to a brief poetic flight: "Some people make a lot of noise, Rejecting grants for little boys." After a Literature Awards Committee meeting, Alfred Kazin wrote: "I am resigning from the Awards Committee and most especially as chairman, in protest against what I consider the totally slanted choices imposed on the committee this afternoon. . . . The awards . . . were ones I formally had to assent to but which I definitely do not agree with and frankly resent."[29] In the end, Kazin stayed on the committee, and poetry survived. Allen Ginsberg, elected in 1973, had assumed the uncontested role of gadfly in residence and promoter of the counterculture from the Heights. He would arrive at meetings in a proper, postsixties three-piece suit carrying a no-nonsense briefcase containing who-knew-what literary bombshells.

The seventies and eighties were impressive for the number and nature of new awards established. Through a combination of generous and unusual gifts and bequests, as well as a substantial endowment, the Academy-Institute always had the means and ability to define and assist the creative artist. It is this expertise in selection and sponsorship and the certainty that the process will be reliable and the awards will matter that has continued to draw gifts from benefactors. Unlike awards from large grant-giving foundations, which filter their money through institutional layers to institutionally connected recipients, the Academy-Institute put its faith—and its bets—on the individual. There is a keen awareness that the prestige of the prize, and the money that accompanies it, given at the right moment, can make a difference in a young artist's career. And although in recent years there have been charges of elitism (only the most self-deprecating or self-deluding members would protest), there is also a clear understanding that as the country's cultural policies continue to downgrade and deny support, practice, and respect for the arts and humanities in education and public life, the program gains in meaning and importance.

The annual ceremony at which the prizes are given out mixes the conservatively dressed, older members with the stylish bearers of fresh ideas and hopes and the excitement and confidence that goes with them; it is an annual celebration of continuity. On that warm (or frequently wet) May day a breath of downtown vitality flows through the solemn uptown halls, with a passing whiff of nostalgia for the members' own early, often rebellious days before they became the Establishment. There is an implicit understanding, tinged with sadness over the loss of time and youth, that these are the artists, writers, and musicians who will be replacing them in the natural order of things.

What is notable about most of the awards is their thoughtfulness, and even unconventionality, beyond the usual "bests," "most promising," and other special categories. Beginning with Archer M. Huntington's frequently acknowledged "princely philanthropy" of the 1920s, the Academy-Institute has been the recipient of a continuing stream of remarkable bequests. Some, like the Charles Ives and E. M. Forster bequests, have assigned royalties to specific uses;[30] others, such as Childe Hassam, Eugene Speicher, Louis Betts, and Gardner Symons, left their paintings to the Academy-Institute with orders to sell them and use the funds to buy the work of younger artists for donation to museum collections.

Perhaps the most unusual bequest is the Mildred and Harold Strauss Livings, established in the 1961 will of the former editor-in-chief of Alfred A. Knopf and his wife, which became operative twenty years later. By then, the principal of the bequest was over one million dollars. The interest, given as a five-year "living," is shared by two writers of published works, who, in the award's guidelines, "are on the verge of public recognition."[31] As of 1988, each Strauss winner receives $50,000 a year; this enables—in fact, requires—the recipients to leave their jobs to devote the next five years exclusively to their writing careers. The only other five-year grant of equivalent value is the highly visible MacArthur Fellowship, the so-called genius award, which is praised, attacked, and publicized in the press and academic circles while the equally remarkable Strauss Livings remain relatively obscure.

The original guildelines proposed by Harold Strauss contained one of the oddest of all grant stipulations in the history of giving. The time so generously freed for writing was not to be devoted to "improvident breeding"—a bizarre twist on family values. When the Strausses first approached the Academy, the population explosion was the world's hot problem; disastrous projections and predictions filled serious publications. It was believed that curbing world population growth would secure health, education, and an adequate food supply for all, a simplistic notion of cause and effect that later generations have labeled naive paternalism at best, genocidal evil at worst, and unfeeling and unrealistic in equal parts. Thus, to devote proper attention to literary output and avoid the profligate production of offspring, Harold Strauss's guidelines limited to three an awardee's dependent children (more generous, certainly, than China's recent one-child rule, and probably, such being the romanticism and natural urges of writers, equally unenforceable without cosmic oversight and Draconian measures).[32]

The Academy-Institute, with Glenway Wescott as negotiator, demurred at the time, asking for some ameliorative clarification and other minor revisions, to which Harold Strauss replied, "I must confess that being as precise as you suggested makes us sound more crotchety than we really are, but we'll have to accept that impression, as well as the impression of eccentricity you mention—although I must say that a great many people I respect share our opinion that the population explosion is the world's most acute problem."[33] It is doubtful that Wescott offered a variation on the punch-line argument of antiabortionists: that if birth control had been required in Elizabethan times, Shakespeare might never have been born. In any case, after her husband's death, Mrs. Strauss fortunately agreed to release the Academy from these conditions: "We all know how conditions change. [Harold] was most anxious to give a deserving writer, or writers, a chance that otherwise might be difficult for him to attain."[34]

The first Strauss Livings were awarded to Raymond Carver and Cynthia Ozick in 1983; the second, in 1988, went to Diane Johnson and Robert Stone.[35] Raymond Carver and Cynthia Ozick were both elected to membership in 1988, after their livings expired. Raymond Carver died the same year; the Strauss Living had allowed him to spend his last years writing.

The Strauss Livings were a hard act to follow, but the bequest of one million dollars from the estate of the master composer of legendary Broadway musicals, Richard Rodgers, was spectacular enough to merit a luncheon for its announcement on May 1, 1978, with a full roster of political and cultural grandees attending, including the mayor. The bequest's unique purpose was to subsidize musical theater by giving awards to pay for the reading, development, and production of new works by writers and composers not already established in the field.[36]

The same year brought a gift of $400,000 from the CBS Foundation in memory of Goddard Lieberson, the composer who had been president of the classical records division of CBS; two music composition awards of $10,000 (in the 1990s, $12,500) each are given annually to "young composers of extraordinary gifts." Also in 1978 the Harold D. Vursell Award of $5,000 was endowed to honor "a recent work in book form that merits recognition for the quality of its prose style." The next year, 1979, the Witter Bynner Poetry Prize was first funded. And in 1984 the Jean Stein Award of $5,000 was set up to honor a writer annually, with rotated awards in nonfiction, fiction, and poetry. (The Stein Award was discontinued ten years later when the donor disapproved of the political bent of the winner).

Awards seemed to pour in from benefactors in these years, earmarked for art, literature, and music. At a time when prizes are notoriously linked to publicity and public relations, those administered by the Academy are conspicuously dedicated to the benefit of art and its practitioners. Their presentation in the upper reaches of Manhattan receives far less notice in the press than do others hyped and promoted in the city's cultural circus.

Among the more notable events of the Academy's ninth decade was the election of the first woman president, Barbara Tuchman, in 1979. In view of the fact that it had been decreed just the year before, during discussion of a candidate's qualifications in "his or her creative work," that "the masculine pronoun shall be understood to include the feminine," gender equality among the literati was moving forward rather quickly. Barbara Tuchman was followed as president by Arthur Schlesinger, Jr., from 1981 to 1984, and John Kenneth Galbraith, from 1984 to 1987. Hortense Calisher became the second woman president in 1987. As if two women elected to the highest office were not radical enough, this was also the decade when the Academy-Institute went off the gold standard: the Gold Medals were becoming prohibitively expensive, and after considerable debate and some ritual regret, pragmatism prevailed; they would be goldplated instead.

A polite exchange of goldplated medals took place in 1982 and 1985, when the Gold Medal for Music was presented to William Schuman by Leonard Bernstein and then by William Schuman to Leonard Bernstein, who claimed not to have been so honored since winning the high jump at summer camp. Neither seemed aware of the devaluation. Nor were many other people, because no official announcement had been made. The only protest on record is from Malcolm Cowley, who, having won the Gold Medal for Belles-Lettres and Criticism in 1981, noted the switch and wrote that the change seemed a "comedown, like being awarded the Order of Chastity, Second Class."[37] Comedown or not, the various departments continued to jockey for the number and distribution of Gold Medals, while categories were debated, consolidated, and eliminated; at various times history and biography, the novel and the short story were put together or torn asunder. Among the recipients in this decade were Jasper Johns, in graphic art; Louise Nevelson, in sculpture; I. M. Pei, in architecture; Edward Albee, in drama; Bernard Malamud, in fiction; Francis Steegmuller, in biography; and Robert Penn Warren, in poetry. All were accepted graciously regardless of carat content.

It was about this time, also, that one of the more traditional social flourishes, the customary postprandial performances at Academy-Institute dinners, was discontinued. It had been the practice to have musical programs or readings of members' work, seriously presented and somnolently received. Two occasions proved to be the kiss of death. One legendary disruption of a musical perfor-

Ceremonial, 1982. The induction of Shirley Hazzard (Mrs. Steegmuller) creates another his/her membership. Left to right: Eleanor Clark (Mrs. Warren), Robert Penn Warren, Francis Steegmuller (winner of the 1982 Gold Medal for Biography), and Shirley Hazzard.

mance was attributed to Virgil Thomson's deafness, although how much he realized his long, loud, irreverent, and somewhat scatalogical soliloquy dominated the evening is still uncertain. But the effect on listeners and performer was unmistakable. A poetry reading by the visiting Soviet celebrity poet and Foreign Honorary Member, Bella Akhmadulina, who attended a dinner in April 1987 with Andrei Voznesensky and newly elected Foreign Honorary Member, Yevgeny Yevtushenko, produced the same unsettling effect. Declaimed, as is the Russian custom, with maximum brio and delivered in a silver outfit from hat to cowboy boots, the result was electrifying. The usual chatter was reduced to stunned silence; this is not a group comfortable with the drama of excess. The two incidents exacerbated continuing dissension about what should be heard and whether the atmosphere was conducive to hearing anything, and the entertainments ceased.

During his term as president, Arthur Schlesinger, Jr., raised the question of the advisability of sponsoring more broadly cultural and socially inclusive programs, a subject that came up with some regularity. The matter became urgent when the Koch administration, facing one of the city's recurring financial crises in the late 1970s, revoked the tax-exempt status of the Academy-Institute and other not-for-profit organizations. Long discussions ensued about the definition and extent of the Academy-Institute's public service role, ranging from narrowly defined requirements to preserve tax exemption to appropriate ways to serve a larger constituency.

After paying $106,000 in real estate taxes in 1980 and 1981, the Academy-Institute decided to sue the city for a tax refund and reinstatement of its tax-exempt status. The mayoral maneuver proved to be a fiscal disaster when the city was forced to reverse itself and refund the taxes, with interest. Another suggestion from City Hall soon followed: that tax-exempt institutions make voluntary payments to the city to cover the cost of municipal services, a sum, it was noted, that would be considerably smaller than real estate taxes. This voluntary contribution was considered and respectfully declined, on the grounds that less well-off institutions would find payment for essential services difficult or impossible and that a problematic precedent would be set. In the more immediate term, a minor remodeling of the auditorium was undertaken to secure it from the administration building, so that it could be open for more community use; at the same time, public school visits to the building and its exhibitions were encouraged.

One event that went beyond the Academy-Institute's customary insular activities was a conference of Soviet and American writers held in May 1978, sponsored and arranged by the Charles F. Kettering Foundation and the U.S. Department of State. The sequel to a similar conference held in Moscow the previous year, the meeting was cochaired by Norman Cousins and Nicolai Federenko, with eight Academy-Institute participants: Edward Albee, William

Jay Smith, Elizabeth Hardwick, Joyce Carol Oates, Harrison Salisbury, William Styron, John Updike, and Kurt Vonnegut. Like the earlier conference, this one combined political, economic, and literary themes; an interchange among representatives of the two cultures centered on the novel as seen and practiced on both sides of the table. Topics ranged from John Updike's discussion of the artist as the custodian of spiritual values, an idea with which the Soviets seemed in agreement, to the future of the novel; accord turned to disapproval when Updike quoted the French view that the novel could not exist without adultery, the Soviets insisting that there was more to life than love.[38] The Americans' concerned emphasis on the fate of dissident writers in the Soviet Union was met by the Soviets' practical complaints about the lack of distribution and sales opportunities for their books in the United States. Perhaps because of the Academy-Institute's remoteness from midtown or the fact that such high-level intellectual and artistic meetings are not easy to arrange or finance, this outreach effort was not repeated.

Although the subject of the buildings' inaccessibility had arisen many times, the idea of relocation had been growing as the nature of the surrounding neighborhood changed. The Acropolis had become an island in an area of inner-city poverty and neglect.[39] The situation was not helped by the negative articles that had begun to appear as far from Audubon Terrace as London, Ontario.[40] After the American Geographical Society pulled out of Audubon Terrace in 1981 and with the fate of the Museum of the American Indian hanging in the balance,[41] the matter came to a head. There had been serious talk of a move as early as 1941. At that time, Walter Damrosch had reported to the board that a smaller, more centrally located building "could be bought for a song," citing a house on East 64th Street then available for $50,000 that "could perhaps be remodeled to our needs for another $20,000."[42] These figures are now in the realm of fantasy; today, houses on ultrachic East 64th Street change hands for millions.

The subject came up again, and urgently, in 1977, when the Academy-Institute was suddenly offered a house on Fifth Avenue facing the Metropolitan Museum of Art. A developer had purchased three fine beaux arts town houses directly across the street from the museum, intending to replace them with a luxury skyscraper. The offer came out of the blue from a protesting group of wealthy and influential neighbors willing to donate one of the houses to the Academy-Institute in order to prevent the erection of a tall apartment building on the site. Immediate interest was discreetly expressed, but the offer had come too late: demolition and construction had already started before a deal could be made or the machinery of official decision making set in motion.

An impassioned discussion of the pros and cons of relocation followed. The familiar arguments were made for something more accessible to members, the cultural community, and the public; some were even concerned that a refusal to move would be seen as a sign of old age. But a majority prevailed in favor of staying put: "The organization was in an ideal spot of great beauty, in an extraordinary building, and should be cherished." Moreover, "it was preferable for the Academy-Institute to remain low-keyed and unambitious, to avoid public relations and to consider austerity and remoteness as virtues, not faults."[43] The group declared itself pleased to be decisively out of step.

At about the same time, in the late 1970s, recession and inflation were shrinking institutional endowments; museums, libraries, and universities, facing rising costs and lowered income, were viewing their futures with alarm and starting urgent capital campaigns. Facing the specter of an uncushioned, or less well-cushioned, existence, the Committee on the Future was once again reactivated to study the problem and consider the possibility of fund-raising activities. Finding itself in unfamiliar territory, the Academy-Institute took an unprecedented step: on the advice of the treasurer, William Schuman, who had shepherded Lincoln Center through financial crisis, a consultant was hired in 1980 to carry out a development study that was to include an analysis of resources and make fiscal and administrative recommendations. As part of the study, the question of relocation was reopened once again, with the value of the buildings and land and relocation costs to be figured into the calculations. This professional real estate assessment was to be carried out independently as a pro bono publico gesture by one of New York's most successful commercial developers, Lawrence Wien, for incorporation into the final report.

The Academy-Institute was in good company with many other nonprofit institutions following the same course; however, subjecting a proudly nonconforming, intellectually and artistically overprivileged group to the limited criteria and spreadsheet mentality of the real world was a doomed effort. At the time, consultants were "dumbing down" all manner of higher institutions in financial trouble with formulaic recommendations for better business management and increased popular outreach. They all got substantially the same advice: a standard mix of stock answers and conventional wisdom guaranteed, if nothing else, to reduce the extraordinary to the ordinary in the pursuit of a broad base of appeal and support. Only President Barbara Tuchman demurred; in fact, she did more than demur: she protested strongly. But the board, feeling the need for expertise that it did not possess, opted for a contract with the kind of consulting service that is the peculiar product of the insecurities and anxieties of the late twentieth century. Its aims and methods were singularly unsuited to those who entertain their own mysterious values and follow no rules or principles that the business world understands. That artists and writers devote themselves to a calling of almost certain financial uncertainty is something that eludes comprehension by those entrepreneurial geniuses who pay outrageous sums for the work of the "hot" names of the moment, usually as status symbols or for investment potential.

Development studies, at best, sell the obvious and at worst, deliver costly, irrelevant surveys based on erroneous assumptions and questionable principles as well as a fairly consistent insensitivity to the real attributes and assets of the organization studied. The Academy-Institute went down the garden path, and $10,000 went down the drain. The recommendations, which included hiring a paid president (a standard suggestion other institutions were following) was delivered in many pages of boilerplate, revised once by request, and ultimately recorded as "unsatisfactory" by a majority of the members of the board.[44] It would be better to go down like the Titanic than to be saved by the forces of convention. Not long after, the market went up, inflation receded, and so did the worry about investments and endowment.

If the real estate survey accomplished nothing else, it pointed up the impracticality of moving, although the idea would continue to resurface. The cost of relocation balanced unfavorably against the value of the property and the difficulty of selling, since the buildings' quality counted far less than the potential for profitable reuse. There was no way to provide figures for the fact that the tradeoff for accessibility would be a distinguished identity nurtured and expressed in an irreplaceable complex of the building and decorative arts. The board concluded that "both financial and sentimental considerations favor staying where we are."

In fact, Audubon Terrace, with its museums and institutional buildings, had been designated a New York City Historic District the year before, in 1979. Emboldened and hopeful, the chancellor of the Academy, I. M. Pei, accompanied by Ralph Ellison and Hortense Calisher, descended from Parnassus into the 157th Street subway station, where they were joined by local political and civic leaders in making a public plea for subway improvements and the renaming of the station as Audubon Terrace. In the way of New York City, where memory and money are short, that has not happened. But in the cyclical history of cities, where what was up goes down and up again, noticeable neighborhood improvements were taking place.[45]

The crowning event of the decade was the exhibition of portraits from the Academy-Institute's collection held at the National Portrait Gallery of the Smithsonian Institution in Washington in 1987.[46] As with cities, cycles in art are both inevitable and unpredictable. Nothing could epitomize the changes from the founding years of the Academy more effectively than the manner and the subjects of these paintings; the men and, eventually, women of the Academy-Institute, at once lifelike and larger than life, formal in expression and attire, standing and seated, singly and in groups, give a remarkably revealing picture not only of their world but also of the changes in art and the attitudes toward it. It is a world that now seems as remote as Mars; its look, feel, customs, beliefs, and behavior are matched by the fabrics, settings, and stances.

Casual was not a word in vocabulary or haberdashery. The frock coat was the garment of choice. Poses were struck. A contemporary photograph of F. W. Ruckstull, the sculptor of a bust of Nicholas Murray Butler, shows the artist standing next to his work looking immensely pleased, in hat, tight collar, and tie; in some minor bohemian gesture he has removed his jacket and pushed his hat back on his head. Otherwise absolute decorum prevails.

Paradoxically, the classical revival known as the American Renaissance was considered progressive by many at the time; then the style fell so out of favor that even the name was forgotten until reinstated by recent revisionist art historians. The timing of the National Portrait Gallery show was just right for that moment when the old becomes new and a scholarly revival takes place. But in spite of the ambitious claims made by the style's practitioners—of sponsoring innovation within tradition—it was Establishment all the way: resolutely conservative, it dominated important commissions and guarded the portals of privilege and custom.

This work was done in the same decades that saw the sinuous sweep of art nouveau, the inventive crosscurrents of the Vienna secession and the Scottish

A wintry effort in 1979 to install signage for the Academy in the local subway station. Left to right: *Margaret M. Mills, executive director; Ralph Ellison, Institute secretary; Hortense Calisher, Institute president; and I. M. Pei, Academy chancellor.* (Christina Wohler)

arts and crafts movement, the innovative buildings of Frank Lloyd Wright and the American Prairie School, and the early European modernism of Le Corbusier. But for Academicians it was as if the Armory Show of 1913 had never happened. It is easy to know what the immortals thought of that: the barbarians were at the Academy's American Renaissance gates, where Kenyon Cox's "classic spirit" held the barricades, an ideal, in Cox's words, that "asks of a work of art not that it shall be novel or effective, but that it should be fine and noble."[47] While "fine and noble" could be splendidly vague, it was clearly understood that these radical trends were a free fall from classical grace.

What is evident today is that many of these portraits are admirable paintings, skillfully rendered, insightful documents of art, history, and personality. What we like about them now is their competence, dignity, and certitude, their aesthetic elegance and irreproachable propriety, the fine, painterly surfaces and keen sensitivity to the subject, the studied awareness of how the image is to be represented for posterity. This was a time when art and architecture were practiced with technical mastery and a social agenda. There was none of the current dogma about avoiding "the privileging of the eye," a perverse doctrine, favored by academics and laid at Duchamps's door, that denies the visual and sensory nature of art. These pictures give us direct pleasure and a sense of the way it was. After all, this was, and is, the Academy, and the Academy, by its very nature, is not the avant-garde: it is a stronghold of tradition. That is what *academic* means. It celebrates achievement within "the genteel tradition," as George Santayana put it, rather than embracing the rude break with tradition that signals new departures. (At the least, it waits a while to do so.) As defined in the foreword to the catalogue of the exhibition, by Alan Fern, director of the National Portrait Gallery, the Academy's position has been limited to "encouraging new developments in the arts based on an understanding of the values of the past." That sets limitations, but it also gives leeway, and time; it does not make an academy irrelevant.

Time has its value. The changes in art and society have shattered tradition, including the tradition of the academy, and it will take time to sort it all out. The Academy has time on its side. The role of the artist as outlaw, always cultivated by the avant-garde, is by its nature outside the Academy, and that role is increasingly hard to play in a society that condones extremes of conduct and behavior; to transgress the limits of acceptance, sensation must be constantly accelerated. In the final, necessary step of rebellion, art becomes anti-art— declared as such by the artist—the more nihilistic and transient the better. Anti-art is not art for art's sake, and stripped of the need to be judged by traditional values, it becomes political, or propaganda, art (the kind of statement still unwelcome at the Academy). Only time will determine what of it will survive as art, and that, too, is problematic, since at least some of it is meant to self-destruct, and has already begun to do so. But the Academy has the luxury of waiting; it will be there at the end to enshrine the survivors.

If time is on the side of the Academy, so, it would seem, is space. In 1983 NASA invited the Academy-Institute's visual artists, composers, poets, and writers to join the space program as part of a feasibility study for putting artists in space.[48] The idea of being an "artist in residence" on the space station came at a moment when the fascination with space was at its optimistic height. The inquiry, sent on to selected members by Maggie Mills (the criteria for the mailing are unknown, but one suspects they were her reliable gut instincts), got a mixed reaction. There were those who clearly considered it a cosmic boondoggle and those who viewed it as an opportunity to be part of the music of the spheres. An extremely earthbound multiple-choice questionnaire that accompanied the request was so awesomely pedantic that the moondust quickly disappeared. (The funding, obviously, also vanished with later space program cutbacks.)

Only two of those queried wanted to fly: the sculptor Marisol and the poet Allen Ginsberg. Both filled out the questionnaire at great length. Marisol described a specific project—a sculpture of an angel (one hopes it would be carrying one of her characteristic handbags) that would have its own orbit—and Ginsberg offered extensive commentary on the benefits to himself and mankind in Whitmanesque prose of passionately redundant complexity. Of those who received the letter from Maggie Mills, it is recorded that Christo, Roy Lichtenstein, and George Tooker did not answer. Jasper Johns replied politely that he thought it a "wonderful idea that artists should work in NASA's space station." "But," he added, "not me. Please send the others."[49]

From the classical and conventional to a flirtation with the unknowable and unfathomable, the Academy-Institute had managed to remain much the same. It was still an exclusive club ("our Mafia," in Saul Steinberg's immortal words),[50] but with a membership based on diversified creative achievement and an enlarged mission of patronage. Called "a craft guild of the highest order" by Virgil Thomson,[51] it guarded the high ground. One thinks of the changes in literary style and life from Henry James to William Gaddis, of portraits from William Merritt Chase to Chuck Close, of music from Victor Herbert to John Cage. Gilded Age decorative excess gave way to stark modern minimalism as the revolution rolled in like a slow tide. The Academy-Institute had survived a twentieth-century upheaval in society and the arts so radical that only the beaux arts buildings on Audubon Terrace formed a tangible tie to its own past.

NOTES

All archival materials are located in the Academy files unless otherwise indicated.

1. The claim has been made that the 1970s was a decade that consolidated and incorporated the ideas and attitudes of the 1960s in a way that profoundly affected the future. See Nicholas Lemann, "How the Seventies Changed America," *American Heritage* 42, no. 4 (July/August 1991): 39–49.

2. Report of meeting of Committee on the Future to the Academy board, November 13, 1981.

3. President Jimmy Carter to Barbara Tuchman, February 20, 1980.

4. The letter is undated but was received on February 18, 1986. The speech, "On Truth," was distributed at the Ceremonial reception on May 21, 1986.

5. *Proceedings of the American Academy and Institute of Arts and Letters*, 2d ser., no. 30 (1979): 31.

6. Undated; June 22, 1979.

7. June 18, 1979; June 26, 1979.

8. To John Hersey, chancellor of the Academy, and John Updike, secretary, November 23, 1982.

9. To Arthur Schlesinger, Jr., and Hortense Calisher, January 22, 1984.

10. To Hortense Calisher, January 31, 1983.

11. To Margaret Mills, July 23, 1986.

12. To the Academy-Institute, January 23, 1989.

13. To John Kenneth Galbraith, January 27, 1986.

14. To Margaret Mills, November 10, 1981.

15. Minutes of board of directors meeting, December 2, 1988.

16. Minutes of board of directors meeting, January 24, 1979.

17. Minutes of board of directors meeting, April 9, 1981.

18. Margaret Mills to the membership, October 5, 1983.

19. To Margaret Mills, April 25, 1979.

20. To Margaret Mills, May 28, 1982.

21. March 10, 1983.

22. February 2, 1984.

23. To Margaret Mills, July 7, 1987.

24. July 8, 1987.

25. Minutes of Academy-Institute meeting, January 18, 1978.

26. Minutes of Academy-Institute dinner meeting, April 12, 1978.

27. In 1991, however, responding to the argument that architecture was the only field for which no Academy-Institute-funded award existed, the board, with a conspicuous lack of enthusiasm, finally established an Academy-Institute Award in Architecture of $7,500 "to recognize an American architect who has shown great promise through work characterized by a strong personal direction."

28. To Irving Howe, March 20, 1987.

29. To Margaret Mills, February 7, 1986.

30. The E. M. Forster Award, for a stay in the United States for an English writer, was based on the American royalties of his novel *Maurice*. Sales had slowed to the point where the award might have had to be abandoned when the Merchant-Ivory film made of the book increased sales and renewed the stream of funds.

31. Award guidelines.

32. Harold Strauss originally stipulated that "no living is to be granted to a writer with more than two dependent children, the stipend to be reduced by one third for each dependent child in excess of two" (to Glenway Wescott, August 29, 1961). Six weeks and more negotiations later, he wrote to Wescott, "We understand that the [board] has cer-

tain reservations regarding the proposal. . . . Among several revisions is the following . . . 'no living is to be granted to a writer with more than three dependent children.' Thus the sliding scale is eliminated." He requested that this restriction remain in force for forty years. The board of directors found these conditions unacceptable and appointed Jacques Barzun, C. Vann Woodward, and John Hersey to negotiate terms.

33. August 20, 1961.

34. To Jacques Barzun, November 16, 1977.

35. The third livings, for 1993–1997, were given to John Casey and Joy Williams.

36. The recipients include *Rent*, by Jonathan Larson, which was awarded a staged reading in 1994, and *Juan Darien*, by Julie Taymor and Elliot Goldenthal, given a production in 1989, and *Violet*, by Brian Crawley and Jeanine Tesori, given a production in 1997.

37. To Arthur Schlesinger, Jr., May 27, 1981.

38. "Saturday Review: Outlooks, Editorial: When American and Soviet Writers Meet," *Saturday Review*, June 24, 1978.

39. For a personal history of the neighborhood, see the next chapter, by Hortense Calisher, who grew up in the area when it was a substantial middle-class enclave and has charted its changes.

40. See "Environment Plagues Cultural Center," London, Ontario *Free Press*, May 7, 1983.

41. The Museum of the American Indian left in 1994, when the collections were taken over by the Smithsonian Institution, which plans to install them in a new museum to be constructed on the Mall in Washington, D.C. A New York branch has been established in the Old U.S. Custom House, a restored beaux arts landmark on the Battery.

42. Minutes of the meeting of the board of directors, May 7, 1941.

43. Dinner discussion, November 9, 1977.

44. Minutes of the board, April 3, 1980.

45. During Kevin Roche's presidency in the 1990s, the Academy-Institute buildings were to be beautifully restored and carefully updated, including a painstaking restoration of the organ in an auditorium known for some of the city's best acoustics.

46. Hortense Calisher, who oversaw the effort as president, gives a comprehensive account of the conception and execution of the exhibition in the following chapter.

47. Quoted in *Portraits from the American Academy of Arts and Letters* (Washington, D.C.: National Portrait Gallery, Smithsonian Institution, 1987), p. 22.

48. James Pridgeon to Margaret Mills, August 31, 1983.

49. October 18, 1983.

50. Geoffrey T. Hellman, "Some Splendid and Admirable People," *The New Yorker*, February 23, 1976, p. 81.

51. Ibid., p. 80.

CHAPTER TEN

1988–1997

DECADE OF REUNION

Hortense Calisher

THE MEMBERS' ROOM of the American Academy of Arts and Letters is a nineteenth-century chamber; no matter that the edifice housing it was built in 1923. Down in front are the slender rows of the original academicians' chairs, each with a nameplate on its back. Rising on an incline from these, in seminary style, are rows of anonymous chairs, quite comfortable. Some members dare the front seats naturally or without forethought; others noticeably avoid them. Those who go for the upper tiers have the best part of it. At five o'clock of a winter afternoon, in air that would be a brown fug if it weren't so august, their heads loom, gone to physiognomy rather than face, the men out of Rembrandt, the women Vermeer.

This is the room where meetings of the members at large enact the general business, after which the eulogies for the recent dead are delivered. Though the room could not possibly seat the full two hundred and fifty, their opinions have sifted here, by vote, the testimony of committees, or more direct avenue if they so choose. Actual presence is an extra virtue.

One dinner meeting is for members only. At the others, a member's spouse or guest may attend in part. At the moment when business is done and eulogy is about to begin, the big doors are opened wide, and the waiting invitees, augmented by the families of those to be eulogized, stream in and are quickly seated. This is a moment when the separation from the general populace that marks any academy is perhaps too sharply evident. Can't be helped. And the eulogies will take care of that. By custom, each comes from another member. As we listen to these tributes to the life and works of the deceased, we, the dead, and that outer world in which so many of them have figured, are all a company.

Meanwhile, the scene at the broad window has another meaning for me, as it will each time I come. Across the street to the south, brilliant in the sun

Duke Ellington, elected in 1970.   —*David Redfern*

ABOVE: Charles Ives Centennial Festival, October 17, 1974. Aaron Copland speaking in the Academy's library.

BELOW: 1975 Ceremonial. (l to r) Terrence McNally, winner of an Academy–Institute Award in Literature, with members Tennessee Williams and Edward Albee.

ABOVE: 1978 Ceremonial. Robert Rauschenberg and Marisol Escobar at the reception following their induction. —*Michael Hintlian*

BELOW: 1978 Ceremonial. Induction of Joyce Carol Oates into the Institute with (l to r) Edward Albee (partial view), Hugo Weisgall, Clyfford Still, Dwight Macdonald, Marisol Escobar (partial view), and Jack Levine. —*Michael Hintlian*

ABOVE: 1978 inauguration of the Richard Rodgers Production Award. (l to r) Dorothy Rodgers, Jacques Barzun (President of the Institute), Mayor Edward I. Koch, and Richard Rodgers.   —*Michael Hintlian*

BELOW: 1979 Ceremonial. (l to r) Eleanor Clark, Eudora Welty, and Institute President Barbara Tuchman.   —*Christina Wohler*

1992 Strauss Livings Committee. (l to r) Kurt Vonnegut, Alison Luric, E. L. Doctorow, Paul Theroux. Strauss Livings awards are given to two writers every five years. Each recipient receives $50,000 annually for a period of five years.

—*Timothy Greenfield-Sanders*

ABOVE: 1984 Ceremonial. (l to r) Jacob Lawrence, Chaim Gross, and Lukas Foss cele-brate their induction into the Academy. —*Wagner International Photos Inc.*

BELOW: 1989 Ceremonial. (l to r) Elizabeth Hardwick, John Cage, and Mary McCarthy.

ABOVE: 1983 Ceremonial. John Kenneth Galbraith with Jaqueline Kennedy Onassis.
—*Wagner International Photos Inc.*

BELOW: 1983 Ceremonial. George Rickey with Louise Nevelson, winner of the Gold Medal for Sculpture.

Centennial Committee, November 11, 1994. First row (l to r): Hugo Weisgall, Eliza-beth Hardwick, Ada Louise Huxtable. Second row: Will Barnet, Cynthia Ozick, John Updike (Chairman), John Guare. Third row: Richard Lippold, Jack Beeson, Ned Rorem.   —*Timothy Greenfield-Sanders*

Nominating Committee, December 3, 1996. (l to r) Will Barnet, Hortense Calisher, David Diamond, Elizabeth Hardwick, Varujan Boghosian.

—*Timothy Greenfield-Sanders*

Members Dinner, November 10, 1994. Allen Ginsberg and Arthur Schlesinger, Jr.

—Timothy Greenfield-Sanders

1992 Literature Award Committee. Seated (l to r): Harold Bloom (Chairman), Hortense Calisher. Standing: Ann Beattie, Donald Justice, James Merrill, Eric Bentley,
Mark Strand.   —*Timothy Greenfield-Sanders*

Members Dinner, January 17, 1996. John Heliker and William Maxwell.

—*Benjamin Dimmitt*

1994 Richard Rodgers Committee. Seated (l to r): Terrence McNally, Stephen Sondheim (Chairman), R.W.B. Lewis. Standing: Francis Thorne, Jack Beeson, Richard Maltby, Jr., John Guare. —*Benjamin Dimmitt*

ABOVE: Art Purchase Committee, September 9, 1996. Front row (l to r): Jane Wilson, Paul Cadmus, Jane Freilicher. Back row: William Bailey, Dimitri Hadzi, Ibram Lassaw.
—*Benjamin Dimmitt*

ABOVE (PREVIOUS PAGE): Authors of *A Century of Arts and Letters* in the Academy's Members Room, May 21, 1997. Seated (l to r): Hortense Calisher, John Updike. Standing: Arthur Schlesinger, Jr., Richard Lippold, R.W. B. Lewis, Ada Louise Huxtable, Louis Auchincloss, Jack Beeson, Wolf Kahn, Cynthia Ozick. Not present for the photograph: Norman Mailer. —*Timothy Greenfield-Sanders*

BELOW (PREVIOUS PAGE): Members' Dinner Meeting, January 18, 1995, group of artists and architects. First row: John M. Johansen. Second row (l to r): Philip Pearlstein, Will Barnet, George Rickey, Kenneth Snelson, Chuck Close, Jack Levine. Third row: George Segal, Jane Wilson, William Bailey, Paul Cadmus, James Ingo Freed, Wolf Kahn, David Levine. Fourth row: Paul Resika, John Chamberlain, Hugh Hardy, Kevin Roche. —*Benjamin Dimmitt*

LEFT: Virginia Dajani, executive director since 1990, in the Academy's library.

—*Henry Groskinsky*

BELOW: 1997 Ceremonial. John Ashbery (l) receiving the Gold Medal for Poetry, presented to him by John Malcolm Brinnin (r).

—*Dorothy Alexander*

or luminously gray, in a light that any ordinary resident of these blocks knows to be cast by the Hudson River just past the viaduct, are the trees and low stone walls of the cemetery that in my childhood belonged to the Chapel of the Intercession, the big church up on Broadway. None seem to walk there as freely now; it belongs to Trinity Church. We ten-year-olds treated it as an amiable pathway either to the rocky outcroppings in the street below—New York's basic mica-schist from which we mined what we called "ising-glass"—or to that hollow we never dared, where there was a great, peaked American Gothic, black as an eagle, that we called the "haunted house." Reputed to have been John James Audubon's, and long since gone, under an apartment block.

That view from the Members' Room, in an edifice built six blocks from where I lived until my teens and just about then, remains the same and is likely to, unless either the Academy or the boneyard moves (I won't lay bets). But on our way through the decades, the neighborhood into which an academy purporting to be an icon of its nation's culture inserts itself deserves its brief archivist.

Washington Heights in the 1920s had the floating gentility promised by its name: broad avenues, some like Amsterdam still cobbled, river and intermittent parkland, a federalist tinge from Madame Jumel's mansion (once Washington's headquarters), as well as the much-touted "good air" of its riverside, at its northern tip verging toward Spuyten Duyvil and Riverdale. There was also an institutional flavor: the Academy for the Deaf, the Presbyterian Hospital on its way, Christian churches including an old French one, Mount Neboh synagogue, a Carnegie library branch. Foodshops European in flavor, many "honest craftsmen" in the old Jacob Riis style. A settled population; mildly trafficked streets. Above all space, likely to satisfy the beaux arts taste for plazas and for buildings with enough marble to suit both the nation and the plutocrat.

An academy can reflect the state of a nation's art from any site. Especially so if its moral position is that it does not legislate art's direction, leaving that to the individual, as so much American ethic does. Nor does this one cling dangerously close to government. Yet the building's location per se—on the East Coast and at Manhattan's less accessible end—will often give pause. One doubts that the men who built

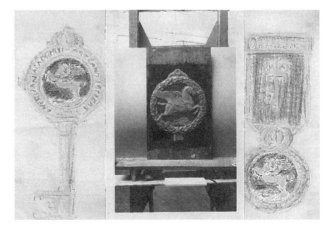

Herbert Adams's sketches for the Academy key and a photograph of the completed symbol. The symbol, which measures eighteen by twelves inches, hangs in the Members' Room.

it knew enough about the neighborhood either to recognize or ignore that it was a very mixed one, already rumbling with sociological change. Though one thinks of some earlier members who might have approved. "Mark Twain," for instance, whose pseudonym, in riverboat language, is what the pilot calls out to signify "two fathoms sounded."

By 1923 any new residential building in the area was rare, about the last having been the Hempstead-Letchworth apartments, occupying a square block—160th and 161st Streets on Broadway—where the tenancy was nominally lace-curtain Irish, Jewish, and German. In the tenement blocks between Broadway and Amsterdam were the railroad flats, same ethnic strains with less money: half a floor of three tiny rooms, inside toilet. Farther east, Harlem, still partly Italian and black (hall toilets for some). For others, fancy Sugar Hill, home of the Harlem Renaissance. On Riverside Drive, some of the city's younger smart set or demimonde might well be perched in that building on a curve of the street just beyond the Academy, one of whose apartments is said to have been the setting for a scene in *The Great Gatsby*. Almost all the neighborhood children of any status went to the same public school, P.S. 46, walking home and back whatever their distance from it, four times a day. The school had no marble but much wood, including the privies.

By 1939 the Hitler refugees arrive; by then the better-off local Jews have moved downtown or to the suburbs, the lower-middle Irish and Germans to the other boroughs or to Jersey, the middle-class blacks to lower Riverside Drive. On Broadway and Amsterdam, Haitian and Dominican will move in. By 1980 so has the drug trade and all the other ills of the poor. By 1990 a good part of Washington Heights, including the blocks just north of the Academy, will be gunshot territory. But in the way a city changes, and New York particularly, by the end of the decade young professionals and artists will once again settle in.

One of the Academy's neighbors on the plaza, the Museum of the American Indian, planned a remove in the 1980s to a federally owned building on Manhattan's nether tip, after a scandal in which certain of its trustees were alleged to have purchased certain artifacts from its seriously neglected collection (we kids used to "go to see the mummy," a tiny shrunken South American dignity). The Numismatic Society considered moving. The "Spanish Museum"—the Hispanic Society of America, where we used to marvel at the great murals of provincial Spain and pretend we were in Valencia—is still there, somnolent grandee, aloof from the Latino culture now surrounding it. Shortly, having acquired the vacated building of the Museum of the American Indian, it will even expand to exhibit more of its collection, one of the great, and little-known, splendors of New York.

The Academy has made what gestures to the community its quarters and security allow. A senior citizens' group has been meeting there every Friday for the last thirty years. The Academy actively participates in the annual

"Uptown Treasures," a day of group tours of Washington Heights and Inwood cultural institutions, such as The Cloisters, Malcolm X Museum at the Audubon Cultural Center, Dyckman Farmhouse Museum, Morris-Jumel Mansion, Yeshiva University Museum, and our other neighbors on Audubon Terrace. Recurrently it will consider how it might function—better? more widely? more publicly?—without compromising aims partisan to art only. Or trying vainly to engage a membership far-flung, honorary, and generally busy at its own creations.

One public ceremony in mid-May attracts hundreds, many of whom cherish their place on the ticket list or scramble for one. Is it merely to see the honors and the cash given out? And to decode from their programs the identities in the body of members lined in tiers on the stage, facing them like a not quite vestigial photograph? Old people mostly, or fast getting there. Luckily interspersed with fresh-faced first-time honorees, some of whom may one day be on the platform for good. Who, warmed as they are by being chosen, may also be wondering, as I would one day in 1968, whether even the most benevolent body could monitor the "best," or even the "good," considering all the wilder ferocities of art? Or should?

I first saw that ceremony as audience, about 1949 or 1950. A Miss Elizabeth Sergeant, a resident of my up-Hudson town, had dropped in on me, having heard of me through her sister, E. B. White's wife, Katharine, an editor of *The New Yorker*. In Miss Sergeant's youth she had interviewed Willa Cather, later writing of her and others in a book called *Fire in the Andes*. She was now writing on Robert Frost. She wore the winged, high-crowned hat of my aunts and had the same sweetly immovable manners, as well as two requests. She wished to tour my house and to have me as her guest at "the May ceremony," whatever that was. On the tour, it devolved that she wanted to rent quarters for herself, a weekly maid, and a dachshund that had heart trouble—and was amazed that I had never heard of "the Academy." We did not rent rooms, but the hat (and maybe Willa Cather) was persuasive. So, on a sunstruck day, at the point in the ceremony when audience and those onstage finally mix and meet, I first saw that plaza as apart from childhood's rim. And met Thornton Wilder.

I recall his kindness to Miss S.'s gushiness and his courtly if abstract greeting to the neophyte she so proudly presented. He was not going to reveal impatience or lack obligation. Or show the bored tolerance that can affect artists dealing with admiration face on. But that was not why I was to store away this incident. Rather, it first brought home to me that there could be a continuity, merging many traditions and modes yet celebrating what each of us was trying to do singly.

By the time one is tapped for membership, one may have forgotten about an academy. Other awards may have been won, newer avenues opened. There may be already enough elegy in one's life. Enough activity. And with the honor, isn't there a certain obligation? . . . Better decline. (I even wrote the letter.) Group action through one's work had always seemed to me dubious, propelled as it was by group thought. Communism had been the allure for a generation before me; Freudian allegiance now surrounded me. In France it was indeed respectable to rebel in the arts, en masse, as with Dada. Or to congeal behind a thinker existentially, e.g., by following Sartre's nose. Such orthodoxies are not for some of us. Yet many an artist is a society watcher, a sucker for the café. In New York enclaves are cherished; they humanize. Was that the attraction here?

On further thought, in my country, where *elite* is a cussword to the democratically confused who equate equal opportunity with equal ability, maybe it's wiser, and braver, of these platform people to dare to be elite, even in such large number? As for me, I remind myself that they're only citing me, not immortalizing me. (Twenty years later, on the other side of the fence, as their president, I'll remind myself again.) As for the building, it is certainly not Bohemia. But I already know that there's no proper dress for our trade, no prescribed village. Our trades can hang out anywhere. Maybe these slightly chipped, offside arenas were the best? A monument too well kept can have an official glare.

This enclave purports to speak for the nation—to a degree. Hierarchy might be both its business and its plague. But it spoke gently, in terms to which any in the arts might accede. *Mon semblable, mon frère.* And, within limits—*ma soeur.* In the arts there can sometimes be a kind of duration, akin to the musical term *sostenuto*, or in the contiguous portraiture that painters make of us. Concepts that leap over language and down the ages, as with the kinship between Villon's "Où sont les neiges d'antan?" and Yeats's "When you are old and grey," two fires in front of which age, and experience, sit. One in the late nineteenth century, one in the fifteenth.

Meanwhile, the plaza is still there, and the building to which downtown taxis have to be guided. Something is continuous there, more even than the company you keep. Perhaps it is the light up there, benedictory even on a smog day. Where so many practice under the art aura, there are few halos. One gathers, in a naughty world, for the expenditure of good will.

A decade is a sometime thing. Originally merely a series of ten, then transmuted to mean "ten years," the term was also used to signify ten days, replacing the week in the French Republican calendar of 1793. Its literary significance was also early, meaning a work divided into ten parts. In modern usage, a factual convenience for critics and historians has often been parlayed into heady or clumsy analyses that a harder look at the inhabitants of such a period, and the stereotypes they are pushed toward, will not sustain. By the time ten decades or so become the balloon called an era we are in the land as much of Euclid as of Herodotus. So, for instance, the "Victorian" era swells and congeals into a fantasy of detail, wherein corsetry provokes psychoanalytic conclusion, men and women repress sex yet have offspring by the dozen, eat enormously from gilt-edge menu cards or are found starved on the steps of the jail—and eventually much of the British empire hangs by theory on the skirts of the old lady in black bombazine. Vintage wine attracts. As does theory. So we get the waxworks we very likely crave. Still, definite events occur and are reportable; only lean not too heavily when interpreting them.

This is the decade when what the gods of communication have wrought becomes clear. Computers, television, fax, cyberspace, virtual reality, Internet begin to combine toward a new kind of mental space or environment already foreseeable in the young. All the details of the human span, once seen as a general road from birth through death via family and country, no matter where, are now visible and discussable, no matter where. With fictionalizing and fantasy not standing by, and computer visual art already on its way.

Foremost on the political scene, the third-world concept will collapse, powerless against all that creeping information. The German wall will fall. The Soviet Union as a military and economic threat will be revealed as a concept half in our own heads. Asia will emerge for us as more than a source for Japanese runabouts, meditational philosophies, acupuncture. Islam will arrive on the world scene and in Western consciousness, terror in one hand, religious discipline in the other. And once again, the threat of the big bomb, while smaller versions here and there practice up.

On the domestic rialto, what's on? Cities used to hide the poor in unmentionable slums: in New York alcoholism in the Bowery, violence in Hell's Kitchen, wastelands in Brooklyn that only the gas company appeared to monitor. Now we walk among street people nationwide and are inured. Guns, yes, too, instead of boys with bloody noses; and on the screens, vampires whom kids see instead of read about, couples in bed rather than the ritual "talk" with pa or ma. Yet thanks to the computer screen, doctors miles apart also now consult *en face*, surgeries can be seen or even cooperatively performed between distant points. Science no longer waits for publication for its experimental results to disseminate; the computer reinvents physics and astronomy, to the surprising end that some in those sciences now dare to hypothesize God. While rights, whether or not human, circumnavigate the talking planet far sooner than they are practiced.

In the nineteenth century "by hand" was superseded by "machine-made," only later reascending to a certain status. Now we ourselves are in an analogous situation. The receptor or creator, teacher or practitioner, will need to be less and less on hand. In the arts this is so as well, from music, which is already on the air principally, to museums, and to books as we know them or need them (a process already under way in scholarly research). While in the virtual novel, where the computer user may wield the mouse to choose alternate paths or passages offered, making author only an instigator, and reader a col-laborator—who calls the tune?

When so much that was private and local is now public and national and manipulable, not only the audience changes or departs—or mutates. The val-ues do. When *peacekeeping*, say, can mean military action seeable every evening on the earth's circumference, some of the world may still see it as colonialism. Conversely, the fan who has all a rocker's records may have an uncontrollable need to participate in concert with those who are his kin. It could be, some now say, that rather than keeping to the stigmatized couch position in either entertainment or the cyberspace of ideas, a communicant will crave to be in the very presence of what is going on: in the hall, in the gallery, at the poetry reading. The arts might well benefit from all this electronic fakery. It could be that the stereotypic American who considers art to be merely entertainment may find that, along with other intelligences, the arts have become part of the daily, offered, necessary grain of life.

As for the "greediness" of the decade, it appears clearly, as one would expect, in the arts coverage, the prices at the auction houses, or for film or book rights. At times, or in the *Times*, it will seem that an arts section breathes money mainly. But Maecenas is always news, especially so, it is said, with us Americans—or do we merely conceal it less? The real reportage does go on, if so valiantly that Bohemia, whose birthright is the city, is scarcely born before it gets to be estab-lishment. A trend, such as a bit of melody returning to music, or in painting the human figure taking the field over the long reign of the abstract, is spotted and dissected before it can reach maturity. What may be worse, there are fewer provinces, or provincials, the traditional lifeblood of "educated" art. While the brouhaha as to what is "high" art or "pop"—we don't say "low," dear—engages the critics and is ignored by the righteous contenders from Reverse Press and Honkytonk Row.

Does this sound like any decade, if you look close? Nothing new under the sun? As any artist surveying the centuries will blithely admit? While swearing inwardly to challenge that personally.

The arts profited in this decade. Architects—or developers—had more money to build. Patrons could be more lavish, even if mostly the big and the visible benefited: museums and performance art. But in the smaller art purposes, it was the National Endowment, and the states' arts funds where these existed, that seeded the nation, and well outside the cities. Young artists cropped up, older ones were helped to survive, children were attracted, community inter-est fused. Small literary magazines, art shows, concerts, art classes sprouted in the backwater and the city slum. The barrio took to what was in its bones nat-urally, and the Native American reservations also. Small local "opera" houses with perfect wood-enclosed acoustics, a late-nineteenth-century network, were here and there restored, bringing chamber ensembles and other reper-toire to quite ordinary local audiences. Much of the substantive art produced might be transient or even amateur, but what was important was that the habit of art, its acceptance as a necessary endowment of the citizenry, was becom-ing normal. The U.S.A. was only embarking on what other, often poorer nations had long since admitted: that art hunger is inborn, its satisfaction brings benefices, and state support is a constitutional right. Humdrum story, but this was the decade also.

Upstairs, among the professionals, some of the new art as usual inflamed the old guard. Painters and sculptors once again took to incorporating words, axioms, in plastic work, or went referential, making new work by quoting and assembling from old sources. Music became part environment in which one submerged. Environmental art became indoor installation. Photography and sculpture adopted noise. Media became mix. Film in the popcorn palaces grew by leaps of ten-thousand-dollar-a-page ads and special-effects bounds, while the cult films —for which read those that appealed to the serious—were no longer only foreign: we were fostering our own. And the list of minority participants in every art was growing. The arena arts, rock to gangsta, loosened the vocabu-lary. Some critics wondered, could art still heal? Or must it only incite? Was all intelligence by now a "cult"? Deconstruction, flown over from France when it was already moribund, ate into our academic language like moths into wool and was sucked into the holes it had made.

And what of the Academy?

An academy is no mirror of the times, except as its members may be indi-vidually—or in that changing platform photograph. Rather, it's like a buoy, sedately riding the waves of whatever, occasionally rocked, but persisting on. Since artists are opinionated, and free with the expression thereof, an academy's collectively mild role—a consensus verging on silence—can mystify outsiders. Some members find acceptance of that hard also. The Hocking-Lippman report, a 1950 scrutiny of what we might or ought not say as a body, and usu-ally referred to as our guide, contains caveats sufficient to restrain most action, much less a prompt one.

The more honorary an organization is, the less constant will be its atten-dance and its member energy, the more sporadic its memory, and the shorter its appetite for the merely topical. Meanwhile, the same long-standing issues are always cropping up and are confronted by an ever-changing cast. The executive director, capable of both the long view and the short one, will often seem the only permanent member in the house.

By the time we were associated, she had long known all of the Academy-Institute's affairs, managing efficiently the working details of a double-bar-reled organization: meetings, committees, voting procedures, exhibitions, din-ners (including seating demands and menus to suit certain palates), correspondence both internal and external, supervision of staff—plus the care of an archive, a valuable art collection, an aging building—and constituency. At the Ceremonial, which is a production in three parts: luncheon for members, honorees, and guests; awards and speeches; reception for the audience in the open plaza. For the speeches, scores of "stars" and awardees must be conducted through tortuous backstage corridors, polite staff waving them on to the platform, where they won't quite hear the speakers behind whom they sit. They will however have seen the citations, books, artwork, musical scores in the upper gallery, then lunched, merrily, bashfully, importantly, according to their lights, under a vast tent in case it rains; it often has.

One saw Miss Mills fleetingly through this, a naturally elegant woman, medium size, in black chic enough for the occasion, wearing the familiar modicum of gold jewelry, on scrutiny seen to be fine examples from the Brazil where, though she had been born in England, the family had had a farm that she for a spell would manage after her father's death. A lady, though never too ladylike, she has a humor that could be acerb, that wouldn't sentimentalize us; she serves but is never servile and has an intelligence that can deal with anybody. One watches her coping, though scarcely giving evidence of it, kindly seeking out a new recruit to introduce her or him or just imperious enough to quell the visiting grandee who wants to commandeer the staff and the telephones. On one day she will cope with a flood. On another, a fire.

An academy runs by influence, a fusion of member opinion, judgment, worldly status, and the weight of individual character. Of this she was well aware. When consulted, she spoke up, and was often consulted. There was never any doubt that she harbored a strong sympathy for the Academy-Institute's aims, and affection for many of its members, much returned. Most called her Maggie. Whether on duty in committee or at dinner socially, she was open, though never tiresomely so; never gossipy, though she could be anecdotal. She was set on administering our collection of influences as decently as she could. And did.

Since she is now dead I have taken the liberty of describing her as she seemed to me.

When she came to tell me of my nomination for president of the Institute, I told her I would have to refuse. My tenure as president of P.E.N., an agreed-on one year only, had been so because for the following year my husband would be for some months on a fellowship in France, and I would accompany him. She thought for a minute, inquired for what months I would be away, then said: "You would only have to be here three times during that period. We could fly you over. And consult by phone in between." Whether or not she had to check this out with the nominating committee I never knew, but so it was done.

According to the record, this was a time when the Academy proper, that separate group of fifty, was having discussion, grave to troubled, as to whether it should dissolve. Of this I was, of course, unaware at the time. Miss Mills, present at every meeting, was not. I would shortly realize that she had come to be much more than the trusted go-between, depended on merely for her knowledge of history and procedure. She had a commitment, private but glimpsed, to the end that the organization must not lapse into a mere respectability and seniority excused once a year by its partial honoring of the young. Yet she knew the boundaries set by charter and precedent better than any of us. There was only so much she could do behind the scenes to keep us as lively and responsive as we could be. But she was determined to work through those better situated, who might help effect that. This was revealed gradually by her approval or even encouragement of efforts toward that end I myself proposed, minor though those might be, as well as by a nudge now and then toward what I hadn't envisioned but might be possible.

As an Institute member, I had a mild agenda of my own. It had seemed to me that an academy, like any assembly that judges by vote, will always be in danger of verging toward the median and the safe—and in our case the generational, of which we would all likely be guilty in our time. Artists could be more tolerant of difference than most, I had thought. But perhaps only of what did not impinge on their own art. For, looking about, I could see instances where we had ignored some considerable achievers among those "wild beast" artists the world calls *fauve*, a term preferable to *avant-garde*, since it signifies the deviant rather than the new (if often, as well, the threatening manners that can accompany work already exciting enough).

The manners on 155th Street are engaging: a courteousness tuned to the building and its occasions, where cronies may tip the wink to alliances encountered only at safe intervals, pomp can be sure of like companions, and the certainty of high intelligence, lined to a generous cause, can produce a lightsome calm. But an academy that cherishes too much the even tenor of its ways is not representative—and may be in peril.

I had no trouble in finding seconders for a few shockers I'd nominated now and then, not all of them literary.[1] It's a catholic place, always with like-minded compatriots. Perhaps it merely took a spot of bother. The surprise was that Miss Mills, who'd been watching such sponsorships, approved, no doubt as consonant with her own aims, though discreetly; she hadn't yet spoken to me of the Academy proper. For the first time, however, as we talked of the calendar to come, I became aware of how subtly this upper group was there, a presence always in the Institute's doings, since Academicians were, of course, members of both. And often functioned so. A strange muddle, surely. No accepted path, except to keep to the main issues. In the record I find certain letters of my own that I would not normally impose on a history. They show two transitions: a personal one, that may have relevance, and the far side of the Academy-Institute split that would finally occur.

I had been in China during the fall of 1986, just prior to my term. Answering Maggie's request for a vita, to include a report on the trip, I appended: "All good wishes to you for the new year. As you might know, some of its pleasant prospects for me will be the thought of working with you. I'm still bemused—and amused, by having gone public so recently. (Well recalling a remark I once made to you—that 'no artist would want the job'—of Institute president.) Well, perhaps we're needed now and then. And I have come to feel that, whatever the mild inter-art squabbles, more concentrated good will is expressed on 155th Street, than in many places."[2]

The Academy proper always gave a once-a-year luncheon to which Institute members were invited, the date falling while I was away. As I recall, Maggie would not have been averse to my flying back for it. My decision was not to; instead I sent a letter to be read:

> Since I'll be in France when this luncheon occurs I wish to send you my greetings. Living here, where the French Academy is an entity known to most, and an expected if fractious arbiter of the language, it is tempting to consider what role the Academy-Institute might further play in our own national life. We would not wish to be arbiters—as a group; we are the opposite of that. But might we be more of an influence on the general welfare of the arts than we are? If so—how?
>
> Every generation here has in some way considered that question. This may be a time to ask it again—and in the hope of involving the entire membership. For as you here today are aware, neither our pleasant and heartening social occasions, nor our constant and necessary flow of business meetings, are shared by as many members as could do so across the country, if interest truly called.
>
> We hope soon to query the membership on these matters—meanwhile, ideas and suggestions are ever welcome.
>
> Bon appetit.[3]

When I returned, in a conversation where Maggie was clearly sounding me out, I reminded her of a letter I'd written to Arthur Schlesinger, Jr., then president of the Institute, while I was a board member, then had not sent but had later shown her, as pertinent to some continuing board discussions.

> It seems self-evident that any mortal group must both renew its membership and interest its members in serving it.
>
> The Academy-Institute concentrates on the former, leaving the latter to the accidents of friendship, locale, or to the efforts of the executive secretary. Seems to me that in the matter of both welcoming and informing the new member, something more active might be done.
>
> . . . One of the delights here is the opportunity of elder company, and most of us would hope to survive to become that. The question of

Academy-Institute service or control oughtn't be more a matter of gray-beard against young than human nature makes it. But possibly new recruits might be more actively solicited to serve than they are, and more educated toward it.

What's it like to come in?

Most new members of whatever age are likely to be in full career, and already used to some honor. The first impulse is to take the honor—thanks very much—and go. By very breed we're more often those who tend to ignore organizational ambition or disdain it, or are shy or cynical about the panoply that goes with an academy—from platform-sitting to medals. We'll have long since formed our allegiances and habits in the realm of social protest, and whether or not we favor timely Academy-Institute expression on artistic matters vital to the world or to us, we're unlikely to be drawn to it as our prime vehicle for that, preferring to express ourselves singly. Nor do we want study-groups—except possibly to lead them. On Olympus—as was very clear last evening, most of us prefer to be Olympian—if we come at all.

Added to that, the Academy-Institute has to deal with its own division into two, which does alienate some by suggesting that their own presence or service might be regarded as fledgling or subordinate, at a time of life when they may well be used to the opposite. Again, I think that altering the division in the letter might be no more fruitful than doing so in the spirit—by actively soliciting and engaging new members in the work to be done.[4]

This letter described some confusions confided to me by new members and recognizable as once mine. It reflected also a misconception as to what response might be possible. "Activities" sustain the ordinary organization yet may be antithetical to the very intent—and impersonal calm—of the honorary one. A proposed modest concert or two, perhaps, paying young musicians to perform (as at dinner meetings on occasion), drawing on the work of members or honorees, and showing off the revered acoustics for which recording companies pay? As a break with the Academy's imposing silence, might not such an event draw an audience even up this hill, as with those who do attend the once-a-year competitive visual arts exhibit (for nonmembers)?

Indeed not. One's mistake had been to assume that music sends a universal message. The disclaimers were prompt. On our successive boards a serialist composer might well have served amicably with one linked to the diatonic, but going public meant choices. To program would be to champion; we don't. Also, to monitor performance quality, who would find the time? Under the argument the real point was clear, as it would have been for either of the other two disciplines. An academy encourages the arts at the designated place and time. It cannot risk being ordinary.

The executive director let one discover such subtleties for oneself. Yet she did speak to me directly of our double setup, having hoped, she said, that the matter might have been pushed during my predecessor's term; what were my sentiments? Now that I knew more, I told her I would certainly favor one shop, as likely would the 199 other members solely of the Institute. But the impetus would have to come from the Academicians themselves. Certainly no woman could broach it to the conservatives there, as was clear from history. (In 1980 an attempt by Barbara Tuchman had failed.) Though if asked, of course, I would speak my mind. She then mentioned that Jacques Barzun, nominated for the Academy once he had become president of the Institute, had politely refused; what would I think of such an eventuality? I said that I doubted the matter would come up in my case but that, of course, I would feel the same. A single separation, distinguishing anyone from the general republic of the arts, was enough.

As to more women members, efforts had been made, she said, though not nearly enough; she assumed I would help. I explained on which terms I certainly would. The term *politically correct* hadn't yet arrived in full force; I had a bias against such manipulation. Electing token members was also condescending and unnecessary. What was most at fault here was that the associations within the world of the arts were in the American Academy preponderantly male. As well as the knowledge.

Citing names the world knew, I felt that the lack of women among the Honorary Members was particularly shocking, though among my own nominees (not all women), several had been elected. As for nationally: "The celebrities do a little better, in both sexes. It's the middle ground women candidates who often don't get anywhere, compared to the men. Same for the blacks. The ground knowledge is missing."

It's perhaps appropriate here to comment on the history of women members in general. Isabel Bishop, nominated for president in 1955, had been pressured to withdraw, mostly by Malcolm Cowley, who did not feel that a woman could best represent us. (Her letter of withdrawal is a sad artifact.) We are all of our own era. My name had chanced to be on the presidential ballot because, asked if I would allow that, I had agreed, thinking its presence merely token but that a token presence was better than none. You do what you can.

The anecdotes are, of course, endless.

What's it like to preside over a board of directors on which you are the only woman? Well—on congratulating you, first meeting—they kiss you. Jumping from the chairs they sat in. You're amused. Your predecessor, the seven-foot-or-so John Kenneth Galbraith, what if they'd kissed him? You have an image of just that. They could have shaken hands with you, if not clapped you on the shoulder. But you see, in their quite touching expressions, that, men of impeccably formal manners, they're a bit unsure of what to do. You for once know better than they. On reflection, later, you are pleased to have been thought kissable. After that, you never think of it.

What's it like to be president of an eleven-member board of which five (the chancellor, three vice-chancellors, and the secretary of the Academy) are members of another group—capable of meeting, discussing, and ruling, all to some effect—to which you yourself are not privy? Suddenly confronted broadside with the real inner workings of this bifurcate place of which you have so anomalously been put at the head, it flashes over you how a dead friend, the writer C. P. Snow, archnarrator of committee status mongering, would have enjoyed hearing about your situation, but he's beyond reach. After that, you don't think of it.

Some propositions dealt with are of the never-never kind any board is familiar with. They crop up; investigations kill them. One of the first of these, as proposed by Stanley Kunitz and, as always, related to the seniority issue ever with us, is that we cause to be made a video record of all members. The logistics will be difficult, even tetchy. Start with the oldest, to be sure, but after that? Still, we are intrigued. After much investigation of recording groups, their fees, and possible funding sources, we find no tenable means of accumulating such a record, one that might have been of interest well beyond our walls. Possibly, as electronic means broaden and cheapen, the idea may come round again.

The sturdy old building both craves attention and responds. An asbestos problem is dealt with. The platform mike system is revised. The auditorium acoustics are revered by recording artists, but the building's wiring is touch-and-go. (In 1989, when too besieged by a camera crew on the big day, it will burst into flame.) When the building is crowded, the need for toilet facilities is acute; the ladies' line, longer even than in an old-style New York City theater during entr'acte, appalls our guests. I tell the board that an enlarged Ladies' will be a satisfactory tribute to my tenure; under the aegis of Walter Melvin, a specialist in antique structure restorations, it is done, hung with pictures, and viewed by the male board members, who clap.

We are reminded that the art collection, long taken for granted, has increased in value and must be insured accordingly. The financial portfolio, cautiously managed, takes a sudden rise in tune with the market, and we are just about contemplating how we will spend the extra—which we are required to do tax-wise—when the market dips. We are able, however, to increase our benefices—including the general awards, the Strauss Livings, and the fund for artists in need—in tune with inflation.

In the world of flashier prizes and a government subsidy all too soon to be constricted, the Academy-Institute has kept up a persistent bread-and-butter support of the arts. Slender, imperfect as all awards by committee may be, but always noncommercial, this program is like a holdover from federalist days or even the beaux arts period of the country, when the value of the arts to the good life, the moral life, and even the pursuit of happiness went unquestioned—if sometimes shielded from the grosser realities by formal language and the figleaf. In the present-day postsexual revolution in language and mores, it's interesting that the so-called religious right focuses not on the commercial or philistine but on the arts' freedom of representation and speech: part of the liberty for which the protesters' very forefathers may have fled.

Discomfort with member seniority again rises. A proposal within the Academy proper, which is having trouble recruiting members for meetings, that it set up an emeritus status, is defeated, with hot letters from some. On the cusp, of course, is the final action, when, able to see itself as oddly separatist, it will fold itself into the larger group. The Institute board, polled on the emeritus question, opts for the status quo. As the nation's population ages, becoming more self-respectful, then the aging of an arts group may seem more natural.

During this period we will again reconsider our relationship with the American Academy in Rome, a quite separate group to which we have traditionally sent a literary fellow yearly. Such a group, always tied to the social mores of the host country, necessarily seeing itself as a version of international friendship or even diplomacy, must often adopt a more elaborate social tone not always consonant with what all artists expect. Years back, when the Academy in Rome balked at accepting a black candidate, there had been a hiatus during which we sent no one. Now it looked as if we might have to do that again. Italy had become very expensive; our stipend, though increased, did not compare with what their fellows received, often from several sources. Over the years some of our fellows had nevertheless greeted the opportunity for immersion in Italy with ardor; others, however, had complained of unequal treatment, both as to quarters—one small room, as opposed to the ample studios of the visual arts and music fellows—and because of a general pecking order not to their benefit.

As a visitor for a few weeks in the late 1950s, I'd seen that atmosphere: a certain consciousness of contessas and cultivation of Italian grandees, artistic or not, and, among the fellows, special cliques quite evidently taken for granted. The sculptor Carl Milles, then an elderly resident, had told me: "When I was first here, we sculptors had to dine in black-tie." I'd thought of our current art scene: East Tenth Street, hairy underarms, and motorbikes, metal instead of marble.

When, according to some of our recent fellows, quarters and treatment are not adequate or equal, and after a visit and report by Miss Mills, neither well received by the Rome Academy, we again opt out, sending no fellow for the year. A request comes from Rome that we allow them to choose the fellow, which we have to refuse. Subsequently, adjustment having been made on both sides—better quarters from them, more money from us—plus a feeling that we should not deny the experience to those who might profit from it, the program is resumed.

But the spectacle of the two old organizations jousting did give one pause. Two old buildings, each on its hill, the Rome one far more august than ours and with much of ancient Italy nostalgically in place, though even on the Janiculum the motorcycles spurt and surely in some quarters now—as on the Via Margutta before it became chic—there will be the scruffy blood relatives of East Tenth. While here on Washington Heights, we too maintain a gentility that some treasure, and some consider an anachronism: the two-class membership. In the ever postmodern world, what is our duty?

Looking down the list of Blashfield addresses since the first in 1917, one finds a minihistory, in which the choice of speaker reflects, if shallowly, the cultural stance of the Academy as linked with the thought of the successive decades. The initial concern for language, and for only one tongue, has become, slowly, more various, but the first addresses adhered strictly to the founders' avowed purpose: "the preservation of the English language in its beauty and integrity, and its cautious enrichment by such terms as grow out of modern conditions."[5] They were given by such panjandrums of the subject as the stately critic Paul Elmer More ("English and Englistic," 1917) and Columbia University's arbiter, Brander Matthews ("The English Language and the American Academy," 1918), followed by Bliss Perry ("The Academy and the Language," 1919). In 1922 the seventh address was given by Henry van Dyke, the quasi-philosopher whose richly bound books of preachment for the enlightened well-to-do were to be found on many coffee tables ("A Fringe of Words").

Ten years later the critic Irving Babbitt will worry ("The Problem of Style in a Democracy"). The popular—perhaps in both senses—William Lyon Phelps will in 1934 introduce literature per se ("Five American Novels"), and in 1936 he will unaccountably do it again ("Two American Novels"). In between will come the first female, the essayist and wit Agnes Repplier, reverting to the classical (Horace). Owen Wister, the first novelist; Stephen Vincent Benét, the first poet; and Lewis Mumford and Walter Lippman, essayists with interests widened toward architecture and politics, will all follow in quick succession, and in 1946, Senator J. William Fulbright. In 1947 the second woman will be the disabled and heroic Helen Keller.

Two years later, the first foreigner will be E. M. Forster, to be followed over the years by a long line of Britishers. In the fifties, Aaron Copland will be the first from music; Salvador de Madariaga and Meyer Schapiro will introduce visual art. Mexico first appears with Octavio Paz in 1984.

Some of the speakers have always been recruited from members. So far, in this decade, since 1987, two—Jacques Barzun and Alfred Kazin—have been so; the others to date include Mario Vargas Llosa, Nadine Gordimer, Ada Louise

Huxtable (increasing the number of women to eight out of the seventy-eight so far). In 1995 Henry Louis Gates, Jr., the first black, will speak on Matthew Arnold and multiculturism. What has evolved from an initial concern for language, and for only one tongue, has become, if slowly, more various.

In 1987 when the National Portrait Gallery of the Smithsonian and we join forces for an exhibit in Washington, D.C., of portraits from our collection, we have an immersion in our own beaux arts history. The historian James Flexner's introduction, "The Academy-Institute Today," resonates with what the institution has meant and can mean to the nation's cultural life. Lillian B. Miller of the Gallery, who curated the exhibition, contributes a refreshingly blunt essay on all the cabals between art and money, pomp and scorn for same, that beset our founders but characterizes the collection as not trivia but a valuable record.

Early in the decade we have also begun upgrading the housing and care of our own archives, hoping for further gifts and one day a show of manuscripts. Other proposals—for musical or lecture use of the building—always fall shy, "because of its location." The music and poetry programs often customary at dinner meetings were finally abandoned; what this assemblage wants to do is talk.

Any ceremonial is a pact between speakers and audience, in which the rhetoric flows gently over the predictable. A day of awards is always benign. The crowd, augmented yearly by the awardees and a few invited guests, is largely a repeat mix of art aficionados and professionals, some media, plus a substratum of those come to view the members on the platform as much as to hear the talk. The president of the Institute and the chancellor of the Academy make opening remarks, longer than mere greetings perhaps, but shorter than formal addresses. The subject is usually some portion or version of the Academy-Institute's history, perhaps allusions to the cultural state of the nation and, more recently, pleas for more government support of the arts. The tone may be light to earnest, according to speaker. And in my time, the subject has always been parochial—us.

Ceremonial, 1989. Institute president Hortense Calisher (right) with Foreign Honorary Member Nadine Gordimer, who delivered that year's Blashfield address.

My guess was that few or none of my colleagues viewed us as exempt from the world's melee. But our outer lives and works took care of that. Here we were a modest shrine to the ideal, rendering some small services. Nor did one want to make this amiable audience a forum. Nor, God knows, put one's trust in rhetoric. But mass communication had long since relieved us of comfortable isolation; we had a range of vision on what was happening to many artists abroad who dared openly to pursue that ideal we harbored so peacefully. And "ivory," whether exported as tusk or tower, was getting a very bad press. We also had over seventy-five Foreign Honorary Members, some of them vulnerable and vocal.

Best, surely, to put the Academy-Institute on record as aware. So in 1987, in the president's customary address, the following:

> Artists are individual spokesmen for the human condition. But once we gather together we become a testimony for the untrammeled flow of thought. . . . All here know why I must enunciate this. And will forgive me if I speak for a moment solely as a writer, from the freedom I know best. At this moment there are men and women sitting in silent cells because they have sung out in poetry; dying of diseases of neglect because they have upheld the sanctity of the true word—and in a perversion of the art of healing that reminds one of the Holocaust—confined to psychiatric hospitals because their sanity is a judgment against the state. We hear of welcome change. But the bureaucracy of death moves slowly— and we get news of that too. At this bright celebration we must also breathe for that martyrdom.[6]

The chancellor, Arthur Schlesinger, Jr., addressing his remarks to "the conditions of artistic production" also noted that "the freedom of the artist and the freedom of the audience constitute a measure of the sanity of the society" and concluded: "The fight against the political control of the arts will be in its nature unending. On behalf of the American Academy and Institute, I salute those in all lands who persevere in the worldwide struggle for artistic and intellectual freedom."[7]

At worst one has ignored tradition, but not the world.

Shortly we would have to report worse. By chance I was present at a Fund for Free Expression board meeting (part of Human Rights Watch), to which the head of Viking Press came to inform us, prior to its reaching the press, of Iran's edict against Salman Rushdie, a threat that included his publishers, translators, booksellers.

The protest world is a regularized one. Rights organizations whose business it is—Amnesty International, the Rights Watches—can have considerable clout. International P.E.N. had done much for writers, as had more recently the Committee to Protect Journalists. We could have no illusions that any word from us would much influence Khomeini-Iran, even though we were known not to take stands on such matters ordinarily. In any case, the recognized espousers do better: those who are known to have observers worldwide. What was important was that the Academy-Institute be present in a cause surely of weight to freedom in the arts everywhere and that our members be able to find public expression through us.

The board was polled, Miss Mills phoning round the clock. We had a scoop, she felt, and it would be good, given our nonrecord, if we were not seen as merely on the bandwagon. This was not to be. Over the weekend the news went out, and the agent for the Academy-Institute's public announcements was slow; we did not appear in the *Times* at all. So, having indeed received inquiry from both nonmembers and members as to why we had been silent, it was announced from the May pulpit as follows: "We have been asked . . . what we did on the Rushdie matter. We had news before it broke in the press, midweek. On that Friday, February 19th, the American Academy and Institute of Arts and Letters wired the President of the United States and the Secretary of State asking them to protest publicly this act of international terrorism, and to assure federal protection to those principals threatened here. . . . We were observing Washington's Birthday early, you might say."[8]

During the last of this decade, as American domestic doings honor and support an ever-increasing list of artists old and young and of all kinds, the trends as usual rise and fall, leaving their spoor, or detritus. Deconstruction, liveliest in the universities, will submit the surprising aperçu that all statement has to be examined for its taint of the personal (except its own?). Shortly that muffling blanket will reveal some black holes. Rock beat and rap will invade the concert hall, submerging us in medicine-man tempo. Performance art will project its private images as if there had never before been theater or mime. Architects, blissing on the environment as they are able and on commerce as they must, will project public places that will affect our footsteps and workdays for decades to come. The visual arts have become ever higher investment for some. Bookshops have become chains.

In time of earthquake, war, rapine, racial upheaval, is that when the arts most flourish, or in those sustained peacetimes when historians can better scrutinize them? Or in both? As one enters the Academy-Institute's retrospective marble staircases, spottily personal library and walls hung with art-by-gift, is one stepping into a backwater only? Or are we merely one of the many art clusters that congregate by choice also: museums, galleries, movements, and "schools" among the artists themselves? During this period the intellectual journals and the journalists do a lot of worrying as to what kind of art is "high" or "low." The creators do not.

The building's location continues to prevent its being used less specifically, yet the neighborhood is changing once again. In 1995 Washington Heights and its vicinity is attracting young residents, some in the arts. The history of New York City shows that artists have often colonized poor neighborhoods. More to the point is the Academy's own admission that, centered in New York as its business is, it must make every effort to represent the nation. Perhaps a certain change shortly to come—the end of our bifurcated status—will effect others, though this is not yet clear.

At the end of the eighties there had been certain reachings-out—and retreats. In 1988 I proposed that we solicit the Foreign Honorary Members (who after their induction drop into a zone of silence) to provide us with short accounts of the present state of the arts in their countries. The response was small but worthy. Some contributors restricted publication of these reports; others are available in the published *Proceedings*. All provide a perspective that if continuous might prove a useful document.

In "The Changing Chinese Literature," Honorary Member Ba Jin contributes a brief but fascinating commentary on China's past literary history and the present—or then current—hopes, saying in part:

> Now Chinese writers dare to face the reality of life, think independently, select source material according to their own artistic interests, and express their perceptions of life. . . . When politics no longer fetters literary creation, would it be possible that some weak-willed and short-sighted writers may fall into the quagmire of moneymaking peculiar to commercial society and forget their commitment to the literary cause and society? Therefore, as an old man who has been engaged in literary work for over sixty years, what I would like to say is only that there is never any easy path in the literary field, and the most important thing to an author is his artistic conscience.[9]

In "The Art of Senegal," Leopold Sédar Senghor's three-and-one-half pages illuminate much:

> It is in the plastic arts, in painting and sculpture, that Senegal has particularly distinguished itself in the twentieth century. . . . I organized exhibitions of Senegalese art in the principal European capitals. And I did not forget the United States. . . . One American critic had this to say: "The French . . . believe that the Negro-African artists imitate them when in reality it is the contrary." . . . The chief of the School of Paris and of Cubism was of course Pablo Picasso, whom I visited from time to time. . . . Once, as I was leaving, Picasso said, looking straight at me, "We must remain savages." And looking straight back at him, I answered, "We must remain Negroes." He burst out laughing. We had understood each other.[10]

The list of deceased Foreign Honorary Members, beginning with those elected in 1929, is so extraordinary that one wishes all of them might have been queried. Reporting on one's country to another, or perhaps to the United

States?—and on the common ground of art, is perhaps a unique category, producing statements oddly angled, rare.

In 1990 Allen Ginsberg asked that we join in a public statement opposing proposed legislation on broadcast censorship; a membership meeting voted to do so (with the exception of one paragraph of the statement). At that same meeting Ada Louise Huxtable suggested we might wish to comment on proposed restrictions to the National Endowment for the Arts and the National Endowment for the Humanities.

In a summary of a board meeting months later one finds the following: "It was agreed that the Board would not issue a public statement at this time on the censorship issue at the National Endowment for the Arts. It was noted that the censorship issue is up for a vote in Congress, and that the Board might consider action in the future, depending on the outcome of that vote."[11] So far as one knows, that has not been pursued.

In that brown room with all its nineteenth-century intimations one gets used to the rise and fall of the temporal. One may be amused at the solemn pace of "immortals" anywhere, or resigned to the limitations of protest, all the way to the UN. Outside the Academy-Institute we were watching the great and hopeful wave of the end of Communism in Europe—or so we thought. Whether this loss of a target did fling American conservatives back to local and parochial issues, other historians will assess. As a country we are entering the arena of political correctness for fair; protests, once an arsenal of some effectiveness, now serve as identity cards. But in the arts, perhaps a widening of subject matter has occurred, and more consciousness of what is out there? Which our own awards begin to reflect, if slowly.

By 1991 my own term was finished. As Maggie's long association with us was soon after. During 1989, looking forward, I had suggested to her that the long line of "wordsmith" presidents of the Academy-Institute—i.e., all from literature, none from either music or the visual arts—should by rights be interrupted. We would have our best impact as a collective voice, and this should show us as the tripartite group we are.

It was then she told me she planned to retire at the end of the current term, "While the going is good" and having a chance to live in Florida, where, leaning on her farm-management period in Brazil, she might look forward to starting a flower farm. "Well—you've been through the fire," I said. . . . She'd announced the actual fire from the balcony, I relaying it from the podium, directing the crowd of hundreds how to leave for the plaza, where, sitting or standing, we listened to Nadine Gordimer give the Blashfield address in the sunny air. The arts and its audience had comported themselves well.

Maggie asked me not to reveal her decision. At the November 1989 board meeting, by which time she had herself done so and the composer Hugo

Weisgall had been elected president of the Institute, she noted "that she had not had time to list her recommendations for the future but believed that early in 1990 a meeting of the Committee on the Future should be called to discuss the purpose of the organization, which was 'the furtherance of literature and the fine arts,' and how the organization was carrying it out."[12]

Often she and I would have exchanges on how well or poorly that was happening. As the administrative core, party to everything, actually an admitted influence, discreet but not averse to speaking her mind, she had made her own place and pushed us to serve ours. The Academy-Institute, dealing with her resignation, can be proud of itself as employer and friend. She was appreciated. Regret was great. Saddest was that even in retirement she would not live to witness either the final drama of the Academy-Institute division or, more importantly, a settlement entirely according to her own hopes.

Margaret Mills died in an auto accident in Florida in 1993.

The Academy-Institute has been lucky in attracting staff who understand working in secluded quarters for a declared purpose, enlivened by dealing with a train of personalities, elders ever supplemented by the younger, and seen both in their social moments and when in committee. Virginia Dajani, who came as executive director in 1990 from the Municipal Art Society, would have a special focus on the place in the city of cultural organizations, as well as the personal wit and interest to keep every usual activity ticking during a crucial time. For this mid-decade will see the Academy proper, that shadow congress of fifty, finally voting its own demise.

The history has been long, the new discussions elaborate, but only simmering, never rising to brouhaha, the tone of the exchanges, like all the Academy record, confined within a politesse clearly relished to the full. Reading the record, which must in the main be kept internal, one finds these formal courtesies charming, glossed with occasional pomp but always keeping firmly to what the participants consider themselves to represent. Reporting in any measure on this small, civilized drama, only formal language will do. Listening, as it were, to the minutes of these meetings, words like *lucubration*, *tergiversation*, do come to mind. The intramural jokes are plainly of long standing. One reminds oneself that the arts are like any other sector when they have to resolve the political.

In 1980 when Barbara Tuchman, then president of the Academy-Institute as well as an Academy member, had asked that the division be ended, Malcolm Cowley, who would be ever opposed, wrote an essay to that effect. Tuchman followed with a rebuttal, and the matter was shelved by the full group. The Institute was, of course, not made privy to any of this.

Over the years since, the group will continue to have ever smaller attendance. There is concern among them about their travel and hotel expenses (perks not shared by Institute members) that assure their arriving from wherever. Some worry about the canard, known to be ever circulating, that they keep electing their friends to be Academicians. (Cowley once replied that nominations do indeed come from friendship but that "nobody has enough friends" to effect election.)

Talk will be more and more serious, to the extent that the long-standing division will be termed "invidious" by some. Others will object to that characterization yet edge toward the center. A few of the diehards for the status quo have of course passed on. During Hugo Weisgall's term as president of the Academy-Institute (1990–1993), he will be called in to join the discussion—which had never happened until then—and his calm exegesis has been well received. The painter Jack Levine, who as a former chancellor of the Academy and the next president of the Institute will be the most blunt and persistent champion of dissolution, will remark on what most offended him: that when Academicians died, their tributes were read only at Academy meetings, which were, of course, not attended by Institute members.

On February 12, 1991, Virginia Dajani wrote to John Updike:

> I recently prepared letters to new members telling them that they have just been elected to the American Academy and Institute of Arts and Letters, and found myself wondering if they will feel "put in their places" when they discover that in fact they have been elected only to the Institute. One member of some years' standing has told me that he didn't understand until five years after induction that he was not an Academician. It might come as a surprise for the members to know how many Institute members (especially newer ones who may not have had our internal hierarchy adequately explained to them—they may not get it from the yearbook version either) describe themselves, innocently to be sure, on their C.V.s, as Academicians. . . . I have recently discussed this with William Schuman, a member for 45 years—an Academician for 13—who feels very strongly that our goal should be that we have only one name.

Updike wrote back three days later: "As you remember, the Academy when I was Chancellor debated as to whether to vote itself out of existence, and voted, rather narrowly, and with half the membership abstaining, not to. But maybe the time has come. . . . Having witnessed a number of elections, and read of the rather vague way in which the Academy came into being, I have come to feel the distinction is not very meaningful, and maybe what the initial splinter group, in setting up an Academy, had in mind would be finalized by making the whole Institute the Academy."

As the year went on, a showdown was arranged for the Academy meeting of December 6. Arthur Schlesinger, Jr., framed the motion: "Resolved: that in the interest of removing invidious distinctions within our fellowship and of making our organization more intelligible to the media at home and to our counterparts abroad, the Institute should be abolished and its members absorbed into a single American Academy of Arts and Letters, ways and means to be worked out by the executive committee."

George Kennan, writing on December 4, regretted his inability to be present on December 6th and registered himself in favor of the motion: "I would prefer to see the word 'invidious,' on the second line of the draft Resolution, dropped and replaced by the words 'confusing and no longer appropriate'; but I would not make an issue of this; and you may add my vote to any language of the Resolution that does not distort its general sense and is acceptable to the others present at the meeting."[13]

From Key West, Florida, John Hersey also wrote in support: "I'd like to register with you . . . my support of the move for a complete amalgamation of the Academy and Institute. I still think, as I have said in the past, that the Academy could and should take a more active role in resisting attacks on freedom of expression in the arts, in defense of fellow artists who may be victims of such attacks, and in other forms of support, beyond our awards, of high standards in the arts we represent. . . . A unified Academy could and should be a more effective force in the culture."[14]

From Honolulu, Hawaii, however, a vigorous dissent arrived in the form of an open letter from Leon Edel to the Academy, dated a month after the meeting of December 6 had voted to propose amalgamation in a ballot vote by all the members.

> I want to protest against the wording of the resolution proposing admission of all the members of the National Institute of Arts and Letters to the Academy and the ill-informed discussions that preceded this document. . . .
>
> The only real issue is in itself curious: it is that of the hurt feelings of certain members of the Institute who feel they are put into an "invidious" position by having to wait for possible election to the Academy. The minutes of the discussions show this emotional approach—of ambitions unrealized, or a feeling that an army should consist entirely of generals, and of a confused and undocumented understanding of what is an Institute and what is an Academy. No one seems to have pointed out that we exist to be "invidious"—if you want to use that word. We pick and choose Institute members, rejecting some every year who richly deserve admission; that we are supposed to be highly discriminatory (in the benign sense of the word) in choosing award winners and in bestowing other honors. We scrutinize every candidate's biography and achievement.

The discussion overlooks the essential difference between democratic egalitarianism—the rights of the ballot and the law—and our entire system of hierarchies in business or in the arts. The arts can't be egalitarian. The solution proposed, "Here Comes Everybody" (as Joyce put it), is simplistic in the extreme and unworthy of a deliberative body of Academicians. . . . The French model for our organizations was the *Institut de France*, which is a kind of corporate body that gathers in the academies and other organizations of the Arts and even the best-known French Academy. . . . Our Institute is heterogeneous and broad enough to include satirists, newspapermen, demure as well as resounding poets and poetesses etc., some of whom . . . may not want academicism thrust upon them. There is much more we would need to talk about, and maybe go back to Matthew Arnold's idea of an Academy. We have not succeeded in making it a truly American institution.[15]

On January 15, Louis Auchincloss wrote to Virginia Dajani, "I found Leon Edel's arguments completely convincing . . . and I regret that, overcome with surprise at meeting the problem for the first time at my first meeting in the Academy, I voted for the resolution." And Helen Frankenthaler, through her assistant, communicated support for the Edel position.

Nevertheless, the vote, concluded on June 1, 1992, was thirty-nine to nine for unification. It was decided, per John Updike's suggestion, that everybody in the Institute would become an Academician. The total body henceforth to be known, pure and simple, as the Academy.

There's a certain elegiac sadness to be felt even by an egalitarian reader of these conversations and letters. These voices, one or two mourning postmortem the loss of that smaller company, or even of the special room in which it has met, come as ruefully as those of the shades in Virgil when consigning themselves to the Styx. A custom, not without elegance, even of some usefulness, is so no longer. A group once formative to this body politic has seen itself as no longer necessary, very possibly detractive. And has done so with honor. It has come to their attention that at times they may have been brooding on privilege. Not art.

In the Republic verging toward the twenty-first century, as this small band of 250 arrives at its own centenary, very much more than government support of the arts is at stake. "Anti-intellectualism" is too fancy a phrase for that state of mind, always dormant in the American citizenry, whose adherents have often confused education with elitism, representational art with image-making idolatry, "going to the play" as risking one's mental purity, dancing as contributing to sexual sin, music beyond the hymnal as dilettante or even unnecessary, and even book larnin' as threatening to the holy life. Nor are these attitudes confined to the bible beaters. In the age of movies and college-for-the-kids, those who might once have seen themselves as "God-fearing" now merely mistrust or decry those extra intelligences that only "entertain" or "decorate" and neither justify that nor earn their keep. Art is once again very nearly un-American, as our Congress may well decree. Exempting only folk art, as for and by the people, many of them inoffensively dead.

Oddly coincidental is what has happened to the professional handlers of art, that is, to the values they now impose. Visual art is now baldly spoken of as money investment before it is anything else. Publishers, gone corporate, veer all written matter toward the salable, as the primary aim. Theater? Preferably spectacle, for the high spenders, and shockers for all. Meanwhile, the graying of the classical music audience is whispered in the aisles. From the family room,

Final meeting of the "old" Academy, May 20, 1992, with nineteen of the fifty members present. First row, left to right: Jacob Lawrence, Elizabeth Hardwick, Louis Auchincloss, Lukas Foss, and Ada Louise Huxtable. Second row, left to right: Jack Levine, Milton Babbitt, James Merrill, Hugo Weisgall, Arthur Schlesinger, Jr., Saul Steinberg, and William Gaddis. Third row, left to right: Alfred Kazin, Ralph Ellison, C. Vann Woodward, James Dickey, Richard Wilbur, Kurt Vonnegut, and Harrison E. Salisbury. (Niki Berg)

or the arena, anyone can hear where the young are. Only the architects, always at money's mercy, have become adept at sneaking their own aesthetic in.

Call the situation "reverse philistinism": money is art.

True, to the extent it always has been. Often so in those same periods when the arts indeed have flourished, however "immoral" the patronage. Coercion—of the artist's freedom of style not to mention the loss of personal freedom—is the other spur. When you have both encouragements going on, as now, you have a marvelous jumble: tycoons backing shows on race problems. Rushdie being protected at much cost by the British government. "Minimal" art paid for in staggering sums. An esteemed music critic telling us that pop must be embraced as the new lingua franca to replace classical, because pop's current audience is the mostest.

Not to worry. Art when assaulted (or assimilated) does what any bacterium does, or human being. It creates more. And never quite predictably.

So, what peroration? For any centenary, an account of the present is still the best one. Louis Auchincloss, elected to succeed Kevin Roche as president, is a member from the department of literature, thus carrying on an alternating representation that has worked well. Meanwhile, during the last few years the building itself has been receiving attention, very much within its own terms. Under the executive director's discerning eye, the paintings and drawings that line the interior have been rearranged or supplemented, and the tour itself is instructive of what the Academy has been. Before retiring as president, Kevin Roche instituted a cohesive building plan for the years ahead, much of which has been completed.

Also to the point, the selection of members has been scrutinized. On June 5, 1995, Roche wrote to the members of the Academy:

> In proposing candidates for membership to the Academy, you may wish to consider broadening the selection to include a better geographic, ethnic, and gender representation of our society. This in no way suggests that candidates should be proposed for this reason alone, but it is suggested to encourage looking beyond the usual circle of acquaintances on the East Coast for worthy candidates. . . . There are 14 members in 13 Midwestern states, and three members in nine Western and Southwestern states. More than half the entire membership lives in Connecticut, New Jersey, and New York. . . . Only one sixth of the membership are women, and in 1995, of ten new members elected, ten were male. There are six African-American members and two Asian-American members.
>
>   . . . The distribution of our 75 Foreign Honorary Members reveals that almost two-thirds are writers, one-third coming from Western Europe, Great Britain, and Ireland. There are three Foreign Honorary Members in Africa (not including South Africa) and four in South

America (Brazil, Colombia, and Peru.) In China there are two members, and in Southeast Asia there are none.

Selection is any society's diadem . . . and curse. The Academy is a social structure and an American one, each voter acting according to the canon best known to him, and none bossing the job—which would be tyranny. Collectively, an academy at its best functions as a unit of what John Jay Chapman—the greatest and most neglected of American social critics (and not a member)—called "the class of worthies."

The air on 155th Street is granite-shadowed, the door heavy—with the passage of the decades, no doubt. Entering it, one can feel less honored than honoring, a kind of citizenship. That breath of the ideal which working in and about the arts can sometimes confer—still here, is it?

And in company.

NOTES

Unless otherwise specified, all materials cited are located in the Academy files, which are also the source of any unannotated quotations in the text.

1. They included William Burroughs, George Segal, Gary Snyder, and, as honoraries, Natalia Guinzberg (didn't make it), Anita Desai, Janet Frame, Athol Fugard, Alice Munro.

2. December 23, 1986.

3. November 25, 1987. The quoted message was meant for members by Calisher, who included a handwritten note to Mills at the bottom of the letter.

4. Undated (1983).

5. Quoted from the offer of gift from Mrs. Edwin Howland Blashfield reproduced in the minutes of a meeting of the Academy's board of directors of the Academy, November 15, 1916, and in the preface to *Academy Papers: Addresses on Language Problems by Members of the American Academy of Arts and Letters* (New York: Scribner's, 1925).

6. *Proceedings of the American Academy and Institute of Arts and Letters*, 2d ser., no. 38 (1988): 6.

7. Ibid., p. 9.

8. *Proceedings*, 2d ser., no. 40 (1990): 4.

9. *Proceedings*, 2d ser., no. 39 (1989): 99–102.

10. Ibid., pp. 111–14.

11. Minutes of a meeting of the Academy board of directors, October 11, 1990.

12. Minutes of a meeting of the Academy board of directors, November 2, 1989.

13. To Virginia Dajani, December 4, 1991.

14. To Virginia Dajani, November 26, 1991.

15. January 6, 1992.

APPENDIX
ACADEMY MEMBERS, PAST *and* PRESENT

THE NAMES on this list are followed by letters designating the departments to which members belong(ed) (L = literature department; A = art department; M = music department) and their years of election. In the case of deceased members, department designations are followed by birth and death dates and years of election to the Institute and, when appropriate, to the Academy. In the case of Honorary Members, living and dead, names are followed by dates of election to honorary status, and American Honorary Members are identified by the fields for which they were honored. Note that in the 1993 unification, all Institute members became Academicians.

Current Academy Members (as of January 1998)

	ELECTED		ELECTED
Aaron, Daniel (L)	1997	Barnet, Will (A)	1982
Adams, John (M)	1997	Barth, John (L)	1974
Adler, Renata (L)	1987	Barzun, Jacques (L)	1952
Albee, Edward (L)	1966	Baskin, Leonard (A)	1963
Ammons, A. R. (L)	1990	Bassett, Leslie (M)	1981
Anderson, Lennart (A)	1977	Beattie, Ann (L)	1992
Argento, Dominick (M)	1980	Beeson, Jack (M)	1976
Ashbery, John (L)	1980	Bellow, Saul (L)	1958
Auchincloss, Louis (L)	1965	Bentley, Eric (L)	1990
Babbitt, Milton (M)	1965	Berger, Arthur (M)	1972
Bailey, William (A)	1986	Bloom, Harold (L)	1990
Baker, Russell (L)	1984	Bloom, Hyman (A)	1974
Banks, Russell (L)	1998	Bly, Robert (L)	1987
Barnes, Edward Larrabee (A)	1991	Boghosian, Varujan (A)	1986

Current Academy Members (as of January 1998)

	ELECTED		ELECTED
Bolcom, William (M)	1993	Fine, Vivian (M)	1980
Bourgeois, Louise (A)	1983	Flexner, James Thomas (L)	1976
Bowles, Paul (L)	1981	Foote, Horton (L)	1998
Brant, Henry (M)	1979	Foote, Shelby (L)	1994
Brinnin, John Malcolm (L)	1978	Ford, Richard (L)	1998
Brooks, Gwendolyn (L)	1976	Foss, Lukas (M)	1962
Buchwald, Art (L)	1986	Frank, Mary (A)	1984
Cadmus, Paul (A)	1975	Frankenthaler, Helen (A)	1974
Calisher, Hortense (L)	1977	Freed, James Ingo (A)	1994
Carter, Bennett L. (M)	1996	Freilicher, Jane (A)	1989
Carter, Elliott (M)	1956	Gaddis, William (L)	1984
Celmins, Vija (A)	1996	Gaines, Ernest J. (L)	1998
Chamberlain, John (A)	1990	Galbraith, John Kenneth (L)	1966
Chou Wen-chung (M)	1982	Gass, William H. (L)	1983
Christo (A)	1989	Gay, Peter (L)	1989
Close, Chuck (A)	1992	Gehry, Frank O. (A)	1987
Cobb, Henry N. (A)	1980	Giurgola, Romaldo (A)	1977
Coleman, Ornette (M)	1997	Glück, Louise (L)	1996
Commager, Henry Steele (L)	1952	Graves, Michael (A)	1991
Connell, Evan S. (L)	1988	Graves, Morris (A)	1957
Coover, Robert (L)	1987	Gray, Cleve (A)	1998
Corigliano, John (M)	1991	Gray, Francine du Plessix (L)	1992
Creeley, Robert (L)	1987	Green, Julian (L)	1972
Crumb, George (M)	1975	Guare, John (L)	1989
Davidovsky, Mario (M)	1982	Gwathmey, Charles (A)	1976
DeLillo, Don (L)	1989	Hadzi, Dimitri (A)	1983
Dello Joio, Norman (M)	1961	Hall, Donald (L)	1989
Del Tredici, David (M)	1984	Hancock, Walker (A)	1941
Diamond, David (M)	1966	Harbison, John (M)	1992
Didion, Joan (L)	1981	Hardwick, Elizabeth (L)	1977
Dine, Jim (A)	1980	Hardy, Hugh (A)	1993
di Suvero, Mark (A)	1986	Harrison, Lou (M)	1973
Doctorow, E. L. (L)	1984	Hawkes, John (L)	1980
Dodd, Lois (A)	1998	Hazzard, Shirley (L)	1982
Eberhart, Richard (L)	1960	Hecht, Anthony (L)	1970
Erdrich, Louise (L)	1998	Held, Al (A)	1984
Escobar, Marisol (A)	1978	Heliker, John (A)	1969
Fagles, Robert (L)	1998	Heller, Joseph (L)	1977
Feiffer, Jules (L)	1995	Hoagland, Edward (L)	1982
Fiedler, Leslie (L)	1988	Hollander, John (L)	1979

Current Academy Members (as of January 1998)

	ELECTED		ELECTED
Hovhaness, Alan (M)	1977	Marden, Brice (A)	1998
Howard, Richard (L)	1983	Martin, Agnes (A)	1989
Hunt, Richard (A)	1998	Martino, Donald (M)	1981
Husa, Karel (M)	1994	Matthiasdottir, Louisa (A)	1998
Huxtable, Ada Louise (L)	1977	Matthiessen, Peter (L)	1974
Imbrie, Andrew W. (M)	1969	Maxwell, William (L)	1963
Jacobsen, Josephine (L)	1994	McPhee, John (L)	1988
Johansen, John M. (A)	1979	Meier, Richard (A)	1983
Johns, Jasper (A)	1973	Meredith, William (L)	1968
Johnson, Philip (A)	1963	Merwin, W. S. (L)	1972
Jolas, Betsy (M)	1983	Miller, Arthur (L)	1958
Justice, Donald (L)	1992	Milosz, Czeslaw (L)	1982
Kahn, Wolf (A)	1984	Morris, Wright (L)	1970
Kaplan, Justin (L)	1985	Morrison, Toni (L)	1981
Katz, Alex (A)	1988	Murray, Albert (L)	1997
Kazin, Alfred (L)	1965	Murray, Elizabeth (A)	1992
Keene, Donald (L)	1986	Noland, Kenneth (A)	1977
Kelly, Ellsworth (A)	1974	Oates, Joyce Carol (L)	1978
Kennan, George F. (L)	1962	Oldenburg, Claes (A)	1975
Kennedy, William (L)	1993	Oliveira, Nathan (A)	1994
Kepes, Gyorgy (A)	1968	Ozick, Cynthia (L)	1988
Kiley, Daniel Urban (A)	1996	Paley, Grace (L)	1980
Kinnell, Galway (L)	1980	Pearlstein, Philip (A)	1982
Kirchner, Leon (M)	1962	Pei, I. M. (A)	1963
Kitaj, R. B. (A)	1982	Pelli, Cesar (A)	1982
Koch, Kenneth (L)	1996	Perle, George (M)	1978
Kunitz, Stanley (L)	1963	Poor, Anne (A)	1987
Laderman, Ezra (M)	1991	Powell, Mel (M)	1998
Lassaw, Ibram (A)	1984	Powers, J. F. (L)	1968
Lawrence, Jacob (A)	1965	Price, Reynolds (L)	1988
Levine, David (A)	1983	Puryear, Martin (A)	1992
Levine, Jack (A)	1956	Rauschenberg, Robert (A)	1978
Levine, Philip (L)	1997	Reich, Steve (M)	1994
Lewis, R. W. B. (L)	1982	Resika, Paul (A)	1994
Lippold, Richard (A)	1963	Resnick, Milton (A)	1993
Lurie, Alison (L)	1989	Rich, Adrienne (L)	1990
MacIver, Loren (A)	1959	Rickey, George (A)	1974
Mailer, Norman (L)	1967	Rivers, Larry (A)	1979
Mamet, David (L)	1994	Rochberg, George (M)	1985
Marca-Relli, Conrad (A)	1976	Roche, Kevin (A)	1970

Current Academy Members (as of January 1998)

	ELECTED		ELECTED
Rorem, Ned (M)	1979	Vendler, Helen Hennessy (L)	1993
Rosenquist, James A. (A)	1987	Venturi, Robert (A)	1990
Roth, Philip (L)	1970	Vicente, Esteban (A)	1993
Rothenberg, Susan (A)	1990	Vonnegut, Kurt (L)	1973
Russell, John (L)	1996	Ward, Robert (M)	1967
Ryman, Robert (A)	1994	Weaver, William (L)	1992
Sacks, Oliver (L)	1996	Welty, Eudora (L)	1952
Schlesinger, Arthur, Jr. (L)	1961	White, Edmund (L)	1996
Schuller, Gunther (M)	1967	Wiesel, Elie (L)	1996
Segal, George (A)	1981	Wilbur, Richard (L)	1957
Serra, Richard (A)	1995	Wills, Garry (L)	1995
Shapey, Ralph (M)	1989	Wilson, August (L)	1995
Shapiro, Joel (A)	1998	Wilson, Jane (A)	1991
Shapiro, Karl (L)	1959	Wilson, Olly (M)	1995
Shepard, Sam (L)	1986	Woodward, C. Vann (L)	1970
Simic, Charles (L)	1995	Wright, Charles (L)	1995
Smith, William Jay (L)	1975	Wuorinen, Charles (M)	1985
Snelson, Kenneth (A)	1994	Wyeth, Andrew (A)	1950
Snodgrass, W. D. (L)	1972	Zwilich, Ellen Taaffe (M)	1992
Snyder, Gary (L)	1987		
Sondheim, Stephen (M)	1983		
Sontag, Susan (L)	1979		
Spencer, Elizabeth (L)	1985	**Current Foreign**	
Starer, Robert (M)	1994	**Honorary Members**	
Steinberg, Saul (A)	1968	**(as of January 1998)**	
Stone, Robert (L)	1994		
Strand, Mark (L)	1981	Abakanowicz, Magdalena (A)	1996
Styron, William (L)	1966	Achebe, Chinua (L)	1982
Terkel, Studs (L)	1997	Akhmadulina, Bella (L)	1977
Theroux, Paul (L)	1984	Alberti, Rafael (L)	1975
Thiebaud, Wayne (A)	1986	Amichai, Yehuda (L)	1986
Thon, William (A)	1967	Arciniegas, Germán (L)	1943
Thorne, Francis (M)	1988	Ba Jin (L)	1985
Tooker, George (A)	1983	Bassani, Giorgio (L)	1974
Tower, Joan (M)	1998	Bei Dao (L)	1996
Twombly, Cy (A)	1987	Berio, Luciano (M)	1985
Tyler, Anne (L)	1983	Boulez, Pierre (M)	1966
Updike, John (L)	1964	Caro, Anthony (A)	1979
Van Duyn, Mona (L)	1983	Chillida, Eduardo (A)	1994
		Correa, Charles (A)	1998
		Desai, Anita (L)	1992

Current Academy Members (as of January 1998)

	ELECTED		ELECTED
Dutilleux, Henri (M)	1981	Powell, Anthony (L)	1977
Frame, Janet (L)	1986	Richter, Gerhard (A)	1998
Freud, Lucian (A)	1988	Schnittke, Alfred (M)	1995
Friel, Brian (L)	1996	Sédar Senghor, Léopold (L)	1973
Fuentes, Carlos (L)	1985	Shankar, Ravi (M)	1974
Fugard, Athol (L)	1988	Solzhenitsyn, Aleksandr I. (L)	1969
Gallant, Mavis (L)	1989	Soulages, Pierre (A)	1979
García Márquez, Gabriel (L)	1974	Soyinka, Wole (L)	1986
Goehr, Alexander (M)	1989	Spark, Muriel (L)	1978
Gombrich, E. H. (L)	1985	Stockhausen, Karlheinz (M)	1979
Gordimer, Nadine (L)	1978	Tal, Josef (M)	1981
Havel, Václav (L)	1991	Tange, Kenzo (A)	1966
Heaney, Seamus (L)	1993	Tippett, Michael (M)	1973
Henze, Hans Werner (M)	1982	Vargas Llosa, Mario (L)	1986
Herbert, Zbigniew (L)	1990	Voznesensky, Andrei A. (L)	1972
Hockney, David (A)	1981	Walcott, Derek (L)	1979
Hope, A. D. (L)	1989	Wolf, Christa (L)	1990
Isosaki, Arata (A)	1998	Xenakis, Iannis (M)	1975
Kiefer, Anselm (A)	1990	Yevtushenko, Yevgeny (L)	1987
Knussen, Oliver (M)	1994	Zhang Jie (L)	1992
Kundera, Milan (L)	1986		
Lessing, Doris (L)	1974		
Lévi-Strauss, Claude (L)	1977		
Ligeti, György (M)	1984		
Mahfouz, Naguib (L)	1992		
Matta, Roberto Echaurren (A)	1981		
Menotti, Gian Carlo (M)	1953		
Munro, Alice (L)	1992		
Murdoch, Iris (L)	1975		
Naipaul, V. S. (L)	1981		
Narayan, R. K. (L)	1981		
Niemeyer, Oscar (A)	1964		
O'Brien, Edna (L)	1987		
Oe, Kenzaburo (L)	1997		
Pärt, Arvo (M)	1996		
Paz, Octavio (L)	1972		
Penderecki, Krzysztof (M)	1998		
Petrassi, Goffredo (M)	1977		
Pinter, Harold (L)	1984		

Current American Honorary Members

	ELECTED
Allen, Woody (filmmaker)	1987
Brown, Trisha (choreographer)	1997
Callahan, Harry (photographer)	1997
Cunningham, Merce (choreographer)	1984
Roach, Max (jazz drummer/composer)	1992
Robbins, Jerome (choreographer)	1985
Sokolow, Anna (choreographer)	1993
Taylor, Paul (choreographer)	1989
Tharp, Twyla (chorcographer)	1997
Wilder, Billy (filmmaker)	1984

Deceased Members of the Academy and Institute—1898 to 1997

		ELECTED TO INSTITUTE	ELECTED TO ACADEMY
Abbey, Edwin Austin (A)	1852–1911	1898	1905
Adams, Brooks (L)	1848–1927	1906	
Adams, Charles Francis (L)	1835–1915	1905	1909
Adams, Franklin P. (L)	1881–1960	1946	
Adams, Henry (L)	1838–1918	1898	1905
Adams, Herbert (A)	1858–1945	1898	1912
Adams, James Truslow (L)	1878–1949	1923	1930
Adams, Léonie (L)	1899–1988	1951	
Adams, Wayman (A)	1883–1959	1929	
Ade, George (L)	1866–1944	1908	
Adler, David (A)	1882–1949	1946	
Aiken, Conrad (L)	1889–1973	1941	1956
Aitken, Robert Ingersoll (A)	1878–1949	1915	
Albers, Josef (A)	1888–1976	1968	
Albright, Ivan (A)	1897–1983	1957	1967
Alden, Henry Mills (L)	1836–1919	1898	1910
Alderman, Edwin Anderson (L)	1861–1931	1925	1926
Aldrich, Chester (A)	1871–1940	1937	
Aldrich, Richard (L)	1863–1937	1908	
Aldrich, Thomas Bailey (L)	1836–1907	1898	1905
Alexander, John White (A)	1856–1915	1898	1910
Algren, Nelson (L)	1909–1981	1981	
Allen, Hervey (L)	1889–1949	1936	
Allen, James Lane (L)	1849–1925	1898	
Amateis, Edmond (A)	1897–1981	1952	
Ames, Winthrop (L)	1871–1937	1931	
Anderson, Maxwell (L)	1888–1959	1935	1955
Anderson, Sherwood (L)	1876–1941	1937	
Andrews, Charles M. (L)	1863–1943	1937	1937
Archipenko, Alexander (A)	1887–1964	1962	
Arendt, Hannah (L)	1906–1975	1964	
Arms, John Taylor (A)	1887–1953	1932	1947
Arvin, Newton (L)	1900–1963	1952	
Atherton, Gertrude (L)	1857–1948	1938	
Auden, Wystan Hugh (L)	1907–1973	1948	1954
Ayres, Louis (A)	1874–1947	1944	
Babb, George F. (A)	1836–1915	1907	
Babbitt, Irving (L)	1865–1933	1920	1930

Deceased Members of the Academy and Institute—1898 to 1997

		ELECTED TO INSTITUTE	ELECTED TO ACADEMY
Bacheller, Irving (L)	1859–1950	1920	
Bacon, Henry (A)	1866–1924	1913	1921
Bacon, Leonard (L)	1887–1954	1941	1951
Bacon, Peggy (A)	1895–1987	1956	
Baker, George Pierce (L)	1866–1935	1916	1925
Baker, Ray Stannard (L)	1870–1946	1920	
Baldwin, James (L)	1924–1987	1964	
Baldwin, Simeon E. (L)	1840–1927	1898	
Ballin, Hugo (A)	1879–1956	1908	
Barber, Samuel (M)	1910–1981	1941	1958
Barnard, George Grey (A)	1863–1938	1908	1930
Barnes, Djuna (L)	1892–1982	1959	
Barry, Philip (L)	1896–1949	1930	
Barthelme, Donald (L)	1931–1989	1978	
Bartlett, Frederic Clay (A)	1873–1953	1916	
Bartlett, Paul Wayland (A)	1865–1925	1908	1911
Bassett, John Spencer (L)	1867–1928	1923	
Basso, Hamilton (L)	1904–1964	1955	
Bates, Arlo (L)	1850–1918	1905	
Beach, Chester (A)	1881–1956	1918	
Beal, Gifford (A)	1879–1956	1923	1943
Beard, Charles Austin (L)	1874–1948	1939	1946
Bearden, Romare H. (A)	1912–1988	1972	
Beaux, Cecilia (A)	1855–1942	1930	1933
Becker, Carl (L)	1873–1945	1933	
Beckwith, J. Carroll (A)	1852–1917	1898	
Beebe, William (L)	1887–1962	1939	
Behrman, Samuel N. (L)	1893–1973	1943	
Bellows, George Wesley (A)	1882–1925	1918	
Belluschi, Pietro (A)	1899–1994	1955	1993
Benét, Stephen Vincent (L)	1898–1943	1929	1938
Benét, William Rose (L)	1886–1950	1933	
Benson, Frank W. (A)	1862–1951	1911 (resigned 1934; reelected 1944)	
Benton, Thomas Hart (A)	1889–1975	1942	1962 (resigned 1965; reinstated 1966)
Berenson, Bernard (L)	1865–1959	1922	1937
Bergsma, William (M)	1921–1994	1967	1993

Deceased Members of the Academy and Institute—1898 to 1997

		ELECTED TO INSTITUTE	ELECTED TO ACADEMY
Berman, Eugene (A)	1899–1972	1964	
Berman, Leonid (A)	1896–1976	1976	
Bernstein, Leonard (M)	1918–1990	1961	1981
Berryman, John (L)	1914–1972	1965	
Betts, Louis (A)	1873–1961	1912	
Beveridge, Albert J. (L)	1862–1927	1920	1924
Biddle, George (A)	1885–1973	1961	
Bierstadt, Albert (A)	1830–1902	1898	
Bigelow, John (L)	1817–1911	1898	1905
Bird, Arthur (M)	1856–1923	1898	
Bischoff, Elmer (A)	1916–1991	1988	
Bishop, Elizabeth (L)	1911–1979	1954	1976
Bishop, Isabel (A)	1902–1988	1944	1971
Bishop, Joseph Bucklin (L)	1847–1928	1923	
Bishop, Morris (L)	1893–1973	1973	
Bishop, William Henry (L)	1847–1928	1918	
Bitter, Karl (A)	1867–1915	1910	
Blackmur, Richard P. (L)	1904–1965	1956	
Blashfield, Edwin Howland (A)	1848–1936	1898	1908
Blitzstein, Marc (M)	1905–1964	1959	
Bloch, Ernest (M)	1880–1959	1937	1943
Blum, Robert Frederick (A)	1857–1903	1898	
Blume, Peter (A)	1906–1992	1951	1960
Bogan, Louise (L)	1897–1970	1952	1968
Bolotowsky, Ilya (A)	1907–1981	1982	
Borie, Charles (A)	1871–1943	1937	
Bouché, Louis (A)	1896–1969	1953	
Bowen, Catherine Drinker (L)	1897–1973	1963	
Bowers, Claude G. (L)	1878–1958	1937	
Boyd, James (L)	1888–1944	1938	
Boyle, Kay (L)	1902–1992	1968	1978
Bradford, Gamaliel (L)	1863–1932	1915	1931
Bradford, Roark (L)	1896–1948	1947	
Breuer, Marcel (A)	1902–1981	1965	
Bridges, Robert (L)	1858–1941	1906	
Brinton, Crane (L)	1898–1968	1955	
Brockway, Howard (M)	1870–1951	1910	
Brodsky, Joseph (L)	1940–1996	1979 (resigned 1987)	

Deceased Members of the Academy and Institute—1898 to 1997

		ELECTED TO INSTITUTE	ELECTED TO ACADEMY
Bromfield, Louis (L)	1896–1956	1928	
Brook, Alexander (A)	1898–1980	1942	
Brooks, Cleanth (L)	1906–1994	1970	1993
Brooks, James (A)	1906–1992	1973	
Brooks, Richard E. (A)	1865–1919	1908	
Brooks, Van Wyck (L)	1886–1963	1925	1937
Brown, Arthur, Jr. (A)	1874–1957	1940	1953
Brown, Glenn (A)	1854–1932	1909	
Brown, John Mason (L)	1900–1969	1950	
Browne, George Elmer (A)	1871–1946	1929	
Brownell, William Crary (L)	1851–1928	1898	1908
Bruce, Edward (A)	1879–1943	1939	
Brunner, Arnold W. (A)	1857–1925	1913	
Brush, George de Forest (A)	1855–1941	1898	1910
Buck, Dudley (M)	1839–1909	1898	
Buck, Pearl S. (L)	1892–1973	1936	1951
Bunce, William Gedney (A)	1840–1916	1898 (resigned 1914)	
Bunshaft, Gordon (A)	1909–1990	1960	
Burchfield, Charles E. (A)	1893–1967	1943	1958
Burke, Kenneth (L)	1897–1993	1951	1966
Burliuk, David (A)	1882–1967	1967	
Burnham, Daniel Hudson (A)	1846–1912	1906	
Burroughs, John (L)	1837–1921	1898	1905
Burroughs, William S. (L)	1914–1997	1983	1993
Burt, Struthers (L)	1882–1954	1926	
Burton, Richard (L)	1861–1940	1908	
Butler, Howard Russell (A)	1856–1934	1916	
Butler, Nicholas Murray (L)	1862–1947	1909	1911
Bynner, Witter (L)	1881–1968	1962	
Cabell, James Branch (L)	1879–1958	1937 (resigned 1942)	
Cable, George Washington (L)	1844–1925	1898	1908
Cadman, Charles W. (M)	1881–1946	1932	
Cage, John (M)	1912–1992	1968	1988
Calder, Alexander (A)	1898–1976	1960	1964
Calder, Stirling (A)	1870–1945	1916	
Caldwell, Erskine (L)	1903–1987	1942	1984
Campbell, Joseph (L)	1904–1987	1973	1987
Canby, Henry Seidel (L)	1878–1961	1931	

Deceased Members of the Academy and Institute—1898 to 1997

		ELECTED TO INSTITUTE	ELECTED TO ACADEMY
Capote, Truman (L)	1924–1984	1964	
Carlsen, Emil (A)	1853–1932	1908	
Carman, Bliss (L)	1861–1929	1898 (resigned 1915)	
Carpenter, John Alden (M)	1876–1951	1918	1942
Carrére, John M. (A)	1858–1911	1908	
Carson, Rachel (L)	1907–1964	1953	1963
Carver, Raymond (L)	1938–1988	1988	
Castellon, Federico (A)	1914–1971	1968	
Cather, Willa (L)	1876–1947	1929	1938
Catton, Bruce (L)	1899–1978	1955	1962
Cavallon, Giorgio (A)	1904–1989	1988	
Cawein, Madison J. (L)	1865–1914	1908	
Chadwick, French Ensor (L)	1844–1919	1912	
Chadwick, George W. (M)	1854–1931	1898	1909
Chambers, Robert W. (L)	1865–1933	1909	
Channing, Edward (L)	1856–1931	1911	1926
Chase, Stuart (L)	1888–1985	1938	
Chase, William Merritt (A)	1849–1916	1898	1908
Chatfield-Taylor, Hobart C. (L)	1865–1945	1912	
Cheever, John (L)	1912–1982	1957	1973
Cheney, John Vance (L)	1848–1922	1908	
Churchill, Winston (L)	1871–1947	1908 (resigned 1923)	
Chute, Marchette (L)	1909–1994	1957	1974
Ciardi, John (L)	1916–1986	1957	
Clampitt, Amy (L)	1920–1994	1987	1993
Clark, Allan (A)	1896–1950	1931	
Clark, Eleanor (L)	1913–1996	1968	1993
Clarke, Gilmore D. (A)	1892–1982	1937	1946
Clarkson, Ralph (A)	1861–1942	1912	
Clemens, Samuel Langhorne (L)	1835–1910	1898	1904
Coates, Robert M. (L)	1897–1973	1958	
Coffin, Robert P. Tristram (L)	1892–1955	1946	
Cole, Timothy (A)	1852–1931	1908	1913
Collins, Alfred Q. (A)	1855–1903	1898	
Colum, Mary M. (L)	1887–1957	1953	
Colum, Padraic (L)	1881–1972	1948	1963
Connelly, Marc (L)	1890–1980	1935	
Connolly, James Brendan (L)	1868–1957	1908	

Deceased Members of the Academy and Institute—1898 to 1997

		ELECTED TO INSTITUTE	ELECTED TO ACADEMY
Converse, Frederick S. (M)	1871–1940	1908	1937
Conway, Moncure D. (L)	1832–1907	1898	
Cook, Walter (A)	1846–1916	1908	
Copland, Aaron (M)	1900–1990	1942	1954
Cortissoz, Royal (L)	1869–1948	1908	1924
Cowell, Henry (M)	1897–1965	1951	
Cowley, Malcolm (L)	1898–1989	1949	1964
Cox, Gardner (A)	1906–1988	1957	
Cox, Kenyon (A)	1856–1919	1898	1908
Cozzens, James Gould (L)	1903–1978	1943	
Cram, Ralph Adams (A)	1863–1942	1915	1940
Crawford, Francis Marion (L)	1854–1909	1898	1908
Cret, Paul Philippe (A)	1876–1945	1936	1941
Croly, Herbert (L)	1869–1930	1912	
Cross, John Walter (A)	1878–1951	1947	
Cross, Wilbur L. (L)	1862–1948	1911	1926
Crothers, Rachel (L)	1878–1958	1933	
Crothers, Samuel McChord (L)	1857–1927	1906	
Crowninshield, Frederic (A)	1845–1918	1908 (resigned 1913)	
Cummings, E. E. (L)	1894–1962	1949	1953
Curry, John Steuart (A)	1897–1946	1942	
Dahlberg, Edward (L)	1900–1977	1968	
Dallin, Cyrus E. (A)	1861–1944	1916	
Dalton, Peter (A)	1894–1972	1952	
Daly, Augustin (L)	1838–1899	1898	
Damrosch, Walter (M)	1862–1950	1898	1932
Dannat, William T. (A)	1853–1929	1898	
Davidson, Jo (A)	1883–1952	1944	
Davis, H. L. (L)	1896–1960	1956	
Davis, Owen (L)	1874–1956	1923	
Davis, Stuart (A)	1894–1964	1956	
Day, Frank Miles (A)	1861–1918	1908	
De Camp, Joseph R. (A)	1858–1923	1908	
de Creeft, José (A)	1884–1982	1955	1969
Dehn, Adolf (A)	1895–1968	1965	
De Kay, Charles (L)	1848–1935	1905	
de Kooning, Willem (A)	1904–1997	1960	1978
deKoven, Reginald (M)	1859–1920	1898	

Deceased Members of the Academy and Institute—1898 to 1997

		ELECTED TO INSTITUTE	ELECTED TO ACADEMY
DeLamarter, Eric (M)	1880–1953	1938	
Deland, Margaret (L)	1857–1945	1926	
Delano, William Adams (A)	1874–1960	1931	1937
De Lue, Donald (A)	1898–1988	1946	
de Marco, Jean (A)	1898–1990	1959	
de Rivera, José (A)	1904–1985	1971	
Deutsch, Babette (L)	1895–1982	1958	1973
De Voto, Bernard (L)	1897–1955	1948	
De Vries, Peter (L)	1910–1993	1969	1982
Dewey, Charles Melville (A)	1849–1937	1908	
Dewing, Thomas W. (A)	1851–1938	1908 (resigned 1915)	
Dickey, James (L)	1923–1997	1972	1987
Dickinson, Edwin (A)	1891–1978	1956	1961
Dickinson, Sidney E. (A)	1890–1980	1931	
Diebenkorn, Richard (A)	1922–1993	1967	1985
Diederich, Wilhelm Hunt (A)	1884–1953	1938 (expelled 1947)	
Dielman, Frederick (A)	1847–1935	1908	
Dodge, Theodore A. (L)	1842–1909	1908	
Donaldson, John M. (A)	1854–1941	1910	
Dos Passos, John (L)	1896–1970	1937	1947
Dougherty, Paul (A)	1877–1947	1908	
Druckman, Jacob (M)	1928–1996	1978	1993
Du Bois, Guy Pène (A)	1884–1958	1942	
Du Bois, W. E. B. (L)	1868–1963	1944	
Dubos, René Jules (L)	1901–1982	1979	
Duchamp, Marcel (A)	1887–1968	1960	
Du Mond, Frank V. (A)	1865–1951	1918	
Dunne, Finley Peter (L)	1867–1936	1908 (resigned 1931)	
Durant, Will (L)	1885–1981	1959	
Duveneck, Frank (A)	1848–1919	1898	
Eames, Charles (A)	1907–1978	1977	
Eaton, Walter Prichard (L)	1878–1957	1918	
Eby, Kerr (A)	1889–1946	1937	
Edel, Leon (L)	1907–1997	1964	1972
Edman, Irwin (L)	1896–1954	1941	
Edwards, George Wharton (A)	1869–1950	1925	
Edwards, Harry Stillwell (L)	1855–1938	1912	
Egan, Maurice Francis (L)	1852–1924	1908	1919

Deceased Members of the Academy and Institute—1898 to 1997

		ELECTED TO INSTITUTE	ELECTED TO ACADEMY
Eggleston, Edward (L)	1837–1902	1898	
Eiseley, Loren (L)	1907–1977	1971	
Elkin, Stanley (L)	1930–1995	1982	1993
Ellett, Thomas Harlan (A)	1880–1951	1943	
Ellington, Duke (M)	1899–1974	1970	
Ellison, Ralph (L)	1914–1994	1964	1975
Ellmann, Richard (L)	1918–1987	1971	
Embury, Aymar, II (A)	1880–1966	1946	
Ernst, Jimmy (A)	1920–1984	1983	
Erskine, John (L)	1879–1951	1920	
Evans, Rudulph (A)	1878–1960	1926	
Evergood, Philip (A)	1901–1973	1959	
Farrell, James T. (L)	1904–1979	1942	
Faulkner, Barry (A)	1881–1966	1920	1942
Faulkner, William (L)	1897–1962	1939	1948
Fawcett, Edgar (L)	1847–1904	1898	
Feininger, Lyonel (A)	1871–1956	1955	
Ferber, Edna (L)	1887–1968	1930	
Fergusson, Francis (L)	1904–1986	1962	
Fernald, Chester B. (L)	1869–1938	1910	
Finck, Henry T. (L)	1854–1926	1908 (resigned 1914)	
Finley, John Huston (L)	1863–1940	1908	1927
Finney, Ross Lee (M)	1906–1997	1962	1993
Firkins, Oscar W. (L)	1864–1932	1912	
Fisher, Dorothy Canfield (L)	1879–1958	1931	
Fisher, M. F. K. (L)	1908–1992	1991	
Fiske, Willard (L)	1831–1904	1898	
Fitts, Dudley (L)	1903–1968	1957	
Fitzgerald, Robert (L)	1910–1985	1962	
Flanagan, John (A)	1865–1952	1923	
Flanner, Janet (L)	1892–1978	1959	
Fletcher, Jefferson Butler (L)	1865–1946	1918	
Fletcher, John Gould (L)	1886–1950	1949	
Folinsbee, John F. (A)	1892–1972	1953	
Foote, Arthur (M)	1853–1937	1898	
Forbes, James (L)	1871–1938	1922	
Ford, Paul Leicester (L)	1865–1902	1898	
Ford, Worthington C. (L)	1858–1941	1908	

Deceased Members of the Academy and Institute—1898 to 1997

		ELECTED TO INSTITUTE	ELECTED TO ACADEMY
Foster, Ben (A)	1852–1926	1908	
Fox, John, Jr. (L)	1862–1919	1898	
Francis, Sam (A)	1923–1994	1980	1993
Frank, Waldo (L)	1889–1967	1952	
Fraser, James Earle (A)	1876–1953	1915	1927
Fraser, Laura Gardin (A)	1889–1966	1931	
Frederic, Harold (L)	1856–1898	1898	
Freeman, Douglas Southall (L)	1886–1953	1937	1945
Freeman, Mary E. Wilkins (L)	1852–1930	1926	
French, Daniel Chester (A)	1850–1931	1898	1905
Friedlander, Leo (A)	1888–1966	1953	
Frost, Robert (L)	1874–1963	1916	1930
Fuller, Henry B. (L)	1857–1929	1898 (resigned 1909)	
Fuller, R. Buckminster (A)	1895–1983	1963	1979
Furness, Horace H. (L)	1833–1912	1905	1905
Furness, Horace H., Jr. (L)	1865–1930	1911	
Gabo, Naum (A)	1890–1977	1965	1975
Garber, Daniel (A)	1880–1958	1948	
Garland, Hamlin (L)	1860–1940	1898	1918
Gatch, Lee (A)	1902–1968	1966	
Gay, Walter (A)	1856–1937	1898	1934
Gibson, Charles Dana (A)	1867–1944	1898	1921
Giddings, Franklin Henry (L)	1855–1931	1918	
Gideon, Miriam (M)	1906–1996	1975	1993
Gilbert, Cass (A)	1859–1934	1906	1914
Gilchrist, William Wallace (M)	1846–1916	1898	
Gilder, Richard Watson (L)	1844–1909	1898	1905
Gildersleeve, Basil Lanneau (L)	1831–1924	1906	1908
Gill, Brendan (L)	1914–1997		1995
Gillespie, John Birks "Dizzy" (M)	1917–1993		1993
Gillette, William (L)	1855–1937	1898	1995
Gilman, Daniel Coit (L)	1831–1908	1898	1908
Gilman, Lawrence (L)	1878–1939	1908	
Ginsberg, Allen (L)	1926–1997	1973	1993
Glackens, William J. (A)	1870–1938	1936	
Glasgow, Ellen (L)	1874–1945	1932	1938
Godkin, Edwin L. (L)	1831–1902	1898	
Godwin, Parke (L)	1816–1904	1898	

Deceased Members of the Academy and Institute—1898 to 1997

		ELECTED TO INSTITUTE	ELECTED TO ACADEMY
Goodhue, Bertram G. (A)	1869–1924	1915	
Goodrich, Arthur (L)	1878–1941	1927	
Gordon, George A. (L)	1853–1929	1898	
Gottlieb, Adolph (A)	1903–1974	1972	
Gould, Morton (M)	1913–1996	1986	1993
Grafly, Charles (A)	1862–1929	1908	
Grainger, Percy (M)	1882–1961	1950	
Grant, Robert (L)	1852–1940	1898	1915
Graves, Nancy (A)	1940–1995	1990	1993
Green, Paul Eliot (L)	1894–1981	1941	
Greenbaum, Dorothea (A)	1893–1986	1968	
Greene, Balcomb (A)	1904–1990	1976	
Greenslet, Ferris (L)	1875–1959	1908	
Gregory, Eliot (A)	1854–1915	1898 (resigned 1910)	
Gregory, Horace (L)	1898–1982	1964	
Gregory, John (A)	1879–1958	1930	
Griffin, Walter (A)	1861–1935	1923	
Griffis, William Elliot (L)	1843–1928	1898	
Groll, Albert L. (A)	1866–1952	1932	
Gropius, Walter (A)	1883–1969	1962	
Gropper, William (A)	1897–1977	1968	
Gross, Chaim (A)	1904–1991	1964	1983
Grosz, George (A)	1893–1959	1954	
Gruenberg, Louis (M)	1884–1964	1947	
Guérard, Albert L. (L)	1880–1959	1958	
Guérin, Jules (A)	1866–1946	1908	
Gugler, Eric (A)	1889–1974	1942	
Gummere, Francis B. (L)	1855–1919	1913	
Guston, Philip (A)	1913–1980	1972	
Gwathmey, Robert (A)	1903–1988	1971	
Hackett, Francis (L)	1883–1962	1949	
Hadley, Arthur Twining (L)	1856–1930	1898	1908
Hadley, Henry (M)	1871–1937	1908	1924
Hagedorn, Hermann (L)	1882–1964	1920	
Hahn, Emily (L)	1905–1997	1987	1993
Hale, Edward Everett (L)	1822–1909	1905	1908
Hamilton, Clayton (L)	1881–1946	1912	
Hamilton, Edith (L)	1867–1963	1955	1957

Deceased Members of the Academy and Institute—1898 to 1997

		ELECTED TO INSTITUTE	ELECTED TO ACADEMY
Hammerstein, Oscar, II (L)	1895–1960	1950	
Hanson, Howard (M)	1896–1981	1935	1979
Harben, William Nathaniel (L)	1858–1919	1912	
Hardenbergh, Henry J. (A)	1847–1918	1908	
Hardy, Arthur Sherburne (L)	1847–1930	1898	
Harland, Henry (L)	1861–1905	1898	
Harper, George McLean (L)	1863–1947	1911	
Harris, Joel Chandler (L)	1848–1908	1905	1905
Harris, Roy (M)	1898–1979	1944	1978
Harrison, Alexander (A)	1853–1930	1898	
Harrison, Birge (A)	1854–1929	1908	
Harrison, Henry Sydnor (L)	1880–1930	1914	
Harrison, Wallace K. (A)	1895–1981	1960	
Harte, Bret (L)	1836–1902	1898	
Haseltine, Herbert (A)	1877–1962	1935	
Hassam, Childe (A)	1859–1935	1898	1920
Hastings, Thomas (A)	1860–1929	1906	1908
Hawthorne, Charles W. (A)	1872–1930	1920	
Hay, John (L)	1838–1905	1898	1904
Hayden, Robert (L)	1913–1980	1979	
Hazen, Charles Downer (L)	1868–1941	1918	1924
Hellman, Lillian (L)	1905–1984	1946	1962
Henderson, William J. (L)	1855–1937	1914	1933
Hendrick, Burton J. (L)	1871–1949	1923	
Henri, Robert (A)	1865–1929	1908	
Herbert, Victor (M)	1859–1924	1908	
Herford, Oliver (L)	1863–1935	1911	
Hergesheimer, Joseph (L)	1880–1954	1920 (resigned 1933)	
Herne, James A. (L)	1839–1901	1898	
Herrick, Robert (L)	1868–1938	1908 (resigned 1929)	
Hersey, John (L)	1914–1993	1950	1953
Heyward, DuBose (L)	1885–1940	1937	
Hibben, John Grier (L)	1861–1933	1912	
Higgins, Eugene (A)	1874–1958	1943	
Higginson, Thomas Wentworth (L)	1823–1911	1898	1908
Hill, David Jayne (L)	1850–1932	1920	1920
Hill, Edward Burlingame (M)	1872–1960	1916	

Deceased Members of the Academy and Institute—1898 to 1997

		ELECTED TO INSTITUTE	ELECTED TO ACADEMY
Hillyer, Robert S. (L)	1895–1961	1938	
Hindemith, Paul (M)	1895–1963	1947	
Hirsch, Joseph (A)	1910–1981	1967	
Hitchcock, Ripley (L)	1857–1918	1911	
Hocking, William Ernest (L)	1873–1966	1947	1961
Hoffman, Malvina (A)	1885–1966	1937	
Hofmann, Hans (A)	1880–1966	1964	
Homer, Winslow (A)	1836–1910	1905	1905
Hooker, Brian (L)	1880–1946	1912	
Hopkinson, Charles (A)	1869–1962	1935	1941
Hopper, Edward (A)	1882–1967	1945	1955
Hord, Donal (A)	1902–1966	1950	
Horgan, Paul (L)	1903–1995	1956	1993
Howard, Bronson (L)	1842–1908	1898	1908
Howard, Cecil (A)	1888–1956	1938	
Howard, John Galen (A)	1864–1931	1908	
Howard, Sidney (L)	1891–1939	1927	1935
Howe, Irving (L)	1920–1993	1979	1993
Howe, Julia Ward (L)	1819–1910	1907	1908
Howe, Mark Antony DeWolfe (L)	1864–1960	1908	1935
Howe, William H. (A)	1846–1929	1908	
Howells, John Mead (A)	1868–1959	1911	
Howells, William Dean (L)	1837–1920	1898	1904
Hughes, Hatcher (L)	1884–1945	1924	
Hughes, Langston (L)	1902–1967	1961	
Humphries, Rolfe (L)	1894–1969	1953	
Huneker, James Gibbons (L)	1860–1921	1918	
Huntington, Anna Hyatt (A)	1876–1973	1927	1932
Huntington, Archer M. (L)	1870–1955	1911	1919
Hutton, Laurence (L)	1843–1904	1898	
Isham, Samuel (A)	1855–1914	1908	
Isherwood, Christopher (L)	1904–1986	1949	
Ives, Charles (M)	1874–1954	1946	
Jaegers, Albert (A)	1868–1925	1912	
James, Henry (L)	1843–1916	1898	1905
James, Marquis (L)	1891–1955	1953	
James, Philip (M)	1890–1975	1933	

Deceased Members of the Academy and Institute—1898 to 1997

		ELECTED TO INSTITUTE	ELECTED TO ACADEMY
James, William (L)	1842–1910	1898 (resigned 1905)	
Jarrell, Randall (L)	1914–1965	1960	
Jeffers, Robinson (L)	1887–1962	1937	1945
Jefferson, Joseph (L)	1829–1905	1898	1905
Jennewein, C. Paul (A)	1890–1978	1931	
Johansen, John C. (A)	1876–1964	1930	
Johnson, Edgar (L)	1901–1995	1975	1993
Johnson, Owen (L)	1878–1952	1909	
Johnson, Robert Underwood (L)	1853–1937	1898	1908
Johnston, Richard M. (L)	1822–1898	1898	
Jones, Francis C. (A)	1857–1932	1908	
Jones, H. Bolton (A)	1848–1927	1908	
Jones, Robert Edmond (A)	1887–1954	1933	
Josephson, Matthew (L)	1899–1978	1948	
Kahn, Louis I. (A)	1901–1974	1964	1973
Kaufman, George S. (L)	1889–1961	1938	
Kay, Ulysses (M)	1917–1995	1979	1993
Keller, Helen (L)	1880–1968	1933	
Kempton, Murray (L)	1918–1997		1995
Kendall, William Mitchell (A)	1856–1941	1914	1929
Kendall, William Sergeant (A)	1869–1938	1908	
Kennan, George (L)	1845–1924	1898	
Kent, Rockwell (A)	1882–1971	1964	
Kern, Jerome (M)	1885–1945	1945	
Knaths, Karl (A)	1891–1971	1955	
Koch, John (A)	1909–1978	1970	
Kreis, Henry (A)	1899–1963	1951	
Krenek, Ernst (M)	1900–1991	1960	
Kreymborg, Alfred (L)	1883–1966	1949	
Kroeger, Ernest R. (M)	1862–1934	1915	
Kroll, Leon (A)	1884–1974	1930	1948
Kronenberger, Louis (L)	1904–1980	1951	
Krutch, Joseph Wood (L)	1893–1970	1937	1954
Laessle, Albert (A)	1877–1954	1931	
La Farge, Bancel (A)	1866–1938	1898	
La Farge, Christopher (L)	1897–1956	1947	
La Farge, John (A)	1835–1910	1898	1904
La Farge, Oliver (L)	1901–1963	1957	

Deceased Members of the Academy and Institute—1898 to 1997

		ELECTED TO INSTITUTE	ELECTED TO ACADEMY
Lamb, William F. (A)	1883–1952	1950	
Landeck, Armin (A)	1905–1984	1946	
Lathrop, Francis (A)	1849–1909	1898	
Lathrop, Gertrude K. (A)	1896–1986	1949	
Lattimore, Richmond (L)	1906–1984	1965	
Laughlin, James (L)	1914–1997		1995
Laurent, Robert (A)	1890–1970	1970	
Lawrie, Lee (A)	1877–1963	1931	1945
Lawson, Ernest (A)	1873–1939	1918	
Lea, Henry Charles (L)	1825–1909	1905	1908
Lebrun, Rico (A)	1900–1964	1960	
Lefevre, Edwin (L)	1871–1943	1916	
Leighton, Clare (A)	1898–1989	1951	
Leonard, Wiliam Ellery (L)	1876–1944	1926	
Levertov, Denise (L)	1923–1997	1980	
Levi, Julian (A)	1900–1982	1959	
Levin, Harry (L)	1912–1994	1960	1993
Lewis, Sinclair (L)	1885–1951	1935	1937
Lichtenstein, Roy (A)	1924–1997	1979	1993
Lie, Jonas (A)	1880–1940	1929	1937
Lindeberg, Harrie T. (A)	1880–1959	1948	
Lindner, Richard (A)	1901–1978	1972	
Lindsay, Nicolas Vachel (L)	1879–1931	1920	
Lipchitz, Jacques (A)	1891–1973	1961	1962
Lippmann, Walter (L)	1889–1974	1932	1934
Lipton, Seymour (A)	1903–1986	1975	
Lloyd, Nelson (L)	1873–1933	1908	
Lockman, DeWitt McClellan (A)	1870–1957	1931	
Lodge, George Cabot (L)	1873–1909	1908	
Lodge, Henry Cabot (L)	1850–1924	1898	1908
Loeb, Louis (A)	1866–1909	1908	
Loeffler, Charles Martin (M)	1861–1935	1908	1931
Long, John Luther (L)	1861–1927	1908	
Lopatnikoff, Nikolai (M)	1903–1976	1963	
Lounsbury, Thomas R. (L)	1838–1915	1898	1905
Lovett, Robert Morss (L)	1870–1956	1908	
Low, Will H. (A)	1853–1932	1908	
Lowell, Abbott Lawrence (L)	1856–1943	1910	1910

Deceased Members of the Academy and Institute—1898 to 1997

		ELECTED TO INSTITUTE	ELECTED TO ACADEMY
Lowell, Robert (L)	1917–1977	1954	1963
Lowes, John Livingston (L)	1867–1945	1929	
Luening, Otto (M)	1900–1996	1952	1993
Lummis, Charles F. (L)	1859–1928	1908	
Mabie, Hamilton Wright (L)	1845–1916	1898	1908
Macdonald, Dwight (L)	1906–1982	1970	
MacDowell, Edward (M)	1861–1908	1898	1904
MacEwen, Walter (A)	1860–1943	1908	
MacKaye, Percy (L)	1875–1956	1908	
MacLane, Jean (A)	1878–1964	1931	
MacLeish, Archibald (L)	1892–1982	1933	1946
MacMonnies, Frederick (A)	1863–1937	1898	1915
MacNeil, Hermon A. (A)	1866–1947	1908	1926
Maginnis, Charles D. (A)	1867–1955	1944	
Mahan, Alfred Thayer (L)	1840–1914	1898	1905
Malamud, Bernard (L)	1914–1986	1964	1980
Maldarelli, Oronzio (A)	1892–1963	1950	
Mann, Thomas (L)	1875–1955	1950	1951
Manship, Paul (A)	1885–1966	1920	1932
Marin, John (A)	1870–1953	1942	1943
Markham, Edwin (L)	1852–1940	1908	1929
Marquand, John P. (L)	1893–1960	1940	
Marquis, Don (L)	1878–1937	1923	
Marr, Carl (A)	1858–1936	1908	
Marsh, Reginald (A)	1898–1954	1946	
Martin, Edward Sandford (L)	1856–1939	1908	
Martin, Bohuslav (M)	1890–1959	1955	
Mason, Daniel Gregory (M)	1873–1953	1911 (resigned 1913) reinstated 1938)	
Masters, Edgar Lee (L)	1869–1950	1918 (resigned 1931)	
Mather, Frank Jewett, Jr. (L)	1868–1953	1913	1935
Matthews, Brander (L)	1852–1929	1898	1908
Matthiessen, Francis O. (L)	1902–1950	1948	
McCartan, Edward (A)	1879–1947	1924	1944
McCarthy, Mary (L)	1912–1989	1960	1988
McCormick, Anne O'Hare (L)	1882–1954	1947	
McCullers, Carson (L)	1917–1967	1952	
McFee, Henry Lee (A)	1886–1953	1943	

Deceased Members of the Academy and Institute—1898 to 1997

		ELECTED TO INSTITUTE	ELECTED TO ACADEMY
McFee, William (L)	1881–1966	1941	
McGinley, Phyllis (L)	1905–1978	1955	
McKelway, St. Clair (L)	1845–1915	1898	
McKim, Charles Follen (A)	1847–1909	1898	1905
McMaster, John Bach (L)	1852–1932	1898	
McNeil, George (A)	1908–1995	1989	1993
Mead, Margaret (L)	1901–1978	1955	
Mead, William Rutherford (A)	1846–1928	1908	1910
Melchers, Gari (A)	1860–1932	1898	1916
Mennin, Peter (M)	1923–1983	1965	
Merrill, James (L)	1926–1995	1971	1989
Mestrovic, Ivan (A)	1883–1962	1956	1960
Metcalf, Willard Leroy (A)	1858–1925	1908	1924
Mies van der Rohe, Ludwig (A)	1886–1969	1961	1967
Miles, Josephine (L)	1911–1985	1980	
Millay, Edna St. Vincent (L)	1892–1950	1929	1940
Miller, Charles Ransom (L)	1849–1922	1915	
Miller, Henry (L)	1891–1980	1957	
Miller, Joaquin (L)	1839–1913	1898	
Miller, Kenneth Hayes (A)	1876–1952	1947	
Milles, Carl (A)	1875–1952	1947	1951
Millet, Francis Davis (A)	1846–1912	1908	1910
Mitchell, Donald Grant (L)	1822–1908	1898	1908
Mitchell, Joan (A)	1926–1992	1979	
Mitchell, John Ames (L)	1845–1918	1908	
Mitchell, Joseph (L)	1908–1996	1970	1993
Mitchell, Langdon E. (L)	1862–1935	1908	
Moody, William Vaughn (L)	1869–1910	1905	1908
Moore, Bruce (A)	1905–1980	1949	
Moore, Charles (L)	1855–1942	1920	
Moore, Douglas (M)	1893–1969	1941	1951
Moore, Marianne Craig (L)	1887–1972	1947	1955
More, Paul Elmer (L)	1864–1937	1908	1915
Morgan, Wallace (A)	1873–1948	1941	
Morison, Samuel Eliot (L)	1887–1976	1963	1963
Morley, Christopher (L)	1890–1957	1936	
Morris, Benjamin W., III (A)	1870–1944	1944	
Morris, George L. K. (A)	1905–1975	1975	

Deceased Members of the Academy and Institute—1898 to 1997

		ELECTED TO INSTITUTE	ELECTED TO ACADEMY
Morris, Harrison Smith (L)	1856–1948	1908	
Morse, John Torrey, Jr. (L)	1840–1937	1906 (resigned 1915)	
Moss, Howard (L)	1922–1987	1971	
Motherwell, Robert (A)	1915–1991	1970	1982
Mowbray, H. Siddons (A)	1858–1928	1898	
Muir, John (L)	1838–1914	1898	1909
Mumford, Lewis (L)	1895–1990	1930*	1955 (resigned 1967)
Munger, Theodore T. (L)	1830–1910	1905	
Nabokov, Nicolas (M)	1903–1978	1970	
Nakian, Reuben (A)	1897–1986	1974	
Nash, Ogden (L)	1902–1971	1950	
Nason, Thomas W. (A)	1889–1971	1941	
Nathan, Robert (L)	1894–1985	1936	
Neel, Alice (A)	1900–1984	1976	
Neihardt, John G. (L)	1881–1973	1943	
Nelson, Henry Loomis (L)	1846–1908	1898	
Nemerov, Howard (L)	1920–1991	1960	1976
Neutra, Richard J. (A)	1892–1970	1964	
Nevelson, Louise (A)	1899–1988	1968	1979
Nevin, Ethelbert (M)	1862–1901	1898	
Nevins, Allan (L)	1890–1971	1938	1954
Nichols, Hobart (A)	1869–1962	1937	
Nicholson, Meredith (L)	1866–1947	1908	
Niebuhr, Reinhold (L)	1892–1971	1953	1958
Niehaus, Charles H. (A)	1855–1935	1916	
Nin, Anaïs (L)	1903–1977	1974	
Nivola, Costantino (A)	1911–1988	1972	
Noguchi, Isamu (A)	1904–1988	1962	1971
Norton, Charles Eliot (L)	1827–1908	1898	1905
Ochtman, Leonard (A)	1854–1934	1908	
O'Connor, Andrew (A)	1874–1941	1922 (resigned 1927)	
Ogden, Rollo (L)	1856–1937	1923	
O'Hara, John (L)	1905–1970	1957	
O'Keeffe, Georgia (A)	1887–1986	1949	1962
Oldberg, Arne (M)	1874–1962	1915	

*Lewis Mumford resigned from the Institute in 1948 and was reinstated in 1954. He refused to be reinstated in the Academy after resigning in 1967.

Deceased Members of the Academy and Institute—1898 to 1997

		ELECTED TO INSTITUTE	ELECTED TO ACADEMY
Olmsted, Frederick Law (A)	1870–1957	1918	1943
O'Neill, Eugene (L)	1888–1953	1923	1933
Page, Thomas Nelson (L)	1853–1922	1898	1908
Paine, Albert Bigelow (L)	1861–1937	1918	
Paine, John K. (M)	1839–1906	1898	
Parker, Dorothy (L)	1893–1967	1959	
Parker, Horatio William (M)	1863–1919	1898	1905
Parrish, Maxfield (A)	1870–1966	1905 (resigned 1915)	
Patigian, Haig (A)	1876–1950	1927	
Payne, Will (L)	1865–1954	1908	
Payne, William Morton (L)	1858–1919	1908	
Peabody, Robert Swain (A)	1845–1917	1908	
Pearce, Charles Sprague (A)	1851–1914	1898	
Peattie, Donald Culross (L)	1898–1964	1941	
Peck, Harry Thurston (L)	1856–1914	1898	
Peixotto, Ernest C. (A)	1869–1940	1937	
Pennell, Joseph (A)	1857–1926	1908	1921
Percy, Walker (L)	1916–1990	1972	
Perelman, S. J. (L)	1904–1979	1958	
Perkins, James Breck (L)	1847–1910	1898	
Perry, Bliss (L)	1860–1954	1905	1910
Perry, Ralph Barton (L)	1876–1957	1942	
Perry, Thomas Sergeant (L)	1845–1928	1898 (resigned 1914)	
Persichetti, Vincent (M)	1915–1987	1965	
Phelps, William Lyon (L)	1865–1943	1910	1931
Pier, Arthur Stanwood (L)	1874–1966	1908	
Piston, Walter (M)	1894–1976	1938	1955
Platt, Charles Adams (A)	1861–1933	1908	1919
Pond, Irving K. (A)	1857–1939	1912	
Poole, Abram (A)	1882–1961	1930	
Poole, Ernest (L)	1880–1950	1916	
Poor, Henry Varnum (A)	1888–1970	1943	
Pope, John Russell (A)	1874–1937	1916	1927
Porter, Benjamin C. (A)	1845–1908	1898	
Porter, Katherine Anne (L)	1890–1980	1941	1966
Porter, Quincy (M)	1897–1966	1944	
Post, George Brown (A)	1837–1913	1908	1911
Potter, Edward C. (A)	1857–1923	1898	

Deceased Members of the Academy and Institute—1898 to 1997

		ELECTED TO INSTITUTE	ELECTED TO ACADEMY
Pound, Ezra (L)	1885–1972	1938 (resigned 1958)	
Powell, John (M)	1882–1963	1924	
Pratt, Bela L. (A)	1867–1917	1910	
Proctor, A. Phimister (A)	1862–1950	1908	
Putnam, Brenda (A)	1890–1975	1943	
Putnam, Herbert (L)	1861–1955	1925	1937
Pyle, Howard (A)	1853–1911	1898	
Quinn, Edmond T. (A)	1868–1929	1920	
Rand, Edward Kennard (L)	1871–1945	1933	
Ransom, John Crowe (L)	1888–1974	1965	1966
Rapuano, Michael (A)	1904–1975	1959	
Rattner, Abraham (A)	1895–1978	1958	
Rawlings, Marjorie Kinnan (L)	1896–1953	1939	
Redfield, Edward W. (A)	1869–1965	1908	1943
Reid, Robert (A)	1862–1929	1898	
Remington, Frederic (A)	1861–1909	1898	
Repplier, Agnes (L)	1858–1950	1926	1941
Rexroth, Kenneth (L)	1905–1982	1969	
Rhodes, James Ford (L)	1848–1927	1898	1905
Rice, Elmer (L)	1892–1967	1938	
Richter, Conrad (L)	1890–1968	1961	
Riegger, Wallingford (M)	1885–1961	1953	
Riley, James Whitcomb (L)	1849–1916	1898	1911
Rives, George Lockhard (L)	1849–1917	1914	1915
Roberts, Charles G. D. (L)	1860–1943	1898	
Roberts, Elizabeth Madox (L)	1886–1941	1941	
Roberts, Kenneth L. (L)	1885–1957	1935	
Robinson, Boardman (A)	1876–1952	1938	
Robinson, Edwin Arlington (L)	1869–1935	1908	1927
Rodgers, Richard (M)	1902–1979	1955	
Roethke, Theodore (L)	1908–1963	1956	
Rogers, Bernard (M)	1893–1968	1947	
Roosevelt, Theodore (L)	1858–1919	1898	1905
Root, Elihu (L)	1845–1937	1915	1917
Roszak, Theodore J. (A)	1907–1981	1964	
Roth, Ernest David (A)	1879–1964	1933	
Roth, Frederick G. R. (A)	1872–1944	1910	
Rothko, Mark (A)	1903–1970	1968	

Deceased Members of the Academy and Institute—1898 to 1997

		ELECTED TO INSTITUTE	ELECTED TO ACADEMY
Royce, Josiah (L)	1855–1916	1898	
Ruckstull, F. Wellington (A)	1853–1942	1898	
Rudolph, Paul (A)	1918–1997	1971	
Ruggles, Carl (M)	1876–1971	1954	
Rukeyser, Muriel (L)	1913–1980	1967	
Ryder, Albert Pinkham (A)	1847–1917	1908	
Saarinen, Eero (A)	1910–1961	1954	1959
Saint-Gaudens, Augustus (A)	1848–1907	1898	1904
Salisbury, Harrison E. (L)	1908–1993	1972	1985
Sandburg, Carl (L)	1878–1967	1933	1940
Santayana, George (L)	1863–1952	1902 (resigned 1911*)	
Sargent, John Singer (A)	1856–1925	1905	1905
Saroyan, William (L)	1908–1981	1943	
Savage, Eugene Francis (A)	1883–1978	1936	
Schapiro, Meyer (L)	1904–1996	1976	1993
Schelling, Ernest (M)	1876–1939	1913	
Schelling, Felix E. (L)	1858–1945	1911	
Schnakenberg, Henry (A)	1892–1970	1952	
Schofield, W. Elmer (A)	1867–1944	1908	
Schorer, Mark (L)	1907–1977	1962	
Schouler, James (L)	1839–1920	1912	
Schuman, William (M)	1910–1992	1946	1973
Schurz, Carl (L)	1829–1906	1898	1905
Schuyler, Montgomery (L)	1843–1914	1908	
Scollard, Clinton (L)	1860–1932	1908	
Scudder, Horace E. (L)	1838–1902	1898	
Sedgwick, Anne Douglas (L)	1873–1935	1931	
Sedgwick, Ellery (L)	1872–1960	1915 (resigned 1934)	
Sedgwick, Henry Dwight (L)	1861–1957	1908	1933
Seldes, Gilbert (L)	1893–1970	1963	
Sepeshy, Zoltan (A)	1898–1974	1949	
Sert, José Luis (A)	1902–1983	1966	
Sessions, Roger (M)	1896–1985	1938	1953
Seton, Ernest Thompson (L)	1860–1946	1905	
Shahn, Ben (A)	1898–1969	1956	
Shaler, Nathaniel S. (L)	1841–1906	1898	
Sheean, Vincent (L)	1899–1975	1941	

*George Santayana, who lived abroad, was elected a Foreign Honorary member in 1943.

Deceased Members of the Academy and Institute—1898 to 1997

		ELECTED TO INSTITUTE	ELECTED TO ACADEMY
Sheeler, Charles (A)	1883–1965	1963	
Sheldon, Edward Brewster (L)	1886–1946	1918	
Shelley, Harry Rowe (M)	1858–1947	1898	
Shepherd, Arthur (M)	1880–1958	1938	
Shepley, Henry R. (A)	1887–1962	1939	1942
Sherman, Frank Dempster (L)	1860–1916	1908	
Sherman, Stuart Pratt (L)	1881–1926	1918	1923
Sherwood, Robert E. (L)	1896–1955	1937	1949
Shinn, Everett (A)	1876–1953	1951	
Shirlaw, Walter (A)	1838–1909	1908	
Shorey, Paul (L)	1857–1934	1911	1918
Shrady, Henry M. (A)	1871–1922	1910	
Siegmeister, Elie (M)	1909–1991	1990	
Simmons, Edward E. (A)	1852–1931	1898 (resigned 1915)	
Simon, Louis A. (A)	1867–1958	1941	
Simon, Sidney (A)	1917–1997	1996	
Sinclair, Upton (L)	1878–1968	1944 (resigned 1966)	
Singer, Isaac Bashevis (L)	1904–1991	1965	1978
Sloan, John (A)	1871–1951	1929	1942
Sloane, William Milligan (L)	1850–1928	1898	1905
Smedley, William T. (A)	1858–1920	1908	
Smith, David Stanley (M)	1877–1949	1910	
Smith, Francis Hopkinson (L)	1838–1915	1898	1908
Smith, James Kellum (A)	1893–1961	1948	
Smith, Tony (A)	1912–1980	1979	
Sowerby, Leo (M)	1895–1968	1935	
Soyer, Moses (A)	1899–1974	1966	
Soyer, Raphael (A)	1899–1987	1958	1969
Spalding, Albert (M)	1888–1953	1926	1937
Speicher, Eugene (A)	1883–1962	1930	1942
Speight, Francis (A)	1896–1989	1960	
Stafford, Jean (L)	1915–1979	1970	
Stedman, Edmund Clarence (L)	1833–1909	1898	1904
Steegmuller, Francis (L)	1906–1994	1966	1993
Stegner, Wallace (L)	1909–1993	1969	1993
Steinbeck, John E. (L)	1902–1968	1939	1948
Sterne, Maurice (A)	1878–1957	1938	
Sterner, Albert (A)	1863–1946	1929	

Deceased Members of the Academy and Institute—1898 to 1997

		ELECTED TO INSTITUTE	ELECTED TO ACADEMY
Stevens, Wallace (L)	1879–1955	1946	
Stevenson, Burton E. (L)	1872–1962	1928	
Still, Clyfford (A)	1904–1980	1978	
Stillman, William J. (L)	1828–1901	1898	
Stillman-Kelley, Edgar (M)	1857–1944	1898	
Stimson, Frederic Jesup (L)	1855–1943	1898	
Stock, Frederick A. (M)	1872–1942	1912	
Stockton, Frank R. (L)	1834–1902	1898	
Stoddard, Charles Warren (L)	1843–1909	1898	
Stoessel, Albert (M)	1894–1943	1931	
Stone, Edward Durell (A)	1902–1978	1958	
Stravinsky, Igor (M)	1882–1971	1949	1956
Street, Julian (L)	1879–1947	1924	
Strong, Austin (L)	1881–1952	1929	
Strunsky, Simeon (L)	1879–1947	1946	
Stuempfig, Walter (A)	1914–1970	1959	
Sullivan, Thomas R. (L)	1849–1916	1898	
Swartwout, Egerton (A)	1870–1943	1940	
Swenson, May (L)	1913–1989	1970	
Symons, Gardner (A)	1865–1930	1914	
Taft, Lorado (A)	1860–1936	1906	1920
Talma, Louise (M)	1906–1996	1974	1993
Tarbell, Edmund C. (A)	1862–1938	1908 (resigned 1931)	
Tarkington, Booth (L)	1869–1946	1908	1920
Tate, Allen (L)	1899–1979	1949	1964
Taylor, Deems (M)	1885–1966	1924	1935
Taylor, Henry Osborn (L)	1856–1941	1915	1940
Taylor, Peter (L)	1917–1994	1969	1982
Tcherepnin, Alexander (M)	1899–1977	1974	
Thayer, Abbott Handerson (A)	1849–1921	1898	1909
Thayer, William Roscoe (L)	1859–1923	1911	1914
Thomas, A. E. (L)	1872–1947	1924	
Thomas, Augustus (L)	1857–1934	1898	1912
Thomas, Lewis (L)	1913–1993	1984	1993
Thompson, Dorothy (L)	1894–1961	1938	
Thompson, Maurice (L)	1844–1901	1898	
Thompson, Randall (M)	1899–1984	1938	
Thomson, Virgil (M)	1896–1989	1948	1959

Deceased Members of the Academy and Institute—1898 to 1997

		ELECTED TO INSTITUTE	ELECTED TO ACADEMY
Thorndike, Ashley H. (L)	1871–1933	1913	
Tinker, Chauncey Brewster (L)	1876–1963	1931	1937
Tobey, Mark (A)	1890–1976	1956	
Toch, Ernst (M)	1887–1964	1957	
Tooker, L. Frank (L)	1855–1925	1911	
Torrence, Ridgely (L)	1875–1950	1908	
Townsend, Edward W. (L)	1855–1942	1914	
Train, Arthur (L)	1875–1945	1924	
Trent, William P. (L)	1862–1939	1898	
Trilling, Lionel (L)	1905–1975	1951	1975
Trowbridge, S. Breck P. (A)	1862–1925	1915	
Tryon, Dwight W. (A)	1849–1925	1908	
Tuchman, Barbara W. (L)	1912–1989	1968	1971
Twachtman, John H. (A)	1853–1902	1898	
Tworkov, Jack (A)	1900–1982	1981	
Tyler, Moses Coit (L)	1835–1900	1898	
Untermeyer, Louis (L)	1885–1977	1941	
Ussachevsky, Vladimir (M)	1911–1990	1973	
van der Stucken, Frank V. (M)	1858–1929	1898	1929
Van Doren, Carl (L)	1885–1950	1944	
Van Doren, Mark (L)	1894–1972	1940	1948
van Druten, John (L)	1901–1957	1951	
van Dyke, Henry (L)	1852–1933	1898	1908
Van Dyke, John Charles (L)	1856–1932	1908	1923
Van Dyke, Paul (L)	1859–1933	1927	
van Loon, Hendrik Willem (L)	1882–1944	1938	
Van Vechten, Carl (L)	1880–1964	1961	
Van Veen, Stuyvesant (A)	1910–1988	1972	
Varèse, Edgard (M)	1883–1965	1955	
Vedder, Elihu (A)	1836–1923	1898	1908
Viele, Herman K. (L)	1856–1908	1908	
Vinton, Frederick P. (A)	1846–1911	1898	
Volk, Douglas (A)	1856–1935	1918	
Vonnoh, Bessie Potter (A)	1872–1955	1931	
Walden, Lionel (A)	1861–1933	1908	
Walker, Charles Howard (A)	1857–1936	1928	
Walker, Henry Oliver (A)	1843–1929	1898	
Walker, Horatio (A)	1858–1938	1898	

Deceased Members of the Academy and Institute—1898 to 1997

		ELECTED TO INSTITUTE	ELECTED TO ACADEMY
Walker, Ralph (A)	1889–1973	1949	
Ward, John Quincy Adams (A)	1830–1910	1902	1905
Warner, Charles Dudley (L)	1829–1900	1898	
Warren, Austin (L)	1899–1986	1975	
Warren, Charles (L)	1868–1954	1925	1937
Warren, Robert Penn (L)	1905 1989	1950	1959
Warren, Whitney (A)	1864–1943	1908	
Watkins, Franklin C. (A)	1894–1972	1946	
Watrous, Harry W. (A)	1857–1940	1935	
Waugh, Sidney B. (A)	1904–1963	1941	
Weber, Ben (M)	1916–1979	1971	
Weber, Max (A)	1881–1961	1955	
Weems, Katharine Lane (A)	1899–1989	1952	
Weinman, Adolph A. (A)	1870–1952	1910	1931
Weir, J. Alden (A)	1852–1919	1898	1915
Weisgall, Hugo (M)	1912–1997	1975	1991
Wendell, Barrett (L)	1855–1921	1898	1916
Wengenroth, Stow (A)	1906–1978	1942	
Wescott, Glenway (L)	1901–1987	1947	1964
West, Andrew F. (L)	1853–1943	1911 (resigned 1914)	
Wharton, Edith (L)	1862–1937	1926	1930
Wheelock, John Hall (L)	1886–1978	1948	1966
White, Andrew Dickson (L)	1832–1918	1898	1908
White, E. B. (L)	1899–1985	1962	1973
White, Stanford (A)	1853–1906	1906	
White, Stewart Edward (L)	1873–1946	1908	1935
White, William Allen (L)	1868–1944	1908	
Whiting, Arthur (M)	1861–1936	1905	
Whiting, Charles Goodrich (L)	1842–1922	1908	
Whitlock, Brand (L)	1869–1934	1913	1918
Wilder, Thornton (L)	1897–1975	1928	1938
Wiles, Irving R. (A)	1861–1948	1908	
Williams, Francis Howard (L)	1844–1922	1912	
Williams, Jesse Lynch (L)	1871–1929	1908	
Williams, Tennessee (L)	1911–1983	1952	1976
Williams, William Carlos (L)	1883–1963	1950	1958
Wilson, Harry Leon (L)	1867–1939	1908	
Wilson, Woodrow (L)	1856–1924	1898	1908

Deceased Members of the Academy and Institute—1898 to 1997

		ELECTED TO INSTITUTE	ELECTED TO ACADEMY
Winter, Ezra (A)	1886–1949	1937	
Winter, William (L)	1836–1917	1898 (resigned 1901)	
Winters, Yvor (L)	1900–1967	1956 (resigned 1957)	
Wister, Owen (L)	1860–1938	1898	1912
Wolfe, Thomas (L)	1900–1938	1937	
Wolpe, Stefan (M)	1902–1972	1966	
Wood, Thomas W. (A)	1823–1903	1898	
Woodberry, George Edward (L)	1855–1930	1898	1908
Woodbridge, Frederick J. E. (L)	1867–1940	1933	1935
Wortman, Denys (A)	1887–1958	1946	
Wright, Frank Lloyd (A)	1869–1959	1947	1951
Wright, James A. (L)	1927–1980	1974	
Yamasaki, Minoru (A)	1912–1986	1982	
Young, Mahonri M. (A)	1877–1957	1935	1947
Young, Stark (L)	1881–1963	1938	
Yourcenar, Marguerite (L)	1903–1987	1982	
Zantzinger, Clarence C. (A)	1872–1954	1952	
Zorach, William (A)	1887–1966	1953	

Deceased Foreign Honorary Members

		ELECTED
Aalto, Alvar Henrik (A)	1898–1976	1968
Abe, Kōbō (L)	1924–1993	1992
Aragon, Louis (L)	1897–1982	1972
Auric, Georges (M)	1899–1983	1979
Barragán, Luis (A)	1901–1988	1984
Barrie, James (L)	1860–1937	1929
Beerbohm, Max (L)	1872–1956	1943
Berkeley, Lennox (M)	1903–1989	1980
Berlin, Isaiah (L)	1909–1997	1966
Betjeman, John (L)	1906–1984	1973
Blomfield, Reginald (A)	1856–1942	1929
Böll, Heinrich (L)	1917–1985	1974
Borges, Jorge Luis (L)	1899–1986	1971
Bowen, Elizabeth (L)	1899–1973	1961
Bowra, Maurice (L)	1898–1970	1960
Braque, Georges (A)	1882–1963	1951
Britten, Benjamin (M)	1913–1976	1957

Deceased Foreign Honorary Members

		ELECTED
Burle Marx, Roberto (A)	1909–1994	1979
Burri, Alberto (A)	1915–1995	1994
Calvino, Italo (L)	1923–1985	1975
Canetti, Elias (L)	1905–1994	1984
Chagall, Marc (A)	1887–1985	1958
Chaplin, Charles (L)	1889–1977	1976
Chávez, Carlos (M)	1899–1978	1960
Chevrillon, André (A)	1864–1957	1933
Churchill, Winston (L)	1874–1965	1908 (resigned 1923)
Clark, Kenneth (L)	1903–1983	1972
Cocteau, Jean (A)	1889–1963	1957
Colette, Sidonie Gabrielle (L)	1873–1954	1953
Connolly, Cyril (L)	1903–1974	1974
Croce, Benedetto (L)	1866–1952	1934
Dallapiccola, Luigi (M)	1904–1975	1964
Davies, Robertson (L)	1913–1995	1980
Day-Lewis, Cecil (L)	1904–1972	1966
de Andrade, Carlos Drummond (L)	1902–1987	1975
de la Mare, Walter (L)	1873–1956	1955
Dinesen, Isak (L)	1885–1962	1957
Ding, Ling (L)	1904–1986	1986
Dunoyer de Segonzac, André (A)	1884–1974	1955
Elgar, Edward (M)	1857–1934	1929
Eliot, T. S. (L)	1888–1965	1943
Empson, William (L)	1906–1984	1974
Epstein, Jacob (A)	1880–1959	1955
Ernst, Max (A)	1891–1976	1974
Espina, Concha (L)	1879–1955	1938
Fisher, Herbert A. L. (L)	1865–1940	1937
Forster, E. M. (L)	1879–1970	1949
Frisch, Max (L)	1911–1991	1974
Frye, Northrop (L)	1912–1991	1981
Gallegos, Romulo (L)	1884–1969	1943
Galsworthy, John (L)	1867–1933	1929
Giacometti, Alberto (A)	1901–1966	1963
Gide, André (L)	1869–1951	1950
Ginastera, Alberto (M)	1916–1983	1968
Greene, Graham (L)	1904–1991	1961 (resigned 1970)
Guttuso, Renato (A)	1912–1987	1987

Deceased Foreign Honorary Members

		ELECTED
Hauptmann, Gerhard (L)	1862–1946	1932
Hélion, Jean (A)	1904–1987	1978
Hepworth, Barbara (A)	1903–1975	1973
Honegger, Arthur (M)	1902–1955	1955
Hughes, Richard (L)	1900–1976	1963
Hu Shih (L)	1891–1962	1943
Huxley, Aldous Leonard (L)	1894–1963	1960
Jameson, Storm (L)	1894–1986	1978
John, Augustus E. (A)	1898–1961	1943
Jouhandeau, Marcel (L)	1888–1979	1975
Kawabata, Yasunari (L)	1899–1972	1969
Kodály, Zoltán (M)	1882–1967	1963
Koestler, Arthur (L)	1905–1983	1976
Kokoschka, Oskar (A)	1886–1980	1963
Kuniyoshi, Yasuo (A)	1893–1953	1949
Le Corbusier, Charles Edouard J. (A)	1887–1965	1953
Léger, Alexis (St.John Perse) (L)	1887–1975	1960
Lutoslawski, Witold (M)	1913–1994	1975
Lutyens, Elisabeth (M)	1906–1983	1979
Macmillan, Hugh P. (L)	1873–1952	1938
Malipiero, G. Francesco (M)	1882–1973	1949
Malraux, André (L)	1901–1976	1955
Manzú, Giacomo (A)	1908–1991	1964
Marcks, Gerhard (A)	1889–1981	1980
Marini, Marino (A)	1901–1980	1968
Maritain, Jacques (L)	1882–1973	1955
Masefield, John (L)	1878–1967	1930
Masson, André (A)	1896–1987	1977
Matisse, Henri (A)	1869–1954	1950
Mauclair, Camille (L)	1872–1950	1934
Maugham, W. Somerset (L)	1874–1965	1950
Mauriac, François (L)	1885–1970	1958
Messiaen, Olivier (M)	1908–1992	1964
Milhaud, Darius (M)	1892–1974	1943
Miró, Joan (A)	1893–1983	1960
Mistral, Gabriela (L)	1889–1957	1943
Montale, Eugenio (L)	1896–1981	1977
Moore, Henry (A)	1898–1986	1961
Moravia, Alberto (L)	1907–1990	1964

Deceased Foreign Honorary Members

		ELECTED
Nancarrow, Conlon (M)	1912–1997	1992
Nehru, Jawaharlal (L)	1889–1964	1950
Neruda, Pablo (L)	1904–1973	1968
Nervi, Pier Luigi (A)	1891–1979	1957
Nicolson, Harold (L)	1886–1968	1958
Nolan, Sidney (A)	1917–1992	1985
Orozco, José Clemente (A)	1883–1949	1943
Orpen, William (A)	1878–1931	1929
Paderewski, Ignace Jan (M)	1860–1941	1931
Pasternak, Boris (L)	1890–1960	1960
Ponge, Francis (L)	1899–1988	1980
Poulenc, Francis (M)	1899–1963	1958
Pritchett, Victor S. (L)	1900–1997	1971
Read, Herbert (L)	1893–1968	1966
Rhys, Jean (L)	1894–1979	1979
Richards, Ivor Armstrong (L)	1893–1979	1963
Rivera, Diego (A)	1886–1957	1943
Romains, Jules (L)	1885–1972	1943
Rossi, Aldo (A)	1931–1997	1996
Russell, Bertrand (L)	1872–1970	1951
Saint-Exupéry, Antoine de (L)	1900–1944	1943
Sakharov, Andrei (L)	1921–1989	1988
Santayana, George (L)	1863–1952	1943
Sauguet, Henri (M)	1901–1989	1951
Schmidt-Rottluff, Karl (A)	1884–1976	1974
Schweitzer, Albert (L)	1875–1965	1955
Seferis, George (L)	1900–1971	1971
Shaw, George Bernard (L)	1856–1950	1943
Shostakovich, Dmitri (M)	1907–1975	1960
Sibelius, Jean Julius Christian (M)	1865–1957	1937
Silone, Ignazio (L)	1900–1978	1950
Simenon, Georges (L)	1903–1989	1971
Sitwell, Edith (L)	1887–1964	1949
Sitwell, Osbert (L)	1892–1969	1951
Smuts, Jan Christiaan (L)	1870–1950	1943
Snow, C. P. (L)	1905–1980	1961
Spender, Stephen (L)	1909–1995	1969
Stead, Christina (L)	1902–1983	1982
Stirling, James (A)	1926–1992	1990

Deceased Foreign Honorary Members

		ELECTED
Sutherland, Graham (A)	1903–1980	1972
Takemitsu, Torū (M)	1930–1996	1984
Tamayo, Rufino (A)	1899–1991	1961
Tanizaki, Junichiro (L)	1886–1965	1964
Tomlinson, H. M. (L)	1873–1958	1943
Toynbee, Arnold J. (L)	1889–1975	1950
Trevelyan, George Macaulay, (L)	1876–1962	1937
Undset, Sigrid (L)	1882–1949	1943
Vaughan Williams, Ralph (M)	1872–1958	1949
Villa-Lobos, Heitor (M)	1884–1959	1943
Villon, Jacques (A)	1875–1963	1961
Walton, William (M)	1902–1983	1978
Warner, Sylvia Townsend (L)	1893–1978	1972
Watson, William (L)	1858–1935	1930
Wedgwood, Veronica (L)	1910–1997	1966
Wells, H. G. (L)	1866–1946	1943
Werfel, Franz (L)	1890–1945	1943
West, Rebecca (L)	1892–1983	1972
Wilson, Angus (L)	1913–1991	1980
Zorrilla de San Martin, José Luis (L)	1891–1975	1943

Deceased American Honorary Members

Abbott, Berenice (photographer)	1898–1991	1983
Adams, Ansel (photographer)	1902–1984	1983
Balanchine, George (choreographer)	1904–1983	1983
Capra, Frank (filmmaker)	1897–1991	1984
de Mille, Agnes (choreographer)	1905–1993	1992
Graham, Martha (choreographer)	1894–1991	1983
Mamoulian, Rouben (filmmaker)	1897–1987	1984
Slonimsky, Nicolas (musicologist)	1894–1995	1991
Vishniac, Roman (photographer)	1897–1990	1984
Welles, Orson (filmmaker)	1915–1985	1983
Wolff, Helen (publisher)	1906–1994	1985

INDEX

Boldface denotes page numbers in photo insert section. Italic numbers refer to illustrations in the body of the text.

Abbey, Edward, 250

Abbey, Edwin Austin, 20

Abbott, Berenice, 247, *247*

Abstract expressionism, 130, 140, 144, 147, 149–51, 246; Schapiro's statement on, 162

Academia (Blashfield), *80*

Académie française, ix, 1, 2, 30, 48–49, 77, 116; women members, 13

Across the River and into the Trees (Hemingway), 184

Action painting, 150

Adams, Ansel, 247

Adams, Brooks, 24, 29; on women's duty, 33–34

Adams, Charles Francis, Jr., 24; letters, exhibit of, 79

Adams, Henry, 5, 9, 17, 24, 29; letters, exhibit of, 79; Pulitzer Prize, 53; on women members, 100

Adams, Herbert, 26n. 14, 42n. 2, 73, 79, 87; Academy key, *265;* bronze doors, 73, *73*

Adams, James Truslow, 115; member-selection controversy, 110–11, 112

Adams, John, vii, 2

Adams, John Quincy, 2

Administration building, Washington Heights, Manhattan, **2**, 54, *57*, 106, 290; auditorium, *88;* bronze doors, 73, *73*, *139*, *245;* building security, concern with, 182; building staff, 114; cornerstone, 48, 50, 51; cost, 57; frieze, wording for, 57; Hassam Room, *139;* location, concern with, 116, 256–58, 282; Members' Room, 264, 265; repairs to, 277

Advisory Committee on the Arts, 158

Afro-Americans. *See* Black Americans

Age versus youth, in Academy-Institute affairs, 244, 246

Aiken, Conrad, 51, 124

Akhmadulina, Bella, 255

Albee, Edward, **26**, **27**, 188, 254, 255

Albers, Josef, 141

Aldrich, Richard, 64–65

Aldrich, Thomas Bailey, 6, 17, 25n. 13; letters, exhibit of, 79

Alfred, William, 188

Algren, Nelson, 118, 140, 194, 213

Allen, Harvey, 95

Allen, Woody, 226, 247

Alma Mater (bronze by Daniel Chester French), 199

American Academy and Institute of Arts and Letters (1976–1992), x, 204, 205; age versus youth, 244; bylaws, amendment of, 246; development study, 257–58; Druckman-Diamond incident, 241–42; final meeting of, *289;* and National Book Awards, 207–12

American Academy in Rome, 74, 278–79; Williams affair, 173–76

American Academy of Arts and Letters (1904–1976), x, 6, 8; and American Academy in Rome, 173, 176; American speech, concern with, 81, 91, 92; bookplate, 73; Burroughs commemoration, 76–77; caps and gowns, 74; charter, ix; concerts and recitals sponsored by, 80; constitution, 28; federal government, relations with, 157; fiftieth anniversary, *141;* finances, 90, 115, 204–5; first Conference, 17; formation of, ix, 15, 16, 17, 19–24; fund-raising, 34, 54; Garland's programs for, 70; gown and hood, proposal for, 139; grants to nonmembers, 114, 118; Howells memorial meeting, 75; Huntington's gifts and endowment, 29, 54, 80, 89, 106; incorporation, 51; insignia, 74; Institute, amalgamation with, 201–4, 206, 250, 285–88; Institute, relationship with, 273, 274, 275; interim headquarters, West 81st Street, 55, 56; Johnson's influence on, 17, 59; key and symbol, *265;* lapel rosette, *x;* Lowell centennial celebration, 61–63; meetings, (1923) *76,* (1927) *80,* (1940) 113, (1963) *182,* (1964) *183;* meetings outside New York City, 29; Mencken's opinion of, 75–76; Molière anniversary celebration, 77–78; motto, 73; national charter, 28, 29; New York State charter, 29; officers and committee members, obliga-

tions of, xii; public events (1927), 79; public lectures, 74; Pulitzer prizes, judging of, 31; purpose of, 22–23; treasurers, 235; twentieth anniversary, 72; twenty-fifth anniversary, 86; voting, 32; in World War II, 125. *See also* American Academy and Institute of Arts and Letters (1976–1992); American Academy of Arts and Letters (as of 1993)

American Academy of Arts and Letters (as of 1993), 288; art collection, 277; centennial anniversary celebration, xi; Centennial Committee, **32;** Centennial Portfolio, **24;** participation in community activities, 266–67. *See also* Administration building; Membership; Prizes and awards; and names of specific departments

American Academy of Arts and Sciences, 28, 206–7

American Academy of Language and Belles Lettres, 2

American Composers' Orchestra, 151

American cultural awareness, 2, 23

American Honorary Members, xi, 131, 143, 218, 226, 228, 231, 247, 276; creation of category of, 246; lists of, 297, 323–24

American Indian music, 11, 229–30

American Renaissance, 259, 260

American Scene painting, 129, 147, 151

American Social Science Association (ASSA), ix, 1, 3

American speech, 81, 91–92, 170

American Wave in music, 131

Anderson, Sherwood, 53, 101, 109

Anti-art, 260

Anti-Communism, 117–18, 136–37, 156

Anti-intellectualism, 288–89

Antimodernism, 51, 63, 65, 66, 67; of Johnson, 78–79, 92–99

Antin, Mary, 15

Anti-Semitism, **2,** 101, 120–21

Architecture, 8, 9–10, 17, 218, 248–49,

270, 281, 290; mid- and late-twentieth
century, 170; postmodernism, 239;
post-World War I, 61; prizes and
awards, 138, 170, 249, 254, 262*n.* 27
Archives, 280
Arendt, Hannah, 224
Argento, Dominick, 226
Armory Show (1913), 9, 65, 67, 130, 260
Armstrong, Louis, 64
Arnold W. Brunner Award in
Architecture, 138, *188*
Art, 270, 271, 281, 288, 289, (1938–1947)
128–30, (1948–1957) 139–54; Black
artists, 14–15; modernism, 65–67, 79;
portrait exhibition (1987), 258–60,
280; postmodernism, 239; post-World
War I, 61; prizes and awards, 31, 73,
118, 142, 164, 189, 223, 254;
Senegalese, 283; women artists, 13–14
Art, department of, 3, 7–10, 17, 24, 102,
130, 213–16, 218, 219; architects, 248,
249; cantakerousness of, 245–46;
vacancies, 247
Art Censorship, Committee on, 79
Art museums, proposals for, 29, 74, 79
Arts, government involvement in. *See*
Government involvement in the arts
Ashbery, John, **10**, **40**
Ashcan School, The, 9
Asian-Americans, 290
ASSA. *See* American Social Science
Association
Association of American Publishers,
209, 212
Atlantic Monthly, 61
Auchincloss, Louis, **38**, 288, *289,* 290
Auden, W. H., 126, 164, *182,* 223, 224
Audubon Terrace, **1**
Audubon collection, 172
Audubon Terrace neighborhood, 258
Avant-garde music, 131
Award for Distinguished Service to the
Arts, **15**, 221
Award of Merit, 125, 142, 162, 221; for
the Novel, **15**, 184; for Poetry, 126

Awards. *See* Prizes and awards
Awards Committee, 246, 250; citations,
writing of, 242

Babbitt, Irving, 52, 92, 279
Babbitt, Milton, 189, 205, 225, 231, *289*
Bacon, Henry, 73
Bacon, Peggy, 118, 189
Baizerman, Saul, 66
Bailey, William, **38, 39**
Ba Jin, 283
Baker, Russell, 244
Baldwin, James, **21**, 140
Baldwin, Simeon, ix, 1, *3*
Balthus, 219
Bancroft, George, 2
Barber, Samuel, 222–23, 230
Barnard, George Gray, 30, 43*n.* 10
Barnet, Will, **32, 33, 38**, 246
Barth, John, 188
Barzun, Jacques, **28**, 189, 191–92, 193,
201, 202, 203, 205, 206, 212, 243, 276,
279; electronic music, 225; member-
ship in departments, proportion of,
248; on prizes and awards, 220–21;
U.S. population, representation of, in
Academy, 216
Bassett, John Spencer, 52
Beach, Amy Marcy Cheney, 14
Beard, Charles A., 108, 138
Bearden, Romare, 188
Beattie, Ann, **35**
Beauvoir, Simone de, 219
Beaux, Cecilia, 13, 100, 111
Beaux-arts tradition, 9, 65, 261
Becker, Carl, 94, 116
Beckett, Samuel, 219
Beckwith, Carroll, 34, 38
Beebe, William, 95, 108
Beeson, Jack, **32, 37, 38**, 217–18, 219,
226, 230
Behrman, S. N., 123
Bellow, Saul, 128, 140, 157
Bellows, George, 9
Belmont, Mrs. August, 32

Benét, Stephen Vincent, 56, 93, 97, 110, 127, 128, 279
Benét, William Rose, 128
Bentley, Eric, **35**
Benton, Thomas Hart, 128, 129, 151, *199;* and Mumford's anti-Vietnam War speech, 187, 198
Bequests, endowments, and gifts, 16, 204, 251; Hassam's paintings, 114; Huntington's gifts, 29, 54, 80, 89, 90; Ives's copyrights, 131, 232–33; Rodgers's bequest, 233
Berenson, Bernard, 52
Berger, Thomas, 243
Bergsma, William, 118, 232
Berlin, Isaiah, 188
Berman, Ronald, 205
Bernstein, Leonard, **24**, 253
Betts, Louis, 251
Biddle, George, 121, 189
Bigelow, John, 20, 39
Biography, prizes and awards in, 73, 138, 254
Bird, Arthur, 68–69, 227
Bishop, Isabel, 118, 138, 189, 246, 276
Bishop, James Bucklin, 52
Black Americans: artists, 14–15, 129; Blashfield speakers, 280; members, 101, 119–20, 290; music, 11, 15, 64, 131–32, 231; "Negro" designation on list of Institute candidates, 119; Williams, John, and American Academy in Rome, 173–76; writers, 14, 51, 128
Blacklisting, Hollywood, 136
Black Mountain College, 141, 142, 143, 223
Blasco Ibañez, Vicente, 75
Blashfield, Edwin Howland, **3**, 40, 67, 72, *80*
Blashfield, Evangeline Wilbour, 32, 72
Blashfield addresses, 72, 220, 279
Blitzstein, Marc, 118, 131, 226, 230
Bloch, Ernest, 64, 163, 230
Blok, Aleksandr, 53

Bloom, Harold, **35**
Blume, Peter, 118, *183,* 189, 202, 203, 246
Bogan, Louise, 51, 224
Boghosian, Varujan, **33**
Boston Herald, 81
Boulanger, Nadia, 230
Boulez, Pierre, 188
Bowen, Catherine Drinker, 189
Bowen, Mrs. Cochran, 49
Bowers, Claude G., 94
Bowles, Paul, 142, 226
Bowra, Maurice, 220
Boyle, Kay, 157, 158, *247*
Brinnin, John Malcolm, **40**, 143
Brodsky, Joseph, 243
Bromfield, Louis, 128
Bronowski, J., 188
Brooks, Gwendolyn, 118, 219
Brooks, Van Wyck, 91, 115, 125, 126, *141;* March, Fredric, presentation of medal to, 170; robes, *139;* tribute to, 170–71
Brown, Caroline, 143
Brown, Earle, 143
Brown, Trisha, 247
Brownell, William Crary, 30, 73
Brunner Prize in Architecture, **13**, 138, *188*
Brush, George de Forest, 29–30, 32
Bryant, William Cullen, 2
Buchwald, Art, 244
Buck, Pearl S., **14**, 95, 109, 128, 173
Bunce, William Gedney, 32
Burchfield, Charles E., 164–65
Burke, Kenneth, 118, 149
Burnham, Daniel, 8, 9, 10
Burroughs, John, 20, 36, *36,* 79; Johnson's letter to, 42*n.* 2; memorial to (1922), 76–77
Burroughs, William, 109, 194, 213, 214
Burton, Richard, 79
Business and finance: in early 1900s, 4–5; in 1930s, 88–89
Butler, Nicholas Murray, x, **6**, 36, 74, *76, 80,* 86, 87, *87,* 90, 99, 100, 259; Academy member-selection contro-

versy, 107–14; American speech, concern with, 91; anti-German sentiments, 60; Eliot, support for, 94; Huntington, description of, 105; Lewis's opinion of, 96; Mark Twain centennial celebration, 95; Molière anniversary celebration, 77, 78; Pound's animosity to, 121–22; resignation of, 113; on theory of evolution, 39

Bynner, Witter, 56, 57
Bynner Poetry Award, 57, 242, 253

Cabell, James Branch, 53, 109
Cable, George Washington, 39–40
Cadman, Charles Wakefield, 229
Cadmus, Paul, **38**, **39**, 246
Cage, John, **30**, 131, 141, 142, 230
Cahan, Abraham, 15
Caldwell, Erskine, 109, *140*
Calisher, Hortense, **33**, **35**, **38**, 243, 253, 258, *259, 280;* as president of Institute, 272–76, 284
Callahan, Harry, 247
Campbell, Joseph, 142
Canby, Henry Seidel, 101, 118 122
Capote, Truman, **18**, 194
Capra, Frank, 247
Cardell, William E., 2
Carpenter, John Alden, 64, 229
Carrère and Hastings, 248
Carter, Benny, 231
Carter, Jimmy, 212, 240
Carver, Raymond, 252
Cassatt, Mary, 13–14
Cather, Willa, **15**, 53, 73, 100
Catton, Bruce, 189
CBS Foundation, 253
Censorship, 284; in cold war period, 137–38; O'Hara affair, 158–61; Rushdie affair, 281–82
Centennial Committee, **32**
Centennial Portfolio, **16**
Century, The, 58–59
Century Club, 228, 234

Ceremonials, 125, 220, 251, 267, 272, 280, (1941) 114, (1943) 124, (1944) **15**, (1949) **12**, (1951) *143,* (1952) **14**, (1958) 157, (1959) **9**, (1960) **13**, 164, (1961) 168–69, (1962) 173, 174, (1963) 176–77, 179, 181, (1964) 184, *184,* (1965) 157, 185, *188,* 198, (1966) 188–89, (1967) **11**, 194, (1969) **10**, (1972) 222, (1975) **26**, (1978) **27**, (1979) **28**, 241, (1982) *254,* (1983) **31**, *247,* (1984) **30**, (1986) 240, (1989) 280, (1996) 233, (1997) **40**
Chadwick, George W., 10, 35, 64, 79, 80, 227
Chamberlain, John, **38**
Chaplin, Charlie, **3**, 218, 226
Chapman, John Jay, 291
Charles F. Kettering Foundation, 255
Charles Ives Centennial Festival, **26**, 233
Chase, Stuart, 189
Chase, William Merritt, 8
Cheever, John, 128, 188, *188*
Chesnutt, Charles, 14
Chevrillon, André, 77
Chicago, in 1900, 4
Chicago, University of, 148
Chicago World's Fair (1893), 9–10, 14, 248
Chinese literature, 283
Chopin, Kate, 13
Choreography, 218, 246, 247
Christo, 261
Church, Frederic, 8
Chute, Marchette, 138, 189, 212, 214
Ciardi, John, 200–201
Cinema. *See* Motion pictures
Civil War, 23–24
Clark, Eleanor, **28**, 118, *254*
Clarke, Gilmore D., 136, *141,* 161, *183*
Clemens, Samuel L. (Mark Twain), 2, **4**, 5, 7, 16, 17, 24, 59; centennial celebration (1935), 95; Kipling's opinion of, 103*n.* 39; and women members, 12, 13
Close, Chuck, **38**
Cold War, 127, 136–38, 149, 156, 191, 239

Cole, Timothy, 49, 73–74, 79
Coleman, Ornette, 231
Columbia University, 211; Electronic Music Center, 226; in Vietnam War era, 199
Commager, Henry Steele, 189–90
Committee of Six, 137
Committee on Art Censorship, 79
Committee on Government and Art, 138
Committee on Progress, 201, 203
Committee on the Future, 205–6, 213, 234, 239–40, 257, 285
Congress, U.S., 28–29
Connelly, Marc, 137
Conrad, Joseph, 53
Converse, Frederick S., 64, 79, 229
Cooke, Alistair, 92
Copland, Aaron, 11, **26**, 63, 130, 131, 151, 230, 235, 279
Copyright law, 24–25, 59, 206; musical works, 231–32, 233
"Correspondance School" (Johnson), 143
Cortissoz, Royal, 66, 67
Cousins, Norman, 255
Cowell, Henry, 64, 142, 181, 231; tribute to Charles Ives, 176
Cowley, Malcolm, 118, 124, 137, 138, 157, 172, *179, 183,* 189, 204, 254, 276; censorship question, 159–61; and Franklin Library, 211; members, selection of, 107, 112, 215–16, 286; and unification of Institute and Academy, 250, 285; Updike, John, introduction of, 182; and Williams affair, 174, 175
Cox, Kenyon, 67, 79, 260
Cozzens, James Gould, 128
Crane, Hart, 51
Crane, Stephen, 6
Crasto, Frank P., 55, 56, 113, 114, 121
Crawford, F. Marion, 2
Creston, Paul, 125
Cross, Wilbur L., 74, 95, 97, 98, 100, 113
Crothers, Rachel, 100
Crucible, The (Miller), 226

Cubist movement, 67
Culhane, Stephen, 139
Cummings, E. E., 51, 118, 122, 124
Cunliffe, Joan, 208
Cunningham, Merce, 141, 143, 247
Curry, John Steuart, 128, 129, 147
Curtis, H. Holbrook, ix, 1, 3

Dada movement, 53
Dajani, Virginia, xii, **40**, 285, 286
Dalton, Peter, 118
Damrosch, Walter, x, 31, 35, 63, 97, 98, 99, 111–12, 117, 130, 227, 235; Academy headquarters, relocation proposal, 256; Academy member-selection controversy, 110–14; American speech, concern with, 91; Huntington, description of, 105; Pound's letter, response to, 122; remaking of Academy-Institute, 114–15, 127; in World War II, 125
David, Owen, 52
Davidovsky, Mario, 225
Davidman, Joy, 120
Davidson, Jo, **3**
Davis, Elmer, 125
Davis, Stuart, 130, 145
Davison, Jo, 130
Day-Lewis, Cecil, 188
Deceased members: lists of, 297–324; tributes to, 224, 264
Deconstruction, 271, 281
deKay, Charles, 79
de Kooning, Willem, 141, 142, 147, 150, 151–52
deKoven, Reginald, 64, 228
Deland, Margaret, 95, 100, 119
Delano, William Adams, 137, *141*
Dello Joio, Norman, 118
de Mille, Agnes, 247
DeMuth, Charles, 130
de Niro, Robert, Sr., 151
Depression years, 88–91
Deutsch, Babette, 202
De Vries, Peter, 118, 211

Dewey, John, 118

Diamond, David, **33**, 118, 188, 241–42, 247

Dickey, James, 188, *289*

Dickinson, Edwin, *183*

Dickinson, Emily, 38–39

Diederich, William Hunt, **2**, 120–21

Disney, Walt, 95

Distinguished Service to the Arts Award, **15**, 205

di Suvero, Mark, 240

Doctorow, E. L., **29**

Dondero, George A., 137

Donnay, Maurice, *77*

Doolittle, Hilda (H. D.), 51

Doro, Edward, 120

Dos Passos, John, 73, 101, 109, *141,* 189

Douglass, Frederick, 14

Drama. *See* Theater

Dreiser, Theodore, 7, 9, **15**, 73, 97, 98; Award of Merit, 125–26

Druckman, Jacob, 241–42

Du Bois, Guy Pène, 130

Du Bois, W. E. B., 14, 101, 119, 120

Dubuffet, Jean, 219

Duchamp, Marcel, 142

Dugan, Alan, 173, 174, 175

Dumas, Alexandre, 39

Dunbar, Paul Laurence, 14

Dunne, Finley Peter, 34, 90, 95

Duyckinck, Evert, viii

Dvorak, Antonin, 11

Eakins, Thomas, 8

Earlham College, 57–58

Eastman Group (musicians), 130

Eaton, Walter Prichard, 94, 96, 100–101

Eberhart, Richard, 189, 250

Edel, Leon, 189, 191, 202, 203, 243; and unification of Academy and Institute, 287–88

Eggleston, Edward, 2, 7

Eisenhower, Dwight D., 138

Electronic music, 225–26

Eliot, Charles W., 21, 32

Eliot, T. S., 51, 94, 122, 153

Elitism, 251, 268, 288

Ellington, Duke, **25**, 64, 131, 224, 231

Ellison, Ralph, 140, 184, *188,* 189, 208, 245, 258, *259, 289*

Emeritus category, proposal for, 217, 243, 278

Emerson, Ralph Waldo, 80

Endowments. *See* Bequests, endowments, and gifts

English language, preservation of, 30, 279; Blashfield donation for, 32

Entertainments, 227, 254–55

Environmental art, 271

Erskine, John, 52, 95, 111, 136

Escobar, Marisol, **27**

Evolution, theory of, 39

Executive directors, xii, 271

Existentialism, 150

"Farewell Academia" (Vanamee and Crasto), 113

Farwell, Arthur, 11, 230

Faulkner, Barry, *141, 183*

Faulkner, William, 108, 109, 128, 173, *222*

Federal Advisory Commission on the Arts, proposal for, 138

Federenko, Nicolai, 255

Feldman, Morton, 143

Ferber, Edna, 97, 100, 116, 125

Fergusson, Francis, 189

Fern, Alan, 260

Films. *See* Motion pictures

Finance. *See* Business and finance

Finley, John Huston, 79, *80*

Finney, Ross Lee, 130, 214, 230

Fisher, Dorothy Canfield, 100

Fitzgerald, F. Scott, 73, 94–95, 128

Flanagan, John, *91*

Flexner, James Thomas, 219, 280

Foch, Ferdinand, 48, *48,* 50; trowel incident, 56

Follet, Jean, 145

Foote, Arthur, 35, 64

Foreign Honorary Members, 70, 143,

145, 146, 163, 188, 199, 218, 226, 235, 243, 255, 281, 283, 290–91; Blashfield addresses, 220; lists of, 296–97, 320–23
Formalist art, 151
Forster, E. M., 251, 279
Forster Award, 262n. 30
Forty Immortals, 2
Foss, Lukas, **30**, *289*
Foster, Stephen, 11
Fox, John, Jr., 7
Frankenthaler, Helen, 205, 213, 246, 288
Franklin Library, 209–13
Franklin Mint, 207, 209, 211, 213
Fraser, James Earle, *80*
Fraser, Laura, 100
Freed, James Ingo, **38**
Freedom of representation and speech, 278, 281, 282, 290. *See also* Censorship
Freeman, Mary E. Wilkins, 13, 72, 100; bronze doors honoring, *245*
Freilicher, Jane, **39**, 146
French, Daniel Chester, 8, 20, 66, *76,* 199; Gold Medal, design of, 31
Frost, Robert, 72, 79, 90, 92, 124, 127, 167–68, 193; Johnson's opinion of, 78
Fulbright, J. William, 126–27, 279
Fuller, Buckminster, 141, 143, 223–24
Fuller, Henry Blake, 6
Furness, Horace Howard, 20
Future, Committee on the. *See* Committee on the Future

Gaddis, William, *289*
Galbraith, John Kenneth, **31**, 188, 253, 276
Galsworthy, John, 62
Gardner, John B., 189
Garland, Hamlin, 4, 6, 69–72, *76,* 81, 98, 101; Academy member-selection controversy, 111; American speech, concern with, 91, 92; Blashfield address, 108–9; on local color in literature, 40
Gates, Henry Louis, Jr., 280
Geffen, Felicia, xii, 114, 119, 139, *140,* 157, 189; Dreiser's award, 126; Parker,

correspondence with, 163; Pound's letter, response to, 123; Sexton, correspondence with, 178; Steinbeck, correspondence with, 180–81; and Williams-Rome Academy affair, 174
"Genius" (Huntington), 54–55
Genteel tradition, the, 47, 260
German expressionists, 146
Germany, prejudice against, 36–37, 60–61
Gibson, Charles Dana, *76,* 110, 112, 113
Gide, André, 53, 154
Gifts. *See* Bequests, endowments, and gifts
Gilbert, Cass, 26n. 14, 79, 87, *87,* 88, 93, 94, 102, 248; Academy auditorium, *88;* arched facade, proposal for, *89;* drawing by, *74*
Gilbert, Henry F. B., 11
Gilder, Richard Watson, 2, 12, 13, 20, 58–59; "Molière," 77
Gillespie, Dizzy, 131, 231
Ginsberg, Allen, **10**, **34,** 194, 213, 251, 261, 284
Glanville-Hicks, Peggy, 142
Glasgow, Ellen, 100, 110
Glyn, Elinor, 87
Goethe, Johann Wolfgang von, 154
Gold Medal, 142, 221; of the Academy, 25, 31, *31;* for Architecture, 170; for Belles-Lettres, 73, 198; for Belles-Lettres and Criticism, 254; for Biography and History, 73; for Drama, **9**, 163, 221; for Essays and Criticism, 119, 164; for Fiction, **14**, **15**, goldplated medals, 253–54; for History, 173; of the Institute, 25, 28, 30–31, 40, 210, *210,* 211; for Music, 189, 222, 253; for the Novel, *222;* for Painting, 164–65; for Poetry, **40**, 181; for Sculpture, **31**, 73, 189, 223
Goodman, Benny, 131
Goodnough, Robert, 146
Gordimer, Nadine, 279, *280,* 284
Gorky, Arshile, 130, 145

Government and Art, Committee on, 138

Government involvement in the arts, 138, 157, 158, 163–64, 171, 172, 185, 193, 205, 239, 270, 271

Government Participation in the Arts and Humanities, Conference on (1966), 189–93

Graham, Martha, 218, 247

Grainger, Percy, 230

Grant, Robert, 36–37, 93, 94, 96, 98, 99; Academy member-selection controversy, 107, 110

Grant, Ulysses S., 59

Graphic art, 254

Graves, Robert, 169–70

Great Depression, 88–91

Greenbaum, Dorothea, 118

Greene, Balcomb, 219

Greene, Graham, 199–200, 219

Grippe, Peter, 141

Griswold, A. Whitney, 157

Gropius, Walter, 61, *188*

Gross, Chaim, **30**, 189

Guare, John, **32**, **37**, 226, 233

Guston, Philip, 142

Gwathmey, Charles, 219

Hadley, Arthur T., 37, *76*

Hadley, Henry, 35, 229

Hadzi, Dimitri, **39**

Hale, Edward Everett, 13

Hall of Fame, 86

Hamilton, Clayton, 101, 119

Hamilton, Edith, 138

Hammerstein, Oscar, II, 233

Hanks, Nancy, 205

Hans Hofmann School of Fine Arts, 145

Hanson, Howard, 230

Happenings, 146

Hardwick, Elizabeth, **30**, **32**, **33**, 256, *289*

Hardy, Hugh, **38**

Harlem Renaissance, 51, 266

Harold D. Vursell Award, 253

Harper, George McLean, 116

Harriman, Joseph W., 90

Harriman National Bank, 90

Harris, Joel Chandler, 20

Harris, Julie, 173

Harris, Roy, 130

Harrison, Birge, 40–41

Harrison, Edward, **4**

Harrison, Lou, 131, 142

Harte, Bret, 7, 26*n.* 29

Hartigan, Grace, 151, 152

Hassam, Childe, **5**, 8, 16, 79, 102, 114, 251

Hassam, Maude, **5**

Hassam Room, Academy building, 139

Hastings, Thomas, 66

Hawthorne, Nathaniel, viii, 80

Hay, John, 17, 19, 24

Haymarket Square riot (1886), 5

Hazzard, Shirley, 188, *254*

Heckscher, August, 189

Heliker, John, **36**, 142

Hellman, Lillian, 181, *183,* 194, 208, 221, 224

Hemingway, Ernest, 73, 97, 98, 128, 184

Hendrick, Burton J., 52

Henri, Robert, 9

Herbert, Victor, 64, 79, 229

Herbst, Josephine, 188

Hergesheimer, Joseph, 52

Herlihy, James Leo, 142

Hersey, John, 128, *129, 183,* 189, 208, 287

Hesse, Hermann, 53

Higgins, Eugene, 130

Higginson, Thomas Wentworth, 12, 13; and Dickinson, 38–39; letters, exhibit of, 79; on Norton, 38; Perry's tribute to, 38, 39

High art, 244

Hightower, John B., 189

Hill, Edward Burlingame, 64

Hirsch, Joseph, 118

Hispanic Society of America, 106, 266

History, 23–24; prizes and awards, 73, 138, 173

Hitchcock, H. Wiley, 130

Hocking, William Ernest, 137

Hofmann, Hans, 145–48, 150, 151

Hollander, John, 82

Holmes, Oliver Wendell, Sr., 2

Homer, Winslow, 8, 20, 24

Honorary category, 131. *See also*
American Honorary Members;
Foreign Honorary Members

Hooker, Brian, 79

Hoover, Herbert, 99

Hopkinson, Charles, *141*

Hopper, Edward, 129–30, *183,* 194,
224

Horgan, Paul, 242

House of Representatives, U.S., 28–29

House Un-American Activities
Committee (HUAC), 136, 137

Hovhannes, Alan, 142

Howard, Cecil, 119

Howard, Sidney, 98, 99

Howe, Irving, 250

Howe, Julia Ward, 2, **4**, 12–13, 33, *33,* 34,
68, 100; letters, exhibit of, 79

Howe, Mark Antony DeWolfe, 96

Howells, John Mead, 101

Howells, William Dean, 2, 15, 16, 17, 22,
24, 51, *52,* 59; adverse imagination,
5–6; anti-German sentiments, 37, 60;
letters, exhibit of, 79; memorial meeting (1921), 75; popularity of, 6

Howells Medal, *52,* 221, (1925) 72,
(1945) 126, (1954) 140, (1965) 188;
women recipients, 100

HUAC. *See* House Un-American
Activities Committee

Hughes, Langston, 51, 118

Human rights, 240, 281

Huneker, James Gibbon, 52

Hunt, Richard Morris, 9, 10

Huntington, Anna Hyatt, 100

Huntington, Archer Milton, x, **1**, 29,
54–55, *76,* 80, 86, 87, 89–90, 99,
105–6, 251; Academy members, controversy concerning selection of,
106–14; resignation from Academy,
113

Huxley, Aldous, 162, 173

Huxtable, Ada Louise, **32, 38,** 280, 284,
289

Immigration: Jewish, 15; post–World War
I, 67–68

Impressionism, 8, 147

Indian music. *See* American Indian music

Innovation and tradition, conflict
between, 241

Institut de France, ix, 1

Institute Award for Distinguished
Achievement, 135*n.* 102

In Zikh movement, 51

Irving, Washington, 2

Isherwood, Christopher, **23**

Israel, Al, 145

Ives, Charles, 10, 11–12, **16,** 64, 79,
130–31, 232–33, 251; Cowell's tribute
to, 176

Ives Living, 233

Ives Scholarships and Fellowships, 232–33

Ives Society, 233

Jackson, Helen Hunt, 2

Jaegers, Albert, 42*n.* 2

James, Henry, 2, 17, *18,* 21, 22, 24, 32–33,
59; adverse imagination, 5; British citizenship, 29; *Collected Travel Writings,*
79; Harrison's criticism of, 40–41; letters, exhibit of, 79

James, William, 20–22, 220, 243

Jansen, Mrs. Horst W., 175–76

Jazz, 131, 132, 231

Jean Stein Award, 253

Jeffers, Robinson, 94, 101, 109, 128

Jefferson, Joseph, 15, 19–20

Jewett, Sarah Orne, 13

Jews, 15; artists, 129; awards to, 120; and
Diederich's letter, 120–21; members,
101

Johansen, John M., **38,** 226

Johns, Jasper, 143, 246, 254, 261

Johnson, Diane, 252

Johnson, Lester, 147, 148, 152

Johnson, Lyndon B., 184–85
Johnson, Owen, 98
Johnson, Philip, **22**, 205, 207, 213, 224
Johnson, Ray, 142, 143
Johnson, Robert Underwood, ix, 16, 17, 25, 28*n*. 2, 49, *49, 50*, 70, 71, 72, *76,* 82, 83, 86–87; Academy, influence on, 59; Academy members, selection of, 107; American Academy of Arts and Sciences, controversy with, 28; American speech, concern with, 81, 92; antimodernism, 51, 54, 78–79, 92–99; art museums, proposal for, 74; and Barnard's Lincoln, 43*n*. 10; at *The Century,* 58–59; education, 57–58; fund-raising, 34–35, 54; Gold Medal, design of, 31; illness and death, 98, 99; Kneisel Quartet, concert by, 35; Lowell centennial, 62–63; poetry, 59; Poetry Society and, 56; post–World War I, 61; purpose of the Institute, 117, 156; Saint-Gaudens, tribute to, 39; Sandburg, opposition to, 109; on slackers within the Academy, 42n. 2; social concerns, 59; "Temple, The," 50; vision of the Academy, 109; and women Institute members, 69; "Work and Functions of an Academy in America, The," 22–23
Jones, Howard Mumford, 109
Jones, James, 194
Joplin, Scott, 15
Josephson, Matthew: robes, *139*
Journalism, 243–44
Joyce, James, 53
Justice, Donald, **35**

Kahn, Louis I., **13**, 224
Kahn, Wolf, **38**, 243
Kaprow, Allen, 146
Karnap, Rudolph, 148
Katz, Alex, 150
Kaufman, Edgar, Jr., 142
Kaufman, George S., 101, 109

Kay, Ulysses, 118, 231
Kazin, Alfred, 58, 179, 250, *289*
Keller, Helen, 119, 127, 279
Kennan, George F., 157, 185, *188,* 189, 192–94, 205; and Greene's resignation, 200; and Mumford's anti-Vietnam War address, 187; and unification of Academy and Institute, 287
Kennedy, John F., 164, 165, 169, 171, 172, 173
Kenner, Hugh, **10**
Kent, Rockwell, 95
Kern, Jerome, 230, 233
Kipling, Rudyard, 75, 103*n*. 39
Kirkpatrick, John, 130
Kirstein, Lincoln, 247
Koch, Mayor Edward I., **28**
Klee, Paul, 145
Kline, Franz, 147, 150
Kneisel Quartet, 35
Krehbiehl, Henry E., 228
Kroll, Leon, 137, *141,* 147, *183*
Krutch, Joseph Wood, 101, 123
Kunitz, Stanley, 277
Kuniyoshi, Yasuo, **12**, 147

La Farge, John, 16, 17, 24
Landor, Walter Savage, 51
Lardner, Ring, 94
Lassaw, Ibram, **39**
Lathrop, Gertrude, 118
Laurent, Robert, 66
Lawrence, Jacob, **30**, 129, *289*
Lazarus, Emma, 15
Lea, Henry Charles, 79
Lea, Tom, 129
Leacock, Stephen, 62
Léger, Alexis, 173
Levin, Harry, 189
Levine, David, **16**, **38**
Levine, Jack, **27**, **38**, 118, 129, 286, *289*
Lewis, R. W. B., **37**, **38**, 203
Lewis, Sinclair, 56, 57, 96–99, 109, 116, 126, 128, 219; Academy member-selection controversy, 111

Lexicon of Musical Invective, The
    (Slonimsky), 228
Library of Congress, 2–3
Lichtenstein, Roy, 246, 261
Lie, Jonas, 107
Lieberson, Goddard, 253
Lindeberg, Harrie, 138
Lipchitz, Jacques, *183,* 189
Lippmann, Walter, 110, 137, 189, 279
Lippold, Richard, **32, 38,** 223
Literature, 6–9, 41, 128, 139, 270, 289;
    Black writers, 14; Chinese, 283;
    Garland's protest against coarsening
    of, 108–9; Howells Medal, 72; Jewish
    writers, 15; modernism, 51, 78–79;
    post-World War I, 53, 56, 72–73;
    prizes and awards, 72, 73, 118, 120,
    125, 126, 127, 138, 139, 142, 162, 164,
    173, 181, 184, 189, 198, 252, 253, 254,
    262*n.* 30; Soviet and American writ-
    ers, conference of, 255–56; Strauss
    Livings, 252; women writers, 13
Literature, department of, viii, 3, 17, 19,
    24, 219; charter members, 5–6; Jewish
    members, 101; and Johnson's anti-
    modernism, 92–99; modernist writ-
    ers, 101–2; post-World War I, 52;
    vacancies, 247; women members,
    12–13, 100, 138
Livingston, Brockholst, 2
Lodge, Henry Cabot, 28, 37
Loeffler, Charles Martin, 229
Loines Award for Poetry, 120, 173,
    189
London, Jack, 7
Lounsbury, Thomas, 16, 17, 24
Lowell, Abbott Lawrence, 71
Lowell, James Russell, 2, 61–63
Lowell, Robert, 118, 144, *183,* 224;
    tribute to Marianne Moore, 176
Luening, Otto, 118, 130, 225
Luks, George, 9
Lurie, Alison, **29**

Mabie, Hamilton, 12

Macdonald, Dwight, **27,** 218
MacDowell, Edward, 10–11, 16, 17, 79,
    204, 228, 229
MacKaye, Percy, 79
MacLeish, Archibald, 97, 115, 124, 128,
    137, *141,* 203
MacMonnies, Frederick, 8; on Barnard's
    Lincoln, 30, 43*n.*10
Madariaga, Salvador de, 279
Maeterlinck, Maurice, 75
Mahan, Albert Thayer, 20, 24
Mailer, Norman, **11,** 194–95, 213
Malamud, Bernard, 211, 254
Maltby, Richard, Jr., **37**
Mamoulian, Reuben, 247
Manship, Paul, **8,** 137, *141,* 142, *183*
Marca-Relli, Conrad, 219
March, Fredric, 170
Margetson, Edward, 120
Marin, John, 130, 147
Marisol, 261
Markham, Edwin, 70, 92
Marquand, John, 128
Marquis, Don, 52, 79, 91
Marsh, Reginald, 130
Martinelli, Ezio, 188
Mason, Daniel Gregory, 116, 229
Masters, Edgar Lee, 52, 118
Matisse, Henri, 146, 150
Matthews, Brander, 15, 50, 56, 279; anti-
    German sentiments, 60; frieze across
    Academy building, wording for, 57
Matthison, Edith Wynne, 81
Maugham, Somerset, 53
Maxwell, Elsa, 119
Maxwell, William, **36,** 189, 200
McCarthy, Mary, **30,** 245
McClure, Samuel S., **15**
McCormick, Anne, 127
McCullers, Carson, **20,** 118, 128, 138, 194
McGinley, Phyllis, 138
McKeon, Richard, 148
McKim, Charles Follen, 3, 8, 17, 57,
    248
McKim, Mead & White, 57

McNally, Terrence, **26**, **37**

Mead, Margaret, 138

Mead, William Rutherford, 248

Medal: for Good Diction on the Radio, 91, 92; for Good Diction on the Stage, 120; for Good Speech, 138; for Good Speech on the Stage, 170, 173; for Spoken Language, **15**, 92. *See also* Gold Medal; Howells Medal

Melville, Herman, viii, 153

Melvin, Walter, 277

Membership: Academy, 16–17, 25, 49, 70, 250; Black members, 14, 101, 119–20, 290; eastern members, 29; historians, 24; Institute, 3–6, 10, 25, 28; Jewish members, 101; limits, 25, 28; lists, 293–324; midwestern members, 7, 29; rejection of, xi, 21, 56, 94, 95, 98, 118–19, 219, 243; resignations and reinstatements, xi, 32, 95, 113, 119, 124, 187, 219, 242–43; selection, 214–19, 244; selection controversy (the Row), 105–14; seniority, 278; southern members, 6, 7, 29; western members, 6, 7, 29; women members, 12–13, 68–69, 100–101, 245, 276, 290. *See also* American Honorary Members; Foreign Honorary Members

Mencken, H. L., 53, 75–76, 82, 92, 94–98, 126

Mennin, Peter, 118

Menotti, Gian Carlo, 226

Meredith, William, 189, 203, 204, 219

Merrill, James, **35**, *289*

Merwin, W. S., 219

Middle Western members, 7, 29

Mies van der Rohe, Ludwig, 170, 224

Mildred and Harold Strauss Livings, 251–52, 277

Milhaud, Darius, 64

Millay, Edna St. Vincent, 100, 121

Miller, Arthur, **9**, 157, 163, 226, 250

Miller, Henry, 109, 156, 194, 195

Miller, Joaquin, 7

Miller, Lillian B., 280

Milles, Carl, 278

Mills, Margaret, xii, 202, 206, 216, 218, 234, *259,* 261, 272–74, 276, 278; and art department, 245, 246; death, 285; and department infighting, 247; Druckman–Diamond incident, 241–42; Fuller, Buckminster, award ceremony, 223–24; and National Book Awards, 209, 210; resignation, 284–85; Rushdie affair, 282

Mills, Wilbur, 206

Minimalism, 261, 290

Minorities, 271

Miró, Joan, 145

Mitchell, Joan, 146

Mitchell, Joseph, 211, 213

Mitchell, S. Weir, 21

Modernism, 81, 82, 110, 129, 147, 151, 239, 244; in art, 65–67; Institute's recognition of, 102; international, 78; Johnson's war against, 78–79, 92–99; in literature, 51; in music, 63–65

"Molière" (Gilder), 77

Molière anniversary celebration, 77, 78

Monroe, Marilyn, **9**

Moore, Bruce, 66

Moore, Douglas, 118, 130, 136, 137, *141,* 157, 168–69, *183,* 224, 230, 235; Bloch, tribute to, 163; censorship question, 161; and proposal for national cultural center, 165, 172; and Williams affair, 174

Moore, Marianne, 51, 118, 127, *182, 183;* Lowell's tribute to, 176

More, Paul Elmer, 93, 279

Morison, Samuel Eliot, 94, 95, 173

Morley, Christopher, 95

Morris, Harrison Smith, 53–54, 90, 91, 101, 107; Academy member-selection controversy, 109; anti-Semitism, 120; purpose of the Institute, 117–18

Motherwell, Robert, 150, 214, 218, 246

Motion pictures, 108, 132, 136, 218, 246, 247, 271

Motley, Archibald, 129, 130
Motley, John Lothrop, 2
Muir, John, 7
Muller, Jan, 146
Mumford, Lewis, 138, 157, *183, 184,* 279;
    Brooks, tribute to, 170–71; Kennedy,
    Jacqueline, condolences to, 181–82;
    resignation from Academy, 187, 198;
    speech at 1963 Ceremonial, 176–77;
    Vietnam War address, 185–87, 198
Mural art, 128–29
Murdoch, Iris, 220
Murrow, Edward R., 92, 138
Museum of Modern Art, 140, 149
Museum of the American Indian, 266
Music, 80, 130–32, 142, 143, 151, 270,
    271, 275, 281, 288, 289, 290; American
    Indian, 11, 229–30; Black composers
    and performers, 11, 15, 64, 131–32,
    231; copyrights, 231–32, 233; elec-
    tronic, 225–26; German, 60, 227;
    modernism, 79; and poetry, 226–27;
    postmodernism, 239; post-World War
    I, 61, 63–65; prizes and awards, 118,
    142, 143, 189, 222, 232–33, 253;
    women composers, 14
Music, department of, 3, 10–12, 17, 102,
    130–31, 214, 216, 219, 225–35; compo-
    sitions by members of, 35; enlarge-
    ment of, 247–48
Musical theater, 233, 253

Nabokov, Vladimir, 128
NASA (National Aeronautics and Space
    Administration), 261
Nathan, Robert, 95, 109; robes, *139*
National Academy of Design, 15
National Aeronautics and Space
    Administration (NASA), 261
National Book Awards (NBA), 207–12
National Center for the Performing
    Arts, 172
National Council on the Arts, 157, 189
National cultural center, proposal for,
    158, 163–67, 172

National Endowment for the Arts
    (NEA), 205, 206, 270, 284
National Endowment for the
    Humanities (NEH), 205, 206
National Institute of Arts and Letters, **2**,
    4; Academy, amalgamation with,
    201–4, 206, 250, 285–88; Academy,
    relationship with, 273, 274, 275;
    Audubon collection, 172; board, 277;
    charter members, 3, 5–6, 10;
    Communist front allegation, 137;
    copyright bill, support of, 24–25;
    dues, 16, 34, 90; expulsion of
    Diederich from, 120–21; federal gov-
    ernment, relations with, 157; finances,
    16, 88–90, 204–5; formation of, ix, 3;
    fund raising, 34; grants to non-mem-
    bers, 114, 118; lapel rosette, *x;* last
    meeting of, 104; letters and letter
    excerpts, printing of, 116; meetings,
    15–16; meetings outside New York
    City, 29; modernism, recognition of,
    102; national charter, ix, 28, 29; public
    meetings, 4, 10; purpose of, 4, 117–18,
    156; relief fund, 90–91; robes, *139;*
    voting, 32; in World War II, 125. *See
    also* American Academy and Institute
    of Arts and Letters (1976–1992);
    American Academy of Arts and
    Letters (formed 1993)
National Institute of Arts, Science and
    Letters, ix, 1, 3
National Institute of Letters, Arts, and
    Sciences, 2
National Portrait Gallery, Washington,
    D.C., 258–60, 280
National Sculpture Society, 65
Native American music. *See* American
    Indian music
Naturalism. *See* Realism and naturalism
NBA. *See* National Book Awards
Neel, Alice, 219
Negroes. *See* Black Americans
Nevelson, Louise, **31**, 254
Nevin, Ethelbert, 228

Nevins, Allan, 137, 157, 158, 172, 173, 189
New Criticism, 128
New Deal, 91
Newhall, Nancy and Beaumont, 141
New York City, in 1900, 4
New York Public Library, 248
New York School-Second Generation, 152
Nin, Anaïs, 109
Nobel prizes, 61, 99, 173; Lewis, Sinclair, 96, 97
Norris, Frank, 6, 7, 9
North American Review, 61
Norton, Charles Eliot, 5, 17; Higginson's discussion of, 38; *North American Review,* 61
Note-Book in Northern Spain, A (Huntington), 106

Oates, Joyce Carol, **27**, 256
Ogden, Rollo, 52
O'Hara, John, 158–60, 184
O'Keeffe, Georgia, 151
Olmsted, Frederick Law, 2
Onassis, Jacqueline Kennedy, **31**
O'Neill, Eugene, 52, 98, 110, 128
Opposing self, Trilling's notion of, 5
Osborn, Henry Fairfield, 77
Ozick, Cynthia, **32**, **38**, 252

Page, Thomas Nelson, 7
Paine, John K., 10, 228
Painting, 7, 8, 17, 79, 128–30; 1948–1957, 139, 146–54; post-World War I, 61; prizes and awards, 118, 142, 164
Palmer, Erastus Dow, 65
Parker, Dorothy, 163, 194, 224
Parker, Horatio, 10, 12, 15, 20, 37, 60, 64, 79
Parkman, Francis, 2, 228
Paz, Octavio, 279
Pearlstein, Philip, **38**
Peattie, Donald, 116
Pei, I. M., 189, 254, 258, *259*
Pennell, Joseph, *76,* 79

Pension plan, 139
Perelman, S. J., 158
Performance art, 281
Perkins, James Breck, 16, 26n. 24, 28
Perry, Bliss, 33, *76, 93,* 279; Academy member-selection controversy, 110; Higginson, memorial to, 38, 39; Pound controversy, 123
Pershing, John J., 99, 107
Phelps, William Lyon, 92, 95, 97, 98, 100, 279; Academy member-selection controversy, 110; on realism in fiction, 41; on Stoessel's death, 124
Photography, 218, 246, 247, 271
Pinching of the Trowel, 55–56
Plantation songs, 11
Poe, Edgar Allan, viii
Poetry, 72, 128; modernism, 78–79; music and, 226–27; prizes and awards, 120, 126, 127, 173, 181, 189, 253, 254
Poetry Society of America, 56
Pop art, 151
Pop music, 290
Popular art, 244
Populism, in music, 131
Porter, Katherine Anne, 119, 171, 203
Postimpressionism, 67
Postmodernism, 81, 82, 239, 241
Pound, Ezra, **7**, 51, 102, 109, 115, 118, 121–24, 145; Academy member-selection controversy, 110
Powell, John, 64, 65, 79
Prendergast, Maurice, 8
Prizes and awards, 25, 28, 277–78, (1908–1917) 30, 31, (1918–1927) 72, 73, (1928–1937) 30, 91, 92, (1938–1947) 118, 120, 125, 126, (1948–1957) 138, 139, 142, (1958–1967) 162, 163, 164, 170, 173, 181, 184, 188, 189, (1968–1977) 143, 198, 205, 220–24, (1978–1987) 250–54; citations, writing of, 242; Druckman-Diamond incident, 241–42. *See also* names of specific prizes and awards
Proceedings, 219–20, 221, 224; censorship

question, 161; Foreign Honorary Members, statements by, 283; papers published in (1908–1917), 37–41
Progress, Committee on, 201, 203
Prohibition, 69
Prown, Jules, 8–9
Public events, sponsorship of, 74, 79, 80, 227
Public relations, 118
Public statements, policy on, 137, 159–60, 200–201, 239, 271
Pulitzer prizes, 31; Frost, Robert, 72; post-World War I, 53
Purchase Committee, **39**
Purchase program, **5**

Rachmaninoff, Sergei, 64
Racial ideas: in Osborn's commemoration of Burroughs, 77
Radio award, 91, *91,* 92
Ransome, John Crowe, 51
Rascoe, Burton, 52, 53
Rattner, Abraham, 147
Rauschenberg, Robert, **27**, 142, 143
Rawlings, Marjorie, 108
Read, Herbert, 188
Reagan, Ronald, 239
Realism and naturalism, 6–9, 41, 126, 246; Garland, Hamlin, 69
Recordings, 227
Redding, J. Saunders, 119
Regionalism, 128
Religion, in 1900, 4
Remainders, taxing of, 240
Remembered Yesterdays (Johnson), 58
Repplier, Agnes, 13, 100, 279
Resika, Paul, **38**, 146
Revolving Fund, 124
Rhodes, James Ford, 20, 24, 69
Rice, Elmer, 101, 109, 119, 189
Richard and Hinda Rosenthal Foundation Award, 138
Richard Rodgers Production Award, 233, 253
Richards, I. A., 173

Richards, M. C., 141
Rickey, George, **31**, **38**, 214, 216–17, 218, 244, 245, 247
Ripley, George, 2
Rivera, Diego, 137
Rivers, Larry, 146, 148, 151, 226
Roach, Max, 131, 231, 247
Robbins, Jerome, 247
Roberts, Kenneth, 95
Robeson, Paul, **15**, 92, 120
Robinson, Edwin Arlington, 56, 79; Johnson's opinion of, 78
Roche, Kevin, xii, **38**, *188,* 249, 290
Rockwell, Norman, 129
Rodd, Reynolds, *80*
Rodgers, Dorothy, **28**
Rodgers, Richard, **28**, 231, 233
Rome Fellowship in Literature, 138
Roosevelt, Theodore, 17, 19, *19,* 24; on nationalism in literature and art, 41
Rorem, Ned, **32**, 226
Rosenthal Foundation Award, 138
Roszak, Theodore J., 211, 218
Rothko, Mark, 153
Row, the, 105–14, *117*
Royce, Josiah, 16
Ruckstull, F. Wellington, **6**, 74, 259; Barnard's Lincoln, attack on, 43*n.* 10
Rukeyser, Muriel, 118
Rushdie, Salman, 240, 281–82, 290
Russell, Bertrand, 87
Russian revolution, 44*n.* 28
Ryder, Albert Pinkham, 145

Saarinen, Eero, **13**
Sabbaticals, 193
Saint-Gaudens, Augustus, 3, 8, 16, 17, 24, 65; Gold Medal, 31; Johnson's tribute to, 39; Taft's comments on, 40
Sakharov, Andrei, 240
Salinger, J. D., 140
Salisbury, Harrison E., 205–12, 250, 256, *289*
Sanborn, Franklin B., 26*n.* 24

Sandburg, Carl, 53, 56, 94, 97, 109, *141,* 194

Santayana, George, 122, 260

Sargent, John Singer, 3, 20, 24, 40

Saroyan, William, 219

Schapiro, Meyer, 162, 219, 279

Schlesinger, Arthur, Jr., **34, 38,** 118, 165, 189, 191, 243, 253, 255, 281, *289;* and unification of Academy and Institute, 286–87

Schoenberg, Arnold, 64, 135*n.* 102

Schuller, Gunther, 224, 231, 232

Schuman, William, 118, 125, 130, 205, 235, 253; Barber, Samuel, presentation of award to, 222–23; development study, 257; and National Book Awards, 209, 212; and unification of Academy and Institute, 286

Schurz, Carl, 20

Scollard, Clinton, 79

Scudder, Horace E., 61

Sculpture, 7–8, 17, 139, 271; post–World War I, 61, 65–67; prizes and awards, 31, 73, 189, 223, 254

Secularism, in 1900, 4

Sedgwick, Anne Douglas, 100

Segal, George, **39,** 146, 246

Senate, U.S., 28–29

Senegalese art, 283

Senghor, Leopold Sédar, 283

Sergeant, Elizabeth, 267

Sert, José Luis, 188

Sessions, Roger, *141*

Sexton, Anne, 178–79, *179,* 180

Shahn, Ben, 129, 137, 151

Shapiro, Karl, 118

Shaw, George Bernard, 235

Shaw, Irvin, 118

Sheeler, Charles, 130, 147

Shelley, Harry Rowe, 227

Shepley, Henry R., *141*

Sherwood, Robert E., 127, *141*

Shinn, Everett, 9

Simmons, Edward, 3

Sinclair, Upton, 7

Sissman, L. E., **10**

Sitwell, Dame Edith, **12**

Sitwell, Sir Osbert, **12**

Six, Committee of, 137

Slave songs, 11

Sloan, John, 9, 102; robes, *139*

Sloane, William Milligan, 22, 25, 28, *48,* 51–52; American speech, concern with, 81; English language, preservation of, 30, 32; Gold Medal, 73; on guarding tradition, 66–67

Slonimsky, Nicolas, 228

Smith, Lawrence, 123

Smith, William Jay, 256

Snelson, Kenneth, **38**

Snow, C. P., 212

Snyder, Gary, 188, 213, 214

Sobotnick, Morton, 241

Social concerns, 240; of charter members, 5–6; Vietnam War, 185–87, 199–201; Washington Heights community, 266–67. *See also* Censorship

Socialism, 7

Social realism, 129

Sokolow, Anna, 247

Solomon, Joseph, **17**

Sondheim, Stephen, **37,** 226, 231, 233

Southern members, 6–7, 29

Sowerby, Leo, 230

Soyer, Isaac, 129, 130

Soyer, Moses, 129, 188

Soyer, Raphael, 118, 129

Space program: artist-in-residence proposal, 261

Spark, Muriel, 220

Speicher, Eugene, 147, 251

Spender, Stephen, 220, 224

Stafford, Jean, 118, 211

Stalin, Joseph V., 138

Starr, Harry, 189

State, U.S. Department of: Soviet and American writers, conference of, 255

Stedman, Edmund Clarence, 13, *13,* 16, 21–22, 58, 94; letters, exhibit of, 80

Steegmuller, Francis, 188, 254, *254*

Stein, Gertrude, 73, 97, 131
Stein Award, 253
Steinbeck, John, 108, 109, 128, 180–81
Steinberg, Saul, 261, *289*
Stella, Frank, 243
Stevens, Roger L., 189, 190–91, 193, 208
Stevens, Wallace, 12, 51, 127
Stevenson, Adlai, 161–62
Stieglitz, Alfred, 82
Still, Clyfford, **27**, 146
Stockhausen, Karlheinz, 143
Stock market crash (1929), 88
Stoddard, Richard Henry, 80
Stoessel, Albert, 124–25
Stone, Robert, 252
Story, William Wetmore, 2
Stowe, Harriet Beecher, 2
Strachey, Lytton, 53
Strand, Mark, **35**
Strauss, Harold, 252
Strauss Livings, 251–52, 277; Committee, **29**
Stravinsky, Igor, 64
Strong, Austin, 95, 116; Fulbright's Blashfield address, 127; robes, proposal for, *139;* Stoessel's death, 124–25
Strong, George Templeton, 2
Styron, William, 188, 256
Sulgrave Institution, 30
Sullivan, Louis, 9–10
Symons, Gardner, 251

Taft, Lorado: on sculpture, 40
Tanner, Henry, 14–15
Tarkington, Booth, *80,* 99; Academy member-selection controversy, 111; Howells Medal, 126
Tate, Allen, *183,* 202
Taubman, Howard, 189
Tax-exempt status, 29, 137, 138, 255
Tax laws, 206, 240
Taylor, Deems, 125, 137, *141,* 229, 235
Taylor, Paul, 247
Taylor, Peter, 224
Television, 139

"Temple, The" (Johnson), 50
Ten North Frederick (O'Hara), 159
Tetractys Club, viii
Thayer, Abbott Handerson, 21; Henry James, drawing of, *18*
Tharp, Twyla, 247
Thayer, William Roscoe, 81
Theater, 218, 289; drama prizes and awards, 126, 127, 163, 221, 254; musical theater, 233, 253
Theater Guild, 53
Theroux, Paul, **29**
Thomas, Augustus, 15, *76,* 90
Thomas, Edith M., 72, 79
Thomas, J. Parnell, 136
Thompson, Dorothy, 109
Thomson, Virgil, 63, 131, 142, 165, 181, 189, 224, 226, 230, 255, 261; wine cellar, 242
Thorne, Francis, **37**
Thurber, James, 119
Tinker, Chauncey Brewster, 103*n*. 32, 126
Tocqueville, Alexis de, 23
Tooker, George, 261
Toomer, Jean, 51
Tourtellot, Arthur, 210
Tradition and innovation, conflict between, 241
Train, Arthur, 114, 115, 120; Academy member-selection controversy, 107, 112; Pound controversy, 123–24
Trilling, Lionel, 5
Trinity Church cemetery, 250, 265
Tuchman, Barbara, **28**, 138, 202–3, 250, 253, 257, 276, 285; Druckman-Diamond incident, 241–42
Twachtman, John H., 8
Twain, Mark. *See* Clemens, Samuel L.
Twombly, Cy, 143
Tworkov, Jack, 151

UNESCO (United Nations Educational, Scientific, and Cultural Organization), 138

Updike, John, **32**, **38**, 182, 183, 234; Soviet and American writers, conference of, 256; and unification of Academy and Institute, 286, 288
Ussachevsky, Vladimir, 225

Vacancies, distribution of, 247
Vanamee, Grace Davis, xii, **6**, 17, 55–56, 86–87, 90, 99–102, 108; American speech, concern with, 81; anti-Semitism, 120; Pound's letter, response to, 122; resignation of, 113, 114, 122; on women's exclusion from the Institute, 68
Van Doren, Dorothy, 195
Van Doren, Mark, 137, *141, 182;* censorship question, 160, 161; Pound controversy, 123; Sandburg, tribute to, 194
van Druten, John, 126
van Dyke, Henry, 3, 75, 96, 279
Van Dyke, John Charles, *76, 80*
van Loon, Hendrik Willem, 123
Van Vechten, Carl, **17**
Varèse, Edgard, 61, 63, 142, 151, 225, 230
Vargas Llosa, Mario, 279
Vedder, Elihu, 139
Vidal, Gore, 219
Vietnam War, 157, 198–201; Mumford's speech on, 185–87
Vonnah, Bessie Potter, 100
Vonnegut, Kurt, **29**, 208, 242–43, 256, *289*
Voznesensky, Andrei, 255
Vursell Award, 253

Ward, John Quincy Adams, 17
Ward, Robert, 118, 226, 232
Warner, Charles Dudley, 1, 3, 4; purpose of the Institute, 117
Warren, Charles, 136
Warren, Robert Penn, 24, 124, *254;* censorship question, 160, 161; Williams, tribute to, 181
Warren, Whitney, 68

Washington, Booker T., 14
Washington Heights, Manhattan, 265–67, 282; Audubon Terrace, 258
Weber, Ben, 142
Weber, Max, 129
Weinman, Adolph A., 244; bronze doors, *245;* Gold Medal designed by, *210*
Weir, J. Alden, 8
Weisgall, Hugo, **27**, **32**, 205, 211, 234, 235, 248, 285, 286, *289*
Welles, Orson, 219, 247
Welty, Eudora, **28**, 118, 128, 138, 140, *222;* Faulkner, tribute to, 173
Wendell, Barrett, 12
Wescott, Glenway, **12**, 138, 157, 172, *183,* 189; censorship question, 160; and Franklin Library, 211; Frost, Robert, relations with, 167–68; Keller's Blashfield address, 127; and proposal for national cultural center, 164–67; and Strauss Livings, 252; and unification of Institute and Academy, 250
West, Andrew, 32
West, Nathanael, 128
West, Rebecca, 53
Western members, 6–7, 29
Wharton, Edith, **4**, 5, 13, 53, 59, 73, 100
Wheelock, John Hall, 189
Whistler, James McNeill, 3, 4
White, E. B., 119, 164, 219
White, Stanford, 8, 57, 248
Whiting, Arthur, 228
Whitlock, Brand, 41
Whitman, Walt, 2, 4–5, 63, 64, 80
Whittier, John Greenleaf, 2, 5
Wien, Lawrence, 257
Wilbur, Richard, 205, *289*
Wilder, Billy, 247
Wilder, Thornton, **14**, 125, 128, *141,* 267
William Dean Howells Medal. *See* Howells Medal
Williams, John, 173–76
Williams, Tennessee, **19**, **26**, 118, 221
Williams, William Carlos, 51, 122, 181

Wilson, Edmund, 118

Wilson, Jane, **38**, **39**, 150

Wilson, Olly, 231

Wilson, Woodrow, 36, 60, 61, 70

Wister, Owen, 68, *76*, 93, 98, 279

Witter Bynner Prize for Poetry, 57, 242, 253

Wolfe, Thomas, 101, 109, 128

Wolff, Christian, 143

Wolpe, Stefan, 142, 146

Women: Academy-Institute presidents, 138, 253; Blashfield speakers, 279–80; duty of, Brooks Adams's notion of, 33–34; evolving aspirations of, 67–68; members, **4**, 68–69, 100–101, 138, 245, 276, 290; portrayal of, in modern fiction, 108, 109; writers, artists, and composers, 12–14

Wood, Grant, 128, 129, 130, 147, 151

Woodward, C. Van, *289*

Woolson, Constance Fenimore, 2

Woolworth Building, New York City, 248

"Work and Functions of an Academy in America, The" (Johnson, Stedman, and Howells), 22, 23

Works Progress Administration (WPA), 129, 138

World's Columbian Exposition (1893), 9–10, 14, 248

World War: Utterances Concerning Its Issues and Conduct by Members of the American Academy of Arts and Letters, The, 44n. 32, 50, 60

World War I, 34–37, 60

World War II, 124–25

WPA (Works Progress Administration), 129, 138

Wright, Richard, 128

Wuorinen, Charles, 231

Wyeth, Andrew, 194, 224

Xenophobia, 108, 109

Yevtushenko, Yevgeny, 243, 255

Yiddish literature, 51

Young, Mahonri M., *141*; robes, *139*

Youth versus age, in Academy-Institute affairs, 244, 246

Ziff, Larzer, 9–10s

Zorach, William, 66